Sex Discrimination in the Workplace

To the memory of Mady Karsenty, with love.
FJC

To my students for putting up with me.
MSS

Sex Discrimination in the Workplace

Multidisciplinary Perspectives

Edited by

Faye J. Crosby
Margaret S. Stockdale
S. Ann Ropp

Blackwell Publishing

© 2007 by Blackwell Publishing Ltd

BLACKWELL PUBLISHING
350 Main Street, Malden, MA 02148-5020, USA
9600 Garsington Road, Oxford OX4 2DQ, UK
550 Swanston Street, Carlton, Victoria 3053, Australia

The right of Faye J. Crosby, Margaret S. Stockdale, and S. Ann Ropp to be identified as the Authors of the Editorial Material in this Work has been asserted in accordance with the UK Copyright, Designs, and Patents Act 1988.

First published 2007 by Blackwell Publishing Ltd

1   2007

Library of Congress Cataloging-in-Publication Data

Sex discrimination in the workplace / edited by Faye J. Crosby, Margaret S. Stockdale, S. Ann Ropp.
     p.   cm.
   Includes bibliographical references and index.
   ISBN-13: 978-1-4051-3449-1 (hardback)
   ISBN-13: 978-1-4051-3450-7 (pbk.)
1. Sex discrimination in employment—United States.   2. Women—Employment—United States.   3. Sex discrimination in employment—Law and legislation—United States.   I. Crosby, Faye J., 1947–   II. Stockdale, Margaret S.   III. Ropp, S. Ann.

HD6060.65.U5S49 2007
331.4′1330973—dc22
                          2006027521

A catalogue record for this title is available from the British Library.

Set in 10.5 on 13.5 pt Plantin
by SNP Best-set Typesetter Ltd, Hong Kong
Printed and bound in the Singapore
by Markono Print Media Pte Ltd

The publisher's policy is to use permanent paper from mills that operate a sustainable forestry policy, and which has been manufactured from pulp processed using acid-free and elementary chlorine-free practices. Furthermore, the publisher ensures that the text paper and cover board used have met acceptable environmental accreditation standards.

For further information on
Blackwell Publishing, visit our website:
www.blackwellpublishing.com

Contents

Contributors

Theresa M. Beiner is the Nadine H. Baum Distinguished Professor of Law at the University of Arkansas at Little Rock, William H. Bowen School of Law. Her areas of expertise include Employment Discrimination Law as well as Civil Procedure, Federal Jurisdiction, judicial appointments, and Constitutional Law. In 2005, her book *Gender Myths v. Working Realities: Using Social Science to Reformulate Sexual Harassment Law* was published by the New York University Press. Her law school has awarded her its faculty excellence awards for scholarship and teaching. Professor Beiner is the mother of three children. tmbeiner@ualr.edu

Barbara R. Bergmann writes on economic and social policy. She formerly served as Professor of Economics at the University of Maryland and at American University in Washington, DC. She received the PhD in economics from Harvard University. Dr. Bergmann served as a senior staff member of the President's Council of Economic Advisers during the Kennedy Administration. Other government experience includes service as Senior Economic Adviser with the Agency for International Development, and as an economist with the Bureau of Labor Statistics. She has served on advisory committees to the Congressional Budget Office and the Bureau of the Census. In the early 1980s, she wrote a monthly column on economic affairs for the *New York Times* Sunday Business Section. She has served as President of the Eastern Economic Association, the Society for the Advancement of Socio-Economics, the American Association of University Professors and the International Association for Feminist Economics. She is currently working on a book entitled *The Decline of Marriage and What to Do About It*. brbergmann@verizon.net

Susan Bisom-Rapp is Professor of Law and Director of the Center for Law and Social Justice at Thomas Jefferson School of Law. She is a founder of the law school's Women and the Law Project. Professor Bisom-Rapp's scholarly work focuses on globalization and the workplace, legal sociology, and employment discrimination law, subjects upon which she has written and lectured widely. Her co-authored casebook, *The Global Workplace: International and Comparative Employment Law* (Cambridge University Press, 2007), is the first law school text in that emerging field. Before beginning her academic career, she practiced labor and employment law in New York City. susanb@tjsl.edu

Eugene Borgida is Professor of Psychology and Law and Adjunct Professor of Political Science at the University of Minnesota. He is a Morse-Alumni Distinguished Teaching Professor of Psychology. He is a Fellow of the APS and an APA Fellow, and has served on the Board of Directors for the Association for Psychological Science and the Social Science Research Council. He received his BA from Wesleyan University and PhD from the University of Michigan. He has written on the use of psychological science in court and served as an expert witness in both class action and single-plaintiff sex discrimination cases. Borgi001@umn.edu

Wayne F. Cascio is US Bank Term Professor of Management at the University of Colorado at Denver and Health Sciences Center. He has written extensively on human resource management issues, including downsizing, restructuring, and the economic impact of behavior in organizations. An elected Fellow of the Academy of Management, the American Psychological Association, and the National Academy of Human Resources, he received the Distinguished Career award from the Academy's HR Division in 2000, and an honorary doctorate from the University of Geneva (Switzerland) in 2004. Currently he serves on the Boards of Directors of CPP, Inc., the Society for Human Resource Management Foundation, and the Academy of Management. Wayne.Cascio@cudenver.edu

Faye J. Crosby is a social psychologist and an expert on affirmative action. She has authored, co-authored, edited, or co-edited 14 volumes and over 100 articles and chapters in scholarly books. Since receiving her PhD in 1976, Crosby has been the fortunate recipient of numerous awards including an honorary degree from Ball State University, the Carolyn Sherif Award from Division 35 of the American Psychological Association, and the Kurt Lewin Award from the Society for the Psychological Study of Social Issues. Crosby is Professor of Psychology at the University of California, Santa Cruz, where she has been Chair of the Academic Senate since 2005. fjcrosby@ucsc.edu

Colleen E. Crangle was born in South Africa. She spent her childhood in Zimbabwe (then known as Southern Rhodesia), Miami Beach, USA, and South

Africa. In 1980 she immigrated to the United States for graduate study. Born to an Irish father, she held Irish citizenship until 1991 when she became a citizen of the United States. She holds a PhD in Philosophy from Stanford University and a Master's degree in Computer Science from the University of South Africa. She has two teenage children who live with her in Palo Alto, California. crangle@ix.netcom.com

Paula England is Professor of Sociology at Stanford University. She is the author of *Comparable Worth* (Aldine de Gruyter, 1992) and *Households, Employment, and Gender* (Aldine de Gruyter, 1986, with George Farkas). From 1994–1996 she was editor of the *American Sociological Review*. She was the 1999 recipient of the American Sociological Association's Jessie Bernard Award for career contributions to the study of gender. pengland@standford.edu

Susan T. Fiske, Psychology Professor at Princeton, has investigated gender bias since graduate school at Harvard. Fiske expert-witnessed in a landmark gender discrimination case, *Hopkins v. Price Waterhouse*. With Glick, she developed Ambivalent Sexism Theory in lab, survey, and cross-cultural contexts, and now in close relationships. With Cuddy and Glick, her Stereotype Content Model identifies universal dimensions of intergroup bias. She authored *Social Cognition* (McGraw Hill 3rd ed., in press) and *Social Beings* (Wiley, 2004); she edits the *Handbook of Social Psychology* (McGraw Hill and Oxford University Press) and the *Annual Review of Psychology* (Annual Reviews). Fiske was elected President of the Association for Psychological Science (formerly American Psychological Society). sfiske@princeton.edu

Peter Glick (AB, Oberlin College, 1979; PhD, University of Minnesota, 1984) is Professor of Psychology at Lawrence University and a Fellow of the American Psychological Association and the Association for Psychological Science. His work on ambivalent sexism (with Susan Fiske of Princeton University) was recognized with the 1995 Gordon W. Allport Prize for best paper on intergroup relations. This theory and related empirical work challenge conventional views of prejudice as an antipathy by showing how "benevolent sexism" (subjectively positive, but patronizing attitudes toward women) as well as hostile sexism is related to gender inequality. peter.s.glick@lawrence.edu

Barbara A. Gutek is Professor and Eller Chair in Women and Leadership in the Department of Management and Organizations, University of Arizona. She authored over 100 books and articles. In 1994, Gutek received the Sage Scholarship Award from the Gender and Diversity in Organizations Division of the Academy of Management, the American Psychological Association's Division 35 Heritage Award for a "substantial and outstanding body of research on women and gender" and the Committee on Women in Psychology Award as a "Distinguished Leader for Women in Psychology." *The Brave New Service*

Strategy (AMACOM, 2000), with T. Welsh, was selected one of the 30 best business books of the year 2000 by Soundview, publishers of Business Executive Summaries. bagutek@aol.com

Ann Branigar Hopkins is a gardener, carpenter, speaker, and occasional writer. She was born in Texas, the oldest child of a career army officer and a nurse. As an army brat, she grew up in Germany and moved a lot. She earned degrees in mathematics from Hollins College (BA, 1965) and Indiana University (MA, 1967) and began her professional work as a theoretical physicist at IBM in the late sixties. In the early seventies she moved from technical work into project management and became a management consultant at Touche Ross & Co and later at Price Waterhouse. Along the way she married and had three children. In the eighties, she was involved in a seven-year discrimination litigation with Price Waterhouse that ended in the early nineties when she returned to the firm as a court ordered partner. After eleven years as a partner, she retired in 2002. annhopkins@earthlink.net

Anita Kim is a graduate student in the social psychology doctoral program at the University of Minnesota. She is interested in a variety of fields within social psychology, including its application to the legal system. She received her BS in psychology from the University of California at San Diego in 1999, and has also worked in litigation consulting and market research. kimx0917@umn.edu

Ellen B. Kimmel retired in 2003 from the University of South Florida where she was Distinguished Professor of Psychology. A prolific writer, and the recipient of numerous grants and awards, Kimmel has been recognized as a leader in the fight for gender equity. She has served as president of the Southeastern Psychological Association and of Division 35 of the American Psychological Association. Her current interests center on issues of wellness. kimmel@tempest.coedu.usf.edu

Linda Hamilton Krieger is a Professor of Law at the University of California, Berkeley School of Law (Boalt Hall). She is a graduate of Stanford University (BA 1975) and the New York University School of Law (JD 1978). Before entering law teaching, Professor Krieger worked as a civil rights lawyer, serving as a Staff Attorney at the Employment Law Center in San Francisco and as a Senior Trial Attorney for the United States Equal Employment Opportunity Commission, where she litigated sex, race, national origin, age, and disability discrimination cases, including class actions. Her legal scholarship centers on the application of insights from cognitive social psychology to issues in antidiscrimination law and policy in particular, and on the role of science in law and legal policy more generally. lkrieger@law.berkeley.edu

Jocelyn D. Larkin is the Director of Litigation and Training for The Impact Fund, a legal foundation that provides funding and representation in support of complex public interest litigation. Her practice focuses on complex employment discrimination and class action practice on behalf of plaintiffs. She currently serves as class counsel in the gender discrimination class action, *Dukes v. Wal-Mart Stores*, the largest certified civil rights class action in history. Ms. Larkin is the co-chair of the Employment Subcommittee of the ABA Litigation Section's Class Actions and Derivative Suits Committee. jlarkin@impactfund.org

Maureen O'Connor is Associate Professor and Chair of the Psychology Department at John Jay College of Criminal Justice and has appointments on the faculty of the doctoral programs in Forensic Psychology, Social/Personality Psychology, and Criminal Justice at the Graduate Center of the City University of New York. She received her JD and her PhD with specialization in Law, Psychology, and Policy, from the University of Arizona (with a minor in Organizational Behavior). Research interests focus on the intersection of gender, psychology, and law, and include stalking and sexual harassment, with particular attention to lay and legal definitions of those concepts. moconnor@jjay.cuny.edu

Deborah L. Rhode is the Ernest W. McFarland Professor of Law and Director of the Stanford Center on Ethics at Stanford University School of Law. She is the former Chair of the American Bar Association's Commission on Women in the Profession, former president of the Association of American Law Schools, and former director of Stanford's Institute on Women and Gender. She is the author or co-author of 17 books and over 150 articles in the areas of gender and professional ethics. Her publications include *The Difference "Difference" Makes: Women and Leadership* (Stanford University Press, 2003), *Gender and Law* (Aspen, 2006, with Katherine Bartlett), and *Women/Leadership* (Forthcoming, Jossey Bass, with Barbara Kellerman). rhode@stanford.edu

Cecilia L. Ridgeway is the Lucie Stern Professor of Social Sciences in the Department of Sociology at Stanford University. Her research addresses the role that social hierarchies in everyday interaction play in stratification and social inequality, especially in regard to gender. She is the author of *Gender, Interaction, and Inequality* (Springer-Verlag, 1992) and articles on this topic in *American Journal of Sociology*, *American Sociological Review*, *Social Forces*, and *Journal of Social Issues*. She is past editor of *Social Psychology Quarterly* and recipient of the 2005 Cooley-Mead Award for career contribution to social psychology. ridgeway@leland.stanford.edu

S. Ann Ropp has been an assistant professor of psychology at the University of Alaska, Southeast, and is currently the program director at AWARE, a local women's shelter in Juneau, Alaska. She received her PhD in social psychology from the University of California, Santa Cruz, in 2003. She has published in the area of discrimination and inter-group relations. Ropp has received a number of awards for her outstanding teaching. ann.ropp@uas.alaska.edu

Donna Ryu earned a BA from Yale University and a JD from University of California, Boalt Hall, where she was a founding member of the Berkeley Women's Law Journal. She serves on the clinical faculty of Hastings College of the Law. Prior to that, she was the Associate Director of the Women's Employment Rights Clinic at Golden Gate University Law School. She spent the first 12 years of her career in private practice, specializing in civil rights class actions. During her partnership in Ryu, Dickey and Larkin, an all-women's civil rights firm, she and Jocelyn Larkin litigated the sex discrimination class action described in Chapter 7. ryud@uchastings.edu

Margaret (Peggy) Stockdale is Professor of Psychology and Area Head of Applied Psychology at Southern Illinois University Carbondale (SIUC). She holds a MS and PhD in Industrial-Organizational Psychology from Kansas State University and is pursuing a Master's of Legal Studies at SIUC's School of Law. Her research focuses on gender issues in the workplace, with specific attention to sexual harassment and sex discrimination. She has served as an expert witness on both single-litigant and class action sex discrimination cases for both plaintiffs and defendants. pstock@siu.edu

Richard S. Ugelow has been a member of the faculty of the Washington College of Law, American University, Washington, DC, since June 2002. Prior to joining the law school faculty, he was a Deputy Section Chief of the Employment Litigation Section, Civil Rights Division, U.S. Department of Justice. Over the course of his 29-year career at DOJ, he supervised and lead investigations and litigation to enforce Title VII of the Civil Rights Act of 1964. Mr. Ugelow was also the government's lead trial attorney in defending challenges to the constitutionality of federally sponsored affirmative action programs, particularly statutes and programs designed to provide contracting opportunities to minority, disadvantaged, and women-owned businesses. Before joining the Department of Justice, Mr. Ugelow served in the Army's Judge Advocate General's Corps for four years. rugelow@wcl.american.edu

Jonathan D. Wetchler is a partner in the law firm of Wolf, Block, Schorr and Solis-Cohen LLP, where he heads the Employment Service Department's employment litigation practice. Mr. Wetchler has extensive experience in handling employment litigation of all kinds, including but not limited to class actions involving FLSA, ERISA and employment discrimination claims, as well as cases concerning covenants against competition, employment contracts and the wide variety of other statutes governing the employment area. Mr. Wetchler also works closely with clients in the development and implementation of executive employment contracts and policies and practices to reduce potential exposure to liability in all areas of employment. His practice includes training employers and employees about sexual harassment, the Americans with Disabilities Act and other work-related legal issues. He received his BA degree, summa cum laude, from the State University at Buffalo and his JD degree from

Northwestern University. Mr. Wetchler is a member of the Philadelphia, Pennsylvania and American bar associations. jwetchler@WOLFBLOCK.com

Joan C. Williams is Distinguished Professor of Law, and founding Director of the Center for WorkLife Law at University of California, Hastings College of the Law. A prize-winning author and expert on work/family issues, she is author of *Unbending Gender: Why Family and Work Conflict and What To Do About It* (Oxford University Press, 2000), which won the 2000 Gustavus Myers Outstanding Book Award. She has authored or co-authored four books and over fifty law review articles. She co-edited, with Monica Biernat and Faye Crosby, a special issue of the *Journal of Social Issues* (2004), which was awarded the Distinguished Publication Award by the Association for Women in Psychology. Williams@email.uchastings.edu

Preface

Every book has a story. This is ours.

Feeling perhaps a little too proud of ourselves for the success of our previous collaboration, *The Psychology and Management of Workplace Diversity*,[1] and a vaguely formed idea that *the book* on sex discrimination hadn't been written yet (or that it was time for a new one), Faye Crosby and Peg Stockdale sat down to breakfast with Christine Cardone at a Washington DC hotel in September, 2004. The point was to brainstorm what would the book look like. What would it contain? What would it accomplish? Our first thought was – multidisciplinary.

Although Peg and Faye were well versed in the psychological research on sex discrimination, we knew that ours was not the only voice in the wilderness. Faye quickly rattled off the names of preeminent scholars who could write handbook-style chapters representing their discipline's approach to the subject: Peter Glick and Susan Fiske; Cecilia Ridgeway and Paula England; Barbara Bergmann; Deborah Rhode and Joan Williams. Then we thought that what's missing from most scholarly treatises are the voices of people who have actually been in the trenches – the plaintiffs, their lawyers, defense lawyers, and expert witnesses. We envisioned fairly short but highly autobiographical essays that would bring the academic concepts and theories to life. Finally, we knew we could not leave this hanging without forward-looking chapters that would consider "remedies" or possible means for diminishing sex discrimination.

Christine Cardone of Blackwell was excited and willing to take the risk with us and to convince her editors to support this project. Faye then suggested that a newly minted PhD scholar, Ann Ropp, join us. The project and the team were in place.

Unlike most edited books that are accomplished as individual works that the editors weave together, those of us who could – editors and contributors – gathered for a weekend in Lake Tahoe in early November, 2005, to read and discuss preliminary drafts of the chapters, brainstorm ideas for chapters that had not yet made it into print form, and to encourage each other through the revision process. We also hiked, swam in the hot springs pool, and had great meals together.

As with any great idea, however, things change. By the time we finished, we realized that the book would be better organized as four sections instead of three. Thus, we could start with two powerful chapters that remind employers and potential complainants (and those who research them or what they do) about how sex discrimination incidents play out in typical workplaces, and what their responsibilities and options are to avoid or deal effectively with such instances.

We give full credit to our contributors, among whom are some of the nation's leading experts on the topic of sex discrimination. We recognize that editing a book of this nature was at times like herding cats. We thank the authors for their patience, flexibility to bend when we needed them to, and their foresight to stick to their guns when they had a better vision than we did. We appreciate all of our authors who cooperated in the revision process, long and tortured as it was.

We also give thanks to our support network that surrounded us throughout this project. Christine Cardone and Sarah Coleman of Blackwell are a terrific editing team. They were always encouraging, completely responsive to our needs, and helped us make intelligent decisions about the various twists and turns we needed to take to complete the project. Thanks go to Marilyn Patton, who staffed the Tahoe meeting, and to Amanda Crabe, Justin Lin, and Phil Seneca for their editorial assistance. We also thank our partners and families for doing what they do so well – being there for us!

FJC, MSS, SAR

Note

1   Stockdale, M. S., & Crosby, F. J. (Eds.) (2004). *The psychology and management of workplace diversity*. Oxford: Blackwell.

Part I

What Employers and Employees Should Know about Sex Discrimination

1

Introduction: Understanding Sex Discrimination

Faye J. Crosby and
Margaret S. Stockdale

"Judge Certifies Suit Accusing Wal-Mart of Sex Discrimination," read the headline of a front-page article in the June 22, 2004 copy of the *New York Times*. Although the case was three years old at the time the article appeared, and thus hardly news, a federal judge had just decided to classify the case as a class action lawsuit. At a single stroke, the stakes in the Wal-Mart case enlarged dramatically. If it were to be determined that Wal-Mart has discriminated against the women who have brought the suit, the remedy would thus extend to all 1.6 million women who have worked or who do work for Wal-Mart. Still pending, the case is the largest sex discrimination case ever to be brought.

Sex discrimination in employment is clearly a newsworthy topic. For ethical as well as legal reasons, few employers today wish to risk being labeled as sex-discriminatory. And many Americans, perhaps the majority of Americans, today genuinely disapprove of female workers being put at a disadvantage relative to male workers. One does not have to think of oneself as a feminist to approve of and even to work for gender equality at work.

What is sex discrimination in employment? In the broadest sense, sex discrimination occurs when a person is or people are treated unfairly in the work context because of gender. Unfair treatment can concern levels of compensation, as for example, when a woman receives less pay than an equivalent man. Sex discrimination can also occur in terms of non-monetary rewards, in terms of opportunities, and in terms of on-the-job treatment. Sexual harassment is one particular form of on-the-job sex discrimination.

Sex discrimination in employment is the topic of this collection of essays. The book falls into four parts. In the first part, we discuss the basics outlining what every employer and every employee should know about sex discrimination.

Chapter 2 of our volume, by Jonathan Wetchler, is intended to help employers avoid situations in which they might be successfully accused of sex discrimination. Chapter 2 should also be of interest to any person who thinks she or he may have grounds for action. In contrast, Chapter 3, by Terri Biener and Maureen O'Connor, speaks directly to those who think they may have been the victims of discrimination and is also informative to employers who wish to avoid having disgruntled employees.

Part II of the volume puts human faces to the concepts presented in Part I. Together the chapters of Part II illustrate the difficulties and pains for those individuals who use American law to help make the American workplace less discriminatory than it has been, even when the plaintiffs like Ann Hopkins, like Colleen Crangle, and like Ellen Kimmel and her associates are victorious in their quests. In the accounts of the lawyers (Ryu and Larkin; and Ugelow) and expert witnesses (Borgida and Kim; Gutek; Cascio), furthermore, we get a glimpse of the interpenetration of disciplines, foreshadowing the materials in Part III. Increasingly, American jurisprudence is recognizing the applicability of the social sciences. Increasingly, too, social scientists are understanding how to use what they know about the laws of human nature to help influence the rule of law in the United States.

If the chapters in Part II of the volume show clear consistency about the workings of sex discrimination when seen at the level of the individual, the chapters in Part III also show remarkable consensus about the dynamics of sex discrimination in employment, when subjected to scholarly analyses. In Part III four major disciplinary analyses of sex discrimination in employment are presented. Peter Glick and Susan Fiske offer a psychological analysis, while Cecilia Ridgeway and Paula England give a sociological analysis. Barbara Bergmann represents the approach of a well-known economist, and Deborah Rhode and Joan Williams represent current legal thinking on sex discrimination in employment. The chapters in Part III give the reader broad overviews of the issues and also delve deeply into such questions as: What is the extent of sex discrimination in America today? How can we determine the extent of sex discrimination among parts of society or within organizations or individuals? What explains variations in the amount of sex discrimination?

Not unexpectedly, the analyses have proceeded according to the dictates of the scholars' disciplines. Psychologists, for example, have distinguished between sex discrimination and sexual prejudice and sex stereotyping. Sex discrimination concerns behaviors. Sexual prejudice, including sex stereotyping, has to do with thoughts and feelings. Psychologists have investigated in depth the connections between thoughts and feelings (i.e., prejudices), on the one hand, and behaviors (i.e., discrimination), on the other. Meanwhile, sociologists have typically approached the question of prejudice and discriminatory behavior by first noting the role of social structures in determining both thoughts and behaviors. Economists rule out the rational explanations for gender differences in workplace outcomes to sharpen our focus on what is discriminatory, and legal scholars examine the efficacy of the law and legal structures as tools of justice.

Although they take quite different approaches to the question of the extent of sex discrimination, all four sets of experts in Part III of the volume come to the conclusion that discrimination has diminished over the years but still persists to a surprising degree in American society today. In the United States today, it is still more difficult for women to obtain and retain employment than it is for men, even equating for qualification. It is still more difficult for women to be promoted than it is for similarly qualified men to be promoted. Gaining qualifications is also more arduous, even today, for women than for men. Women are still sexually harassed at work much too frequently and much more frequently than men.

Not only do the chapters of Part III show a general agreement in the conclusions they reach, starting from their different origins and proceeding along their different disciplinary paths; the chapters also illustrate how contemporary scholars cross disciplinary boundaries. The sociologists, economists, and lawyers all make use of psychological concepts. Meanwhile, legal rulings figure in the analyses of the psychologists, the sociologists, and the economists. Sociological and economic facts penetrate the psychological and the legal analyses.

The two chapters of Part IV confront squarely the issue that in some sense motivates the entire volume: how to reduce sex discrimination. Approaching the issue from the point of view of the organization (Bisom-Rapp, Stockdale, and Crosby), and the legal system (Krieger), the chapters integrate the different disciplinary approaches represented in Part III. Like the chapters throughout the book, the final two essays contain some intertwined lessons that are simple but also critically important. First, an antidiscriminatory system can help prevent problems. Second, systems are never changed by individuals acting in isolation, but rather are changed by individuals acting in concert with each other. Third, concerted action is facilitated when we understand the general principles that govern the workings of sex discrimination which, in turn, we can do by learning what scholars have found in their systematic studies and by seeing how the principles play out in the lives of actual women and men.

The present volume, with its eminent contributors, is intended to help students, scholars, employers, and lawyers better understand sex discrimination in contemporary American society. We hope that such knowledge may result directly and indirectly in the continued diminution of sex discrimination in the economy of the United States. Perhaps one day in the near or middle future tales of sex discrimination and of the fights against it will only infrequently splash across the front pages of the newspapers – not because people will have grown blasé or cynical – but because people will have come to find themselves less and less either the victims or the perpetrators of unfair treatment based on gender.

2

Avoiding Sex Discrimination Litigation and Defending Sex Discrimination Suits

Jonathan D. Wetchler

This chapter addresses the preventive steps employers should take to avoid claims of sex discrimination and the strategies employers should consider in defending sex discrimination litigation in the event that suit is filed. In the chapter I provide views based on my years as an attorney defending employers against charges of sex discrimination. Not only have I represented defendants in sex discrimination cases, I have also counseled employers about how to minimize the chances of being sued.

Many employers recognize that discrimination (not only on the basis of gender, but on any grounds) is synonymous with ignoring qualifications and merit, and is therefore inimical to advancing the employer's business interests. Similarly, the Supreme Court has recognized that "[t]he harassing supervisor often acts for personal motives, motives unrelated and even antithetical to the objectives of the employer."[1] It is safe to say that being sexually harassed is likely to negatively impact upon an employee's ability to perform his or her job and at the extreme, may cause the employee to quit.[2] Although many employers are committed to preventing discrimination for these reasons, for some, to be sure, complying with the law and avoiding the costs of litigation and payment of damages are also significant incentives.

Good preventive measures make good business sense. The preventive steps are not only important for stopping sex discrimination from taking place; they also provide a mechanism for remedying workplace conduct that is unacceptable to responsible employers and that can create a potential exposure to liability. In the event that litigation does ensue, the preventive steps (or their absence) will be important evidence regarding an employer's attempts to comply with its obligation to provide a workplace that is free of discrimination.

Definitions

At the outset, it is important to define unlawful sex discrimination. Title VII of the Civil Rights Act of 1964 ("Title VII") is the federal statute that prohibits employment discrimination against any individual on the basis of their sex.[3] It is expressly unlawful for an employer to take an adverse employment action against an applicant or employee because of his or her sex.[4] Title VII provides: "It shall be an unlawful employment practice for an employer to . . . fail or refuse to hire or discharge any individual or otherwise to discriminate against any individual with respect to his compensation, terms, conditions, or privileges of employment, because of such individual's . . . sex . . ."[5] Accordingly, actions such as refusing to hire, failing to promote, providing a lower rate of compensation, demoting, or firing an individual because of his or her gender are examples of adverse employment actions that are prohibited by Title VII. Discrimination of this kind is often referred to as gender-based "disparate treatment."

Sexual harassment

Sexual harassment is also a form of sex discrimination that is prohibited under Title VII. The term *quid pro quo* harassment is often used to describe circumstances in which a supervisor takes an adverse employment action against a subordinate for refusing to submit to the supervisor's sexual advances, which is plainly prohibited by Title VII.[6] The term "hostile environment" harassment is used to describe circumstances in which ". . . the workplace is permeated with discriminatory intimidation, ridicule, and insult that is sufficiently severe or pervasive to alter the conditions of the victim's employment and create an abusive working environment . . ."[7]

When courts are attempting to determine whether or not unlawful discrimination has occurred, the nature of the discrimination or harassment that is alleged will often determine the focus of the inquiry. For example, in a claim of quid pro quo harassment or gender-based disparate treatment, the question is usually whether the employer (through its supervisors or managers) acted with discriminatory intent. In other words, was the action taken because of the employee's refusal to submit to sexual advances (in the case of a quid pro quo claim) or because of the employee's gender (in the case of a disparate treatment claim)?

In the case of a hostile environment claim, the focus of the inquiry is typically upon whether the harassment was severe or pervasive enough to rise to the level of a violation of Title VII. "[I]n order to be actionable . . . a sexually objectionable environment must be both objectively and subjectively offensive, one that a reasonable person would find hostile or abusive, and one that the victim in fact did perceive to be so."[8] In order for these determinations to be made, the first question to be answered is whether the alleged conduct was welcome or unwelcome by the person making the complaint.[9] If the behavior is found to be unwelcome, additional questions arise as to the "frequency of the . . . conduct; its severity; whether it is physically threatening or humiliating, or a mere offensive utterance; and whether it unreasonably interferes with an employee's work performance."[10]

Sex Discrimination Policies and Training

In order to decrease the likelihood of sex discrimination or related claims and to increase the likelihood of prevailing in court in the event that litigation is brought, employers should consider: (1) adopting and implementing an effective equal employment opportunity ("EEO") and antiharassment policy; (2) training management and employees about discrimination, diversity, and harassment; (3) evaluating and compensating managers based upon their compliance with these policies; (4) periodically auditing the employer's overall compliance with its policies; and (5) formal or informal mentoring programs. In today's legal and business environment, the first two steps are virtually always warranted.

An EEO and antiharassment policy should: (1) describe the employer's commitment to complying with its obligations under the applicable federal, state and local laws prohibiting employment discrimination; (2) specify the types of discrimination and harassment that are prohibited; (3) describe the aspects of employment to which the nondiscrimination prohibition applies; (4) specifically state that the policy prohibits inappropriate conduct or comments (whether or not unlawful) relating to any protected class of persons under the policy or directed to any person because of their membership in any protected class; (5) include detailed examples of the type of conduct that is inappropriate so that there can be no misunderstanding or confusion about what is prohibited; (6) provide an effective internal complaint procedure for addressing conduct or comments that violate the policy; (7) state that the employer will endeavor to handle complaints in a confidential manner but that it reserves the right to disclose information to the extent that it deems necessary or appropriate to enforce the policy; (8) guarantee that no employee who raises a claim of discrimination, harassment, or retaliation or who cooperates with any investigation under the policy will be retaliated against; and (9) plainly state that any employee who violates the policy will be subject to disciplinary action up to and including the termination of employment.

In drafting the policy, employers should keep in mind the following key points. In order to be effective, the policy should specifically prohibit discrimination and harassment on the basis of membership in groups or classes protected by law, such as sex, race, age, national origin, religion, citizenship, disability, and any others protected by federal, state, or local law. However, not all jurisdictions prohibit discrimination on the basis of sexual orientation or marital status. Since discrimination on grounds such as these are as inimical to an employer's business as any other, employers should also prohibit discrimination and harassment on the basis of sexual orientation and family status.

It is very important that the policy prohibit inappropriate conduct and comments, not merely unlawful harassment. If a manager tells a blatantly sexist and degrading joke at a business meeting to the embarrassment of the only female employee who is present, standing alone, the comment is typically neither severe nor pervasive enough to constitute a hostile environment under Title VII. Nevertheless, the manager should be disciplined for violating the policy, without labeling him a sexual harasser or his statement as unlawful. This approach enables the employer to: (1) require that its workforce in general, and managers in particular, conduct themselves in a professional manner; (2) prohibit and disavow conduct that may be evidence of discriminatory intent and, if allowed to continue, which could rise to the level of a hostile environment; and (3) avoid labeling unacceptable conduct as unlawful (whether it is or not), which is unnecessary for taking corrective action and maintaining a professional work environment. As most employers are not expert in determining whether conduct rises to the level of a hostile environment under Title VII, nor are they required to be, refraining from labeling conduct as unlawful will help avoid both defamation suits by the accused as well as admissions that could be potentially damaging in litigation brought by the complainant.

The complaint procedure should be "user friendly." In other words, an employee should be able to complain to someone other than his or her supervisor, such as a human resources representative. The persons to whom complaints may be made under the policy should, if at all possible, include members of the same groups as those protected under the policy to help ensure that employees will be reasonably comfortable in making complaints. However, if the persons designated to receive complaints are not qualified or of sufficient stature in the workplace, their selection may be perceived as "tokenism" and negatively impact both the credibility of the employer's commitment to EEO and the efficacy of the policy.

It is also advisable for employees to have multiple avenues for raising complaints. For example, it is often prudent to provide field employees with the option of complaining to someone at the location where they work, at a regional or home office, and through an EEO "hotline." The idea is that employers should want to get complaints through their internal procedure, so that they can address any inappropriate or potentially unlawful conduct that occurs. The less desirable alternative is having the complaints addressed through a governmental agency, such as the Equal Employment Opportunity Commission, or in court.

In organizations with strong values and an openness to addressing employee concerns, inappropriate conduct can often be successfully addressed through informal means, without invoking the policy complaint procedure, but it is important that human resources be informed of the issue and resolution, if only to ensure that the resolution was effective and that "repeat offenders" are properly handled. For example, assume that a female employee complains to her manager that a male co-worker is "acting like a jerk" and upon inquiry it is learned that he is verbally bullying her. He can be reprimanded by the manager to "knock it off," which should be documented, along with the specific nature of the complaint. The bully may well correct his behavior based upon the oral reprimand and may be more likely to work in a reasonable manner with the employee who complained if the antiharassment policy is not invoked. And if the complainant is later disciplined for an unrelated event and contends that she has been retaliated against by the employer for making a gender discrimination claim, the employer may be able to successfully assert that she did not make a gender-based claim or otherwise engage in activity that is protected from retaliation under Title VII. Of course, if the bullying does not stop after the oral reprimand, the employer should take more extreme disciplinary action and if the complainant is not satisfied with the result and feels that she is being bullied because of her gender, she may later raise a formal claim for resolution under the policy.

Training should be conducted so that managers and employees alike have an understanding of: (1) the employer's commitment to providing a workplace that is free of discrimination and harassment; (2) a general understanding of what is meant by sexual harassment and the forms it may take; (3) the specific types of conduct and comments that the employer considers to be inappropriate; (4) how to raise harassment and discrimination claims under the policy; (5) the employer's intention to treat complaints as confidential to the extent practicable in conjunction with conducting a reasonable investigation and take prompt and appropriate remedial action in the event that its policy is violated; and (6) the employer's commitment to ensure that no employee is retaliated against for raising a complaint under the policy or cooperating with an investigation. In addition, supervisors and managers should be trained regarding their obligations to address any inappropriate conduct that comes to their attention as well as to report to human resources: (1) inappropriate conduct, even in the absence of a complaint; and (2) all formal and informal complaints of discrimination, harassment or inappropriate conduct prohibited by the policy, even complaints employees request be kept confidential.

Litigation

Disparate treatment litigation

Once litigation ensues, the strategies to be considered by the employer will depend in large part upon the nature of the claim. In a disparate treatment case, the plaintiff is first required to establish a prima facie case of discrimination. In a failure to promote case, for example, the prima facie is typically established by showing that: (1) the plaintiff is a member of a protected class; (2) the plaintiff was qualified for the promotion; (3) the plaintiff was denied the promotion; and (4) the position was open and was ultimately filled by a member of the opposite gender.[11]

Once the plaintiff establishes the prima facie case (which may also be shown by other means, such as direct evidence of discrimination) the burden of producing evidence shifts to the defendant, who must articulate a legitimate nondiscriminatory reason for the challenged action. If the defendant meets this burden of production, the plaintiff must then prove that the reason articulated by the defendant was not its real reason for the action. If the jury concludes that the employer's articulated reason was not the real reason for its action, the jury may – but is not required to – conclude that the plaintiff was unlawfully discriminated against.[12] What this means is that even if the jury thinks that the reason given by the employer is a pretext, (i.e., false), but that the real reason is not due to unlawful discrimination (e.g., dislike of a nasty or disagreeable person), then the jury is not required to conclude that the plaintiff was unlawfully discriminated against. But for reasons including the inclination of many juries to favor an individual over a large organization, a determination that the employer lied about its reasons will often lead to a verdict for the plaintiff.

Although in some gender cases the question of whether the plaintiff has proved a prima facie case is hotly contested, it would appear that many more cases center upon whether the plaintiff has been able to establish that the business reason articulated by the employer was really a pretext for unlawful discrimination. In the hypothetical promotion case described below, the litigation would focus on the employer's intent; namely, whether the decision maker failed to promote the plaintiff on the basis of gender. A plaintiff may try to prove their case through the use of evidence such as the following: (1) statements made by the employer suggesting gender bias; (2) evidence that the plaintiff is really more qualified than the person who was promoted, so the reason given by the employer for the promotion is not true; and (3) testimony of former employees who state that they were also discriminated against on the basis of gender.

In mounting the defense, the employer will need to assess whether the statements arguably suggesting gender bias are inadmissible because they are hearsay, because their probative value is outweighed by their prejudicial effect, or because they are evidence of wrongs that may not be used to prove the character of the employer. Heresay typically consists of an out-of-court statement offered in court to prove the truth of the matter asserted therein. Assume that a female plaintiff offers her own testimony that she heard that management only wanted to promote women if they were "eye candy" and that because the employer routinely promoted men who are not particularly attractive, this practice constitutes sex discrimination. If the plaintiff testifies that she heard a particular manager make the statement, it will not be excludable as heresay, because it will be considered an admission of the opposing party in the litigation, and under the Federal Rules of Evidence, such statements are admissible. On the other hand, if the alleged statement was just a rumor and the plaintiff can't remember where she heard the statement, it is properly excludable as hearsay.

Even if the "eye candy" statement is not hearsay, it may be inadmissible if the court determines that its probative value is outweighed by its prejudicial effect. The trial judge exercises broad discretion in conducting this inquiry under Federal Rule of Evidence 403. The judge will consider factors such as who allegedly made the statement and when it was allegedly made as a part of the inquiry. If the statement was made by the manager who made the decision not to promote the plaintiff and the statement was made during the time period when he was considering which employee to promote, the statement should be admitted. On the other end of the continuum, if the statement was made five years before the plaintiff was passed over for promotion by a first level supervisor in an unrelated department, the statement should not be admitted because it has marginal probative value regarding the intent behind the decision not to promote the plaintiff, and it could well prejudice or confuse the jury. The employer may also assert that statements of this nature are inadmissible under Federal Rule of Civil Procedure 404(b), which mandates that evidence of prior wrongs or acts may not be introduced ". . . to prove the character of a person in order to show action in conformity therewith." Statements offered to show discriminatory intent that are excluded from evidence under Rules 403 and/or 404(b) are often referred to as "stray comments."

When the employer defends against the plaintiff's argument that she was more qualified than the man who was promoted, it is very important to focus upon the criteria that the employer applied in making its decision. For example, if the plaintiff argues that she was more qualified based upon criteria other than that which were applied by the employer, the employer may be able to obtain dismissal of the claim on the grounds that it has the right to apply the criteria it deems appropriate, as long as they are not gender based. There are numerous cases stating that the courts do not sit as "super personnel departments" second-guessing the business decisions of employers.[13]

Of course, a plaintiff may always prove discrimination by showing that the employer's criteria were applied in a discriminatory manner. In addition to the use of direct evidence of discrimination, such as statements (like in the example above) from which the jury may infer discriminatory intent, the plaintiff will attempt to use comparators to show discrimination. In other words, the treatment of men and women who are similarly situated will be used to illustrate whether the criteria for promotion were applied in a gender-neutral way. Thus, if the employer can show that there were numerous male candidates with the same qualifications and performance levels as the female plaintiff and that they too were passed over for promotion, the plaintiff will have a steep uphill battle to avoid dismissal of the case by motion, let alone prevail at trial. In the same way, if the plaintiff can show that there are female employees (in addition to herself) who have been passed over for promotion but are similarly situated to men who have been promoted to the job she seeks, she would have a promising case, even in the absence of statements providing direct evidence of discriminatory intent.

In the event that the plaintiff seeks to introduce the testimony of other employees or former employees of the same gender that they were also passed over for promotion on the basis of sex, the employer should consider seeking to preclude the testimony under Rule 403. The asserted basis for exclusion under these circumstances is typically that the probative value of this evidence is outweighed by the time it will take to be presented, since the employer will be obliged to present evidence to explain the basis for its treatment of each of the witnesses who would testify that they were discriminated against, resulting in multiple mini-trials. The employer will also assert that there is a substantial risk of confusion to the jury when discrimination against persons other than the plaintiff is raised.

Sexual harassment litigation

In sexual harassment litigation, claims are often brought against the alleged harasser under various state law theories, in addition to the claims brought against the employer under Title VII. The first strategic decision for the employer to make in such cases is whether or not the same lawyer representing the employer can or should represent the alleged harasser as well. If it is clear that the principal defense in the case will be that the harassment did not take place, the same lawyer may be effective in representing both parties. But if the employer wishes (or may come to wish, depending upon developing facts) to distance itself from the alleged harasser's conduct, separate counsel should be engaged.

Where the basis of the claim is that the plaintiff was subjected to unwanted sexual advances, the case may focus upon whether the advances were indeed welcome. Evidence may include cards, letters, notes, and emails exchanged between the plaintiff and the alleged harasser, in which the plaintiff expresses his or her feelings about the alleged harasser. Any writings by the plaintiff about the harasser are typically fair game for exploration in the discovery process. So, for example, the plaintiff may be requested to produce any emails he or she authored about the alleged harasser, any diary notes about the harasser, and so forth.

Written documents that are obtained through discovery are often important for what they do not say, in seeking to establish that conduct was welcome. For example, diary entries or email communications to friends that are made at or about the time of the harassment that describe difficulties or problems faced by the plaintiff, yet do not include a description of the alleged harassment, can be used to show that the conduct complained of either did not occur or was welcome.

Similarly, the plaintiff will typically be asked in deposition who he or she told about the harassment. If the plaintiff did not tell friends or family members about it, the inference may be that either the conduct allegedly constituting harassment did not take place, or if it did, it was welcome[14]. To the extent that during a deposition the plaintiff withholds information about whom he or she told of the harassment to protect friends or family members from becoming involved as witnesses, the plaintiff damages his or her case (in addition to violating the obligation to testify truthfully).

A major area of inquiry will almost always be whether the plaintiff utilized the claims procedure included in the employer's antiharassment policy to complain about the harassment that is the subject matter of the suit. The failure to do so may be fatal to a hostile environment harassment claim that does not result in a tangible adverse employment action that is adverse to the plaintiff. As explained by the Supreme Court:

> An employer is subject to vicarious liability to a victimized employee for an actionable hostile environment created by a supervisor with immediate (or successively higher) authority over the employee. When no tangible employment action is taken, a defending employer may raise an affirmative defense to liability or damages, subject to proof by a preponderance of the evidence. See Fed. Rule Civ. Proc. 8(c). The defense comprises two necessary elements: (a) that the employer exercised reasonable care to prevent and correct promptly any sexually harassing behavior, and (b) that the plaintiff employee unreasonably failed to take advantage of any preventive or corrective opportunities provided by the employer or to avoid harm otherwise. While proof that an employer had promulgated an antiharassment policy with complaint procedure is not necessary in every instance as a matter of law, the need for a stated policy suitable to the employment circumstances may appropriately be addressed in any case when litigating the first element of the defense. And while proof that an employee failed to fulfill the corresponding obligation of reasonable care to avoid harm is not limited to showing an unreasonable failure to use any complaint procedure provided by the employer, a demonstration of such failure will normally suffice to satisfy the employer's burden under the second element of the defense. No affirmative defense is available, however, when the supervisor's harassment culminates in a tangible employment action, such as discharge, demotion, or undesirable reassignment.[15]

Based upon this standard, when a plaintiff does not bring a claim through the employer's claims procedure, the litigation will center upon whether the failure to do so was based upon matters such as the employer's failure to adequately communicate the terms of the procedure, concerns about retaliation based upon prior employer actions, and other reasons the plaintiff asserts form a reasonable basis for not using the procedure.

Under Title VII, the plaintiff may recover for emotional distress. The plaintiff often introduces testimony about the extreme emotional distress he or she suffered to prove that element of their damage case (not necessarily their liability case). Discovery will often involve a review of plaintiff's medical and psychological counseling records, if any. If the plaintiff does not report to his or her health care providers or therapists the emotional distress alleged to have been incurred as a result of the alleged harassment or any physical manifestations thereof, that may be a basis for the employer to assert that the employee's claims are overstated or fabricated. Similarly, a plaintiff's failure to exhibit changes in behavior and lifestyle after allegedly severe and distressful harassment may be used in the same manner. Psychological and psychiatric examinations of a plaintiff, conducted by an expert engaged by the defendant, may be ordered by the court when necessary to gain an understanding of the impact of the alleged harassment upon the plaintiff's emotional well-being. It should be noted that while Federal Rule of Evidence 412 protects plaintiffs from unwarranted inquiry into their past sexual conduct and predisposition, this protection does not apply to the inquiries into emotional distress described above. Furthermore, Rule 412(b)(2) permits evidence concerning past sexual conduct and predisposition under certain circumstances.

Personal Advice

Although it may seem idealistic, in many ways litigation is a search for the truth and a battle for the moral high ground. Perhaps what I mean may be illustrated by the following two brief anecdotes, based upon two cases that I handled years ago. The first case involved a sexual harassment claim in which the plaintiff claimed that she was sexually assaulted in her apartment one evening by a male co-worker, and that the employer subjected her to a hostile work environment by not firing the co-worker when she informed them of the incident. The second also involved a sexual harassment claim, with the claimant asserting that she was fired for fighting off her manager when he attempted to sexually assault her. The first case eventually was voluntarily withdrawn by the plaintiff after it was discovered that she had falsely sworn a criminal complaint against her live-in boyfriend, in which she accused him of assaulting her. She later withdrew the criminal complaint and admitted that it was false. In the second case, a settlement was reached after it was determined that the employer had minimal documentation with which to support its defense that the plaintiff's performance was so poor as to justify her involuntary termination.

Had the first case proceeded to trial, the plaintiff would have had to admit that she was the kind of person who would swear a false complaint. Perhaps the plaintiff was concerned that the jury would view her as a dishonest person who could not be relied upon to tell the truth about the alleged sexual assault or the atmosphere at work. Did the fact that she swore a false complaint against her boyfriend mean that she fabricated the co-worker's alleged assault? In the second case, the employer settled. Had that case been tried, the manager who fired the plaintiff would have been subject to sharp cross-examination about how the plaintiff's performance could have been so poor as to warrant termination, given the scant documentation of performance difficulties. Did the fact that he fired the plaintiff without informing her in writing about her performance problems, what she needed to do to improve, and that if she did not improve she would be fired, mean that he tried to sexually assault her and fire her for refusing to submit?

The goal for the reasonable employer, of course, should be to avoid litigation by treating employees in a businesslike manner, promoting an atmosphere demonstrating management's commitment to business ethics and fairness, and maintaining effective policies and procedures to address any improper conduct that may be engaged in by rogue employees or supervisors. If an employer does these things and litigation ensues, it should be well positioned to prevail. And in the event that a reasonable employee is poorly treated in such an environment, he or she should have suitable avenues for correcting the problem without resorting to litigation. With these truisms stated, I suspect that employment litigation will continue to be prevalent for many years to come.

Notes

1 Burlington Industries v. Ellerth, 524 U.S. at 757, 118 S.Ct. at 2266.

2 In order to show that sexual harassment is severe enough to support a constructive discharge claim, the former employee must establish ". . . working conditions so intolerable that a reasonable person would have felt compelled to resign." Pennsylvania State Police v. Suders, 542 U.S. 129, 147; 124 S.Ct. 2343, 2354 (2004).

3 42 U.S.C. Sec. 2000e-2(a). Title VII also prohibits discrimination on the basis of race, color, religion, or national origin.

4 Title VII prohibits discrimination against both men and women because of sex.

5 42 U.S.C. Sec. 2000e-2(a)(1).

6 Burlington Industries, Inc. v. Ellerth, 524 U.S. 742, 753–754; 118 S.Ct. 2257, 2265 (1998).

7 Harris v. Forklift Systems, Inc., 510 U.S. 17, 21; 144 S.Ct. 367, 370 (1993) (internal quotations and citations omitted).

8 Faragher v. City of Boca Raton, 524 U.S. 775, 787, 118 S.Ct. 2275, 2283 (1998) (citing Harris v. Forklift Systems, Inc., 510 U.S. at 21–22, 144 S.Ct. at 370–371).

9 The Supreme Court has explained that the issue is whether the alleged harassment is welcome, not whether the complainant's participation is voluntary. Meritor Savings Bank v. Vinson, 477 U.S. 57, 68; 106 S.Ct. 2399, 2406 (1986). As the Court explained: "the correct inquiry is whether respondent by her conduct indicated that the alleged sexual advances were unwelcome, not whether her actual participation in sexual intercourse was voluntary."

10 Faragher v. City of Boca Raton, 524 U.S. 775, 788, 118 S.Ct. 2275, 2283 (1998) (internal quotations and citations omitted).

11 See, e.g., St. Mary's Honor Center v. Hicks, 509 U.S. 502, 506; 113 S.Ct. 2742, 2747 (1993) (describing prima facie case shown in race discrimination case challenging failure to promote and termination).

12 St. Mary's Honor Center v. Hicks, 509 U.S. at 511; 113 S.Ct. at 2749.

13 See e.g. Millbrook v. IBP, Inc., 280 F.3d 1169, 1180–1181 (7th Cir. 2002).

14 Editors' comment: However, see Beiner and O'Connor's (this volume) discussion of why targets of harassment or discrimination are generally unlikely to voice their complaints to others – at least not initially.

15 Faragher v. City of Boca Raton, 524 U.S. 775, 777–778, 118 S. Ct. 2275, 2278–2279 (1998) (citing Burlington Industries, Inc. v. Ellerth, 524 U.S. 742, 118 S. Ct. 2257 (1998)).

3

When an Individual Finds Herself to be the Victim of Sex Discrimination

*Theresa M. Beiner and
Maureen O'Connor*

For a person who believes her employer has engaged in sex discrimination, there are a variety of approaches that she[1] can use to address the problem. Ranging from trying to solve the problem informally with the person engaging in the discrimination to filing a lawsuit seeking relief, depending on what the employee seeks to gain and the nature of the discrimination, there are numerous possible options. First, the employee can try to work out the problem informally with the person who is perpetrating the discrimination. In addition, it is common for employers to have some sort of internal grievance mechanism or complaint process that permits an employee to make a more formal complaint. Sometimes there are alternative dispute resolution resources such as mediation or arbitration that are available through the Equal Employment Opportunity Commission (EEOC), directly through the employer, or through a private entity that the employee can use in an attempt to remedy the situation. Finally, if all else fails, the employee can file a lawsuit and pursue a variety of claims and remedies.

Individuals often try to resolve problems informally before moving to formal means of resolution. While quite understandable, a person's reluctance to engage in adversarial encounters can have an unfortunate consequence if too much time elapses after the occurrence of the incident or incidences. In many jurisdictions, a victim has only 90 days in which to file a grievance with the Equal Employment Opportunity Commission if she wishes to exercise her right to bring a lawsuit. In fact, in some instances, the EEOC may recommend that the plaintiff and the defendant enter into mediation or arbitration rather than proceeding directly to litigation. In order to keep open various options, the person who thinks she may have been the victim of employment discrimination should consult with the EEOC at the earliest possible moment, even while exploring informal means of conflict resolution.

This chapter examines various options from the perspectives of both law and psychology. We explore psychological studies that might bear on the efficacy of potential remedies. We start by looking at informal attempts; then move to the use of mechanisms in the place of employment; then consider alternative modes of resolution (mediation and arbitration and then litigation). At the end of the chapter, we consider the advantages and disadvantages of various alternatives.

Our chapter does not contain a separate section on settlement as a tool for resolution. Most legal disputes are settled. Indeed, mediation, one of the methods described in this chapter, is designed to facilitate the parties reaching a settlement. The parties always have the opportunity to open a dialogue and settle the problem between them either informally or with the aid of lawyers. Settlement is not unique to sex discrimination claims, but occurs in most civil lawsuits. For sex discrimination, the plaintiff or her lawyer can simply call or write the employer or its attorney, as is ethically appropriate, to propose a set-tlement. In any event, once a lawsuit is filed, all federal courts require parties to participate in a settlement conference.[2] Thus, settlement is always an option through all phases of a sex discrimination dispute.

Informal Responses

After a casual, mutually agreed upon lunch between Kerry Ellison and a co-worker, Sterling Gray, Gray continued to ask Ellison out and pester her at her work station.[3] When he wrote her an odd note saying he had "cried over her" last night, she showed the note to her supervisor, but told him she wanted to handle it herself. She asked a male co-worker to let Gray know that she was not interested in further contact with him. These informal efforts did not, however, deter Mr. Gray, who continued to pursue Ms. Ellison, leading eventually to full-scale sex discrimination litigation that went all the way to the U.S. Court of Appeals for the 9th Circuit.

Why would Ms. Ellison try to handle this matter informally, without esca-lating it to the level of a formal complaint? Why didn't she just complain through official workplace channels? Most people believe and report that if they were faced with potential discrimination, they would themselves confront the person engaging in that discriminatory behavior.[4] Shelton and Stewart found, for example, that women asked to imagine a discriminatory job interview report that they would confront the perpetrator regardless of the social cost of the sit-uation (e.g., whether successfully obtaining the job based on the interview was a strong goal).[5] Yet, the reality appears to be to the contrary. During simulated interviews, most women did not actually confront the discriminator in contrast to the hypothetical results, especially in situations where the social costs of con-frontation might be high.[6]

In actuality, what might be even more surprising to feminist scholars and others who study the experience of discrimination or other victimization is that

Ms. Ellison mentioned it to anyone at all.[7] There is no reliable estimate about how much discrimination goes completely unreported. Yet, there are a number of reasons to suspect that much discriminatory behavior is either not dealt with at all, or handled through informal channels.

As we know from crime reporting rates, only a small proportion of crimes, even violent crimes, are ever reported to authorities.[8] Similarly, comparisons of the proportion of survey respondents who report experience with discriminatory behavior with the number of claims filed reveal significant under-reporting.[9] This has been examined empirically to a significant extent in the sexual harassment context. Bond points to evidence that the proportion of sexual harassment claims actually reported is low.[10] Livingston found that although 42% of female federal workers reported experience of an unwanted social-sexual experience in their workplace (e.g., sexual harassment), only 11% of those workers told someone in authority about their experience. Moreover, less than 3% used formal complaint channels.[11] Gruber concluded that between 10% and 15% of targets of harassment respond assertively to the perpetrator either by confrontation or complaint.[12] In its 1994 sexual harassment survey, the U.S. Merit Systems Protection Board reported that while "doing nothing" continued to be the most common response, 35% of targets reported asking or telling the offender to stop, and nearly 60% of both men and women reported that doing so made the situation better.[13]

Possible explanations for chronic under-complaining range from the psychological, social, cultural, to the political, legal, and pragmatic. Some evidence suggests that people may not necessarily perceive potentially discriminatory behavior as discrimination that would warrant a formal dispute mechanism,[14] and therefore do not opt for formal complaint mechanisms. Some people may, for example, simply have difficulty naming the behavior as discrimination when it occurs (sometimes the conduct involves sexual innuendo and ambiguity).[15] Others may minimize their reaction to it to avoid negative consequences from acknowledging it.[16] Kaiser and Miller, however, challenged the minimization of discrimination hypothesis in a series of studies showing that the cognitive processes involved in these situations are more complex than originally conceived.[17] A sense of self-blame or embarrassment about the situation can also contribute to underreporting.[18] In any event, it is clear that the manner in which people react psychologically to potentially discriminatory behavior will affect the choice of responses to it.

In addition to individual factors that might be involved, there are "negative social consequences" when people attribute events and behavior to discrimination.[19] After reviewing the interview-based literature exploring the social consequences of claiming discrimination, Kaiser and Miller found convincing evidence that the social costs can be severe, ranging from worsening an already tense situation, to damage to social and professional relationships and negative reactions from co-workers.[20] Particularly for targets of discrimination from groups that have experienced long-standing discrimination, e.g., women and ethnic minorities, assigning blame to someone in a position of power can be especially problematic.[21]

Additional political and legal costs that can arise include potential retaliation by co-workers or managers; loss of job/economic well-being; strained work relationships with the concomitant stress associated with heightened tension; mental and physical health consequences; or a realistic appraisal of the difficulties involved in litigating a discrimination claim. Studies have confirmed these are realistic fears for those who complain, particularly those in sexualized, non-traditional, and unsupportive work environments.[22] It may be, therefore, that more calculated weighing of the costs and benefits associated with complaining leads to lower rates of formal complaints, especially with less severe forms of discrimination.[23]

Whatever reasons might explain the responses by many discrimination targets, the evidence is strong that only a small proportion of targets respond by formally complaining about the perpetrator of the behavior.[24] Instead, many targets use less formal, less direct responses that can take many forms.[25] One response, for example, is essentially a non-response, what Fitzgerald and colleagues have called silent tolerance of the behavior.[26] Many targets simply ignore the behavior or actively seek ways to avoid it and its perpetrator as much as possible.[27] Estimates on the prevalence of this response range from a fifth to a third[28] to a full half of one study of female Naval officers.[29] This "discrimination management" approach may be perceived as the best option for workers who are simply trying to keep their jobs and who hope the offending behavior will cease. As Riger explained, these informal responses have as their goal to end the harassment, not to punish or judge the offender.[30]

A different type of response is to go along with the problematic behavior by telling jokes, bantering, and so forth; what Fitzgerald and her colleagues call the "instigator-in-kind" response.[31] In his review of studies examining target responses, Gruber found evidence for attempting to diffuse the situation with humor, and for playing along with the problematic behavior as well,[32] though for approximately two-thirds of the respondents to the U.S. Merit System Protection Board 1994 survey, such a response made no difference, and for one-third of women it made the situation worse.[33] And, as it turns out, Kerry Ellison's initial response of turning to a friend or co-worker is more prevalent than lodging a formal complaint with a supervisor or union official.[34]

A non-confrontational, but certainly not passive, strategy is to leave the workplace altogether.[35] A 1988 survey of federal workers, for example, reported that 36,000 women had left their jobs because of harassment.[36] One of the most important early studies of working women reported as many as 1 in 7 had quit their jobs because of harassment.[37]

Internal Employer Mechanisms

Since the growth of equal employment opportunity law began in the 1960s, employers (working with human resources staff and lawyers) have adopted an array of mechanisms for dealing with disputes, grievances, hiring and firing, and other employment issues in the workplace.[38] Bisom-Rapp cites one large-scale study of nearly 500 large companies, for example, which found that 80 percent had formal performance appraisal mechanisms in place.[39] Studies by Edelman[40] and by Dobbin[41] have tracked the significant growth in a broad range of personnel policies, including grievance mechanisms, that parallels the development of equal employment opportunity law. A 1999 survey by the Society for Human Resources Management revealed that 97 percent of the responding organizations had written sexual harassment policies in place.

The U.S. Supreme Court has contributed to the growth in EEO compliance policies and procedures by articulating a directive to employers who want to avoid liability in discrimination cases: Have clear and well-communicated antidiscrimination policies in place. The U.S. Supreme Court dealt with the issue of employer liability in a series of cases in the 1990s, and developed a template for liability that goes beyond the former reliance on agency principles.[42] Where an employee has suffered some tangible harm in the workplace from harassment, the employer has no real defense to such a lawsuit regardless of prior employer knowledge because an employer is presumed to be responsible for supervising the supervisors at its worksite.

Where a harassed employee has *not* suffered any adverse action on the job, however, the liability scheme changes. In that circumstance, an employer may assert an affirmative defense if it exercised reasonable care in preventing or promptly correcting any sexually harassing behavior and the employee unreasonably failed to take advantage of the preventive and/or corrective opportunities offered by the employer or otherwise failed to avoid the harm.[43]

The EEOC has suggested that reasonable care "generally requires an employer to establish, disseminate, and enforce an anti-harassment policy and complaint procedure and to take other reasonable steps to prevent and correct harassment."[44] The presence or absence of a sexual harassment policy is not a guaranteed defense, but it is certainly an essential first step.

The other component of the Supreme Court's affirmative defense scheme concerns the plaintiff's failure to complain. As Beiner points out, trial courts in particular have been highly skeptical of plaintiffs who fail to assertively complain right from the outset.[45] Yet, as we saw above, the targets of harassment respond in multi-layered and psychologically complex ways to potentially offending behavior – some actively complain, some never complain, some simply leave, others try to manage the situation, etc. As O'Connor and Vallabhajosula state, failure to complain may in fact be a reasonable response, especially in situations where the policy does not provide the affected employee with neutral options for complaint.[46]

Neither the U.S. Supreme Court nor the EEOC has specified the exact elements of an antidiscrimination policy that must be in place in order for it to satisfy legal muster. A veritable industry of consultants, trainers, and lawyers has weighed in on what such a policy should contain.[47] In its 1999 survey, the Society for Human Resource Management found that most of the respondent companies that had sexual harassment policies included the following elements in nine out of ten policies: a statement that sexual harassment is unlawful sex discrimination; a definition of what constitutes sexual harassment; and a chain of command specified for complaints. Prohibitions against retaliation, commitment to eradicating sexual harassment, and statements about confidentiality of complaints were contained in 78–80 percent of the policies.[48] One former Chairman of the EEOC recommends that an effective harassment policy have the following elements: be in writing; define what constitutes harassment; establish a complaint procedure; involve training and education programs; include a prompt and thorough investigation of every complaint; and provide for prompt corrective action.[49]

The legal framework has led to an increased focus on so-called "zero-tolerance" policies, which are now considered by some to be the "lynchpin" to preventing and defending discrimination claims.[50] Yet, little empirical support exists for the effectiveness of such policies, and some scholars predict they may only provide the illusion of a solution.[51]

The existence of a complaint procedure is not sufficient to ensure successful antidiscrimination policies.[52] The policy must be effectively communicated to employees and there must be support for EEO goals at the top.[53] One study found that leadership was a mediator of the relationship between organizational climate and the target's tendency to report the discrimination, suggesting the importance of leaders' commitment to the organization's policies.[54]

Alternative Dispute Resolution: Mediation and Arbitration

One way to avoid the difficulties associated with litigation, which are described more fully later in this chapter, is for a complainant to use an alternative dispute resolution program. There are several avenues open to sex discrimination victims. These include mediation programs (either through the EEOC, the employer, or some other organization) and arbitration. Each has advantages and disadvantages for sex discrimination victims. However, the overall advantage they both purportedly offer is that they tend to be swifter and less expensive than litigating a case through trial. This section will set out the nature of each dispute resolution tool, including a discussion of their pros and cons.

Mediation

Mediation has become increasingly accessible to sex discrimination victims largely because of the EEOC mediation program. Since April of 1999, some complainants filing charges of sex discrimination with the EEOC could voluntarily participate in that organization's mediation program if the employer likewise agreed to mediate. In addition to the EEOC's mediation program, private employers sometimes offer mediation programs of their own. Finally, the parties simply can agree to mediate at any time – prior to a charge being filed or even after a lawsuit is filed – in an effort to settle the dispute.

Mediation is conducted by a neutral third party who facilitates an agreement between the parties. A mediator is not a decision maker, but instead helps the parties reach and craft their own solution. From both parties' perspectives, this provides much more control over the outcome of the dispute than if they took the case to trial, where there would necessarily be a winner and a loser. Mediation allows for creative solutions as well, because the parties are not limited to relief that normally would be available in the legal system. For example, in the context of sexual harassment, one outcome can be that the harasser apologizes to his victim. As the EEOC explains:

> Mediation gives the parties the opportunity to discuss the issues raised in the charge, clear up misunderstandings, determine the underlying interests or concerns, find areas of agreement and, ultimately, to incorporate those areas of agreement into resolutions.[55]

Mediations have several stages. As mediator Mori Irvine explains, mediation can involve overlapping stages: "introduction of the process by the mediator"; "presentation of viewpoints by each of the parties"; emotional expressions by the parties; "caucusing [the mediator meeting privately with a party] to discuss confidential information"; "exploration of alternative solutions"; and forging an agreement that the parties find acceptable.[56]

Mediators facilitate discussion of the dispute with all parties present and, at other times, through "caucusing" with each party individually. During caucuses, the parties split up to discuss their individual positions, including confidential information that they would prefer the other side not know. The mediator will move between the two groups, facilitating the conversation.

There are three basic types of mediator styles: facilitative, evaluative (also known as directive), or a hybrid of both.[57] A facilitative mediator helps the parties reach their own settlement without evaluating the strengths or weaknesses of each side's case. An evaluative mediator will provide occasional "reality checks" (usually during caucuses), whereby the mediator will tell one side or the other about the weaknesses of its position.[58] Both styles can be helpful in settling a case and some mediators employ both, depending on the positions of the parties. It is noteworthy that, while the EEOC trains its mediators to be facilitative, a study of EEOC mediations suggests that nearly half of EEOC mediators use an evaluative approach during mediations.[59] The EEOC drew that conclusion from a study in which EEOC mediators described the behaviors that they believed facilitated resolution of the case. In 46 percent of the cases, mediators used behaviors associated with evaluative mediations.[60] Thus, parties entering an EEOC mediation should be prepared for either a facilitative or evaluative mediation style.

Because mediations are essentially a type of settlement conference, what occurs during them is considered confidential. The EEOC requires the mediator and the parties to sign an agreement stating that matters revealed during mediation will be kept confidential. For this reason, the EEOC keeps the charge process separate from mediations, which essentially act like confidential settlement negotiations. They do not want the charge investigator to be biased by what was said in mediation. It would undermine the mediation process (deter full candor) if what was said in the mediation could come back to haunt a party in the charge investigation process. EEOC mediators, then, only mediate charges; they do not participate in investigations.[61] The information revealed during mediation appears to have an impact on the ability of the parties to resolve the dispute. In their survey of mediators, the EEOC found that the most common variables that caused a turning point in the mediation were "communication and discovery-related" variables, such as "changes in the charging party and respondent position, demands, or behavior due to information obtained at the mediation."[62] Thus, the parties might learn things in the mediation process that are helpful to resolving the dispute, such as the reason the employer promoted a person other than the charging party or the sex discriminatory words said to the plaintiff during her termination. EEOC mediations generally last about 3–4 hours and may take a longer or shorter period of time, depending on the case.[63] There is no fee for this mediation.

Mediations allow for creative solutions, including non-monetary relief. According to the EEOC, in almost half of the cases it mediates, the settlement involves a non-monetary benefit. "Since the program's inception, in approximately 15% of cases, the only benefit involved in settlement is non-monetary."[64] Studies of settlement information suggest that it may be to an employer's advantage to simply apologize for any discriminatory behavior.[65] In a survey of EEOC mediators, 13% of mediators surveyed responded that the dispute they mediated was resolved by "apology/admission/remorse, empathy or recognizing the charging party's concerns."[66] Another 5% were resolved by the respondent "addressing and/or understanding the charging party's concerns."[67] In addition, "acknowledgment of feelings and culpability" served as a turning point in 9% of mediations studied by the EEOC.[68] Thus, an apology or expressing understanding can help resolve such disputes. However, the most common response by mediators about the conduct of both charging parties and responding parties that contributes to resolving disputes during mediation is flexibility and openness, that is, on the part of charging parties, "honesty, flexibility, openness, realism, straightforward dealing, good problem solving skills, taking some responsibility for the dispute and other similar types of behavior,"[69] and on the part of responding parties, "willingness to negotiate and/or to explore settlement options, act in good faith, flexibility, expression of a desire to keep the responding party as an employee, and other such conduct."[70]

The EEOC apparently engages in a triage process to determine which cases are appropriate for mediation. For charges that appear to be meritorious, or those that require additional information in order to determine if they are meritorious, the parties will be offered the opportunity to mediate.[71] This usually occurs shortly after the charge is filed. However, the EEOC permits parties to request mediation at any point in its administrative process.[72] The only exception is charges that the EEOC determines are without merit, which are ineligible for mediation under this program.[73]

Of course, the parties can always hire a mediator to help them resolve the dispute outside of the EEOC's mediation process. The American Arbitration Association (AAA), along with other organizations, provides mediation services. Indeed, the AAA has rules governing employment mediations and arbitrations, which are more fully discussed in the arbitration section of this chapter. In such cases, the parties usually split the cost of the mediator, although there is some flexibility in fee arrangements. Some employers have internal mediation programs that are free to the employee. However, as the employer is paying the mediator in these programs, there is some concern that the mediator may be biased in favor of the employer.

Mediations can occur with or without an attorney, depending on how the parties or the program is structured. Both parties are permitted to bring attorneys to EEOC mediations. Plaintiffs are well advised to bring an attorney to mediation if they are interested in monetary damages. In their study of EEOC mediations, McDermott and Obar found that a complainant who does not have an attorney present during mediation is at a disadvantage when it comes to the amount of any settlement as charging parties represented by counsel obtained higher monetary settlements in evaluative mediations.[74] However, those who participated in facilitative mediations were more satisfied than those who participated in evaluative mediations.[75] Where the charging party was not represented by counsel, evaluative mediation led to lower settlements than mediations during which an attorney represented the charging party.[76]

Where possible, parties deciding to use mediation should inquire as to whether the mediator has a preferred style – facilitative or evaluative. A complainant should be cognizant of what she wants out of the process and the relationship between her desired outcome – whether it be monetary or non-monetary – and mediator style. Thus, although a charging party is not required to have an attorney, it is wise to do so if a large monetary settlement is important to the charging party. In any event, it is prudent for a complainant at least to consult an attorney prior to attending a mediation so that she knows what her legal rights are should the mediation fail. In addition, consulting an attorney provides a complainant with information that will allow her to determine whether she is being offered a reasonable settlement in the mediation or should go ahead with a lawsuit instead.

Mediation in the employment discrimination context has been rather successful. For example, the EEOC's program has resolved many charges of discrimination. "From 1999 through 2003, over 52,400 mediations have been held and more than 35,100 charges, or 69%, have been successfully resolved in an average of 85 days."[77] This compares favorably to the traditional charge investigation process, which on average takes 160 days to go through the investigative process.[78] Thus, the EEOC process is fast and relatively successful. Likewise, the United States Postal Service implemented a mediation program that resulted in disputes being resolved 61% of the time in an average of four hours.[79]

The EEOC has found mediation more popular with employees than employers, with 80% of complainants invited to mediate being willing to do so, whereas only 36% of employers accepted the EEOC's invitation to mediate.[80] A study of those who participated in EEOC mediations found that 96% of all respondents and 91% of all charging parties who had used the program would use it again.[81] This is consistent with other studies of mediation, which show high rates of client satisfaction.[82]

The EEOC also now mediates some charges where it has found discrimination. However, unlike mediations that occur prior to the completion of the official investigation, in post-investigation mediations, the EEOC actually sits as a participant in "conciliation" mediations,[83] because once it has found that discrimination is likely present, it has an interest in the resolution of the dispute.

Arbitration

The Federal Arbitration Act (FAA) was enacted in 1925 and expressed a "liberal federal policy favoring arbitration agreements."[84] The Act provides that written arbitration agreements "shall be valid, irrevocable, and enforceable, save upon such grounds as exist at law or in equity for the revocation of any contract."[85] Initially, the Act was not thought to apply to Title VII claims because that statute did not mention arbitration, but instead provided for a judicial forum for resolution of such claims.[86] After the Supreme Court's 1991 decision in *Gilmer v. Interstate/Johnson Lane Corp.*, holding that the FAA applied to an Age Discrimination in Employment Act (ADEA) claim, courts and employers began to use arbitration agreements to resolve statutory employment discrimination claims.[87] Initially not all courts agreed that the reasoning of the ADEA case extended to Title VII cases. However, a later Supreme Court case, *Circuit City Stores v. Adams*,[88] interpreting the FAA is thought to have laid the issue to rest, with Title VII cases also being arbitrable.[89] The Supreme Court has also held that state employment discrimination claims, unlike the indecision with respect to Title VII, are subject to mandatory arbitration agreements.[90] In fact, arbitration of employment discrimination suits became increasingly common after a Supreme Court decision in 1991 that endorsed the use of arbitration to resolve employment discrimination suits.[91]

Arbitration may be thought of as a procedure that lies between mediation and litigation. Unlike mediation, during which the parties essentially resolve the dispute themselves, in arbitration an arbitrator sits as a fact finder and decision maker. In arbitration, as in litigation, there will be a winner and a loser. Arbitrations are essentially expedited, informal mini-trials. The parties can present witnesses and evidence to support their positions, both of which are subject to cross-examination. However, unlike litigation in court, the rules of evidence for arbitration tend to be looser and the proceedings much less formal. In addition, there is generally less opportunity for pre-arbitration discovery (i.e., the compulsory disclosure of information related to the litigation at a party's request), than would occur in litigation where discovery has broad reach and the discovery phase of a trial can be protracted.[92] Instead, in arbitration the discovery provision simply provides that the arbitrator may order discovery he or she "considers necessary to a full and fair exploration of the issues in dispute, consistent with the expedited nature of arbitration."[93] This reduces the likelihood of the sort of full-blown discovery disputes that are common in civil litigation. Finally, there is no jury; instead the arbitrator makes the decision in the case. Sometimes, a team of three arbitrators decides the case.[94]

Because of concerns regarding fairness, various arbitration organizations have adopted a due process protocol for arbitration of employment disputes.[95] The protocol establishes a right to have a representative during the arbitration, permits access to "information reasonably relevant to . . . arbitration of their claims" (including depositions), and provides for the authority of the arbitrator.[96] Some arbitration clauses permit the employee to have an attorney, and other agreements provide that if the employee represents herself, the company will not use an attorney either.[97] In addition, the American Arbitration Associatio(AAA) has adopted National Rules for the Resolution of Employment Disputes, which include rules related to discovery, qualifications of arbitrators, and evidence, among other things.[98] Although the AAA rules govern many aspects of the arbitration (as well as mediation) process, they are written in a manner that emphasizes flexibility and the expedited nature of the process.[99]

The employer and employee can enter into an arbitration agreement either before or after an employment dispute arises. These agreements generally provide that any dispute that arises out of the employment relationship will be resolved through arbitration rather than litigation in the court system. The parties to the agreement can choose to have the agreement governed by rules of independent arbitration organizations, such as the AAA.

One issue that arises in arbitration is who picks and pays the arbitrator. Most agreements permit both parties to have input on the choice of arbitrator. Generally this is accomplished by each side striking names from a list generated by an arbitration organization.[100] Another issue involves costs. The costs associated with arbitration include the fee for the arbitrator, travel costs, filing fees, hearing costs including room charges, and other costs associated with carrying out the arbitration. The parties generally designate in the arbitration agreement which side will pay the costs of the arbitration. Sometimes the employer agrees to pay for the arbitrator and in other instances the employer and employee split the costs. According to Section 48 of the AAA rules, there is a filing fee of $150 for the claimant and a higher filing fee for employers. The AAA's position is that the hearings fees themselves will be paid by the employer.[101]

The agreement will generally dictate how the arbitrator is paid. Sometimes, the employer pays the full cost of the arbitrator. Other times, the employee and employer split the cost of the arbitrator, or an employee pays a set reasonable sum, such as $50, toward the cost of the arbitrator. The AAA due process protocol recommends that the parties split the cost in order to assure impartiality, although it contemplates that there may be situations in which a party does not have the financial means to pay for the arbitration.[102] Under these circumstances, the parties can agree to an arrangement that shifts all or more of the fees to the employer or lets the arbitrator decide the fee allocation.[103] Some courts will not enforce arbitration agreements where the employee must pay part of the cost of the arbitrator, noting that had the plaintiff brought her case in court under Title VII, she would not be required to pay for the cost of the judge.[104] A study of AAA arbitrators found that arbitrators shift their fees (compensation, travel costs) to the employer in 70.25% of cases; fees associated with the hearing itself, such as room costs, in 71.3%; and some or all of filing fees in 81.12%.[105] Even where the arbitrator has found in the employer's favor, the arbitrators shifted some or all of these fees in 65% of the cases.[106] Thus, as a practical matter, most complainants may not end up incurring large costs in arbitration. Finally, in some jurisdictions, there are *pro bono* arbitrators who work for free.

There are very limited rights to appeal from the decision of an arbitrator. Under the FAA, review in courts essentially is limited to acts of fraud or misconduct.[107] Courts also have overturned an arbitrator's decision if it showed "manifest disregard of the law."[108]

Arbitrations, like mediations, also generally are not open to the public. They take place privately. So, to the extent that either side wants to limit or to increase publicity about the case, arbitration may or may not be an appropriate dispute resolution mechanism.[109]

Some employers require employees to sign arbitration agreements as a term of employment. The U.S. Circuit Courts of Appeal are divided on whether such agreements are enforceable under Title VII. Seven circuits enforce them; five circuits do not.[110] In addition, even in jurisdictions in which such agreements are enforced, courts only enforce them if they are "fair."[111] Any waiver of the statutory rights protected by Title VII must be "clear and unmistakable" in the agreement.[112] Parties who do not wish to arbitrate can litigate these issues, increasing the costs of arbitration.

State and Federal Lawsuits

The federal government and most states[113] have statutes prohibiting sex discrimination in employment. In Chapter 15 Rhode and Williams describe the various laws that prohibit discrimination in employment. Therefore, those laws will not be canvassed here. Instead, one facet of the pre-litigation process under Title VII of the Civil Rights Act of 1964 – the EEOC charge process – will be discussed in this section as well as the potential remedies available to plaintiffs through the litigation process.

The EEOC charge process

Before a plaintiff can file a claim for sex discrimination under Title VII in court, she must first file a charge, detailing the wrongdoing, with the EEOC or the equivalent state agency.[114] The EEOC is the federal agency charged with enforcing Title VII. It receives over 24,000 charges of sex discrimination each year.[115]

The EEOC charge process takes place prior to litigation and provides several avenues for resolving the dispute prior to filing a lawsuit. In fiscal year 2004, the EEOC settled 11.3% of the charges filed. It found reasonable cause to believe there was discrimination in 6.4% of the cases, which it then attempted to conciliate. In 58.2% of the charges disposed of in 2004, it found no reasonable cause to believe the employer discriminated. Another 19% were administratively closed, and 5.1% were withdrawn without any benefits. All in all, in 2004, the EEOC was responsible for recovering for victims $100.8 million.[116] This does not include cases that were resolved through litigation.

The EEOC charge process is designed to operate swiftly. To begin with, a complainant has a limited amount of time to file such a charge. The plaintiff must file her charge within either 180 or 300 days after the discriminatory act, depending on the state in which she resides.[117] If she does not file the charge within the requisite time period, her claim will be considered untimely, and she will not be able to pursue her claim with the EEOC or in the federal court system under Title VII. The 180 day deadline is used in states where there is no work share agreement between the EEOC and a state equivalent of the EEOC. To avoid duplication of effort by the EEOC and state agencies, Congress provided a longer time period in which to file charges if the state set up a fair employment agency that agreed to cooperate with the EEOC in its investigation process.[118] Thus, a complainant has 300 days to file a charge in those states that have an EEOC equivalent and are under a work share agreement with the EEOC. The EEOC advises complainants to file charges with both the EEOC and the state agency, if one exists.[119] While most states have such an agency, three do not.[120] A plaintiff should file her charge with the EEOC as early as possible so that she does not risk losing her claim by waiting. The reason for this short time frame is to encourage prompt complaints that can be settled expeditiously and, hopefully, without resort to the court system.

After receiving a charge, the EEOC engages in a triage process, separating charges into three categories: (1) those in which discrimination is likely; (2) those in which additional information is needed to make a determination; and (3) those in which discrimination is unlikely.[121] Parties to the first two categories of cases are offered the opportunity to mediate. If the parties do not agree to mediate, the EEOC proceeds with an investigation, requesting information from the employer. Due to the number of charges filed, commentators have noted that the EEOC rarely completes a meaningful investigation of the charge.[122] After the EEOC investigates, it has several options. First, should the EEOC decide that there is reason to believe the employer discriminated, it will attempt to conciliate the dispute, during which it will try to work out a settlement between the employer and employee.[123]

The EEOC also can bring a lawsuit on behalf of the individual plaintiff. However, such lawsuits are rare. For example, in fiscal year 2004, the EEOC filed 415 lawsuits total for all categories of discrimination (including race, color, religion, sex, national origin, etc.).[124] This amounts to 0.5% of all charges filed for that year.[125]

The EEOC also issues "right to sue" letters, which give plaintiffs permission to pursue their lawsuits on their own. A plaintiff must file the lawsuit within 90 days of receiving such a letter.[126] Regardless of whether the EEOC finds cause to believe that there may be discrimination, a plaintiff can still pursue a claim in court. The EEOC can also issue a right to sue letter with little to no investigation on its part. As one commentator noted, because of the agency's huge caseload, "the EEOC's case-filing procedures [amount to] an administrative hoop through which plaintiffs with legitimate claims must unfortunately jump."[127]

Relief available under Title VII

One point a plaintiff ought to consider before filing a lawsuit is what she would like to get out of the litigation. Title VII provides for equitable relief and monetary damages. The distinction between the two is of interest to potential plaintiffs.

Equitable relief comes in a variety of forms, including injunctive relief, declaratory relief, back pay, and back benefits. Injunctive relief can encompass, for example, reinstatement to one's job (in the case of discriminatory termination) or a raise in one's salary and back pay (in the case of pay inequity). A court can also order an employer to do something more general, such as implement sexual harassment training or stop its discriminatory practices. Declaratory relief is a statement by the court that the employer has discriminated. For complainants who just want to have their story heard and believed, this can be satisfying. Back pay and benefits as well as front pay (the amount needed to compensate for job loss until the employee can find a new job) are also considered forms of equitable relief even though they result in a monetary award. Unlike compensatory and punitive damages, the monetary aspects of equitable relief are not subject to statutory damages caps that vary with the size of the employer.

The law prescribes the size of monetary damages, whether they are compensatory or punitive. For employers of more than 14 and less than 101 employees, the maximum compensatory and punitive damages is $50,000. For an employer of more than 100 and less than 201, the cap is $100,000. For employers of more than 200 and less than 501, the cap is $200,000. Finally, for employers of more than 500 employees, the cap is $300,000.[128] Employers of less than 15 employees are not covered by Title VII. Thus, sex discrimination plaintiffs seeking relief from small employers only have recourse through state laws, to the extent they cover such employers.

Compensatory damages are only available to plaintiffs who can show that they were a victim of intentional discrimination. This means that disparate impact cases, because they do not depend on the employer's intent to discriminate and therefore are not considered instances of intentional discrimination, do not trigger liability for compensatory or punitive damages.[129]

Congress added compensatory and punitive damages as remedies under Title VII through the Civil Rights Act of 1991. Prior to that time, the equitable relief described above was all that was available to a plaintiff. This was especially problematic in certain types of cases. For example, in sexual harassment cases, if the plaintiff was not fired for not acquiescing to the sexual demands of her supervisor, but instead was treated in a derogatory manner and had no adverse employment action taken against her, she was limited to a finding that the employer had discriminated along with an injunction that the employer stop. Yet, some targets of sexual harassment suffer from psychological problems and/or emotional distress as a result of the harassment and need counseling. The employer, prior to the Civil Rights Act of 1991, was under no obligation to pay for any expenses or resulting psychological damage to the plaintiff. The Civil Rights Act of 1991 corrected this to a certain extent.[130] Because of concerns by small businesses that a single suit could put them out of business, damage caps were implemented.[131]

In addition to the intentional discrimination requirement, if a plaintiff is seeking punitive damages, she must show that the employer acted "with malice or with reckless indifference to the federally created rights of an aggrieved individual."[132] In *Kolstad v. American Dental Association*, the United States Supreme Court interpreted this section to mean that an employer will not be liable for punitive damages if the unlawful employment practice was "contrary to the employer's 'good-faith efforts to comply with Title VII.'"[133] The practical consequence is that it is very difficult to prove what is necessary for a punitive damages award against an employer who has an antidiscrimination policy about which it trains and/or disseminates information to employees or has some other program to prevent discrimination. The Court wished to give credit to employers who were attempting to eliminate discriminatory practices at their workplace, even though there may be a bad actor or two among their employees.

It is noteworthy that Title VII does not provide for liability against individual discriminatory employees (including managers). Instead, the plaintiff's only recourse is against the company. Other state civil rights statutes do apply to individual discriminators as well as employers.[134] However, because individuals are likely to have less assets to use toward a judgment, it may not make economic sense to pursue an individual even when a state law permits it.

Other possible state law claims

Most sex discrimination plaintiffs are not limited to seeking relief through Title VII of the federal Civil Rights Law. In many cases, they can use state laws instead of federal ones. Often, plaintiffs can make claims in both federal and state courts simultaneously. Although space precludes a thorough discussion of the procedural and jurisdictional issues that can arise from the appending of state law claims to federal lawsuits,[135] a number of the more typical claims that could be filed in addition to Title VII claims are described briefly below.[136]

In response to the Title VII claiming framework, many states established their own fair employment practice laws and procedures to minimize duplication of paperwork and simplify the investigation of claims.[137] For example, nearly all states have their own state sexual harassment law. Although there is much overlap in content between the federal and state laws in this area, some key differences in content might make it advantageous for a plaintiff to assert a claim under the state law.[138] Title VII applies only to employers with at least 15 employees, for example, whereas state laws may apply to all employers.[139] Other state antidiscrimination laws may cover more protected categories, e.g., sexual orientation, or may have different or fewer limits on damage awards.[140] Hawaii's law allows for lawsuits against persons who "aid and abet or incite" discrimination, whereas Title VII focuses liability on the employer, and precludes individual liability.[141] Statutes of limitations and filing deadlines may differ as well.

Beyond differences in content, differences in interpretation of otherwise parallel components of antidiscrimination law might make it advantageous for a plaintiff to assert a state claim. As a general rule, state courts give great deference to federal court interpretations of state provisions that are based largely on equivalent federal law.[142] Long[143] argues that as statutory construction of federal discrimination laws has grown more complex, however, and as Congress has sought to curtail or augment judicial interpretations, an increasing number of state courts have crafted or may be likely to craft differing interpretations.[144] Whether an employer can be held vicariously liable is one issue discussed by Long for which such divergence has appeared.[145] Particularly for those issues without a definitive interpretation from the federal courts, plaintiffs might be well served to assert state discrimination claims.

In many instances, and of course, depending on the particular factual circumstances of the case, a plaintiff might also file claims under state tort law in addition to or in lieu of a statutory discrimination claim. A tort is a civil "wrong," or a breach of duty that the law imposes on people in particular relationships, for which liability can be imposed. Tort law is that portion of civil law in America that concerns wrongdoings that are not criminal and that do not involve contracts. In addition to the possibility of enhancing the likelihood of success by expanding the potential bases of liability, other advantages of appending tort claims to a discrimination claim might accrue. These include the possibility of obtaining higher monetary damages (which are limited under federal law), and an ability to circumvent statutory filing deadlines[146] or other limitations, such as the number of employees in the workplace.[147]

One of the most common tort claims deriving from alleged discriminatory conduct is intentional infliction of emotional distress.[148] This claim arises when an employee believes he or she was treated or terminated in an unfair, abusive, coercive, or retaliatory manner.[149] This tort has itself a rather long and tortuous history as courts were historically reluctant to award damages for emotional harm alone.[150] Although it is now uniformly accepted as a viable cause of action, because of concerns about the difficulty in setting limits on the tort courts tend to set high standards for proof in these cases. The challenge for most plaintiffs raising the claim of emotional distress is establishing that the alleged conduct was outrageous as most courts require.[151] While the discrimination itself forms the primary legal claim, the manner in which the discriminatory behavior occurred can give rise to the additional tort claim if it is sufficiently outrageous. The type of behavior often delineated in a sexual harassment claim – for example, ongoing and repeated exposure to sexually abusive language and conduct, improper sexual advances, or abusive behavior coming from someone with power over the plaintiff – has been deemed sufficiently outrageous by some courts.[152] One additional challenge for employees bringing this claim against their employer is asserting vicarious liability for the behavior – balancing the emphasis on the outrageousness of the behavior with the likelihood that such behavior would be less likely viewed as arising within the course of employment.[153]

Where there is actual physical contact or threatened physical contact between the parties, the plaintiff may assert claims for battery, assault, false imprisonment, or invasion of privacy.[154] Assault arises if the defendant intends to cause harm or offensive contact, or creates imminent apprehension in the plaintiff. Battery generally involves intentional touching in an offensive manner, behavior that is often at the heart of a discrimination claim. When that touching results in detention, then false imprisonment can arise and when it leads to an invasion of physical solitude, it can be invasion of privacy. In one not atypical case, repeated and offensive touching of the plaintiff satisfied the battery requirements, that same touching of the plaintiff's private parts constituted invasion of privacy, pinning her against the wall and refusing to allow her to escape was false imprisonment, and the sum total of all the behavior constituted intentional infliction of emotional distress.[155]

One other important state tort claim that could accompany a discrimination claim is defamation. One court said, for example, that any drawing (or cartoon, in that case) that imputes a lack of chastity to a female is actionable *per se*.[156] Statements made to potential employers about the reasons a plaintiff was terminated can also form the basis of this type of claim, though again, there is a line to be drawn between offensive, actionable statements and expressions of opinion which are not actionable.[157]

In addition to these traditional tort claims, discrimination plaintiffs might also file claims based on the existence of an employment contract (implied or explicit) that has been violated by the discriminatory conduct. Two common claims are tortious interference with a contract and wrongful discharge. The threshold challenge for plaintiffs in these cases is establishing the existence of an employment contract, either grounded in a written contract, collective bargaining agreement, legislation, or judicially created exception. Otherwise, employment is at will and no cause of action would accrue for termination. Once that is accomplished, the plaintiff must then show unlawful breach of that contract.

Tortious interference with a contract requires intentional behavior that was directed toward the termination of the plaintiff's contract, and in at least some states, that improper methods were used in so doing.[158] In *Magnuson*, the plaintiff's allegations were sufficient to survive summary judgment[159] where the person accused of discriminating against her made false statements about her to her supervisors thereby adversely affecting her contract.

Wrongful discharge in violation of public policy is a claim created as a judicially-created exception to the employment at-will doctrine.[160] It states simply that, although employees can be fired at will for no reason or for good reason, they cannot in most states[161] be fired for a bad reason. And, at least some states recognize sex discrimination in violation of Title VII as a bad reason, thereby giving plaintiffs a basis upon which to sue for wrongful discharge.[162]

This is by no means an exhaustive review of additional state and federal legal claims that could be available to a sex discrimination plaintiff in addition to the basic Title VII claim. The complexities involved in constructing a case, dealing with the jurisdictional and procedural issues related to pursuing multiple claims, weigh heavily in favor of consultation with an experienced employment lawyer before plunging into discrimination litigation.

Pros and Cons of Various Response Strategies

The individual who feels she has suffered discrimination might weigh the advantages and disadvantages of different remedies. Taking no formal action is a path that is both risk-free and risky. Certainly, it is sometimes easiest not to "rock the boat." But if the assaults on dignity escalate, the woman who does nothing has much to lose.

Internal employer mechanisms

Making use of the company's in-house mechanisms may be sufficient. To use the in-house complaint procedures can save time and expense and can protect privacy. Using discreet in-house procedures can help the woman keep her friends and allies at work.

But relying solely on the in-house mechanisms can also be a bad idea in some instances, particularly when the in-house mechanisms are little more than window dressing. One criticism of employer policies and grievance mechanisms is that they are designed as liability-avoidance measures rather than as discrimination-prevention measures. As one commentator stated, "Why does sexual harassment persist despite nearly three decades of attempts to eliminate it? . . . because the rules of employer liability for harassment are calculated to ensure that employers adopt basic policies and procedures with respect to workplace harassment, not, surprisingly, to ensure that they actually prevent it."[163] Bisom-Rapp makes a convincing case that employment discrimination law as it is being implemented in employer policies and procedures is "increasingly limited in its ability to remedy workplace discrimination," especially given the focus on strategies that prevent litigation rather than strategies that prevent discrimination.[164]

Thus, a victim may wish to make use of formal procedures. Mediation, arbitration, or litigation are all options that can seem daunting. They are also options that may have some benefits, relative to informal response and using only in-house mechanisms.

Mediation and arbitration

There are various pros and cons to the use of mediation or arbitration. The pros include the speed and nature of the processes, their purported lower costs, and their confidential nature. Some of these advantages are more likely to result from one method than the other. Also, mediation has some unique advantages and disadvantages that are not present in arbitration. However, there are significant cons that both methods have in common as well as cons that are unique to each method. A complainant should carefully weigh the pros and cons of these two dispute resolution tools before any decision to use them.

Arbitration and mediation are considered faster and less expensive than litigation.[165] While this appears to hold true for mediation that results in resolution of the dispute, it is not clear that arbitration is significantly less costly and time consuming than litigation.[166] Also, the less costly nature of successful mediation has led some to argue that it provides less deterrence of actual discrimination because employers can use this much more cost-effective method of dispute resolution.[167] There is no empirical support for the proposition that arbitration is less costly than litigation.[168] As arbitration becomes more and more like litigation, the proceedings can become protracted. Indeed, there are cases in which the arbitration process ended up taking longer than litigation.[169] A factor that increases costs of arbitration is the lack of clarity about whether mandatory pre-dispute arbitration agreements are truly enforceable for purposes of resolving Title VII disputes.

Another issue related to costs that affects use of these methods is who pays for the mediator or arbitrator. This is less of a factor in mediation, because there are cost-free mediation programs available, such as the EEOC's program. However, not all cases qualify for this program. Although it may seem obvious that the employee would want the employer to pay for the costs of the arbitrator or mediator, there are significant disadvantages to having the employer pay. If the employer pays the arbitrator, he or she may be inclined to rule in the employer's favor. Likewise, if the employer pays the mediator, he or she may bias his or her characterization of the case in the employer's favor.

An associated problem, especially for arbitration, concerns the "repeat player" phenomenon. Because an employer is more likely to be a repeat player in arbitration, it will have an advantage over a "one-shotter," generally the employee, who is likely to use the system only once. While this phenomenon can occur in mediation, studies have found the effect in employment arbitration in particular. Professor Lisa Bingham studied 203 cases decided by the American Arbitration Association from January 1, 1993 through December 31, 1995. These cases were decided under the AAA's Employment Dispute Resolution Rules. She tracked employers who were repeat players, i.e., those who used arbitration more than once in the sample. She found that "[e]mployees lose more frequently when the arbitrator is one the employer has used at least once before."[170] In another computation she completed for the American Bar Association, Professor Bingham found that of 232 arbitration cases brought by employees, those up against a repeat player succeeded in only one out of five cases, whereas the odds for those cases against non-repeat players were about five out of seven cases.[171]

So, should the employer and employee split the costs of the arbitrator or mediator? Yet, the employee's paying half of the arbitrator's or mediator's fee may increase the costs substantially for the employee. However, if overall arbitration or mediation is less costly than litigation, this additional cost for the arbitrator or mediator may still render these methods more economically feasible than litigation. Much depends on the factual circumstances of the case. It does appear that the increased costs associated with arbitration largely come from challenges by the employee to the arbitration agreement itself. To the extent that employees have control over this additional process, they can make the proceedings more or less costly and more or less time consuming. Thus, it will not necessarily act as a detriment to the employee, but instead give the employer less control.

An advantage to both mediation and arbitration is that they make justice accessible to employees who might not be able to obtain legal representation. Indeed, a 1995 survey of plaintiffs' lawyers indicated that they take only approximately 5 percent of the employment discrimination cases that come to them.[172] This is due to the relatively low damages recoverable in many cases, especially those involving employees who have relatively low salaries.[173] Thus, arbitration may be a readily available means of adjudicating employment discrimination suits for low income workers.[174] Generally, these processes do not require a complainant to hire a lawyer, although it is generally wise for a complainant to do so.

Another advantage to both processes is that they are not held in open court. Thus, there is a degree of privacy involved. This may be significant for the complainant who is embarrassed by the employer's discriminatory actions. It has obvious advantages for the employer, because it will keep its name out of the newspapers as a potential (or proven) discriminator. Mediation is more confidential than arbitration, which is generally not subject to the same confidentiality requirements. Also, arbitration decisions are open to appeal, and therefore the facts may ultimately be revealed in court documents.

There are also significant downsides to this confidentiality. The private nature of both mediation and arbitration potentially lessens civil rights enforcement because other employers and employees will not have the benefit of knowledge about the case and its outcome.[175] High profile cases may lead to more people realizing they experienced discrimination, which may in turn lead to more charges filed.[176] In addition, they provide a wake-up call to employers who might be engaged in similar discriminatory practices. This leads, in turn, overall, to better enforcement of the civil rights laws, which necessarily depend on individual complainants who are willing to file lawsuits. Civil rights advocates thus fear that mediation and arbitration will lead to inadequate civil rights enforcement. Indeed, given that some EEOC mediations result in no employee compensation, complainants may not be obtaining the relief they deserve through mediation and employers may be insufficiently deterred from continuing their discriminatory practices because of the low monetary implications. To the extent that an employer has a company-wide problem, resolving individual disputes using mediation may not get at the overall structural issues at the workplace that contribute to the discrimination.

Another problem with the private nature of these processes is that the victim herself may want public vindication. If she is in a he said/she said sexual harassment dispute, for example, having a third party – whether it be a judge or jury – believe her may provide the vindication she psychologically needs.[177] While having an arbitrator agree with the complainant's view of the case may be sufficient, it is not the same as having one's views vindicated in open court.

There are other advantages that are unique to mediation. One is that it permits the employee and employer to have control over the outcome of the dispute. In litigation and arbitration, the outcome is necessarily at the will of the adjudicator, whether it be judge, jury, or arbitrator. Because mediation allows both sides to agree on the outcome, it provides an opportunity for both sides to win, or, at least, not lose. For example, the plaintiff will return to her job without fear of continued harassment by a co-worker and the employer will now have a workplace free of discriminatory harassment and not be subject to a lawsuit. Anecdotal evidence suggests that a sexual harassment victim is more likely to receive monetary benefits through mediation, while employers are less likely to pay high damage amounts as a result of mediation.[178] In addition, mediation provides an opportunity for parties to continue their working relationship. When an employee files a lawsuit against her employer, this often signifies the end of the employment relationship. Mediation allows the parties to work out their disagreement in a manner that can result in a continued relationship.[179]

Another positive feature of mediation is the informal nature of the process. There are two aspects of the informality of the process that make it advantageous. First, it can lead to better communication between the employee and employer,[180] with resulting benefits for morale and turnover. Also, if people have an opportunity to participate in the decision that creates the remedy, they generally have bought into the solution in a manner that makes it more likely that they will comply with it.[181] Thus, mediation remedies may involve less enforcement problems.

Commentators also have argued that the informal nature of mediation is more suitable than litigation for disputes involving harassment.[182] As one commentator noted, "[b]ecause [mediation] creates a safe environment for telling the story, mediation better meets the needs of women who have been harassed."[183] Indeed, in this sense, mediation can be empowering.[184] To the extent sexual harassment results from misunderstandings or a lack of understanding of another gender's perspective, mediation may provide an opportunity to clear up such errors.[185] Further, there are power imbalances inherent in other tools used to redress sex discrimination.[186] Although mediators may directly counter power imbalances during the mediation process, it is unclear how judges and arbitrators can counteract such imbalances given the formality of those processes. For these reasons, mediation may be a useful tool in resolving sex discrimination disputes.

Not all commentators agree about the advantages of mediation. Some feminists have criticized mediation in the context of gender-based claims and sexual harassment claims specifically. Because women generally have less power in society, female employees may be at a negotiating disadvantage in a mediation.[187] It is generally agreed among mediators that if there is a substantial power disparity between the parties, the dispute is not appropriate for mediation.[188] While much has been written about power imbalances in the context of domestic abuse, some have argued that some of the same concerns that counsel against mediation in that context also counsel against mediation in sexual harassment cases.[189] As one commentator explained:

> [T]here is usually some destructive power imbalance present in sexual harassment cases. In the workplace, particularly where women occupy sex-atypical jobs, gender-based power and its potential for being destructive becomes more acute. The power exercised by a harasser can manifest itself with many of the same characteristics as coercion and intimidation from which abused wives suffer. Like spousal abuse, the harassment can include: relentless criticism, isolation from the group, "intimidation, name-calling, mind games, shouting," threats, and unwanted touching.[190]

If a sex discrimination dispute involves physical abuse, the potential for intimidation and power imbalances is very real, and mediation would not be appropriate. Certainly, there are cases in which employees are physically assaulted by their harassers, and those cases would be inappropriate for mediation.[191]

Finally, there are problems unique to arbitration. There are problems inherent in the arbitration agreements themselves. Most arbitration agreements are drafted by employers and will likely work to the employer's benefit.[192] Often employees cannot meaningfully bargain about the terms of the agreement.[193] Thus, there is potential for employer abuse in the design of the agreement. Because an arbitration agreement may be binding on an employee, she should have the agreement reviewed by counsel before signing it. Unfortunately, that is not always possible, due to costs as well as the sense that the employer may not present the arbitration agreement as a negotiable term of employment.

One very significant disadvantage of arbitration is that some courts have thrown into question the legality of arbitrated settlements. Some courts have held or suggested that employment arbitration agreements are unenforceable because (1) they are inconsistent with federal antidiscrimination laws,[194] (2) they violate state contract law principles,[195] or (3) they are unconscionable.[196] The FAA itself states that arbitration agreements are enforceable "save upon such grounds that exist at law or in equity for the revocation of any contract."[197] Thus, just because a sex discrimination victim has signed such an agreement to arbitrate does not mean a court will actually enforce it. Litigation on the enforceability of arbitration agreements increases the costs and time involved in arbitration and litigation. In addition, the United States Supreme Court has made clear that even where an employee does enter into a binding arbitration agreement that would cover a discrimination claim, the EEOC can always pursue the claim itself on behalf of the employee.[198]

Litigation

Filing a lawsuit generally is viewed as a last resort for resolving sex discrimination in employment. There are several reasons why. First, lawsuits are time consuming and expensive. Although some of the statutes and claims discussed herein are fee generating, so that a successful employee will have his or her attorneys' fees paid, some claims are not fee generating. An employee who does not win in court is also liable for any out-of-pocket expenses (such as filing fees) that the lawyer incurred pursuing the lawsuit. In addition, it can take a long time for a sex discrimination case to work its way through the state or federal court system. The median time from filing to trial in the federal court system is nearly two years.[199] A former employee may find it difficult to search for a new job while the case makes its way through court because of continued distraction caused by the litigation. For the many Americans who rely on a weekly paycheck to meet basic needs, waiting for a lawsuit to pay out can be very stressful. Yet, this delay often works to the benefit of the employer, who is more likely to possess the resources necessary to pursue lengthy litigation. There is also the stress associated with the lawsuit itself. For example, if the employee claims emotional distress damages, there likely will be inquiry into her psychological well-being that could be quite embarrassing and distressful.[200] Because of the nature of the discovery process in litigation, pre-trial proceedings can be very invasive and time consuming.[201]

It is also commonly thought that filing a lawsuit (or even simply filing a sex discrimination charge with the EEOC) will end the employee–employer relationship.[202] Although this may not be a significant issue for an employee who claims her employer has discriminatorily fired her or who already has chosen to quit, it can be a factor for an employee who wishes to continue working for the employer. An employee who accuses a supervisor or co-worker of sex discrimination is bound to create enemies at work and may offend her employer. This can lead to a breakdown in the employer–employee relationship and sometimes can result in the employer firing the employee or the employee quitting, as her job becomes more difficult. In addition, "[t]he traditional adversarial process polarizes parties' positions, particularly in the employment discrimination setting."[203] Title VII of the Civil Rights Act of 1964, the main federal statute prohibiting sex discrimination in employment, contains an antiretaliation provision that prohibits an employer from taking action against an employee who accuses the employer of discrimination,[204] but claims of discrimination may be difficult to prove.[205] Indeed, studies suggest that plaintiffs who file employment discrimination claims often quit or are terminated.[206] Thus, while an employer is not supposed to retaliate, that does not mean that the employer will not do so.

The employee also runs the risk of being branded as a troublemaker by her present and subsequent employers. Lawsuits are a matter of public record and there are numerous ways that a subsequent employer or potential employer may become aware of a potential employee's sex discrimination suit. Indeed, the employee may disclose it herself as an explanation for her termination or quitting. In addition, the former employer may disclose the litigation to a potential employer in retaliation. Although such actions, including subsequent employers relying on the knowledge that an applicant had filed a discrimination suit in denying an employment opportunity to her,[207] violate Title VII, it is difficult for the employee to find out if the inappropriate sharing of information has occurred.

It is also difficult to actually win a sex discrimination lawsuit. For example, in 1998, plaintiffs won less than one-third of employment discrimination cases that resulted in a verdict.[208] In addition, the median verdict in these cases was only $137,000. Other studies suggest that plaintiffs fare better in front of juries than judges.[209] Although jury trials are available under Title VII for certain types of claims, many plaintiffs do not make it to the jury because of high rates of summary judgment.[210] Judgments under state laws with no damage caps can be higher, yet the combination of slim chances of winning and low verdicts makes taking a case to trial a risky proposition for both complainants and their lawyers. This has led to issues of access to justice. Commentators have noted that it can be difficult to find a lawyer willing to take discrimination cases.[211] Although many lawyers are willing to take cases on a contingent fee basis, some require a down payment to cover costs. In a study of 15 sexual harassment claimants, Phoebe Morgan Stambaugh found that women made down payments of $250 to $1,500 to the lawyers who represented them.[212] Thus, contingent fee cases have costs that may be a deterrent to an employee who works at or near minimum wage.

There are also psychological implications to the decision to file or forgo a lawsuit. Psychiatrists Sharyn Lenhart and Diane Shrier have noted, based on their clinical experience, that plaintiffs

> who fare best emotionally with litigation are those who (1) set realistic goals; (2) maintain a sense of control of the litigation process; (3) seek out adequate support from at least one significant source (family, therapist, peers, attorney); (4) appreciate and focus energy on restoring the original equilibrium of their lives independent of the litigation process; and (5) adequately acknowledge and grieve the losses inevitably involved even when litigation has a favorable outcome.[213]

They explain that litigation has both emotional costs and benefits. Litigation can exacerbate psychological problems that the complainant already is having and result in retraumatization.[214]

Law Professor Michael Green has identified the downsides of litigation from the employee perspective and its upsides from the employer perspective:

> [T]he current legal regime of enforcement and vindication for employment discrimination has raised a number of concerns for employees and created a host of advantages for employers, despite the existence of the extended remedies and jury trial rights provided by the Act. Those advantages are: problems of proof; inability to afford counsel and legal representation; the requirements of showing intentional discrimination versus discriminatory impact; and the increasing grant of summary judgment. They are provided to employees by a judiciary that appears to be, at most, hostile to these claims and, at least, concerned that these cases are a nuisance to the courts' efforts to clear its dockets.[215]

Because of the advantages litigation provides employers, Professor Green has argued that alternative dispute resolution mechanisms, and arbitration in particular, actually do not provide much advantage to the employer.

For all these reasons, an employee should explore other approaches to resolving a sex discrimination dispute before resorting to litigation. Still, there are good reasons to pursue litigation as well. Victims of sex discrimination report feeling vindicated by having had their day in court.[216] The dignitary damage that is done by sex discrimination is often ignored by the legal literature, where the emphasis is on damages that a plaintiff might receive. But the victim herself may feel satisfied by being able to tell her story and explain why she believes the employer engaged in sex discrimination. As one study showed, "discrimination victims who do file charges report that taking legal action significantly increases personal empowerment."[217]

There is also potential for a sex discrimination suit to function as a wake-up call to an employer who has ignored discriminatory behavior on the part of its employees. If an employee has tried complaining about sex discrimination and the employer has not responded or responded ineffectively, filing a charge with the EEOC and pursuing litigation is likely to get the employer's attention. Indeed, some victims of sex discrimination are acutely aware of and take satisfaction in the idea that their efforts will help other women.[218]

Finally, if an employee wins, she may not only bring about reform at the employer (through injunctive relief), but also receive compensatory, and, in the appropriate case, punitive damages. For those who have been terminated, have been passed over for promotions, or have had their pay decreased because of sex discrimination, back pay awards can provide much needed compensation. In addition, those who have experienced emotional distress may not only be reimbursed for treatment costs, but also receive compensation for the distress itself. Although Title VII sex discrimination claims are subject to damages caps, some state law claims are not.[219] Thus, a plaintiff who files suit may receive the compensation she deserves as well as stop the employer's discriminatory practices.

Conclusion

As described above, each of these problem-solving tools has pros and cons for sex discrimination victims. Discrimination claimants should consider a number of issues in determining which method works best. These include issues of time – will the process be quick or lengthy? Claimants must also weigh the costs of the various methods. Also, there is the degree to which the parties have control over the outcome. There are issues related to control over the process and privacy concerns related thereto. Finally, there are systemic issues that may or may not be relevant to the parties involved, depending on whether they have a more public focus or simply wish to be compensated for individual harm to them. Depending on the needs and resources of the particular claimant, some tools will be better than others. It is up to the claimant, perhaps in consultation with an attorney, to choose the tool that best meets her needs and provides the best chance of the outcome she desires.

Notes

1   We will be using the pronoun "she" throughout the chapter to refer to targets/plaintiffs, but do so only for convenience, as discussion does not nor should not preclude an understanding of or application to male targets/plaintiffs.
2   Craver, C. B. (2001). The use of non-judicial procedures to resolve employment discrimination claims. *Kansas Journal of Law and Public Policy, 11*, 141–176.
3   Ellison v. Brady, 924 F.2d 872 (9th Cir. 1991).
4   Fitzgerald, L. F., & Shullman, S. L. (1993). Sexual harassment: A research analysis and agenda for the 90's. *Journal of Vocational Behavior, 42*, 5–29.
5   Shelton, J. N., & Stewart, R. E. (2004). Confronting perpetrators of prejudice: The inhibitory effects of social costs. *Psychology of Women Quarterly, 28*, 215–223; see also Swim, J. K., & Hyers, L. L. (1999). Excuse me – What did you just say?! Women's public and private responses to sexist remarks. *Journal of Experimental and Social Psychology, 35*, 68–88.
6   Shelton & Stewart (2004).
7   Kidder, L. H., Lafleur, R. A., & Wells, C. V. (1995). Recalling harassment, reconstructing experience. *Journal of Social Issues, 51*, 53–67.
8   Skogan, W. (1976). Citizen reporting of crime: Some national panel data. *Criminology, 13*, 535–549.
9   Riger, S. (1991). Gender dilemmas in sexual harassment policies and procedures. *American Psychologist, 46*, 497–505, p. 497, citing numerous

studies on college campuses and in workplaces demonstrating the discrepancy in official reports and self-report rates of discrimination.

10   Bond, C. A. (1997). Shattering the myth: Mediating sexual harassment disputes in the workplace. *Fordham Law Review, 65,* 2489–2533, p. 2489, citing among other sources Riger (1991) and Hearings on H.R. 1, The Civil Rights Act of 1991: Hearings before the House Committee on Education and Labor, 102d Congress, 1st Sess. 168, 172 (1991) (statement of Dr. Freada Klein) (indicating that more than 90% of sexual harassment victims are unwilling to report the incidents).

11   Livingston, J. A. (1982). Responses to sexual harassment on the job: Legal, organizational, and individual actions. *Journal of Social Issues, 38,* 5–22.

12   Gruber, J. E., & Smith, M. D. (1995). Women's response to sexual harassment: A multivariate analysis. *Basic and Applied Social Psychology, 17,* 543–562.

13   U.S. Merit Systems Protection Board (1995). *Sexual harassment in the federal workforce: Trends, progress, continuing challenges.* Washington, DC: U.S. Merit Systems Protection Board.

14   Ruggiero, K. M., & Taylor, D. M. (1995). Coping with discrimination: How disadvantaged group members perceive the discrimination that confronts them. *Journal of Personality and Social Psychology, 68,* 826–838; Ruggiero, K. M., & Taylor, D. M. (1997). Why minority group members perceive or do not perceive the discrimination that confronts them: The role of self-esteem and perceived control. *Journal of Personality and Social Psychology, 72,* 373–389 (describing the minimization of attributions to discrimination that can occur where the motivation behind behavior directed at them is ambiguous).

15   Kidder et al., (1995).

16   Ruggiero & Taylor (1995; 1997).

17   Kaiser, C. R., & Miller, C. T. (2001a). Reacting to impending discrimination: Compensation for prejudice and attributions to discrimination. *Personality and Social Psychology Bulletin, 27,* 1357–1367.

18   Gruber & Smith (1995), p. 546.

19   Kaiser, C. R., & Miller, C. T. (2001b). Stop complaining! The social costs of making attributions of discrimination. *Personality and Social Psychology Bulletin, 27,* 254–263, p. 255; see also, Crosby, F. (1984). The denial of personal discrimination. *American Behavioral Scientist, 27,* 371–386.

20   Kaiser & Miller (2001b), p. 255.

21   See, e.g., Crosby (1984); Fitzgerald, L. F., Swan, S., & Fischer, K. (1995). Why didn't she just report him? The psychological and legal implications of women's responses to sexual harassment. *Journal of Social Issues, 51,* 117–138.

22   See, e.g., Hulin, C. L., Fitzgerald, L. F., & Drasgow, F. (1996). Organizational influences on sexual harassment. In M. S. Stockdale (Ed.), *Sexual harassment in the workplace: Perspectives, frontiers, and response strategies*

(pp. 127–150). Thousand Oaks, CA: Sage; Gruber, J. E., & Bjorn, L. (1986). Women's response to sexual harassment: An analysis of sociocultural, organizational, and personal resource models. *Social Science Quarterly, 67*, 814–825; Pryor, J. B., LaVite, C. M., & Stoller, L. M. (1993). A social psychological analysis of sexual harassment: The person/situation interaction. *Journal of Vocational Behavior, 42*, 68–83.

23 See, e.g., Kowalski, R. M. (1996). Complaints and complaining: Functions, antecedents, and consequences. *Psychological Bulletin, 119*, 179–196.

24 Gruber, J. E. (1995). Women's response to sexual harassment: A multivariate analysis. *Basic and Applied Social Psychology, 17*, 543–562.

25 A number of social science scholars have developed conceptual frameworks or typologies that emphasize the multidimensional, layered nature of target responses to discriminatory behavior that can be helpful in understanding the complexity of responses just described, see, e.g., Cortina, L. M., & Wasti, S. A. (2005). Profiles in coping: Responses to sexual harassment across persons, organizations, and cultures. *Journal of Applied Psychology, 90*, 182–192; Gruber & Smith (1995); Knapp, D. E., Faley, R. H., Ekeberg, S. E., & Dubois, C. L. Z. (1997). Determinants of target responses to sexual harassment: A conceptual framework. *Academy of Management Review, 22*, 687–729.

26 Fitzgerald et al. (1995) (describing the "silent tolerator" and "instigator-in-kind" as two typical responses to harassment).

27 Gruber & Smith (1995), pp. 544–545 (citing numerous studies); see also McKinney, K. (1990). Sexual harassment by university faculty by colleagues and students. *Sex Roles, 23*, 421–438.

28 Gruber, J. E. (1989). How women handle sexual harassment: A literature review. *Sociology and Social Research, 74*, 3–9.

29 Gruber & Smith (1995), citing Culbertson, A. L., Rosenfeld, P., Booth-Kewley, S., & Magnusson, P. (1992). *Assessment of sexual harassment in the Navy: Results of the 1989 Navy-wide survey* (Report No. TR-92-11). San Diego, CA: Navy Personnel Research and Development Center.

30 Riger (1991).

31 Fitzgerald et al. (1995).

32 Gruber & Smith (1995), p. 545 (citing for example the Canadian Human Rights Commission (1983) study and the U.S. Merit Systems Protection Board studies of 1981 and 1988, which report both responses), see Canadian Human Rights Commission. (1983). *Unwanted sexual attention and sexual harassment.* Montreal: Minister of Supply and Services of Canada; U.S. Merit Systems Protection Board. (1981). *Sexual harassment in the federal workplace: Is it a problem?* Washington, DC: U.S. Government Printing Office; U.S. Merit Systems Protection Board. (1988). *Sexual harassment in the federal workplace: An update.* Washington, DC: U.S. Government Printing Office.

33 U.S. Merit Systems Protection Board (1995), p. 31.

34 Gruber & Smith (1995), p. 545; see also Gruber & Bjorn (1986).

35 Gruber & Smith (1995), p. 545.

36 U.S. Merit Systems Protection Board (1988).

37 Gutek, B. A. (1985). *Sex and the workplace: The impact of sexual harassment and behavior on women, men, and organization.* San Francisco: Jossey-Bass.

38 Bisom-Rapp, S. (1999b). Discerning form from substance: Understanding employer litigation prevention strategies. *Employee Rights and Employment Policy Journal, 3,* 1–64.

39 Bisom-Rapp (1999b), p. 5.

40 Edelman, L. B. (1992). Legal ambiguity and symbolic structures: Organization mediation of civil rights law. *American Journal of Sociology, 97,* 1531–1576.

41 Dobbin, F., Sutton, J. R., Meyer, J. W., & Scott, W. R. (1993). Equal opportunity law and the construction of internal labor markets. *American Journal of Sociology, 99,* 396–427.

42 O'Connor, M., & Vallabhajosula, B. (2004). Sexual harassment in the workplace: A legal and psychological framework. In B. J. Cling (Ed.), *Sex, Violence and Women: A Psychology and Law Perspective* (pp. 115–147). New York: Guilford Press, citing Burlington Industries, Inc., v. Ellerth, 524 U.S. 742 (1998); Faragher v. City of Boca Raton, 524 U.S. 775 (1998).

43 Burlington Industries, Inc. (1998); Faragher v. City of Raton (1998).

44 O'Connor & Vallabhajosula (2004), citing EEOC, *Enforcement guidance on vicarious employer liability for unlawful harassment by supervisors,* EEOC Notice No. 915-002, 14 (1999).

45 Beiner, T. M. (2001). Sex, science and social knowledge: The implications of social science research on imputing liability to employers for sexual harassment. *William and Mary Journal of Women and the Law, 7,* 273–339.

46 O'Connor & Vallabhajosula (2004).

47 Bisom-Rapp, S. (2001). An ounce of prevention is a poor substitute for a pound of cure. Confronting the developing jurisprudence of education and prevention in employment discrimination law. *Berkeley Journal of Employment and Labor Law, 22,* 1–47.

48 Society for Human Resource Management. (1999). *Sexual harassment survey.* SHRM Management Program.

49 Casellas, G. F., & Hill, I. L. (1998). Sexual harassment: Prevention and avoiding liability. Society for Human Resource Management Legal Report.

50 Powers, Kinder, & Keeney. (1999). Prevent sexual harassment the right way. *Rhode Island Employment Law Letter, 4*(4), 6–8.

51 Stockdale, M. S., Bisom-Rapp, S., O'Connor, M., & Gutek, B. A. (2004). Coming to terms with zero tolerance sexual harassment policies. *Journal of Forensic Psychology Practice, 4,* 65–78.

52 Casellas & Hill (1998), p. 21.

53   Day, N. E., & Schoenrade, N. (2000). The relationship among reported disclosure of sexual orientation, anti-discrimination policies, top management support and work attitudes of gay and lesbian employees. *Personnel Review, 29*, 346–363.

54   Offerman, L. R., & Malamut, A. B. (2002). When leaders harass: The impact of target perceptions of organizational leadership and climate on harassment reporting and outcomes. *Journal of Applied Psychology, 87*, 885–893.

55   Equal Employment Opportunity Commission. (2004, November 1). *Facts about mediation*. Retrieved May 27, 2005, from http://www.eeoc.gov/mediate.facts.html

56   Irvine, M. (1993). Mediation: Is it inappropriate for sexual harassment grievances? *Ohio State Journal on Dispute. Resolution, 9*, 27–53, p. 31 (quoting Rogers, N. H., & McEwen, C. A. (1989). *Mediation: Law, policy, practice*. Eagan, MN: West Group, at p. 8); Moore, C. W. (2003). *The mediation process: Practical strategies for resolving conflict*. San Francisco, CA: Jossey-Bass.

57   McDermott, E. P. & Obar, R. (2004). "What's going on" in mediation: An empirical analysis of the influence of a mediator's decision style on party satisfaction and monetary benefit. *Harvard Negotiation Law Review, 9*, 75–113.

58   McDermott & Obar (2004), pp. 81–85.

59   McDermott, E. P. et al. (2001, August 1). *The EEOC mediation program: Mediators' perspective on the parties, processes, and outcomes*. Retrieved February 10, 2005, from http://www.eeoc.gov/mediate/mcdfinal.html

60   McDermott et al. (2001, August 1). Behaviors associated with evaluative mediations include providing a "reality check," "evaluating the strengths and weaknesses of the charge," "providing knowledge of the law/process," "exploring/proposing options," and "negotiating actively."

61   McDermott et al. (2001, Aug. 1), p. 2.

62   McDermott et al. (2001, Aug 1), p. 22. This led to a turning point in 44% of cases.

63   Equal Employment Opportunity Commission. (2005, March 21). *Questions and answers about mediation*. Retrieved June 13, 2006, from http://www.eeoc.gov/mediate/medation-qa.html; McDermott et al. (2001, Aug. 1), pp. 1–12, table VI.

64   Equal Employment Opportunity Commission (2005, March 21), p. 3.

65   Robbennolt, J. K. (2004, Spring). Apology – Help or hindrance? An empirical analysis of Apologies' influence on settlement making. *Dispute Resolution Magazine, 10*, 33–34.

66   McDermott et al. (2001, Aug. 1), p. 14.

67   McDermott et al. (2001, Aug. 1), p. 14.

68   McDermott et al. (2001, Aug. 1), p. 23.

69   McDermott et al. (2001, Aug. 1), p. 13.

70   McDermott et al. (2001, Aug. 1), p. 14.

71   Craver (2001), pp. 145–146; St. Antoine, T. J. (1995). Mandatory arbitration of employee discrimination claims: Unmitigated evil or blessing in disguise? *Thomas M. Cooley Law Review, 15*, 1–19.

72   Equal Employment Opportunity Commission. (2003, November 19). *History of the EEOC mediation program.* Retrieved July 15, 2005, from http://www.eeoc.gov/mediate/history.html

73   Equal Employment Opportunity Commission. (2003, November 19).

74   McDermott & Obar (2004), pp. 103–104.

75   McDermott & Obar (2004), p. 107.

76   McDermott & Obar (2004), p. 107.

77   Equal Employment Opportunity Commission. (2003, Nov. 19), p.1.

78   Equal Employment Opportunity Commission. (2005, March 21), p.3.

79   Lacy, D. A. (2002). Alternative dispute resolution or appropriate dispute resolution: Will ADR help or hinder the EEOC complaint process? *University of Detroit Mercy Law Review, 80*, 31–59.

80   Sternlight, J. R. (2004). In search of the best procedure for enforcing employment discrimination laws: A comparative analysis. *Tulane Law Review, 78*, 1401–1499.

81   Equal Employment Opportunity Commission. (2004, Nov. 1), p. 2.

82   Guthrie, C. & Levin, J. (1998). "Party satisfaction" perspective on comprehensive mediation statute. *Ohio State Journal of Dispute Resolution, 13*, 885–907.

83   Equal Employment Opportunity Commission (2005, March 21), p.1. These are called conciliation mediations because the EEOC uses them, among a variety of tools, to try to settlement the case during the conciliation process that occurs after the EEOC has determined that there is reason to believe that the employer discriminated.

84   Gilmer v. Interstate/Johnson Lane Corp., 500 U.S. 20, 25 (1991) (quoting Moses H. Cone Mem'l Hosp. v. Mercury Construction Corp. 460 U.S. 1, 24 (1983)); 9 U.S.C. §1.

85   9 U.S.C. §2.

86   Strickler, G. M. (2004, July 29–31). Arbitration of employment discrimination claims. *ALI-ABA CLE, Current Developments in Employment Law, Course Number SK013*, 801–813, p. 803.

87   Strickler (2004), p. 805.

88   Circuit City Stores v. Adams, 532 U.S. 105 (2001).

89   Strickler (2004), pp. 806–807.

90   See Circuit City Stores, Inc. v. Adams, 532 U.S. 105 (2001).

91   Green, M. Z. (2000). Debunking the myth of employer advantage from using mandatory arbitration for discrimination claims. *Rutgers Law Journal, 31*, 399–471, p. 409.

92   Sternlight (2004), pp. 1425–1426.

93   American Arbitration Association. (2004, January 1). *National rules for the resolution of employment disputes.* Retrieved July 26, 2005, from http://www.adr.org/sp.asp?id=22075, Section 9.

94   Sternlight (2004), p. 1425.

95   Dunlop, J. T. & Zack, A. M. (1997). *Mediation and arbitration of employ-
     ment disputes.* San Francisco, CA: Jossey-Bass; Cooper, L. J., Nolan, D.
     R., & Bales, R. A. *ADR in the workplace* (2nd ed.). St. Paul, MN: Thomson
     West, p. 596; American Arbitration Association. (1995, May 9). *A due
     process protocol for mediation and arbitration of statutory disputes arising out
     of the employment relationship.* Retrieved July 26, 2005, from
     http://www.adr.org/sp.asp?id=22078

96   American Arbitration Association. (1995, May 9), p. 2.

97   Cooper et al. (2005), pp. 651–652.

98   American Arbitration Association. (2004, January 1).

99   American Arbitration Association (2006, July 1). *Employment arbitration
     rules and mediation procedures.* Retrieved July 15, 2006, from www.adr.org/
     sp.asp?id = 28481

100 American Arbitration Association. (1995, May 9).

101 For a more thorough discussion of the fees involved, see
     www.adr.org/sp.asp?id = 28481, or go to www.adr.org, and follow the
     links to employment arbitration rules.

102 American Arbitration Association. (1995, May 9).

103 American Arbitration Association. (1995, May 9).

104 Craver (2001); Morrison v. Circuit City Stores, 317 F.3d 646, 658–59 (6th
     Cir. 2003) (en banc) (acknowledging that the "Tenth, Eleventh, and D.C.
     Circuits have suggested that such cost-splitting provisions *per se* deny liti-
     gants an effective forum for the vindication of their statutory rights").

105 Hill, E. (2003). Due process at low cost: An empirical study of employ-
     ment arbitration under the auspices of the American Arbitration Associ-
     ation. *Ohio State Journal on Dispute Resolution, 18,* 777–827, at p. 812.

106 Hill (2003).

107 9 U.S.C.A. §10a (West 2003).

108 Halligan v. Piper Jaffray, Inc., 148 F.3d 197 (2d Cir. 1998); Landrum,
     M. A. & Trongard, D. A. (1998). Judicial marphallaxis: Mandatory arbi-
     tration of statutory rights. *William Mitchell Law Review, 24,* 345–406, at
     pp. 373–80.

109 Brunet, E. (1992). Arbitration and constitutional rights. *North Carolina
     Law Review, 71,* 81–120.

110 Sherwyn, D. (2003). Because it takes two: Why post-dispute voluntary
     arbitration programs will fail to fix the problems associated with employ-
     ment discrimination law adjudication. *Berkeley Journal of Employment and
     Labor Law, 24,* 1–69, p. 13.

111 Sherwyn (2003), p. 13.

112 Wright v. Universal Maritime Service Corp., 525 U.S. 70, 80 (1998).

113 The only state that apparently does not have a law prohibiting sex dis-
     crimination in employment is Alabama.

114 42 U.S.C.A. §2000e-5(e)(1) (West 2003).

115 United States Equal Employment Opportunity Commission. (2005,

January 27). *Sex-based charges FY1992–2005*. Retrieved July 15, 2005, from http://www.eeoc.gov/stats/sex.html

116 United States Equal Opportunity Commission. (2005, January 27).

117 42 U.S.C.A. §2000e-5(e)(1) (West 2003).

118 Catania, A. (1983). State employment discrimination remedies and pendent jurisdiction under Title VII: Access to federal courts. *American University Law Review, 32*, 777–838.

119 Equal Employment Opportunity Commission. (2001, February 13). *State and local agencies*. Retrieved July 15, 2005, from http://www.eeoc.gov/employers/stateandlocal.html

120 Apparently, only Alabama, Arkansas, and Mississippi have no fair employment practices agencies. Hawai'i Civil Rights Commission. Fair employment practices agencies in other states. Retrieved May 27, 2005, from http://www.state.hi.us/here/OtherStates.htm

121 Equal Employment Opportunity Commission (2005, March 21).

122 Craver (2001).

123 Sternlight (2004).

124 Equal Employment Opportunity Commission. (2005, April 22). *Litigation statistics, FY 1992–2004*. Retrieved July 15, 2005, from http://www.eeoc.gov/stats/litigation.html

125 This is a rough estimate. The EEOC filed 415 lawsuits in Fiscal Year 2004 and took in 79,432 discrimination charges. Equal Employment Opportunity Commission. (2005, April 22); Equal Employment Opportunity Commission. (2005, January 27). *All statutes FY1992–2004*. Retrieved June 13, 2006, from http://www.eeoc.gov/stats/all.html

126 42 U.S.C.A. §2000e-5(f)(1) (West 2003).

127 Sherwyn (2003), pp. 6–7.

128 42 U.S.C.A. §1981a(b)(3) (West 2003).

129 42 U.S.C.A. §1981a(a)(1) (West 2003).

130 Beiner, T. M. (2005). *Gender myths v. working realities: Using social science to reformulate sexual harassment law*. New York: New York University Press.

131 Beiner (2005).

132 42 U.S.C.A. §1981a(b)(1) (West 2003).

133 Kolstad v. American Dental Association, 527 U.S. 526, 545 (1999).

134 See, e.g., Broomfield v. Lundell, 159 Ariz. 349 (Ct. App. Div. 1 1988); Wallace v. Skadden, Arps, Slate, Meagher & Flom, 715 A.2d 873 (D.C. 1998); Black v. City & County of Honolulu, 2000 WL 1275818 (D. Hawaii 2000) (Hawaii state law); Morehouse v. Berkshire Gas Co., 989 F. Supp. 54 (D. Mass. 1997) (under Massachusetts law); Hall v. State Farm. Ins. Co., 18 F. Supp. 2d 751 (E.D. Mich. 1998) (under Michigan law); DeLoach v. American Red Cross, 967 F. Supp. 265 (N.D. Ohio 1997) (under Ohio law); Brown v. Scott Paper Worldwide Co., 98 Wash. App. 349 (Div. 1 1999); Kief, S. C. (2000). Individual liability of supervisors, managers, officers or co-employees for discriminatory actions under state civil rights act. *American Law Reports 5th, 83*, 1–102.

135   See, e.g., Woodford v. Community Action Agency of Greene County, 239 F.3rd 517 (C.A. 2, N.Y., 2001); see also Cavico, F. J. (2003). The tort of intentional infliction of emotional distress in the private employment sector. *Hofstra Labor and Employment Law Journal, 21*, 109–182.

136   For a thorough discussion of this issue in the context of Title IX, see Miller, R. C. (originally published in 2001). Liability, under state law claims, of public and private schools and institutions of higher learning for teacher's, other employee's, or student's sexual relationship with, or sexual harassment or abuse of, student. *American Law Reports 5th, 86*, 1–57; see also Beck, J. (2006). Entity liability for teacher-on-student sexual harassment: Could state law offer greater protection than federal statutes? *Journal of Law and Education, 35*, 141–151.

137   Simmons, A. M. (2005). Sixth annual review of gender and sexuality law: IV. Employment law chapter: State sexual harassment. *The Georgetown Journal of Gender and the Law, 6*, 597–613, 597.

138   Simmons (2005), p. 599.

139   Simmons (2005), p. 599 and n.4.

140   Simons, D. F. (2005). Employment law that fits our state. *Hawaii Bar Journal, March*, 4–12.

141   Simons (2005), p. 6.

142   Long, A.B. (2006). "If the train should jump the track...": Divergent interpretations of state and federal employment discrimination statutes. *Georgia Law Review, 40*, 469–557, p. 473 and n.12.

143   Long (2006), p. 473.

144   See also Chamallas, M. (2004). Title VII's midlife crisis: The case of constructive discharge. *Southern California Law Review, 77*, 307–396, 309 ("After more than a decade of litigation under the revised [Civil Rights Act], it is fair to say that Title VII law has never been more complex and confusing").

145   Long (2006), n. 17, citing Chambers v. TrettcoW, Inc., 614 N.W.2d 910, 917–18 (Mich. 2000).

146   But see Hoffman-LaRoche, Inc. v. Zeltwanger, 144 S.W.3d 438 (Tex. 2004) (plaintiff precluded from filing separate intentional infliction of emotional distress claim for same conduct to circumvent statutory limits).

147   Simmons (2005), p. 610.

148   The tort of negligent infliction of emotional distress can also arise, but is not as prevalent.

149   Cavico (2003), p. 110.

150   Dobbs, D. B. (2000). *The Law of Torts*. St. Paul, MN: West Group.

151   Cavico (2003), p. 113, 115; see also Godfrey v. Perkin-Elmer Corp., 794 F.Supp. 1179, 1188 (D.N.H. 1992) "[c]omplete emotional tranquility is seldom attainable in this world, and some degree of transient and trivial emotional distress is a part of the price of living among people. The law intervenes only where the distress inflicted is so severe that no reasonable man could be expected to endure it, citations omitted."

152   See Wolman, B. A. (1988). Verbal sexual harassment on the job as inten-
       tional infliction of emotional distress. *Capital University Law Review, 17,*
       245–272.
153   Cavico (2003), p. 152–153.
154   Note that the complex relationship between discrimination, tort, and
       workers' compensation claims is beyond the scope of this chapter. Injuries
       that are determined to arise out of the course of employment may have
       workers' compensation as their exclusive remedy, though, as one court
       indicated, a reasonable female employee should not expect sexual
       harassment as part of her job so as to bring her injuries under a Workers'
       Compensation law, Pryor v. U. S. Gypsum Co., 585 F.Supp. 311 (W.D.
       Mo., 1984); see also Cavico (2003), p. 163–165.
155   See Stockett v. Tolin, 791 F.Supp. 1536 (S.D. Fl. 1992).
156   Linebaugh v. Sheraton Michigan Corp., 198 Mich.App. 335, 338 (1993).
157   Kryeski v. Schott Glass Technologies, Inc., 426 Pa.Super. 105, 116, 626
       A.2d 595 (1993).
158   Magnuson v. Peak Technical Services, Inc., 808 F.Supp. 500 (E.D. Va.
       1992).
159   Summary judgment means that the court has made a determination or
       judgment without a full trial.
160   Wagenseller v. Scottsdale Mem'l Hosp., 710 P.2d 1025 (Ariz. 1985).
161   Rosenberg, S., & Lipman, J. (2005). Survey: Developing a consistent
       standard for evaluating a retaliation case under federal and state civil
       rights statutes and state common law claims: An Iowa model for the
       nation, *Drake Law Review, 53,* 359–420 (for a state-by-state summary of
       current law).
162   See, e.g., Chamberlin v. 101 Realty, Inc., 915 F.2d 777 (1st Cir. 1990).
163   Grossman, J. L. (2003). The culture of compliance: The final triumph of
       form over substance in sexual harassment law. *Harvard Women's Law
       Journal, 26,* 3–75, p. 3; see also Eller, M. E. (1990). Sexual harassment:
       Prevention, not protection. *Cornell Hotel and Restaurant Administration
       Quarterly, 30,* 84–89 (employers should concentrate on prevention of
       harassment, not the prevention of lawsuits).
164   Bisom-Rapp (1999b).
165   Sherwyn (2003).
166   Green (2000).
167   Schwartz, D. S. (1997). Enforcing small print to protect big business:
       Employee and consumer rights claims in an age of compelled arbitration.
       Wisconsin Law Review, 1997, 33–132.
168   Green (2000).
169   Reuben, R. C. (1996, August). The lawyer turns peacemaker. *ABA
       Journal, 82,* 54–62.
170   Bingham, L. B. (1998). On repeat players, adhesive contracts, and the
       use of statistics in judicial review of employment arbitration awards.
       McGeorge Law Review, 29, 223–259, at p. 238.

171 Reuben (1996, August), at p. 61.
172 Howard, W. M. (1995, Oct.–Dec.). Arbitrating claims of employment discrimination: What really does happen? What really should happen? *Dispute Resolution Journal, 50,* 40–50.
173 Howard (1995, Oct.–Dec.); Hill (2003).
174 Estriecher, S. (2001). Saturns for rickshaws: The stakes in the debate over predispute arbitration agreements. *Ohio State Journal on Dispute Resolution, 16,* 559–570.
175 Harkavay, J. (1999). Privatizing workplace justice: The advent of mediation in resolving sexual harassment disputes. *Wake Forest Law Review, 34,* 135–169, pp. 162–64; Summers, C. W. (2004). Mandatory arbitration: Privatizing public rights, compelling the unwilling to arbitrate. *University of Pennsylvania Journal of Labor and Employment Law, 6,* 685–734; Sternlight, J. R. (2003). The rise and spread of mandatory arbitration as a substitute for the jury trial. *University of San Francisco Law Review, 38,* 17–38.
176 The Anita Hill-Clarence Thomas hearings are thought to have led to an increase in EEOC charges of sexual harassment. Bernard, T. H,. & Rapp, A. L. (2005). Are we there yet? Forty years after the passage of the civil rights act: Revolution in the workforce and the unfulfilled promises that remain. *Hofstra Labor and Employment Law Journal, 22,* 627–670.
177 Harkavay (1999), pp. 161–162.
178 Harkavay (1999).
179 Lacy (2002), p. 45; Harkavay (1999), pp. 156–163.
180 Lacy (2002), p. 44.
181 Lacy (2002), p. 45.
182 Gazeley, B. J. (1997). Venus, Mars, and the law: On mediation of sexual harassment cases. *Willamette Law Review, 33,* 605–647.
183 Gazeley (1997), p. 632.
184 Gazeley (1997); Harkavay (1999).
185 Gazeley (1997).
186 Bond (1997).
187 Evans, M. R. (2001). Women and mediation: Toward a formulation of an interdisciplinary empirical model to determine equity in dispute resolution. *Ohio State Journal on Dispute Resolution, 17,* 145–183; Irvine (1993), pp. 36–39.
188 Irvine (1993), p. 36.
189 Irvine (1993), pp. 37–39.
190 Irvine (1993), p. 38 (quoting Corcoran, K. O. & Melamed, J. C. (Summer 1990). From coercion to empowerment: Spousal abuse and mediation. *Mediation Quarterly, 7,* 303–316, at p. 305).
191 Beiner (2005).
192 Stone, K. V. (1996). Mandatory arbitration of individual employment rights: The yellow-dog contract of the 1990s. *Denver University Law Review, 73,* 1017–1050.

193   Stone (1996); Bales, R. A. (2004). The laissez-faire arbitration market and the need for a uniform federal standard governing employment and consumer arbitration. *Kansas Law Review, 52*, 583–630.

194   See, e.g., Cole v. Burns Int'l Security Services, 105 F.3d 1465, 1482 (D.C. Cir. 1997).

195   See, e.g., Hooters of America, Inc. v. Phillips, 173 F.3d 933, 938 (4th Cir. 1999).

196   See, e.g., Circuit City Stores, Inc. v. Adams, 279 F.3d 889, 892 (9th Cir. 2002).

197   9 U.S.C.A. §2 (West 2003).

198   See EEOC v. Waffle House, 534 U.S. 279, 306 (2002).

199   United States Courts. (2004). U.S. district courts: District court profile. Retrieved June 13, 2006, from http://www.uscourts.gov/cgi-bin/cmsd2005.pl

200   Stambaugh, P. M. (1997). The power of law and the sexual harassment complaints of women. *NWSA Journal, 9*, 23–42.

201   Eighth Circuit Gender Fairness Task Force. (1997). Final report and recommendations of the Eighth Circuit Gender Fairness Task Force. *Creighton Law Review, 31*, 9–181. The task force found that 52.5% of plaintiff's lawyers agreed that discovery in sex discrimination cases was "inappropriately invasive" into the personal lives of parties and witnesses sometimes, often or many times. Stambaugh (1997).

202   Beiner (2005).

203   Lacy (2002), p. 48.

204   42 U.S.C.A. §2000e-3(a) (West 2003).

205   Brake, D. L. (2005). Retaliation. *Minnesota Law Review, 90*, 18–105.

206   Beiner (2005).

207   42 U.S.C.A. §2000e-3(a) (West 2003).

208   Craver (2001).

209   Clermont, K. M., & Eisenberg, T. (1992). Trial by jury or judge: Transcending empiricism. *Cornell Law Review, 77*, 1124–1177.

210   Maltby, L.L. (2003). Employment arbitration and workplace justice. *University of San Francisco Law Review, 38*, 105–118.

211   Sternlight (2004); St. Antoine (1995).

212   Stambaugh (1997).

213   Lenhart, S. A., & Shrier, D. K. (1996). Potential costs and benefits of sexual harassment litigation. *Psychiatric Annals, 26*, 132–138, p. 133.

214   Lenhart & Shrier (1996).

215   Green (2000), pp. 448–49 (footnotes omitted).

216   Green (2000); Stambaugh (1997).

217   Stambaugh (1997), p. 24 (citing McCann, M. W. (1994). *Rights at work*. Chicago, IL: University of Chicago Press).

218   Lenhart & Shrier (1996); Stambaugh (1997).

219   See, e.g., Hall v. Consolidated Freightways Corp. of Delaware, 337 F.3d 669, 678 (6th Cir. 2003) (Ohio law); Martini v. Federal Nat'l Mortgage

Ass'n, 178 F.3d 1336, 1350 (D.C. Cir. 1999); Connecticut General Statutes Annotated §46a-104 (West 2004); Washington Revised Code Annotated §49.12.175 (West 2002). For the federal caps, see 42 U.S.C.A. §1981a(b)(3) (West 2003).

Part II

From the Trenches

Individual Narratives from Plaintiffs,
Attorneys, and Expert Witnesses

4

Opposing Views,
Strongly Held

Ann Branigar Hopkins

William Glaberson, a reporter for the *New York Times Magazine* wrote an article entitled, "Determined to be heard." It appeared the day before the 1989 Supreme Court term started. I was one of several litigants discussed in that article. When Bill interviewed me for it, he commented that interesting stories often emerge when people have "opposing views, strongly held." This is such a story.[1]

In 1978, at age 35, I joined Price Waterhouse as a management consultant. About the same time Betsy (Elizabeth Anderson) Hishon, an Atlanta attorney, sued the law firm of King & Spalding alleging sex discrimination in the partnership promotion process.

At Price Waterhouse I started work with the Department of the Interior as client under the management of Lew Krulwich, the man who hired me and a newly promoted partner. Over the next couple of years, I expanded the consulting business I managed to the Department of State and worked for Tom Beyer, the managing partner of my office.

In August 1982, at the end of a nomination process that began in June, the partners in my office, with Tom and Lew leading the charge, proposed me as a candidate for the partner class to be admitted in July of 1983. I was the only woman among 88 candidates. Six of the firm's 667 partners were women. About ten percent of the partners were consultants. When I was told I would not be among the 47 members of the partner class of 1983, I was miserable, depressed, furious, disconsolate, and inconsolable in cycles. Tom was in a state of controlled depression. Lew was visibly sad.

It was unusual that Joe Connor, the senior partner of the firm, invited me to New York to explain why I wasn't admitted. Explanations by the senior partner were rare, but then my sales record was rare – no senior manager had a record to match mine. When I met with Joe, he was pleasant, but there was no warmth about him. He summed up the paperwork that partners had submitted with their votes on me. By his analysis, "Admit" votes from three partners who knew me well represented strong support. My downfall was negative comments from 26 partners who did not know me well, some of whom were supposedly supporters. The 26 voted: 10 to admit, seven not to admit, one to hold over for another year, and eight abstained for lack of information.

Joe read the comments to me. A few of the more memorable ones were; "Needs a course in charm school"; "Matured from a tough-talking somewhat masculine hard-nosed manager to an authoritative, formidable, but much more appealing lady partner candidate"; "Macho"; "Overly aggressive, unduly harsh, difficult to work with and impatient with staff"; "Overcompensated for being a woman"; and "Universally disliked." Clearly a number of partners did not like me.

After the next nomination cycle I was told I would never be a partner. What more could I do? The firm had the business I had been instrumental in winning, and I was a failed partner candidate in an "up or out" profession. Lacking a reasonable explanation for what appeared to be an irrational business decision, my husband suggested that I "sue the bastards," which I did. August 30, 1983, as first step on the path to litigation, I filed a sex discrimination claim with the Equal Employment Opportunity Commission (EEOC) alleging that Price Waterhouse had violated Title VII of The Civil Rights Act of 1964 (the Act). I left Price Waterhouse in January, 1984.

Pre-Trial

Hishon v. King & Spalding

Hishon v. King & Spalding[2] was under consideration by the U.S. Supreme Court in 1984. At issue was whether a partnership was subject to Title VII of the Civil Rights Act of 1964. In the lower courts, King & Spalding claimed that its constitutional right to freedom of association was paramount in decisions to admit partners to the firm. Betsy Hishon alleged that she had been discriminated against and was entitled to relief. The lower courts weighed the competing constitutional and legislative claims, agreed with King & Spalding that the constitutional claim prevailed, and denied Betsy her day in court.

Because *Hishon* raised questions about federal jurisdiction over discrimination in partnership decisions, *Hopkins v. Price Waterhouse* entered the court system on March 21, 1984 as a matter before the Superior Court of the District of Columbia alleging violation of the DC Human Rights Act. At issue was whether Price Waterhouse had discriminated against me when it failed to make me a partner.

In the summer of 1984, the Supreme Court ruled on *Hishon*: decisions concerning advancement to partnership are governed by Title VII, 42 U.S.C. & 2000e, and must therefore be made without regard to race, sex, religion, or national origin. *King & Spalding* was subject to the Civil Rights Act of 1964. Betsy settled with the firm – the terms of the settlement undisclosed. Her discrimination case was never tried.

Legal Strategy

In a day when discrimination cases were won by "smoking guns," situations in which an obvious villain pursued an obviously discriminatory course of action, Doug Huron, one of my two attorneys, came up with the novel notion that more subtle behavior, stereotyping, can result in organizationally discriminatory results without an obvious villain. He based his notion on the pattern of remarks in the materials that Price Waterhouse submitted during the pre-trial discovery phase. The materials included documents and notes related to partner votes on all partner candidates in my class and minutes and notes taken at several years of Partner Admissions Committee and Policy Board meetings.

Doug discussed his theory with Donna Lenhoff of the Women's Legal Defense Fund. She and Doug had worked together on legal matters in which they shared a common interest. Donna referred him to Sarah E. "Sally" Burns who then worked at the Georgetown Sex Discrimination Clinic, but shortly thereafter joined the National Organization for Women (NOW) Legal Defense Fund. Sally suggested that Doug solicit the testimony of an expert on stereotyping and recommended Dr. Susan T. Fiske, a Harvard PhD who was an associate professor of psychology at the Carnegie Mellon Institute. Sally had worked with Susan on a case involving the General Accounting Office (GAO) but Susan never testified because the GAO matter was settled the night before trial. Doug, who was already worried that his novel theory of the case might fail, also worried that the judge might not qualify Dr. Fiske as an expert.

As Doug worked to develop his theory of the case, we prepared for depositions, which consume hours of attorney time and incur travel costs. Doug and Jim Heller, my second attorney, wanted to keep the number and locus of depositions to a minimum. They decided to depose the four partners who had voted on me, partners representing the Partner Admissions Committee and the Policy Board, and Joe Connor. The decision limited out-of-town travel to Philadelphia and New York. All the lawyers agreed to take all Washington depositions at the offices of Price Waterhouse's attorneys, Gibson, Dunn, & Crutcher (GD, double entendre intended).

Price Waterhouse believed I had serious interpersonal skills problems and was rejected because I was overly assertive, aggressive, and abrasive. In the depositions, the GD lawyers asked questions intended to demonstrate these problems and bring out all my personality defects. By contrast, my attorneys wanted to show a track record of remarkable accomplishments and were hoping to find a "smoking gun."

By and large, the ten days or so of depositions that I attended were long, boring, anxiety-producing, exhausting, and depressing. They were also quite polite. On occasion, they were interesting and entertaining.

On one occasion, Doug and I had spent the entire day closeted in a windowless conference room while he took Tom Beyer's deposition. At close to 5.00 pm, just before we quit for the day, Doug asked Tom what advice he offered to better position me as a partner candidate after I failed the first time. Tom was trying to be helpful when he offered his advice. It was often quoted in the newspapers: ". . . walk more femininely, talk more femininely, dress more femininely, wear makeup and jewelry . . ." That remark was the closest thing to a smoking gun that we ever found.

Doug contained himself until the revolving door whooshed behind us as we left the building. Then the normally somber man broke into a broad grin and said "The walk, talk, dress femininely stuff didn't hurt." The grin stayed on his usually serious face for most of the time it took us to walk the four or five blocks back to Doug and Jim's office at Kator, Scott & Heller.

Hopkins v. Price Waterhouse

In September 1984, *Hopkins v. Price Waterhouse* (*Hopkins*) was entered on the docket of the DC District Court within the federal court system. My attorneys had decided that a victory in the federal system would assure a victory in the DC court, and a loss in the federal system would not necessarily lead to a loss in the DC court. In the federal case, I alleged discrimination and constructive discharge. I alleged that Price Waterhouse had discriminated against me when it failed to make me a partner because of gender stereotyping in the partnership evaluation process. Concerning constructive discharge, I alleged that Price Waterhouse had, in effect, forced me to leave the firm. I sought admission to the partnership, back pay, legal fees, and court costs.

A year later, in September 1985, Judge Gerhard A. Gesell, the District Court judge held that Price Waterhouse had discriminated. Specifically, Judge Gesell wrote:

> Whenever a promotion system relies on highly subjective evaluations of candidates by individuals or panels dominated by members of a different sex, there is ground for concern that such "high level subjectivity subjects the ultimate promotion decision to the intolerable occurrence of conscious or unconscious prejudice." . . . Such procedures "must be closely scrutinized because of their capacity for masking unlawful bias." . . . This scrutiny comprehends examination of evaluation procedures that permit or give effect to sexual stereotyping. Differential treatment on account of sex, even if it is not obviously based on a characteristic of sex, violates Title VII. An employer who treats a woman with an assertive personality in a different manner than if she had been a man is guilty of sex discrimination. . . . A female cannot be excluded from a partnership dominated by males if a sexual bias plays a part in the decision and the employer is aware that such bias played a part in the exclusion decision.
>
> This is not a case where standards were shaped only by neutral professional and technical considerations and not by any stereotypical notions of female roles and images. . . . Discriminatory stereotyping of females was permitted to play a

part. Comments influenced by sex stereotypes were made by partners; the firm's evaluation process gave substantial weight to these comments; and the partnership failed to address the conspicuous problem of stereotyping in partnership evaluations. While these three factors may have been innocent alone, they combined to produce discrimination in the case of this plaintiff. The Court finds that the Policy Board's decision not to admit the plaintiff to partnership was tainted by discriminatory evaluations that were the direct result of its failure to address the evident problem of sexual stereotyping in partners' evaluations.[3]

Judge Gesell also found that I had failed to show constructive discharge and was, therefore, not entitled to be a partner. I appealed the constructive discharge result. Price Waterhouse appealed the discrimination result.

After a couple of years – on August 4, 1987 – the Court of Appeals for the District of Columbia Circuit upheld the lower court on the discrimination result, reversed it on the constructive discharge result, and remanded the matter to the lower court for trial on remedy. Although Price Waterhouse appealed to the Supreme Court on the discrimination issue, constructive discharge was never appealed. In the DC Circuit, *Hopkins* expanded the definition of constructive discharge to include career-ending situations.

Price Waterhouse v. Hopkins

Better known than *Hopkins* is the firm's appeal to the Supreme Court, *Price Waterhouse v. Hopkins*[4] (*Price Waterhouse*). In that appeal, the firm offered several arguments on the issue of liability. They claimed:

- There was no discrimination.
- Freedom of association is paramount in partnerships.
- Stereotyping is inadequate evidence of discrimination.
- The burden of proof should never have shifted to the firm to prove that absent the discriminatory behavior the firm would have made the same decision not to admit me into partnership.
- The evidentiary standard required when the firm had the burden of proof was too high. (The firm had to prove its point by clear and convincing evidence, while I had to prove mine by only a preponderance of the evidence.)

After another couple of years, on May Day 1989, in six opinions, the justices of the Supreme Court discussed their views and related rulings, one of which affected me. The Court ruled that plaintiffs and defendants should be held to the same evidentiary standard – preponderance of the evidence. The case was reversed and remanded to lower courts for reconsideration by the lesser evidentiary standard. The District Court would have to reconsider the firm's argument that it would not have made me a partner even if there had been no discrimination and then decide whether a preponderance of the evidence indicated whether or not there was discrimination.

What made the case famous, among other things, was that the Supreme Court recognized stereotyping as a way of showing evidence of discrimination.

The Court also characterized cases in which an employment decision is made for both lawful and unlawful reasons as "mixed-motive" cases. In such cases, once a plaintiff proves that an unlawful reason is a substantial or motivating factor in a decision or action, the burden of proof shifts to the employer to prove that it would have made the same decision or taken the same action in spite of the unlawful reason. The Court went on to rule that an employer may avoid all liability – including attorney's fees and court costs – if it succeeds with this "same-decision" defense.

The *Price Waterhouse* decision was one of nine Supreme Court decisions issued in May and June of 1989 that narrowed in some respect the scope of key civil rights laws. Partly in response to the Court's decisions, Congress passed the Civil Rights Act of 1991. Because of the *Price Waterhouse* decision, Congress amended Title VII of the Civil Rights Act to state: "Except as otherwise provided in this subchapter, an unlawful employment practice is established when the complaining party demonstrates that race, color, religion, sex, or national origin was a motivating factor for any employment practice, even though other factors also motivated the practice."[5] The 1991 amendments also overruled *Price Waterhouse*'s holding that an employer could avoid Title VII liability entirely by showing that it would have made the same employment decision in spite of the discriminatory motive. An employer violates the law if unlawful discrimination is a motivating factor for the employment practice. The legislation does, however, allow an employer to limit its liability if it shows that it would have taken the same action absent the discrimination.

Hopkins v. Price Waterhouse on Remand

When the District Court judge got *Hopkins* back from the Circuit Court, he was irritated at being overruled by the Court of Appeals for the DC Circuit and then told by the Supreme Court to reconsider the evidence. Except for a bankruptcy case or two, *Hopkins* was the oldest case on his docket. His "bosses," as he referred to the judges on the Court of Appeals, had reversed him on constructive discharge, thereby precipitating a trial on remedy, and their "bosses" (the justices of the Supreme Court) had told him to reconsider the firm's position on discrimination by a different evidentiary standard.

In October 1989, at a scheduling conference for the much amended case, Judge Gesell scheduled oral arguments for reconsideration of the evidence and a trial on remedy. He also announced that he would offer his opinions on reconsideration and remedy simultaneously. Because his calendar was clogged with criminal cases, he scheduled the trial on remedy for February 1990.

A year after the Supreme Court ruled on *Price Waterhouse*, the District Court judge ruled that his opinion on discrimination was unchanged after reconsideration by the new evidentiary standard and ordered that Price Waterhouse admit me to the partnership and pay lost wages, legal fees, and court costs. The ruling was given on May 13, 1990. Price Waterhouse appealed the discrimination result again.

In September, 1990, the Court of Appeals got the case for the second time. The case's legal name was "*Hopkins v. Price Waterhouse (District Court for the District of Columbia 1985), affirmed in part and reversed in part (Court of Appeals for the District of Columbia Circuit 1987), affirmed in part and reversed and remanded in part, Supreme Court (1989)*."[6] I was as weary by then as the title was long.

One of the judges on the appeals panel had been the Chief Judge on the panel that considered the first appeal. The Court of Appeals was only slightly less anxious than the District Court to be rid of the case. Three months later, the Court of Appeals unanimously affirmed the District Court on all issues.

Early in 1991, the firm paid what it was ordered to pay, and I rejoined the firm as a partner with compensation and benefits set at the average of the partner group admitted in July 1983. I received checks for court-ordered back pay, attorneys' fees that I had paid, and for back pay earned between the date of the court order and when I returned to the firm. When the dust settled, I paid almost $300,000 in income taxes for 1991. My attorneys were paid about $500,000.

Nothing Personal

With litigation, for a case to "succeed" surely means to prevail on liability and to achieve the desired remedy. By that definition, *Hopkins*, after it finally got through two trials, two appeals, and a trip to the Supreme Court, was successful. But if you break *Hopkins* into the cases that constitute its parts, some were more successful than others. In the initial case on liability, I won a declaratory judgment and lost constructive discharge with the result that I earned no back pay and no partnership. On the first appeal I won liability again, with a split opinion, won constructive discharge, and earned a trip to the Supreme Court, another trial, and another appeal on liability. Technically, I lost the Supreme Court case – it was reversed and remanded. I "re-won" liability and earned attorneys' fees, back pay, and a partnership in the case on remedy, although I lost an amount roughly equal to the back pay award for failure to mitigate damages. When the litigation ended with the final appeal, I had lost seven years of my career.

There is, however, more to discrimination cases than "winning." In recent years, I have had the pleasure on several occasions of meeting Kay Oberly, the lawyer who argued on behalf of Price Waterhouse before the Supreme Court. "Nothing personal; litigation polarizes," she said when we were first introduced. The warmth of her smile and the sincerity that radiated from troubled eyes banished any recollection I had of her at the arguments. I gave her a ride to the airport once. I was driving to work and noticed her unsuccessfully trying to hail a cab. We chatted about being single parents and the trauma of divorce proceedings, matters that we had in common. I liked and still do like Kay.

"Nothing personal. Litigation polarizes." I'm sure it wasn't personal to her, but it was to me. Discrimination cases tend to get very personal, very fast. My life became a matter of public record. Attorneys pored over my tax returns. People testified about expletives I used, individuals I chewed out, work I reviewed and criticized, and they did so with the most negative spin they could come up with. I am no angel; but I'm not as totally lacking in interpersonal skills as the firm's attorneys made me out to be. How did I survive the personal onslaught? How did I go on to achieve success?

That the case, considered as a whole, was personally successful is due to the work of a lot of people. I attribute the success to me, my firm, my family, my friends, my attorneys, the trial judge and the judges on the appeals panels, my predecessors, and some people I never even met. People on both sides of the litigation made the case successful. Had I been less accomplished, my firm less prominent, my family less involved, my attorneys less brilliant, the trial judge less insightful, the appeals panels less liberal, my predecessors less sympathetic, and others in the civil rights community less committed, the outcome could have been dramatically different. I might have become a nut case.

Advice

I have listened to hundreds of litigants or potential litigants describe their situations in the workplace and ask for advice about what to do. These people included women and men; African Americans, Asian Americans, Hispanic Americans, and White Americans; gays, lesbians, and heterosexuals. They were attorneys, accountants, consultants, polygraphers, research scientists, doctors, administrators, clerks, bureaucrats, and senior executives. They were all between 25 and 60 years old. Each felt displaced by someone in the corporate majority who was less qualified. Most were sad and frustrated. Many were angry. Many felt powerless. A few believed they could make money out of their plights. Another few, typically attorneys who had retained attorneys to represent them, were absorbed in managing their own litigations to the exclusion of getting on with their lives.

I have offered advice reluctantly. That said, I have suggested to most of the potential litigants that they ask themselves "If I win, will the prize be worth the price? At what cost is litigation worth it?" Is one more grade or step in the civil service hierarchy worth a year of life struggling through internal administrative processes and the EEOC? What's the human cost in time lost to self, family, and career? Considered in the greater context of life, is this the hill to die on?

In my own case, I failed to consider any of these questions until it was too late. I got into litigation emotionally, almost on a whim. I fired the opening round with a lawsuit and then I was dragged through years of appeals. It seemed ill advised to quit because each trial or appeal was, at least in part, favorable to me. In retrospect, perhaps I would advise: be sure to blow the opposition away with the opening round – you may not get a second shot.

I have also suggested to those who appeared not to have scored an early and total victory that they get on with their lives. One potential litigant sat for months at a desk near the water fountain with nothing to do, waiting for some administrative process to change her plight. Others spent all their time for months, even years, micromanaging their attorneys in hope, usually dashed, for a dramatic positive outcome. "Get on with your life, your career, your other interests," was usually somewhat unwelcome advice. Yet, six month later, those who did so were much happier people than they had been at the time they came for my advice.

Notes

1   For a longer account, see: Hopkins, A. B. (1996). *So ordered: Making partner the hard way*. Amherst, MA: University of Massachusetts Press.
2   Hishon v. King & Spalding, 467 U.S. 69 (1984).
3   Hopkins v. Price Waterhouse, 618 F. Supp. 1109, 1119 (D.C.D.C., 1985).
4   Price Waterhouse v. Hopkins, 490 U.S. 228 (1989).
5   42 U.S.C.A. §2000e-2 (1991).
6   Hopkins v. Price Waterhouse 920 F.2d 967 (C.A.D.C., 1990).

5

Gender Equity at Stanford University: A Story Behind the Statistics

Colleen E. Crangle

In the autumn of 1980, I moved to the United States to enroll in a PhD program at Stanford University. It was an interdisciplinary program in logic, the philosophy of language, and the philosophy of science offered by the Philosophy Department. I had been teaching computer science in South African universities for six years and doing research in what was then a new area of computer science called artificial intelligence. My special interest was in getting computers to understand human languages, so that you and I could talk to them using ordinary English and they would understand what we were saying. Stanford was perhaps the only place in the world, at that time, where I could combine my scientific expertise with the intellectual insights of philosophy.

My arrival at the San Francisco airport that year was not the first time I had set foot in the United States. Almost 20 years earlier, in 1961, I had sailed into New York harbor on the Queen Mary, an immigrant along with my mother, father, younger sister, and older brother. My father, a citizen of Ireland, had taken advantage of the generous immigrant quotas for the Irish that still existed up to the early 1960s, and had fulfilled his lifelong dream of coming to America. What I remember most clearly about the day we arrived was my mother's call to us as the ship approached land, a call that, without her knowledge, echoed the cry of generations of immigrants. "Come quickly," she said. "There's the Statue of Liberty!" It was a gray, drizzly day, and I remember expecting the statue to be bigger and thinking, for some reason, that the lady with the lamp was facing the wrong way. But we were in America, and we began our new life. Family circumstances forced us to move one year later to my mother's homeland, South Africa, and that was where I finished my education. I completed an undergraduate degree in computer science and mathematics and two graduate degrees in computer science before coming to Stanford to join the interdisciplinary PhD program. I had always thought of the United States as my second home and I was delighted to be back.

After graduating from Stanford in 1984, I joined the academic staff of the research institute headed by my thesis advisor, Patrick Suppes. We co-authored a book in 1995 that summarized the ten years of research we had done on getting machines to understand natural language. This work had a practical side and a theoretical side. The practical side entailed experimental work carried out with researchers funded by the Department of Veterans Affairs. Their aim was to design robotic aids for the physically disabled, robots that could respond to spoken commands from a quadriplegic and help in tasks of daily living – preparing meals, brushing teeth, taking items off a shelf, and so on. The book we published thus represented about ten years of theoretical and applied research in medical robotics.

The Facts

Late in 1995, I was invited to join a project in the School of Medicine that needed my expertise in natural language understanding. This project was in SMI, short for Stanford Medical Informatics. Medical Informatics is an interdisciplinary field concerned with the theory and application of information science in medicine. With the successful sequencing of the human genome and that of other organisms, the term "bioinformatics" is now often used to encompass medical informatics and this new area of biology. I was delighted to join SMI. I threw myself into my work and very quickly established a reputation for excellence both within Stanford and outside with our collaborators in industry. I was the lead author on several publications, invited speaker at conferences, and was developing important collaborations within Stanford and elsewhere in the world. Microsoft invited me to give a talk on my work, and I was invited to Singapore to explore joint work on a project funded by that government. I also received an award at the premier scientific meeting in medical informatics.

But subtle signs had been appearing that suggested something was not quite right. My promised formal appointment in the School of Medicine had not yet materialized. I was told that there could be major friction with the other research scientists in the group, all of whom were men, if I were appointed at a higher level than them, at the same time being assured that this higher-level appointment was entirely appropriate. The appointment was delayed for many months. I felt increasing tension with the colleague who had recruited me to SMI, Larry Fagan. He and I were both senior research scientists in SMI and we both reported to Ted Shortliffe, who was an associate dean in the School of Medicine. He was Larry Fagan's long-time colleague and mentor. In fact, all the senior men in SMI had either worked together for a long time or were each other's former students. There had never been a woman on the faculty or senior research staff of SMI in all its nearly 20 years of existence. I was the first.

I found myself increasingly isolated, not invited to the executive committee meetings, the only senior scientist so excluded. As a result I never quite knew what was going on or what might be going on that I should know about. I was excluded from teaching assignments, even though I had more years full-time teaching experience than all the other senior research scientists. A final signal that something definitely was wrong was when I was told that there was going to be a shortage of funds for my position within a few months – despite the fact that I had helped secure a recent grant that extended for a further two years.

Things came to a head one day in November 1996 when Larry Fagan unexpectedly walked into my office. It was late afternoon. Most scientists and students had already left for the day. "I'm here," Larry said, "to tell you about some restrictions that are going to be placed on you." He said he was reporting the concerns of the head of SMI, Mark Musen. I had met with Mark Musen just a week earlier and he had commended me for what he called my considerable talent. He had encouraged me to widen the scope of my activities and to take on a greater leadership role. Now, in astonishment, I listened to Larry Fagan as he laid out a series of restrictions. I was not to submit proposals for any large grants – to do so would be like "the tail wagging the dog," he said when I asked him for a reason. Furthermore, I was to understand that the work we had been doing together really fell within his research area, and that he had the right to restrict my activities so that I would not be a threat to him. In that meeting and in subsequent emails with Larry Fagan and Mark Musen over the next few weeks, I also discovered that each and every proposal I wrote had to include financial support for Larry Fagan, but I was not ever to expect reciprocal support. I also had to be "sensitive," I was told, to Larry Fagan's fears of my intruding on "his" area of work.

My appointment, like his, was a soft-money appointment, funded entirely by money we brought in from government agencies or from industry. The only way you survived was to write proposals for projects and get them funded. But not only was I made to pay a kind of "tax" to Larry Fagan to be allowed to continue my work in SMI, I was faced with further restrictions that in the end made it all but impossible for me to work. I was told that all my research activities from that point on had to take place physically in my half office (I shared an office with visiting scientists to SMI). That meant that I could not go forward with experiments Larry Fagan and I had jointly been planning with social scientists elsewhere on campus, nor could I move forward with other important collaborations outside the university. This restriction was absurd given the collaborative nature of medical informatics and given the fact that everyone in SMI collaborated with other scientists around the world. I could not believe what was happening.

At this time I began to document some of these discussions, to follow up on meetings with emails that said "I want to make a note of what we discussed at our last meeting so there is no confusion." To my astonishment, I received email replies that would say, "Yes, your understanding is correct."

I don't know if I can adequately convey how utterly bizarre the situation was. My work was widely recognized as excellent. I was highly productive. I gave outstanding presentations. I was a sought-after collaborator. Now, here I was facing the fact that these very achievements were a problem to the men I worked with and who had considerable power over my professional life.

I asked for a meeting with Mark Musen, then the head of SMI. In his office, with Larry Fagan also present, I told them that it was inconceivable to me that the conversations we had been having would have taken place had I been a man and Larry Fagan a woman. I thought the day had long gone when a woman would be asked to curtail her activities to avoid threatening a male colleague. What I wanted, and expected, I said, was to work in an environment where excellence and hard work were rewarded, not squelched because they appeared to pose a threat to a male colleague. I wanted to be treated the same as my male colleagues and no longer excluded from important meetings and other activities of SMI.

Remarkably, these arguments seemed to make sense to Mark Musen and Larry Fagan. In response to my objections, the restrictions that had been placed on me were to be lifted, I was told. My sense of relief was short lived, however. Ted Shortliffe, the man under whom Larry Fagan and I were appointed, had been out of town while these events unfolded. On his return, a week or so later, he called me into his office, closed the door, and said: "Let me tell you how things are around here." Those were his opening words: "Let me tell you how things are around here." We were alone; no one else was going to be hearing the things that were said. Without any preamble, Ted Shortliffe told me that not only would the restrictions I objected to be re-imposed on me, I was now to *report* to Larry Fagan, and I was to understand that my *only* role in SMI was to support Larry Fagan in *his* research efforts. And I was not *ever* to think of myself in any way other than as Larry Fagan's assistant. At the end of this long meeting, in which I tried every argument I had to persuade Ted Shortliffe that what he proposed was improper, I said "It's important that you understand that what you're telling me to do is play a Girl Friday role to Larry Fagan." He thought for just a moment, scrunching up his face on one side as he tended to do when he was uncomfortable and said: "Yes, it is a Girl Friday role, but don't let that worry you – it could just as easily have been a Boy Friday."

The meeting ended in polite but open conflict. After ten days, when Ted Shortliffe did not get back to me as he had promised, I wrote a letter to him, with a copy to Mark Musen, saying that I did not accept the conditions of employment he had presented to me, that they were discriminatory and, I believed, in violation of the law.

We now know that the minute Mark Musen heard about this letter, before he even knew its contents, he sent an email to Ted Shortliffe saying "I'd like to see what options we have right now simply to lay her off." They did not immediately lay me off. Instead Ted Shortliffe immediately assigned me to a position outside of SMI to complete a low-level technical job for a project I had been advising on. In this position, I would have no office, no desk, no phone, and not even a computer that I could reliably use. At this point I put up a fight. I said you cannot do this – it is retaliation. You need to give me equitable working conditions.

The next two months were extremely difficult as I tried to reason with Ted Shortliffe, to persuade him to do the right thing. In the 18 months or so that I had been at SMI, I had noticed what a decent man Ted Shortliffe appeared to be. He came across as straightforward, dedicated to his work and to the scientific field at large, and respectful in his dealings with colleagues. He was particularly thoughtful of the graduate students who came from many different parts of the world to study medical informatics at Stanford. In all my time at Stanford, I had never met a faculty member who paid more attention to orienting students within their chosen field of study. I thought that he must have been misled, that if he understood what had really been happening with Larry Fagan, he would immediately restore my working conditions and make it possible for all staff under his direction to contribute their best to this rapidly growing scientific field of bioinformatics.

My letters and emails to him of that time appear pitifully naive in retrospect. For what Ted Shortliffe had decided to do, at the same time informing an officer in the employee relations department via email, was to ignore me. This we discovered only as part of subsequent legal action. I was desperately trying to get Ted Shortliffe to communicate with me. But he had decided to ignore me. In early March of 1997, I sent him what turned out to be a final email, clearly restating my complaint of discrimination and retaliation and pleading with him to communicate with me. I arrived at work the next day, a Friday, and found in my mailbox a letter informing me that I was being "laid off" effective that day. The reason given was "a lack of funding" – this despite the two-year federal grant I had helped secure. I was told that my computer account would be deactivated, possibly as early as the next morning, and I was to retrieve any files I wanted before then. I returned to my office that evening and worked until the early hours of the morning, trying to salvage several years of work. From that day to this, I have had no access to any of my research files.

That weekend was a difficult one to get through. I suspected that my academic career was over at that point. Academic circles are very small and very tight, and the people I had challenged were some of the most influential in the field. But the stance of resistance was one I had cautiously and deliberately chosen and I was determined to see it through. I was not going to go away and I was not going to keep quiet.

Following standard administrative procedures, I filed a formal written complaint with the university within a week. I had little hope of resolution. The first official response from the university I'd encountered was from an officer in employee relations while I was still at Stanford. She said her responsibility was to "investigate," but she warned me in that very same meeting that Stanford would fight any charge of discrimination I raised. Her response gave me clear notice: make any accusation of discrimination and Stanford will deny it.

Some months after the filing of my official complaint, a hearing was convened. But when I arrived for the first meeting, I discovered that the proceedings would not even touch on my claim of sex discrimination; only the procedure used to terminate my employment would be discussed. In addition, the employee relations officer who was there to record the meeting was the very woman named in my letter of complaint who saw her investigative role as one of establishing credible deniability for the university. I declined to participate in the process and walked out of the meeting. A few months later I filed a lawsuit in Federal Court in San Jose, California.

As these events were unfolding, I found myself waking in the night thinking: this cannot be happening. This is Stanford, a community of scholars who claim to seek knowledge and truth. Stanford had been my intellectual home for close to 20 years. It was the institution I came to this country to join. But the unthinkable had happened. I had stumbled into a cadre of connected colleagues who closed ranks when one of their members, Larry Fagan, needed protection from a woman who didn't know her place. There seemed to be nothing I could do; but nothing would let me just walk away. I had to challenge the institution that seemed to lack in its repertoire of responses the simple admission: What happened is wrong; let's make it right.

It was some months before I understood why I had to fight the discrimination I had encountered, why I had embarked on this hard, lonely road without hesitation and without a moment's doubt. I realized that a lawsuit would hang over my family for a long time. (I thought two years at the most; in the end it was four.) I was living in Palo Alto, on Stanford's doorstep. The community is infused with Stanford connections. Many people are fiercely proud of and loyal to the university. I was afraid I would be ostracized, that neighbors and parents at my children's school might whisper behind their hands that I must have done something to deserve what I got.

But all I knew was: I have to take on this battle; I simply have to. A telephone call at Christmas time from an old South African friend uncovered the reason. This is the story that lies behind.

An Echo out of Africa

Many of my formative years were spent in South Africa, from the early 1960s to the end of the 1970s. There I completed my undergraduate and graduate studies in computer science. I also held my first job in that country. It was at the University of South Africa, an institution that was unusual for its time in that it employed both black and white faculty. The 1970s were perhaps the most repressive years of apartheid in South Africa. I was raised by parents who were absolutely clear in their condemnation of the cruelty of apartheid but who were politically passive. In my early twenties when I worked at the University of South Africa, I came to see that passive condemnation was not enough. One event, in particular, brought this home. It turned out to have eerie reverberations 20 years into my future. This is what happened.

I had a colleague at the University of South Africa. His name was Lott Mamabolo. He was a black South African, one of the few on the professional staff of the university. The year we got to know each other, 1976, was a time of particular turmoil in South Africa with the Soweto student uprising. There was widespread unrest, and a great deal of danger to any black South African who went into work during any of the days of protest when general boycotts were called for by the student leaders. On one of these days, my colleague stayed home to protect his life and his property. The next day, he walked into my office, his arms overflowing with books and papers. He dropped them on my desk. "I've been fired," he said, "for not coming in to work yesterday. They told me to clear out my office today." I said to him, "That can't be. You have an employment contract. You have to be given notice, at the very least." I phoned the employee relations department for confirmation. I was told, to put it bluntly, to mind my own business. And word came down shortly thereafter to the head of my department warning me not to interfere. It turned out that all black professional staff members were hired with contracts that allowed one day's notice of dismissal. Only the black staff, not the white. And it was entirely legal in South Africa at the time.

Well, I did consider this my business, and I didn't leave the matter there. I got some colleagues in the law department involved and they tried to challenge the firing. In the end, though, there was nothing that could be done. Nothing. I realized then that I couldn't stay in a country that permitted and sanctioned that kind of discrimination – and, most importantly, allowed no means of redress.

Lott Mamabolo's story does have a happy ending. He moved to Canada and sought political asylum. He has a wonderful family and is well settled in Toronto. But his new life came at considerable personal cost along the way. No one should have to give up his country for a job.

Again and again as I considered what had happened to me at Stanford, the picture of Lott Mamabolo came into my mind. I had come to this country because I believed that all people could be treated equally here. I did not, and still do not, think that everything that happens here is fair or right. But it is a country built on the notion of equality, however frugally that notion was applied at the time. It is a country in which there are laws that protect individual rights. It is a country in which you can challenge anyone who appears to be breaking those laws. If I could not challenge Stanford's actions, it brought into question the past 20 years of my life. It brought into question the reason I had come to this country. I had to believe that I could lay out the facts of the matter before objective and fair-minded people and have them render judgment on it. I was prepared to accept their judgment, whether in my favor or not. Of course, I would have been very disappointed had they found Stanford's actions acceptable. But what I had to have was the matter held up for judgment.

The Lawsuit

The arguments

Judgment was to come three years and three weeks after Stanford fired me. Before the eight men and women of the jury retired to consider their verdict, they were presented with closing arguments from both my attorney and the lead attorney for Stanford.

"So has everybody lied?" asked the Stanford attorney. "If you accept Dr. Crangle's statement of the facts," he continued, "you have to assume that everybody who got on the stand from SMI lied to you, lied to you under oath. Now is that reasonable to assume?"

Sitting at the plaintiff's table with my two attorneys, I listened as Stanford's attorney continued, daring the jury to believe me and not those who testified on Stanford's behalf – the associate dean Ted Shortliffe, the head of SMI, three senior research scientists, an administrator, and a human resource specialist.

"Let me just finally say that it's not just Dr. Crangle that is affected by what you do here today," said the Stanford attorney in closing. "A charge of retaliation or illegal discrimination in violation of the law is probably the most serious charge you can make against someone that isn't a criminal charge. Everybody knows that. A charge of retaliation supported by this court against any of the people involved will follow them for the rest of their academic careers."

What was Stanford's defense? What was said under oath at trial? First of all, Stanford never attacked my competence directly. Indeed, the attorney acknowledged in his opening remarks to the jury that I "had a distinguished career." Stanford's main argument was that I was simply laid off because there was no funding. Furthermore, when I was offered another assignment, they said, I turned it down. The people at SMI had really been trying to "promote" my career and "assist" me, but I "misunderstood" what they were doing and that misunderstanding "turned into hostility."

However, we submitted documents that showed there was funding for me, and that at the time I was fired I had not turned down the assignment offered me. We produced an email trail illustrating my attorney's assertion that Larry Fagan had been undermining the agreements I was reaching with Mark Musen and Ted Shortliffe about my career at SMI. We produced documents that showed how I protested the treatment I was receiving at Stanford University. We showed the email message I sent to Ted Shortliffe the day before I was fired with less than one day's notice.

Was my experience an isolated incident? In my attorney's closing argument, he addressed the jury with these words. "As you all know," he said, "events do not occur in a vacuum . . . We're talking about events that occur[ed] in the real world at Stanford University, in Palo Alto, California, in November and December of 1996." What was that world like for women? How did others perceive it?

Dr. Frances Conley, a Stanford neurosurgeon, was one of only two people at Stanford courageous enough to testify on my behalf. Frances Conley had come to the medical world's attention some years earlier when she had spoken out about her experiences in the School of Medicine, and more recently with the publication of her book, *Walking Out on the Boys*.[1] Frances Conley's testimony was important, my attorney explained to the jury, "because she told you about the context."

She told the jury about a culture she publicly described as "unfriendly to women," where "often women were not considered to be as good as their male compatriots, where often [a woman] who excelled in a particular field would . . . find herself ostracized, would find herself isolated, would find herself in a situation where she would not be allowed the resources she would need in order to keep her career on track."

"There are certain men in the environment," she continued, "who are very threatened by an accomplished woman and don't want to have her in a position where she is competitive to them for the next advancement . . ." Frances characterized these problems as pervasive around the time I was raising my complaints and still present right up to the day she spoke.

Even a casual look at the statistics suggests something is wrong. At that time of my trial – and there has been no significant change in these numbers – 50% of undergraduates were women, approximately 35% of graduate students were women, but under 20% of tenured faculty were women. Women have been emerging from graduate programs at Stanford and elsewhere for some time, widening the pool of available applicants, yet they still do not rise in significant numbers to senior positions.

Making it to trial

Despite the pervasive problems that Frances Conley described, mine was the first discrimination case against Stanford ever to go to trial. The odds against making it into court, before a jury, are huge. There are so many impediments to gaining your day in court: finding competent and trustworthy lawyers, affording the out-of-pocket legal expenses, withstanding the assaults of the legal process. This ordeal is not for the faint of heart. Just days before the trial opened, Stanford's attorneys made an unlawful attempt to gain access to my medical records, all my records for the 20 years that I had been a patient at the Palo Alto Medical Clinic. They had no legal right to those records, but they almost got them through an improper subpoena.

Fighting a legal battle against a large institution is truly a David and Goliath battle. Stanford hired two outside firms of attorneys to defend themselves against my charges, in addition to their in-house lawyers. By my count, the university had nine attorneys at different times working on the case. That doesn't take into account the associates and paralegals working behind the scenes whom I didn't get to see. And most days it was just me and Liz Johnson, our wonderfully dedicated paralegal, sitting on the floor of a spare room in my attorney's office, sorting piles of documents. This room, high up on the tenth floor of a turn-of-the-century building in Oakland, across the bay from San Francisco, had no furniture, only a dark green carpet that was worn in places and stained. Liz Johnson and I sat on this carpet, surrounded by growing piles of documents, day after day after day, struggling to keep a grueling discovery process going. Discovery, the means by which you retrieve documents relevant to the case from the other party to the lawsuit, was anything but straightforward. We would ask for specific documents, identify the ones I knew existed that Stanford had not given us, then, as was necessary, return to court to force the production of documents. We had to take Stanford before a judge three times to compel the university to hand over documents they were withholding. And when we did receive documents, many were duplicates of documents already provided, only in a different order. We had to sort, read, and analyze thousands of pages. I had to trace every piece of email Stanford produced to identify the related pieces of email they were refusing to give. We hired a forensic computer expert to obtain email from a decommissioned hard drive, but as soon as the judge allowed this expert access to the drive, it suddenly became inoperable. Discovery is painstaking work that is emotionally draining. Every day I spent in my attorney's office, I had to relive my experiences at Stanford and be confronted with the loss of my academic career all over again. And while I was working on the case, I could not get on with building a new career. It was three years and ten days from the time I was fired to the opening arguments of the trial, and for each and every one of those days the Stanford battle was on my mind.

An ocean of support

In addition to the paralegal Liz Johnson, there were, of course, my two attorneys – Anne Weills and Dan Siegel. It was Anne who first told me about the Legal Advocacy Fund (LAF) of the American Association of University Women (AAUW). The LAF adopted my case against Stanford University and provided generous financial support for out-of-pocket expenses related to the legal action. Cases are chosen for support based on their potential significance for women in higher education; the plaintiff's need for financial aid; and a high probability of success. When I received the letter announcing the adoption of my case, I felt as if I had been lifted up and that I was floating on an ocean of support. LAF financial support was essential; it allowed us to do an adequate job of discovery when I wasn't able to earn the money to pay for it. Just as important to me was the knowledge that there were thousands of women across the country who knew and cared about discrimination. I wasn't alone anymore.

Their support sustained me through the years of lonely struggle. They shared the conviction that women in universities are still denied justice in employment. Not every woman believes she is discriminated against. But every one – man and woman, boy, and girl – loses because of the barriers that still exist for women.

The verdict

On March 30, 2000, the jury held the matter up for judgment and found unanimously in my favor on all matters put before them. They reached their decision in under six hours. And they awarded the maximum amount allowed under federal law in compensatory and punitive damages, finding that I had made a good-faith claim of sex discrimination and that in response to it Stanford retaliated against me, acting with malice or a reckless disregard to my protected rights. The jury filled out a form giving their verdict. I kept it on our dining room table for weeks after the trial. I couldn't stop reading it. This is what it said:

1   Dr. Crangle made a good faith claim of discriminatory treatment by Stanford University because of her sex.
2   After she made a claim that she was being subjected to discrimination by Stanford University because of her sex, Stanford took adverse employment actions against Dr. Crangle.
3   The claims made by Dr. Crangle about sexual discrimination were a motivating factor in Stanford University's decision to take adverse employment actions against Dr. Crangle.
4   With respect to each adverse employment action found in 3, Stanford would not have taken the same action based on a legitimate business justification had Dr. Crangle not made a complaint of discrimination.
5   With respect to those adverse actions identified in 4, the total amount of damages suffered by plaintiff caused by defendant Stanford University is $345,000.
6   Stanford University acted with malice toward Dr. Crangle or with a reckless disregard to her protected rights under Title VII, allowing her to recover punitive damages in the amount of $200,000.

Soon after the trial, Stanford gave notice of its intention to appeal the jury verdict and they filed two post-trial motions, challenging the jury's finding and seeking a new trial. Stanford argued that the damage award was excessive, the verdict was against the great weight of evidence, and the Court made errors of law in the admission or exclusion of evidence and the instruction of the jury. Both motions were denied. Several months later, the Court awarded, in full, fees of $492,925.00 requested by my attorneys. This award was in addition to the $545,000.00 awarded to me by the jury at trial. Three months later, the university and I reached a settlement. My family announced a gift of $30,000 to the LAF and, in collaboration with the AAUW of California, we launched The California 2001 Challenge, a fundraiser for LAF with a goal of $200,000 in 2001. The California Challenge is over, but the LAF continues to support women seeking gender equity in their institutions of higher learning.

Women still contend with inequities both subtle and blatant. I don't believe conditions have improved in any substantial way for women at Stanford, even though later in 2001 the university joined with eight other top research universities in a Presidents Workshop on Gender Equity. A unanimous statement issued by this workshop read: "Institutions of higher education have an obligation, both for themselves and for the nation, to fully develop and utilize all the creative talent available." "We recognize that barriers still exist."

Epilogue

My academic career suffered a huge setback because of my stand against Stanford. But I experienced a remarkable journey. The Judeo-Christian tradition that I am a part of believes in a God who loves justice. As I clung to the conviction that justice matters and that I had a part to play in bringing about change for women, I learned that it is possible to prevail against even the most powerful and elite of institutions. I learned that I live in a country that sometimes does administer justice for all, not just those who wield political and financial clout. That knowledge is without price.

I have also gone on to build a new career, taking the research I had been doing at Stanford and applying it to problems in healthcare and biomedicine. Through a small company, ConverSpeech LLC, I am undertaking the most fascinating and challenging work of my professional life, funded in part by two research grants from the National Institutes of Health.

What of Stanford? In addition to having to face other lawsuits, the university is also currently being investigated by the United States Department of Labor. As the recipient of more than $500 million annually in federal contract payments and grants, the university is prohibited from discriminating against anyone because of race, color, religion, sex, or national origin. I was one of 15 women whose complaints against Stanford of widespread gender discrimination in hiring and promotion initiated the government probe. Shortly after the investigation was made public, the number of complainants rose to over 30, including some men and people of color. My experience was not an aberration or an isolated case. Dr. Conley's testimony, ongoing lawsuits, and the Department of Labor investigation – they all provide a disquieting context.

But I find myself asking, was Stanford's attorney right? Did the jury's finding of retaliation and illegal discrimination in violation of the law follow the Stanford people as they continued their academic careers? What has happened to Shortliffe, Musen, and Fagan? Ted Shortliffe left Stanford shortly after the trial to become Professor and Chair of the Department of Medical Informatics at Columbia University. Mark Musen remained as head of Stanford Medical Informatics and Associate Professor of Medicine. Larry Fagan stayed on as a Senior Research Scientist. He also became the Associate Director of the Stanford University Biomedical Informatics Training Program. To my knowledge, not one of the people implicated in my unlawful firing has suffered any consequences from Stanford for his or her actions. The sad fact is that in many of our most prestigious academic institutions it does not really matter how you treat women. That is why I continue to tell my story.

Notes

An earlier shortened version of this story appeared in the April 2002 issue of *The Biochemist.*

1   Conley, F. (1998). *Walking out on the boys*. New York: Farrar, Straus & Giroux.

6

How Did a Nice Girl Like You . . . ?

Ellen B. Kimmel

In the fall of 1997, Distinguished Professor Kristin Shrader-Freshette's name was unaccountably missing from the roll of the awardees of the university-wide Professorial Excellence Program (PEP) at the main campus of the University of South Florida (USF).[1] In fact there were only three women (myself included) on the list of 32 professors selected for this important award, an award that was accompanied by a 9 percent salary increase. Professor Shrader-Freshette had been ranked first by her chair and department committee and by the college dean and college committee. She began investigating what had happened, digging into salary records of all senior women to discover that something was amiss.

After her initial probes, Professor Shrader-Freshette determined not to let the matter rest. She shared her findings with me and other colleagues, and we used my networks to identify a labor lawyer, David Linesh, with experience in class action suits. Seven interested women met with David on January 15, 1998 to explore our options. He oriented us to discrimination litigation. Within three weeks, a group of six senior women filed a $50 million suit, individually and on behalf of all senior women faculty at USF, in federal district court, alleging sex discrimination in pay and promotions.

How had we come to such a pass? This chapter tells the story of the USF suit. It explains how one of the plaintiffs, myself, came to undertake the fight and chronicles how the suit proceeded. In some ways, this is an intensively personal story. It is also a story about the need for vigilance and about the effectiveness of collective action.

My History

How did a "nice girl" like me get involved in a class action suit? The precipitating event was the foul treatment of my friend and colleague and subsequent discovery of inequities for the whole group of senior women, but the story really started over 60 years before. An important theme of this history is the need to redefine the meaning of the term, "nice girl," to embrace agency in helping others and fighting injustice, and to eliminate the insidious ways that phrase has inhibited females young and old from speaking out and rocking the boat. Nice girls, truly nice girls, have strong moral fiber and are capable of moral outrage.

Thousands of studies have examined factors that affect job satisfaction and general well-being. We know that pay and opportunity for advancement (promotions) and recognition play a role in both. When blocked from achieving these, individuals suffer many negative emotions and unhappy attributions that lower a sense of well-being. Only one negative emotion has the opposite effect on mental health, and that is moral outrage, most likely because this emotion alone is correlated with action. Even if the action is directly unsuccessful in eliminating the oppressive situation, it gives the actor a sense of control and purpose that enhances self-esteem. My decision to get involved was motivated by moral outrage, not at the disparities in my own salary, of which I was blissfully unaware in the beginning, but at the treatment of my colleagues.

Just how does a woman come to drop the "nice girl" training? First, she has to wake up. Years ago, *MS.* Magazine had a never-missed-by-me section about the "light bulb" going on when the correspondent-reader detected the presence of sexism in a situation. I was and remain fascinated to read stories of the birth of a feminist consciousness. For over ten years (1975–1986) a woman colleague from the Management Department and I ran a residential summer institute to prepare women for leadership in education.[2] A stated purpose of the program was to foster feminist attitudes for these future leaders whom we hoped could and would actively oppose sexism in the schools. Although most were vaguely sensitive to the paucity of women in leadership roles in public education, very few of our participants, competitively selected by their superintendents or community college presidents, arrived willing to label themselves as feminists. We were open about our wish that they would leave us with a feminist consciousness, and it was exciting to observe their "light bulbs" blinking. Naturally, all this led to reflections on the development of my own attitudes.

Early history

No doubt my family fostered a sense in me that being female was not to be seen as a deficiency. On the contrary, when she was in her eighties, Mother made an offhanded comment that she and Daddy had always thought I'd become President. I was stunned. Never before had she uttered such an astounding notion. Later, I appreciated that, while not to be taken literally, the comment illuminated one source of my belief in the equality of women's and men's worth. On the other hand, the many talks about my future with Mother while I was growing up only envisioned marriage and children, with not a hint in our discussions (usually held while riding our horses) about work outside the home. Mother was a southern lady and aimed for me to be one too. Marry and have children I did, but the lady part only partially took. Despite being voted "most ladylike" in high school, I confess to talking about politics and religion at the dinner table. Still, friends alert me about my tendency to act as a peacemaker and smoother over – the "nice girl" socialization is tough to eschew completely.

Born in 1939, my early years were idyllic, despite the war in Europe. Daddy was the doctor for the Tennessee Valley Authority town of Norris, a government-owned "commune" peopled by several of Roosevelt's brain trust, such as David Lillienthal, our next-door neighbor. The town was sold in 1946, and we moved to nearby Clinton. It was six miles and also light years away, and I felt the constraints of living in rural east Tennessee for the first time. The Depression still existed in the forties in that backwater part of the country. Now Daddy's patients were among the nation's poorest as opposed to the most brilliant, and I spent countless hours accompanying him when he drove deep into the "hollers" to attend to rickets, scurvy, botched childbirth, and every other disease and affliction of the malnourished and impoverished. The poverty was incomprehensible to me, frightening and overwhelming. I railed at the unfairness of things and for the first time questioned God. By the age of 7 or 8, I learned that I was privileged.

Small-town life had its advantages, of course. We kids had free rein of the town on our bikes, and local civic organizations invited me to give speeches when I was 14 (great practice for my life's work). It also was the case that my 8th grade teacher returned a paper on my intended career of pathologist (I liked helping Daddy with his lab work), informing me that women could not be doctors. I accepted this without question, never even thinking to report it to my parents (now I know they would have raised a ruckus), and dropped the whole idea.

From age 9 on Mother conceived of and Daddy funded (talk about traditional gender role division) ways to "get me out of Dodge." Trips to New York City and Washington, DC, England and Europe, summer camps in North Carolina and West Virginia, and, most significantly, enrollment my junior year in high school in the National Cathedral School for Girls (NCS) were all orchestrated by her with me as a most willing beneficiary. In my alumnae address at NCS at my fortieth reunion in 1997, I spoke about the powerful impact on my life's path of those two years in Washington. There, bright women, who tolerated nothing less than our best efforts and who affirmed that women could be fierce in their intellect and warm in their relationships, were my teachers and advisors, admired if a little feared.

Private boarding school had placed no small financial strain on our family, and anyway I was ready to chase boys more seriously. Thwarting the pressures of NCS's dean and faculty to attend a seven-sister school or the like, I matriculated at the almost-free University of Tennessee (UT) in the fall of 1957. Absent women faculty (only one of my classes was taught by a woman, not in my major, psychology, of course) or attention to women in the curriculum, I had no inkling of the existence of such a thing as sex discrimination. The best thing was I got a BA and no MRS (Mrs.). But Mother and I had not discussed this possibility! She had been a high school Latin teacher prior to marrying at 25, but my liberal education was seen only as preparation for the roles of wife, mother, and informed citizen. In 1961, a young college-educated woman had few options. I was tired of school and loath to take the Graduate Fellowship I had accepted from the University of Florida, but I was not qualified to teach or be a nurse. I had avoided (foolishly) learning to type for fear what I might wind up doing.

So off I went to California the day after graduation. After a wearying month pounding the pavements, I landed a job at the Southern California Gas Company in downtown Los Angeles answering telephone calls for emergency gas leaks. We were 100 women working at desks in a large open hall over which our supervisors were suspended in a glass cage. This version of "flippin' burgers" laid waste to fantasies about life in Hollywood and sent me packing right back to academe. I still did not "get it," however. I could not/did not see that my male counterparts were not restricted to the "pink" jobs section of the newspaper and were entering managerial training programs even in the very company where I was relegated to a dead-end job, despite my outstanding grades and honors.

First stirrings of a feminist consciousness

The scales were soon to fall from my eyes. September 1961 in Gainesville, Florida was sweltering with no relief from air conditioning back then except in the University of Florida (UF) library and the local movies. The entering class of 25 psychology doctoral students and the faculty gathered for the orientation were a motley, wilted collection. The only handsome man in the room was a professor, doubtless married I mused (he was divorced). After a few desultory comments by the department chair, the students dispersed to meet with our assigned advisor. As one of the few women in the group, I was assigned to the grey-bearded faculty man who promptly convinced me that I should go into the Masters in Teaching program to prepare for work in a junior college. I wouldn't have to do any research and could accommodate my work to the primary roles of wife and mother he was certain I would fulfill soon. This advice came despite the fact that I was the only one of that cohort of students who had received a coveted Graduate Fellowship (all others had assistantships). Suddenly the handsome man I'd noticed earlier appeared, cursing as he stomped into the room, and announced that I most certainly would *not* consider the Master's program. Further, he ordered me to go to work in his laboratory forthwith. Herb Kimmel was his name, and three months later we were married and obtained legal custody of his three small girls, aged 5, 3, and almost 2. His rescue kept my life on course. What I didn't know then was that the previous spring Herb and my favorite UT professor had made a bet that I would not stay at UF but would go to some better place as my credentials warranted. Herb was never a man to lose a bet.

The incident with the advisor was soon followed by another, similar incident. The University's first Graduate Research Professor was an eminent psychologist. I was flattered when he invited me to lunch and then appalled when he started berating me for accepting the Graduate Fellowship thereby robbing a deserving male. He was certain the MRS was the only degree I'd ever use, even if I finished the program, which he saw as highly unlikely. I was barely able to reply in my defense. Admittedly, I *was* a reluctant student at this point, anxious to find a husband and "start my life," as Mother and I had imagined I would. There was no other image to draw me, no person about whom I could say, "I want to be like her." Yet, I vaguely wanted something and was blessed with good reflexes and good luck to dodge the snares that might have prevented me from finding it. Of course, both my advisor and the research professor were correct. I married and became a mother, no doubt even faster than they anticipated. But these events actually made it possible to discern a path, to discover what would become a rich and satisfying career as a university professor.

From consciousness to action

The proverbial "two-by-four" of sex discrimination hit me squarely in the head as I began seeking employment after graduation (1965); in my first job for three years (1965–1968) at Ohio University (OU) as assistant professor (later "demoted" to research associate once the nepotism rules were discovered that precluded husband and wife from both earning tenure) in the Psychology Department; and in the first three years (1968–1971) piecing together work at USF where Herb served as the Psychology Department's chair and I was required to accept employment in the Educational Psychology Department in the College of Education on a year-to-year contract. The treatment of "faculty wives" then was bragged about and even more egregious than that for women in general. I was juggling my roles as a new professional, wife, and mother of four (Tracy was born at the end of my first semester at OU) and struggling to fit into the all-male department and male-dominated university. There were few women locally with whom I could discuss the struggle (and who had the time, anyway?); so I wrote women psychologists listed in the *American Psychological Association Membership Directory* who appeared to have academic psychologist husbands. I wished to find out how they were faring against the barriers that appeared at every turn. The few who acknowledged my query described similar plights, but no solutions.

My life as a feminist activist began in earnest in the fall of 1970 when I received the new year's contract indicating that my entire nine-month raise was to be the grand sum of $60. Surely a zero was missing?? When the College's business manager assured me the figure was correct, I angrily offered to trade raises. "Nice" was not working. I confronted the Dean about the inequity of the situation, noting that my record clearly exceeded many of my colleagues. I had, for example, exerted intense effort to immerse myself in the College's agenda, taught 12 hours, and continued to do research and publish. My pay – five years after obtaining my PhD – was to be significantly less than that of the two incoming male hires who were still finishing dissertations.

The Dean was a despot no one challenged, certainly not untenured women, but I was furious to the point of not caring about the consequences. The Dean clucked about the obvious discrimination and made vague promises to look into it. No action. I then shot off a letter to him reviewing the conversation and the data presented in it and reminded him that I awaited corrective action. I copied the President of USF, the Chair of the Florida Board of Regents, the Florida Commissioner of Education, and Chair of the Florida Senate's Education Committee. Nothing.

A letter came on a Friday afternoon in December at 4.45 pm, the last day that met the American Association of University Professors (AAUP)'s deadline for notification of termination of faculty whose contracts would not be renewed the next fall. I was fired. Uppityness has a price.

All my life to that point, getting fired seemed to be the worst disgrace one could experience. I did feel horrible, ashamed, even suffered difficulty swallowing, but I was also angry and, unexpectedly, free. What else could be done to me? There was no reason to worry about being nice or pleasing anyone. By now I was reading Simone de Beauvoir and Betty Friedan and participating in informal consciousness-raising (CR) groups. In Gainesville and Athens I had protested injustice against Black Americans – why not fight for women's issues?

In January, 1971 a sympathetic colleague and I organized a meeting of all full-time women faculty to conduct what was for many of them a first CR group targeted to our treatment on campus. The uniformly rotten experiences described by each woman helped the group understand that the problem did not exist within, but without. We agreed to approach the incoming President, a lawyer by discipline.

The rest is wonderful history. The President appointed a Commission on the Status of Women. We documented how lousy women's status was and made recommendations. Then the President set them in motion. One recommendation was to equalize the salaries of all full-time women, and I was asked to oversee this process for each individual woman by negotiating with her chair. (The average difference in salary, after taking into account discipline, years of service, degree, scholarly productivity, etc., was 12% in 1971.) Thus, my first foray into collective action was a smashing success – we were all heady with the power generated by working together and speaking out. My career also got back on track (a long but positive story), I became a dean, served as department chair, headed many major committees on campus, and generally enjoyed 32 more years at USF before retiring in August of 2003.

The Case

There were several unusual aspects of the USF case. First, USF, a relatively new school that had grown rapidly to a size of 40,000, had a record of active attention to women's issues since 1972 and was a trailblazer in such things as salary equalization programs and early establishment and continuing support of a women's studies program and department. Second, the profile of the six lead plaintiffs was not that of a downtrodden group one might expect to raise a fuss. A thumbnail sketch of the group reveals the first woman Graduate Research Professor (Shrader-Freshette), brought in as an internationally renowned philosopher of science and environmental ethics; one of the first women selected internally for the rank of Distinguished University Professor who was a feminist psychologist (myself); the top recipient of federal and state research grant dollars in the history of USF; an eminent classics professor who was serving as president of the local faculty union at the time; and two internationally prominent marine scientists (one of whom left USF subsequent to the settlement to fill an endowed chair at a leading university and the other of whom was featured as one of the world's top coral reef specialists). Diverse though we were, the group shared the luxury of relatively invulnerable positions (tenured, full, or distinguished professors and recognized scholars in our fields). This allowed us to protest loudly a condition that affected all 60 senior women (defined as "the class"), many of whom perceived themselves to be much more vulnerable than we.

In many ways we were the best treated among our peers, at first glance anyway. This appearance of privilege became a factor in our deciding later to settle out of court rather than face a jury who would likely view us as too rich and too greedy. In fact, one of my departmental colleagues (not my favorite person) referred to us repeatedly to any who would listen as a "bunch of rich, whiney bitches." I hasten to note he was among the few who expressed open disdain toward our action, and many faculty, both men as well as women, were very supportive of our cause with notes and calls and "good-for-you's" as we went through our days after the news media announced the filing.

Finally, ironically, of the ten universities in Florida's system in 1998, ours was the only one headed by a woman, President Betty Castor, considered such a trailblazer for women's rights she was in the Florida Women's Hall of Fame. A number of appeals to President Castor, among others, had failed to provoke any relief, leaving us frustrated and convinced that a lawsuit was the only way to get anyone's attention. It did accomplish that much at least, judging from the many newspaper stories that followed the case.

Along with a review of these background variables that were part of the discussion with David Linesh that January morning in 1998, the time frame of events in a suit and fees (in our case 40% of any settlement or award plus expenses) were described. At Linesh's recommendation, we put a few thousand dollars each into escrow for expenses to ensure that the lawyer could hire any needed experts, such as statisticians – a practice we recommend to any group considering a lawsuit. Following the meeting, five of us signed on (the sixth joined after we filed), swearing to secrecy until the filing and agreeing to take Linesh's advice to "build your individual cases" in the meantime.

There were facts left out of the orientation that we unhappily encountered along the way, such as the restrictive statute of limitations on discrimination and the restrictions in federal court as to what constitutes supporting evidence. Nor did we appreciate the difficulties of certifying the "class." Further, large out-of-court-settlements or positive jury decisions occur mainly in cases where there is ample evidence of overt verbal or sexual abuse, not just the more subtle, and sometimes more harmful, accretion of minor injustices. We now understand why our attorney kept asking us for "anecdotal evidence." He was used to representing hourly workers, not women at the top of the hierarchy. We had few recent incidents to report, given that we were too old and too senior to be "hit on" or publicly harassed. We had lots of war stories from our younger days, but those exceeded the time restrictions. Numbers, our weapon, evidently do not speak for themselves in the non-research savvy world – not even for judges and certainly not for juries who, if they understand, are likely to be bored by them.

Initial response

Ours was a classic "ambush" filing: a big number ($50 million) aimed at grabbing headlines and surprising and embarrassing the University. The University assigned a woman staff attorney to respond immediately to the press by flatly denying the allegations and stating that salaries were reviewed for gender disparities each year (true, but the process covered up the problems). We blindsided the administration because their radar was programmed to ignore pertinent data by maintaining such a clear double standard for "women's salaries" that it never occurred to them that the senior women were potential problems. They did expect the Philosophy professor to squawk about the PEP award but probably thought the rest of us came out of the woodwork – we were such a part of the institution's fabric, highly visible in our productivity and faculty leadership roles, all very "nice girls." After the press release the President tried to maneuver each plaintiff individually in a not-so-subtle attempt to divide us. All refused to communicate with her directly. On February 12, 1998 she held a press conference acknowledging that three of the group were paid $15–22,000 lower than male colleagues, but defended the differences with the old saws of disparities in market value, time-in-rank, etc. The logic was faulty since the men were paid above market value in the same fields as the women in question and had less time in service, fewer grant dollars, publications, etc. One of us was in a *better* paying field than the men in question! The implication was that we were paid what we deserved – in fact highly paid – for women!

For example, I *was* the highest paid person in my department in the College of Education, but my fair counterparts were in the Psychology Department in the Liberal Arts College where I held a joint appointment, teaching courses and supervising graduate students.

The hard work begins

Filing suit was relatively easy. Getting ready to go to court required much more effort. First, we had to develop our individual cases. Our materials would serve as models for other senior women whom we needed to contact, persuade to join us, and then help develop their cases. We had to find enough women to be certified as a class. In reviewing curriculum vitae and selecting men closest to me in their records and tenures, I expected to find that I had a very weak case, if any. My participation in the suit was due to the unacceptable treatment of the other lead plaintiffs and the senior women as an aggregate whose plight was not so much hitting a glass ceiling but being nailed to the 80 percent floor set for women's earnings. The discovery that my nearest psychology counterpart earned $32,954 more for nine months (or 42 percent of my salary then) than I did was shocking. He had been named a Distinguished Professor two years before I, had a PhD that was seven years newer, more grant dollars (alcohol abuse research), but considerably fewer grants, publications, offices, awards, etc., and no record of program development or administration (I had been a dean and department chair, presumably salary enhancers). Thus, I was discriminated against in both pay and promotion.

In addition to documenting the inequities for each person in the class, we also dug deeper into the statistics of the class as a whole. We knew our lawyer wasn't a statistician, and four of us were pretty sophisticated in that area so two in particular undertook that work. Salary data for state employees, including state university faculty, are public records published in annual budget reports on file in the university library. The gender disparity for full professors was evident. (Imagine my dismay to discover the exact percentage difference existed in 1998 between the senior women and men at USF that I found in 1972 for all faculty women vs. men!) However, some anomalies hinted that the official annual reports did not tell the whole story. Because of her grants from the National Science Foundation, Kristin had access to the actual payroll records that revealed parallel sets of books that did not match the published records, just as she suspected. The university was routinely hiding the actual earnings of many senior males, irregularities that particularly affected monies from grants and contracts where under-the-table cooking of the books allowed some Principal Investigators to "double dip." She contacted the Vice President for Research and threatened to blow the whistle. Within a few days, the payroll data changed.

All this activity required coordination. We met each Sunday afternoon, often long into the evening, at Kristin's house to report progress on the various fronts. One of us had a lot of space and staff support, and she offered to be the clearinghouse for all the documents we were compiling. We agreed to have Kristin be the spokesperson to the public and the conduit to our lawyer to avoid inundating him with questions and concerns. However, we recognized the need for a publicist to relieve Kristin and to help us "spin" our story to increase public understanding and support in the event of a jury trial. We had already gotten an endorsement from the local National Organization for Women (NOW) chapter, and several groups around the state were interested in how they could both help us and follow our lead. Thus, just the task of communicating was enormous, with press interviews, talking to colleagues, writing missives to faculty about our mission, etc. We were adding at least 20 hours to our already overloaded workweeks, and two in the group still had children at home.

Things get ugly

Shortly after Kristin confronted the VP for Research about the budget irregularities, we began to hear "funny noises" on our home phones, and suspicious vans began to tail Kristin wherever she drove and to hang out in front of her very long driveway (some of her students stayed up all night for several nights videotaping the drivers and their license plates). Local police ran down the plates showing the vans to be owned by known felons who had links to the lawyer the University hired to handle our suit (he was famous for these tactics as we found out from faculty who previously had sued USF). We became (rightfully, I believe) paranoid, especially when we spotted the vans during our Sunday meetings. We switched the meetings to local restaurants where the ambient noise would interfere with listening devices. We never spoke about the case on the phone or even to our spouses in our homes where we feared listening devices could pick up our conversations – talking about the case only when in the car or outdoors and not at predictable times. It was a stressful period, especially for Kristin who bore the brunt of the harassment. Her hair fell out in large chunks. We all lost weight and looked the worse for wear.

The group's dynamics

Each of the six of us was a strong personality, and our interactions were complex and often intense. Each had encountered discrimination in our academic careers; and we all had achieved much. Our ages ranged from early forties to early sixties, and we were married, widowed, divorced, with and without children. We came from every region of the country, were all white, but from different social classes and religious backgrounds. In addition, our experience with the women's movement and with feminist literature and thought varied widely, from being minimal to being the focal point of our lives. Often it was hard to stick to our agendas, but we had little time and so much to deal with, from strategy decision making to the nitty-gritty of putting the data and people all together. We did not always agree, and the press of the work left little time in our process to attend to personal histories. Sometimes feelings got hurt.

With all this, I was proud to be a part of this fierce group of troublemakers, a feeling I think was shared by all. Our differences were a strength and a burden. I found myself in the role of peacemaker (no surprise there – in my defense, also having taught courses on group dynamics I had some expertise in that area). Often, I would bring in a structural, feminist analysis of what I perceived was going on, that is to focus on our common enemies, institutionalized sexism, the bureaucracy, etc. Some of my well-intentioned attempts to foster a productive process backfired, of course.

Our lawyer was having his problems. In retrospect, some of us feel that this brash young man expected to gain a quick settlement from the flashy filing with such prominent clients. He was unprepared for USF's flat rebuttal and unwillingness to yield anything significant in negotiations. By some calculations (1998–1999) high-achieving faculty women earned more than a million dollars less over their career than their male counterparts. The always successful justification for this colossal disparity in lifetime earnings, from Stanford to MIT and used also by USF, was that women contributed less. David was unfamiliar with academe, was thwarted in his quest for useable anecdotal evidence to sway a jury, and was unschooled in the complex statistics we used to parse out pay inequities due to discrimination versus other variables that operate to determine compensation. He worried about the effort required for class certification, and we all worried about the judge we had drawn, a notorious "loose canon" and antifeminist. (Two of us had known her personally when she was an archconservative member of the Florida Board of Regents, hostile to faculty generally and women's studies faculty particularly.) We all worried about our collective health, especially Kristin's.

The resolution

The weeks, then months, dragged on. We remained resolute to continue. The lawyer negotiated, bringing us disheartening reports of those conversations and pleading with us to get more ammunition. The main factor in our favor for any movement was the President's desire to eliminate the bad publicity. She was first and foremost a politician who had basically appointed herself as our president when she held the elected cabinet post as Florida's Commissioner of Education. (She made an unsuccessful bid for U.S. Senate in 2004 as Florida's Democratic nominee.) Many of her primary supporters were women (I myself had given fundraiser parties for her over the years, one of us even ran one of her earlier campaigns, and several local feminists sympathetic to us were planning to run her next one), so it did not look good to have us screaming sexism on her watch.

Five of us became convinced that our chances with a jury were slim and that it was unlikely that USF would offer substantial financial remedy. They had partially gutted our case in the late spring by adjusting the salaries of the two marine scientists, and thereby reduced glaring comparisons to better-paid men scientists. Our attorney later told us that the statistical consultant he used (who turned out to have been the state employee that USF also used . . .) opined that if there had been more scientists among the lead plaintiffs, the case would have made the lawyer a millionaire. Kristin disagreed with the group about the need to settle, by that point feeling that our lawyer had betrayed us, so, sadly, she decided to withdraw from the case and pursue her own with a new lawyer. Also, she accepted the offer of a research chair at Notre Dame and was leaving.

By November we were hammering out language of a settlement that included minor compensation for the remaining five women (we figured 6 cents on the dollar of actual lost wages) and lots of promises for a complete overhaul of USF's compensation program. The University agreed to hire, in full consultation with our group, the services of a nationally recognized compensation consultant. We were to work closely with the consultant designing the new system. No less than $250,000 for each of three subsequent years was to be set aside for a salary enhancement program "with the goal of achieving equity . . ."[3] USF also agreed to appoint an ombudsman to act as a liaison and advocate to the President for salary issues, using our group to select the first appointee. It appeared that these policy concessions could make a permanent difference that our infamous yearly salary "adjustments" never had. We had seen salaries "adjusted" every year and then undone in myriad ways and were anxious to overhaul the system. It's important to note here that juries typically award money not mandate policy. Thus, in late November, 1998 we each signed a settlement agreement absent a non-disclosure clause (a minor victory) that enabled us to discuss the settlement terms.

The aftermath

I would like this story to have a happy ending. But alas, that's not usual when faculty go up against large institutions with a culture of defensiveness and staffs of lawyers to squash the dissenter. Our ending was mixed.

Yes, we did receive some money, as of course did our lawyer. But our euphoria over the promised structural reform – what we had seen as the real victory – was short lived. We spent many hours interviewing for the ombudsman and picking someone (a man from the engineering college!) whose appointment was protested by the Faculty Senate and the position basically gutted; the consultant was hired with virtually no participation by our group.

In the late spring of 1999, I wrote the President stating our dismay at the extent to which the agreement provisions had been ignored. She arranged a meeting where we were invited to present our data to show her the nature and extent of the problem for senior women. Finally! She and the Provost and deans who attended agreed that the problem was clear and could and would be addressed in the next round of salary distributions (the 1999–2000 contracts). Wonderful! The President promptly departed from office to accept a national post in education, and the entire matter was erased from institutional memory.

If anything, after our case, senior women at USF were worse off, since the same insidious factors continued to operate in salary decisions and we lost three of our most outstanding women scholars. The sad realization is that being nice is not effective; yet, cathartic effects aside, stomping one's foot is not a whole lot better. The squeaking wheel gets oiled. Pitching a hissy fit (it's what women do in the south) can enhance one's short-term goals, but always with a price. The best I can say is that the experience gave me a lot to ponder and forged some very strong friendships. The experience reinforced my conviction that truly nice girls must be willing to take the risk and do the work to effect change in academia. But even banding together, nice girls cannot effect change on their own.

Notes

1   University of South Florida. (1998) *1997–1998 University of South Florida fact book*. Tampa, Florida.
2   Kimmel, E., Harlow, D. N., & Topping, M. (1979). Training women for administrative roles: A positive response to Title IX. *Educational Leadership, 37*, 229–231.
3   Settlement Agreement and General Release By and Between the University of South Florida and Ellen Kimmel (or each of the other four plaintiffs). November, 1998, Tampa, Florida.

7

A Gender Discrimination Class Action from the Point of View of Plaintiffs' Lawyers

Donna M. Ryu and Jocelyn D. Larkin

This is the story of how a group of women workers came together with a group of civil rights lawyers to use the legal system to address systemic gender discrimination and sexual harassment in a major U.S. corporation. We describe how the women and their lawyers investigated and identified the causes of discrimination within that workplace and explain the importance of the class action lawsuit as a tool for eradicating discrimination.

The Backdrop

The story behind the lawsuit began with the experiences of several women during their employment with a wholly-owned subsidiary of one of our country's biggest and most powerful corporations, which we refer to in this chapter as "the Company." The Company handled the information technology needs for the entire corporation; as such, its employees ranged from clerical and administrative staff, to highly trained technicians, engineers, and computer specialists, and to mid- and high-level company managers.

Numerous accounts began to emerge about incidents of both gender discrimination and sexual harassment against female employees. One long-time female employee had developed a new strategic information system that was greeted with wide acclaim. But when it came time to implement the system, the Company passed her over and chose a less qualified man to manage the project. She nevertheless had to work behind the scenes to provide invaluable expertise, all without the visible acknowledgment that leads to upward mobility. When the woman voiced her objection, she was told that the man needed a project to prove himself, because he was being groomed for advancement.

Her experiences were echoed by the careers of a number of other talented long-term female employees who had become stagnated in their positions while they watched their male colleagues surge ahead in both status and salary. As she began to complain about the widespread problems, the woman herself became the target of an investigation. Her phone was secretly tapped in an effort to dig up information that could discredit her. She was labeled as a trouble-maker and never rose to positions that truly reflected her abilities.

Gender discrimination in pay and promotions were not the only problems. Women began to speak up about incidents of sexual harassment. One woman, a highly trained computer specialist, received through the inter-office mail system a series of increasingly terrifying and violent pornographic images of women being tortured. She suspected that the perpetrator was a highly placed manager. Again, when she voiced her fears, as well as her factually supported suspicions, the Company turned its investigatory lens on her, tapping her phones and secretly videotaping her movements. By contrast, the male manager was never monitored or even asked basic probing questions about his involve-ment. Other women, running the gamut from clerical employees to highly trained specialists, routinely were subject to inappropriate comments, sexual advances, and sexual "jokes." One such "joke" memo, entitled "Why Beer is Better Than Women," was circulated to dozens of employees. Among the "reasons" given in the memo were "after you've had a beer, the bottle is still worth 10 cents," "if you pour beer right, you always get good head," and "beer doesn't demand equality."

Even though the Company chose to respond to complaints by trying to dis-credit and demonize the victims and to protect the men, as the stories began to surface, other women found the courage to step forward with their own expe-riences. All of the stories were deeply troubling, and painted a picture of a company culture that clearly undervalued women and was hostile to the notion that women should share in the power structure. When viewed in isolation, the experiences seemingly were unrelated; but when taken together, they took on clear patterns: Although women were expected to perform at a high level, they routinely were denied plum positions and promotions to higher grade and salary levels; in fact, women were virtually unrepresented in the top ranks of man-agement. Women were also subject to sexual harassment that was, at the very least, condoned if not actively encouraged. Finally, women who complained about the discrimination and harassment were ignored, were not taken seri-ously, or were labeled as troublemakers and suffered in their careers as a result.

Events reached a crescendo when 28 women banded together and submit-ted a letter to management expressing their strong concern about the negative way in which women as a class were treated within the Company. The letter asked for management's help in resolving the serious issues of sexual discrim-ination and harassment. The next week, a second letter signed by 18 other women and men followed, stating that the women who had signed the first letter were widely known and respected within the company, and if women of that high caliber had been subjected to discrimination and harassment, then the entire company was at risk. In response, the company interviewed the 28 signatories of the first letter. Although the chief interviewer found the women's complaints to be credible, the Company took few, if any, steps to address the problems that had been identified. In fact, one year after the interviews took place, the Company still had not provided basic sexual harassment training to all its employees.

In light of the Company's lukewarm reception to their call for assistance, the core group of women felt they had little choice but to pursue the more formal route of a lawsuit. They contacted a small firm that had a well-earned reputation for excellence and perseverance and for working collaboratively with its clients. After much deliberation, the women and their attorneys decided to file the lawsuit as a class action, rather than as litigation on behalf of just the handful of women who came to enlist the law firm's assistance. A class action is a procedural tool that can be invoked by a party, subject to court approval or "certification," to try to address wrongs on a systemic rather than individualized basis.

Several considerations had to be weighed in the decision to seek class action certification. On the one hand, class certification could lead to broad monetary relief and, through court-ordered injunctive relief, could actually result in companywide changes in policies and practices. On the other hand, class litigation would be more complex, lengthy, risky, and costly. It also presented challenges in communication, since the lawyers and individual plaintiffs whose names would appear on the lawsuit were charged with representing the concerns of the hundreds of women who actually made up the class affected by the discrimination and harassment.

Having decided to proceed as a class action, the lawyers spent over a year preparing the necessary arguments to convince the court to certify the lawsuit for class action treatment. In the end, the court granted class certification for the claims of systemic gender discrimination, but ruled that the sexual harassment claims were too individualized to handle on a class-wide basis.

Because class actions present unique evidentiary challenges the original law firm decided to bring in other lawyers who were experienced in class litigation. At that point, our law firm joined the litigation as co-counsel with the original lawyers. Although our firm was also small, between the three partners we had more than 30 years of experience working on large civil rights class actions. By adding us to the mix, we believed we could successfully go after the Company and prove our case.

The Class Action Litigation

Essentially, the lawyers faced two basic challenges: (1) figuring out how to work with the clients, to understand and develop their stories, to address their concerns, and to tap into their expertise to help shape the litigation; and

(2) figuring out exactly how the discrimination happened, and how to prove its existence.

With respect to the first challenge, one of the fundamental problems stemmed from the women themselves. As noted above, the Company was among the most powerful icons of traditional American capitalism. The subsidiary was headquartered in a fairly affluent and homogeneous community. By and large, its women employees were conservative in their politics, and loath to believe that discrimination existed, or had been hampering their careers. Although suspecting that discrimination *may* have occurred, most were inclined to give more weight to other possible explanations. One of the most powerful experiences in the litigation occurred when the core group of women invited other interested women together, and facilitated meetings during which they shared their stories with each other. Faced with one example after another of careers stalled or stymied, and against the backdrop of stories of sexual harassment, the women experienced a collective and painful dawning of consciousness. Despite their hard work and talent, they had been the victims of discrimination.

With time, the legal team was able to develop close working relationships with a group of women who provided invaluable input, information, and direction, as the lawyers struggled to understand the minutiae of the company's personnel practices and systems in order to pinpoint how discrimination actually occurred.

Investigating and proving the case

To demonstrate a pattern and practice of sex discrimination, it was not enough for us to have a dozen or two dozen women with individual stories of sex discrimination. However compelling those stories were, they would not alone meet the legal standards for systemic discrimination. Those accounts, however, provided strong clues to the bigger picture.

The task of the plaintiffs' lawyer is to understand that bigger picture. She must analyze the specific workplace policies or practices and determine how those practices may be disadvantaging female employees as a group. While that factual investigation may sound straightforward, it rarely is. Typically, the inquiry will require, as it did in this case, reviewing hundreds or thousands of pages of company documents and personnel files, analyzing electronic personnel data, and taking testimony from dozens of company or class member witnesses. The lawyer must then assemble those myriad disparate – and sometimes inconsistent – pieces of information into a coherent picture, which must then be fit into the rigid legal framework for establishing systemic gender discrimination.

Legal theories   What exactly does the law require victims to prove? There are three primary legal theories for proving class-wide gender discrimination. They can be used individually or, more typically, joined as alternative theories of the case as we did here.

A disparate treatment class action alleges that the employer has engaged in a pattern or practice of discriminatory treatment against the class. This theory requires proof of discriminatory *intent*, which is often proven circumstantially by showing that management was aware that its policies were disadvantaging women employees but took no steps to change them.

The disparate impact theory allows victims to challenge employment practices that appear to be neutral, but which are shown (usually through statistics) to have an adverse impact on a protected group. Unlike disparate treatment cases, plaintiffs need not prove the existence of a discriminatory motive. The employer may defend the case by arguing that it needs to use the practice because it is a "business necessity," but this defense will not succeed if the victims can show that this business need could be met with a less discriminatory alternative.

A hostile work environment class action alleges that women as a group have been exposed to a workplace permeated with "discriminatory intimidation, ridicule and insult." The focus of the class action is the employer's knowledge of the hostile environment and its failure to monitor and prevent discriminatory conduct in the workplace.

The trial court in our case certified the claims of disparate treatment and disparate impact but, as noted above, chose not to treat the hostile environment claim as a claim on behalf of the class. Nonetheless, the egregious evidence of pornography in the workplace and other conduct demeaning to female employees remained relevant and admissible to explain the company culture and its influence on personnel decision making.

Use of statistics   One essential building block in a gender discrimination class action is statistical evidence. A plaintiff's lawyer will often rely on statisticians and labor economists to analyze workforce data (e.g. earnings or promotions data) to determine overall differences between the treatment of male and female workers and particularly what company-wide patterns are evidenced by the data. In this case, we used a labor economist to analyze the Company's existing statistical data and to develop our own statistical analyses tailored to the key issues.

Like many large companies, the Company had prepared its own workforce statistical analyses as part of an annual affirmative action plan. Those studies compared the company's "utilization" of women (or minorities) in particular job categories (i.e., how many women there are in the jobs) with their "availability" (i.e., the representation of women in the pool of qualified applicants for those jobs). The Company's affirmative actions plans over a five-year period demonstrated significant disparities – where the utilization of women was below their availability – in most job categories, with little improvement from one year to the next.

The Company had also conducted a smaller statistical comparison of the relative advancement of male and female employees with college degrees (a cohort study), asking how far each group had progressed after 11 years with the company. While women remained clustered in the bottom to middle ranks, the bulk of their male comparators were distributed from the middle to very top ranks.

The Company also compiled a comparison of its own workforce statistics with other large companies within its industry and in other industries. This analysis, often referred to as a benchmark study, again showed the company lagged behind its competitors in the representation of women in supervisory and managerial positions.

This evidence was bolstered by a different kind of statistical evidence, employee attitude surveys, which the Company had also conducted. Among other findings, the results identified a strong perception of a "glass ceiling" based on age, race, and gender and significant doubt among employees that the promotion system selected the most qualified employees.

Taken together, this evidence strongly supported the inference that discrimination against women was a company-wide problem, rather than a few isolated instances. It also supported a finding of discriminatory intent because the company executives were made aware, year after year, of the ongoing problem of under-utilization of women, yet failed to take steps necessary to remedy the problem.

What was causing discrimination against female employees?

While the first step is to determine with statistical evidence whether there is a pattern of disparate treatment between men and women, the next step is to determine what is causing it. What policies or practices are holding women back, and is the policy or practice in fact unlawful?

Women may experience employment discrimination in many different ways, including hiring, promotion, pay, evaluation, assignments, or training. Often numerous different forms of discrimination may explain or contribute to the adverse outcomes that women are experiencing. So, for example, if promotions are based in part on performance evaluation scores, both the evaluation and promotion policies are suspect and must be analyzed. In our case, an individual was more likely to be promoted if the person was given high-profile assignments, which would give him or her an opportunity to show off individual skills to a broader audience than his or her immediate work group. Thus, in addition to the promotion system, we also needed to understand the process by which assignments were made.

The company's pay and promotion system

What we learned was that the Company ordinarily did not post openings for promotional opportunities nor did it provide employees with an opportunity to express their interest in being considered for a particular job opening. Instead, the company used a personnel committee, composed of senior managers (virtu- ally all male), who would meet periodically and select the individual who would be promoted into the open position. The committee typically did not use a fixed set of relevant evaluation criteria against which to measure an employee's quali- fications for a promotion, nor would it necessarily even consider more than one candidate. The group would simply reach a consensus on promoting a particular person, then turn to filling the newly vacated job created by the first promotion.

Annual salary decisions were also made in group manager meetings. Each manager would make a short presentation about the performance of each of the employees within his group. The group would then compare and rank each employee against the others. A fixed pool of money for raises was then split up among the employees based upon their rank. The Company insisted that man- agers keep these deliberations entirely confidential and no notes from the meet- ings were maintained.

Our clients complained that these promotion and pay meetings were fraught with internal office politics and that an individual employee's raise depended largely on his or her supervisor's debating skills. They pointed out that employ- ees who did very different kinds of work (computer programming v. electrical engineering) were being compared to one another. Often managers outside a particular employee's work group would have little understanding of the work being performed and would be in no position to evaluate the employee's performance.

While there was much to criticize about these pay and promotion processes from a fairness standpoint, was there any reason to believe that they were more likely to disadvantage women? Again, we turned to an expert for assistance with this inquiry – a sociologist who specialized in workplace and gender issues. In gender discrimination litigation, sociologists and industrial psychologists are often called upon to analyze workplace policies or employment tests to deter- mine whether they are biased or vulnerable to bias. With the help of our expert sociologist, we focused on the question of how these employment practices encouraged reliance on gender stereotypes.

The role of stereotyping and subjective decision making

One central purpose of the antidiscrimination laws is to prevent employers from making employment decisions based upon "mere 'stereotyped' impressions about the characteristics of males or females."[1] Stereotypes are mental short- cuts by which we process information into categories, automatically and unconsciously. "Gender stereotypes are beliefs about personality traits, role behaviors, physical characteristics and occupational preferences that differenti- ate men and women."[2]

In the past, it was not unusual for gender stereotypes to form the explicit rationale for an adverse employment decision ("she's too emotional for this job," "a woman can't handle the high-level engineering needed for this position"). Today, stereotypes are more likely to operate on an unconscious level.

Sociological research demonstrates that stereotypes are most likely to influence decisions in a workplace where employment decisions are based on subjective and ambiguous evaluation criteria. These include such intangibles as "having good judgment," being "a leader," "a go-getter," or "a team player." While the use of subjective criteria is not *per se* illegal, such criteria are so amorphous that they can easily justify a decision driven by unconscious stereotypes. This risk of stereotyping is compounded when the decision maker lacks accurate, objective, and timely information. People are likely to rely on automatic mental shortcuts unless presented with clear and specific information.

Group ranking and vulnerability to stereotyping

Applying social scientific principles to our facts, it was readily apparent why the Company's group manager meetings might disadvantage women.

- There were no fixed evaluation criteria for salary and promotion decisions. Managers could apply whatever subjective criteria they chose and did not have to do so consistently. So, a male employee could be praised for his hard-driving attitude while a female employee could be criticized for being impatient and too demanding with subordinates.
- Managers had very little information upon which they could make judgments and comparisons. Managers would not review evaluations but instead relied solely on a brief oral presentation made by an employee's direct supervisor. This "condensed" version lent itself perfectly to stereotyped thinking. With many different employees to rank in one session and little information about each, evaluators would fall back on mental shortcuts. The non-supervising managers could simply rely on the evaluation of the director supervisor ("Manager B must know his people"), or assume that the employee is performing in the same way as he or she was the prior year ("I remember, he's solid but no rocket scientist"), or rely on irrelevant information ("Her engineering degree isn't from a top school"), or rely on conscious or subconscious gender and race stereotypes ("She's got kids so she must not put in the hours").
- The assignment process played an additional role. We learned that managers had discretion to assign to particular employees projects based upon their own subjective judgment – there was no process for an employee to express interest in an assignment nor any criteria for deciding who should be selected. With information technology evolving rapidly, there was an enormous advantage to an assignment which involved developing or implementing new technology rather than maintaining an old – and soon to be obsolete – system. We found that managers tended to assign women to the old systems or to the necessary but unglamorous projects, like department budgeting. In the salary and promotion sweepstakes, high visibility, cutting-

edge assignments provided a much greater advantage in the group ranking setting.

- The company culture could also have an influence on these decisions. The Company was in an industry from which women had historically been excluded. The salaried jobs in this division were staffed predominantly by individuals with engineering and computer science backgrounds, again fields in which women have remained a minority. The top management of the Company and the Board of Directors was almost exclusively male. Decision makers simply were not accustomed to seeing women in these higher-level positions and this absence could feed the unconscious stereotype that women do not belong there. This culture was also reflected in the failure of the Company to address complaints of sexual harassment and instead attacking those with the temerity to complain.

The final piece of our case was to develop reliable evidence that women had in fact been injured by the alleged discrimination. The law recognizes that victims of discrimination can be injured both economically and psychologically. While we anticipated that a certain number of individual class members could describe their injuries to the jury, the class was far too large for every woman to testify. Therefore, to augment this anecdotal testimony, we needed to develop class proof of damages.

We relied on our labor economist to calculate the lost earnings for the class, assuming that they had been treated the same as a similarly qualified male employee. While such damage models can be complex, they are objectively quantifiable. Far more difficult is placing a value on the psychological injuries sustained by the class since each woman's experiences and susceptibility to emotional distress varied. We chose to use two psychological experts who had substantial experience evaluating and treating female victims of discrimination and sexual harassment. They each met with and evaluated 10–20 class members to ascertain the patterns of injury that arose as a result of the discriminatory workplace conditions.

The Results

Our trial date was fast approaching and our team, which included by that point a dozen lawyers and paralegals, was furiously preparing for trial. But, as often happens when a court date approaches, the Company recognized the risks of a high-profile trial and thought it should consider settling the case. The parties engaged a mediator specializing in class actions. We met during the day to discuss settlement, while continuing to prepare for trial in the evenings. The negotiations were necessarily complicated because it was not simply a matter of paying money to the class members. A central feature of a civil rights class action is the ability to obtain a consent decree under which the Company would make changes to its practices in order to prevent continuing gender discrimination in the future.

On the eve of trial, the case finally settled. The settlement provided several million dollars for class members to be compensated for their lost wages and emotional distress. The claims process was set up such that a class member could either accept a fixed amount based on a formula (subject to meeting certain minimum proof standards) or seek her actual damages in an arbitration process. If the class member chose arbitration, she could potentially receive larger damages but she also assumed the risk of losing entirely.

The settlement also required the Company to implement changes in the workplace designed to address the challenged practices. The Company was mandated to hire an independent consultant to evaluate its existing personnel policies and practices and recommend improvements to those practices. The settlement also provided for the appointment of an "Ombuds," an official to whom employees could report workplace complaints and seek informal resolution. The Company further agreed to establish a diversity council, sponsored by the company president, to promote diversity issues in the workplace. The Company was directed to sponsor an Annual Leadership Conference heavily focused on women's issues. To ensure its compliance, the Company was required to prepare a series of reports over five years that were provided to us.

We attribute the successful outcome in this case, first and foremost, to the courage of the women who chose to step forward and make their voices heard. Also critical was the effective teamwork of those women, the lawyers, and the experts, all bringing their individual talents to the process of constructing a persuasive story to tell the jury. Through the vehicle of the class action lawsuit, we were able to reform workplace practices and prevent the recurrence of the shocking events that prompted the women to finally speak out.

Notes

1   Los Angeles Dept. of Water & Power v. Manhart, 435 U.S. 702, 707 (1978).
2   Stender v. Lucky Stores, 803 F. Supp. 259, 302 (N.D. Cal. 1992).

8

Title VII of the Civil Rights Act of 1964, the U.S. Department of Justice, and the Gender Integration of Physically Demanding Positions

Richard S. Ugelow

For 29 years, I was a trial attorney or a Deputy Section Chief in the Employment Litigation Section of the Civil Rights Division, United States Department of Justice (DOJ). The Employment Litigation Section is the federal government organization with responsibility for enforcing Title VII of the Civil Rights Act of 1964 against state and local government employers. Title VII is the federal law that prohibits discrimination in employment on the basis of race, religion, sex, and national origin.

In this chapter, I review Title VII's enforcement scheme, provide an overview of how DOJ used its enforcement authority, and then describe litigation with the Buffalo, New York Fire Department to illustrate the practical and legal issues the DOJ addressed in seeking to have women employed as firefighters.

Title VII's Enforcement Scheme

As originally enacted in 1964, Title VII's prohibitions against employment discrimination applied only to private employers. In 1972, Congress extended Title VII's coverage to public sector employers and designated the DOJ as the federal agency with primary enforcement responsibility (the 1972 Amendments).[1] The 1972 Amendments conferred primary enforcement authority for the private sector in the United States Equal Employment Opportunity Commission (EEOC). Title VII lawsuits may be filed by private individuals and organizations or by the EEOC in the case of private employers and by the DOJ in the case of a state and local government employer.

When the DOJ files a Title VII suit, it sues in the name of the United States of America. However, underpinning the DOJ-filed lawsuit may be a charge of discrimination that had been filed by a private party with a statutorily authorized governmental agency, such as the EEOC or a state or local government human rights commission. In addition, the DOJ may file suit when the Attorney General of the United States determines that there exists a pattern or practice of employment discrimination. In either case, the United States and not an individual is the named plaintiff and, therefore, the United States and not an individual is the client. The consideration of "who is the client" may have significant consequences for the manner in which litigation is conducted and for the type of remedial relief sought.

DOJ attorneys are obligated to serve their client, which is the United States and not any particular individual. Individual charging parties often have agendas and strategies that are not consistent with the objectives and purposes of the United States in bringing in the litigation. When these differences exist, the goals and objectives of the United States predominate. The affected individuals may choose to obtain their own counsel and seek to join the ongoing litigation to present their point of view. The important point is that when an individual charging party seeks to have the federal government pursue a claim of discrimination on his or her behalf, the governmental attorney will be pursuing the interests of the charging party only to the extent that such interests overlap with the interests of the United States. As the Buffalo Fire Department case study shows, it is not uncommon for differences to exist between the objectives of the United States and the female applicant who sought to be hired. Most often the United States is interested in systemic changes to the employer's practices, while the individual charging party seeks individualized relief.

Disparate treatment and disparate impact theories of Title VII liability

The two most common legal theories of demonstrating a violation of Title VII are disparate treatment and disparate impact.

To prevail under a disparate treatment theory, a plaintiff has the burden to demonstrate by a preponderance of the evidence (that is, it is more likely than not) that the alleged discriminatory conduct was intentional or purposeful. Since direct evidence of discrimination rarely exists, circumstantial or indirect evidence of discrimination is used by the plaintiff to establish a violation of Title VII. The most common type of circumstantial evidence is to compare how the alleged victim of discrimination (a minority or a female) was treated with the treatment accorded a similarly situated non-minority or male. Claims of disparate treatment typically involve individual allegations of employment discrimination and they constitute the overwhelmingly largest number of Title VII lawsuits.

By contrast, the disparate impact theory does not require evidence of intentional discrimination. In disparate impact cases, the focus is on the effects of the employment practice or the criteria on which the employment decision was based. For example, does a practice – like a physical performance test – eliminate more female than male applicants? If it does, the burden then shifts to the employer to demonstrate that the procedure is a valid predictor of successful job performance.

Disparate impact cases, which seek to eliminate or modify a systemic discriminatory employment practice(s), generally are very complex and expensive to pursue and present resource issues for private plaintiffs. For these and other reasons, the DOJ files most disparate impact cases against state and local government employers and the EEOC files most of the disparate impact cases against private employers.

The Department of Justice's efforts to make employment opportunities available to women

Historically, women have been excluded from being employed in jobs that either are physically demanding or are perceived to be physically demanding. This is certainly true in the firefighting and police professions. The exclusion of women from governmental police and fire departments was perfectly legal until the 1972 Amendments to Title VII.

In 1972, fire and police departments were overwhelmingly white and male. As a matter of practice in 1972 and going forward, the DOJ concentrated its resources to integrate police and fire departments. The DOJ considered police officer and firefighter positions to be highly desirable because of their pay, promotional opportunities, benefits, security, visibility in the community, and prestige.

Women were the victims of both disparate treatment and disparate impact discrimination when applying for firefighter and police officer positions. Thus, a woman could not apply for a police*man*'s position or to be a fire*man*. Even if women had been permitted to apply for such positions, they would have been disproportionately excluded from consideration for employment by a test of physical ability that either they could not pass or that virtually guaranteed a low score when compared to men.

The primary focus of the DOJ was to open protective service jobs to minorities, particularly African Americans and Hispanics. When it came to opening these physically demanding jobs to women, the DOJ was what I would characterize a reluctant partner.

There are many examples of cases filed by the DOJ against police and fire departments that alleged a pattern or practice of employment discrimination against minorities that also included allegations of discrimination against females. The focus of the litigation and the relief obtained, in the form of affirmative hiring relief, back pay, and other remedial relief, almost always was for the primary benefit of minority males, especially in cases involving fire departments.

The physical requirements for police positions were not considered by DOJ to be as physically demanding as those required by firefighters. Therefore, the relief obtained by DOJ in litigation involving police departments often coincidentally was of benefit to past, present, and future female applicants. The DOJ did not seek such relief, to my recollection, in comparable cases involving fire departments.

There are at least three reasons for this differential treatment of minorities and women. First, as I observed earlier, the DOJ decided to focus its limited resources to break down artificial barriers that served to restrict job opportunities for minorities. Any benefit to minority females and females in general was secondary to the primary purpose of the litigation. Second, police jobs were viewed by the DOJ leadership as more cerebral and far less physically demanding than firefighter positions. Indeed, even today one can observe many male (and female) police officers who appear to be physically unfit and yet apparently are able successfully to perform their duties. On the other hand, firefighter positions were perceived by the DOJ to demand more physical skills and ability and, as a group, women were perceived to be physically less able to do the job.

The third reason might be the most important. In its efforts to integrate fire departments, the DOJ's philosophy was to have employers reduce their reliance on cognitive test results and to rely more heavily on physical test performance to make selection. Underlying this decision is a belief that physical ability tests did not discriminate against minority males, while cognitive tests did. This selection process also played into the perception that "more is better." Stated differently, the more strength and more speed a candidate possesses, the better firefighter that candidate will be. Under the "more is better" philosophy, greater numbers of minorities would be hired in the normal course of events without resorting to overt racial preferences.

This selection procedure, pursued by the DOJ in the 1980s, while benefiting minority males had a devastating effect on the ability of females to be hired as firefighters. Interestingly, in proposing this procedure, the DOJ was not concerned with whether a physical abilities test selected the most qualified applicants. Rather, the DOJ was primarily interested whether a physical abilities test discriminated on the basis of race or national origin, which it did not.[2]

Put in the starkest of terms, the DOJ promoted job opportunities for minorities at the expense of women. This tension between the right of minority and female firefighter applicants to equal employment opportunities for me was, and continues to be, among the most difficult issue to address in a principled way.

The DOJ and the Buffalo Fire Department

Given the DOJ's ambivalence in pursuing firefighting positions on behalf of women, it is amazing that the DOJ pursued any such cases. It is fair to say that the DOJ did not affirmatively seek to challenge the selection procedures that adversely affected the ability of women to become firefighters. Rather, it was the courts or the litigants that sought to involve the DOJ. An excellent example is the United States' litigation with the City of Buffalo, New York, which, as this chapter is prepared, remains in active litigation.

The story of Buffalo begins in 1974, when the United States filed suit against the Buffalo Fire Department alleging a pattern and practice of discrimination on the basis of race, sex, and national origin.[3] A similar suit had been filed a year earlier against the Police Department and the two cases were consolidated for trial. After a lengthy trial, the court found that the City had discriminated against minority and female applicants for both the police and fire departments. Among others, the court found that 5'7" height requirement "eliminates the vast majority of American women." In addition, the court found that "No attempt had ever been made to recruit women for the position of [firefighter]."[4] In terms of relief, the court ordered that 50 percent of the Fire Department's hires be minority, but did not order, and the United States did not request, any hiring or other affirmative relief for women.

The court ordered Buffalo to:

> [T]ake affirmative steps to recruit and hire women in numbers commensurate with their interest and with their ability to qualify on the basis of performance related criteria for position as firefighters. Within 18 months from the date of this order the court shall, upon motion of plaintiff and after evidentiary hearing, consider the entry of specific long-term and interim hiring goals for women in [the position of firefighter].[5]

The DOJ vigorously monitored the court's order regarding minority hiring but took no steps to have the City recruit and hire qualified women. Indeed, the DOJ lacked motivation or reason affirmatively to require the hiring of female firefighters. The City certainly did not want to hire women and the DOJ was primarily interested in securing jobs for minorities. Importantly, there was no pressure from the court to secure relief for women. Thus, all parties were content with the status quo.

This all changed in May 1982 when a private attorney in Buffalo, William Price, moved to intervene in the litigation on behalf of his client, Teresa Perger, who wanted to be a Buffalo firefighter. The basis of Mr. Price's plea on intervention was that the court had found that the City was in violation of Title VII and that the United States had not sought or obtained any relief for women.

The DOJ could not and did not oppose Mr. Price's motion to participate in the litigation for two solid reasons. First, Mr. Price's premise was correct. The DOJ had not taken any steps to eliminate barriers to the employment of women in the fire department. Second, the DOJ did not want to be cast as not being supportive of ending gender discrimination. An opposition to the Price motion to intervene would have sent a message to all fire departments throughout the United States that the government did not take the ending of gender discrimination seriously. Nevertheless, the DOJ was not anxious to enter the "hornet's nest" of women in firefighting because it might detract from the relief being sought for minorities or more accurately minority males in Buffalo and elsewhere.

Mr. Price effectively called the DOJ's bluff and caused it to take the necessary steps to have Buffalo comply with the 1974 order of the Court regarding women in the fire department, which is something Buffalo was not about to do voluntarily. Buffalo was quite content to hire minority men and no women. In making his motion, Mr. Price well knew that the DOJ would have to support his cause not only because of the extant court order but also because Judge Curtin, the U.S. District Court Judge hearing the case, was a strong supporter of minority and women's rights. In other words, Mr. Price had a friendly audience and he correctly calculated that Judge Curtin would push and prod the United States to champion the cause of Teresa Perger and females in general. I can personally attest that Judge Curtin was not about to let the United States off the hook.

At the time Mr. Price made his motion, I was the lead DOJ trial attorney assigned to the Buffalo case. It thus fell to me and to my male and female colleagues to respond to Mr. Price and the Court. Interestingly, the trial team consisted of one white male (me), an African American male (Cliff Johnson), and a white female (Ruth Colker). Not only were Mr. Johnson and Ms. Colker accomplished attorneys, they were excellent athletes. I note their athletic accomplishments because the ensuing litigation required substantial knowledge of human physiology and the requirements to perform physically demanding tasks for a sustained time – experiences both Mr. Johnson and Ms. Colker had from their athletic endeavors.

Pursuing Title VII disparate impact litigation is very expensive and complicated. Mr. Price, a solo practitioner, was representing his client and by implication other women without charge. He did not have the resources, time, or expertise to pursue this case on his own. The DOJ, on the other hand, possessed all of those abilities. The only question was whether the DOJ had the commitment to pursue the issue vigorously. I am pleased to say that we did just that. Having said that, it is important to note that the DOJ did not champion Ms. Perger's individual cause to become a Buffalo firefighter. Ms. Perger was not the DOJ's client and the DOJ's objective was different than her personal objective. The DOJ did not seek to eliminate all employment practices, particularly the physical abilities test, that discriminated against females, but rather to secure the employment of a "reasonable" number of female firefighters. It must be remembered that the DOJ's overarching goal was to ensure that Buffalo's employment practices did not discriminate against minority applicants for the fire department. In fact, Ms. Perger unfortunately was never hired as a Buffalo firefighter, even though she bore the brunt of the public criticism and adverse publicity in the Buffalo community.

The Buffalo Fire Department used a physical abilities test that was typical for that era. Such tests placed great emphasis on speed and strength and did not measure other attributes like endurance and flexibility. Males tend to excel on measures of speed and strength, while females perform better on tests of endurance and flexibility. Efforts to include endurance or flexibility in a test battery or to use scoring methods that might reduce the adverse impact upon women were met with claims that the test was designed to lower standards for firefighters. Actually, the inflammatory term in vogue at the time (and today) is "dumbing down." It became clear during the Buffalo litigation that Buffalo and other fire departments using similar tests lacked empirical evidence that their extant physical abilities tests were selecting the "best" or "most qualified" firefighter applicants. The extant tests were used simply because they had always been used and there was no external pressure to change.

In 1982, when Mr. Price joined the case, the United States had already encouraged (if not demanded) Buffalo to make its selection using the rank-ordered results of a physical performance test. Obviously, women were at a severe disadvantage in this type of selection process. As the primary enforcer of Title VII, the DOJ had the ability to exert great influence on the employment practices of state and local governmental employers. Thus, it was not unusual for governmental employers to heed the advice of the DOJ on which selection criteria to use and how they should be used. Because such advice had already been given to the Buffalo Fire Department, the DOJ was foreclosed from demanding that Buffalo use different selection criteria or to use the results of the tests in a different way.

The DOJ goal, then, was to seek to neutralize the disadvantage for women that had been created by suggesting that Buffalo rely upon the rank-ordered results of its physical abilities test to select firefighter candidates. The DOJ retained an expert exercise physiologist, Dr. William McArdle, to compare the physiological demands of the physical performance test administered by Buffalo with actual job requirements. Dr. McArdle reported that, in his expert opinion, firefighters required stamina because they work for sustained periods under extreme duress and that Buffalo's test did not in any way replicate the way fire-fighters perform the job. According to Dr. McArdle, Buffalo tested the candidate's anaerobic ability and not the candidate's aerobic systems, which worked to the disadvantage of female candidates.

Notwithstanding the discriminatory impact of the Buffalo test, Dr. McArdle believed that women could be trained to take and, indeed, excel on the test. At the request of the DOJ and Mr. Price, Judge Curtin directed the Buffalo Fire Department to establish a 12-week training program for women in conjunction with the YWCA. The program was designed by Dr. McArdle in conjunction with the YWCA and consisted of general physical fitness training and, most importantly, training on the exact examination events under examination conditions. The Fire Department provided the YWCA with the exact equipment, such as a balance beam, dummy used to replicate a body drag and hose coupling, that would be used on the test. As the time for the test approached, the women had the opportunity to run through all of the events at the test site. The test results were staggering. Two women were among the top ten highest scoring candidates[6] and five women ranked in the top hundred.[7] I recall that the City's response was equally staggering. The Chief of the Fire Training Academy told me in effect that the physical abilities test must be flawed if women did so well. In other words, according to Fire Department officials, the physical abilities test could not possibly be job-related and predictive of successful job performance if women scored well on it! Nevertheless, the City hired ten female firefighters from that testing cycle.

A number of factors, in addition to the hostility of Fire Department officials to women, coalesced to foreclose the likelihood that women would be hired by the Buffalo Fire Department in the future. Today, like many municipal fire departments, Buffalo's is all male.

Buffalo firefighters, like most civil servant employees, are hired off of a list of eligibles (eligibility list), which is a rank-ordered list of individuals who are deemed by the employer to be qualified for the job. Generally, the longer an eligibility list remains in place the fewer females and minorities remain interested in the position because they have taken other jobs. The life of Buffalo's firefighter eligibility list was almost five years and the availability of qualified and interested females was quickly exhausted. Moreover, during that five-year period, there was no recruitment for female applicants and thus no effort was made to maintain the interest of women in becoming firefighters. Further, there were frequent stories in the press about the difficulties the females encountered in the fire training academy and on the job. For example, it was reported that women had difficulty starting the motor on power saws that are used on the job by firefighters. We learned that the Fire Department training officers assumed that women knew that a ballistic action was necessary to pull the starter rope. When Dr. McArdle was given the opportunity to teach the female cadets the ballistic action (the same action used to start a power lawn mower), they were able easily to start the power saw. Similarly, other tasks performed by firefighters, such as wall climbing or the use of certain tools, assume the knowledge of techniques that for social reasons are known to males and not females. The point here is that the Fire Department either did not know or ignored the differences in social experiences that men and women have and the training offered in the fire training academy did not recognize those differences.

There are other social and institutional obstacles that serve as barriers to the full employment of women in firefighter positions. For example, fire departments and firehouses have been male bastions for many decades. Thus, they typically lack bathroom and sleeping facilities for women. It is not uncommon for fire departments to argue that it is too expensive or difficult to retrofit firehouses to accommodate females. When such accommodations are made they are often inadequate and women are made to feel like second-class citizens. There is also the issue of overt hostility of incumbent males to female firefighters. There is the attitude that she has to be one of the "boys" and accept guy talk and pinup pictures.

Not all of these issues can be changed by the courts through aggressive law enforcement. Obviously, attitudinal changes from the employer and incumbent employees are also required. The DOJ, as the lead Title VII federal law enforcement agency, needs to be aggressive in the courts and to use its bully pulpit to jawbone fire departments to remove obstacles that impair the fair and full employment of women as firefighters.

Notes

1   The Equal Employment Opportunity Act of 1972.
2   What I find perplexing is that employers seem perfectly content to rely on the results of a physical abilities test that is often administered and scored up to a year or more before a candidate is hired. Consequently, the employer has little or no knowledge of the applicant's ability to perform at a high physical level at the time he or she is actually hired as a firefighter.
3   United States v. City of Buffalo, 457 F. Supp. 612, 625 (W.D.N.Y. 1978).
4   United States v. City of Buffalo (1978), p. 629.
5   United States v. City of Buffalo, 20 EPD ¶ 31,112 (W.D.N.Y. 1978).
6   *The Buffalo News*, June 10, 1989.
7   *The Buffalo News*, July 22, 1995.

9

Reflections on Being an Expert Witness in Class Action Sex Discrimination Litigation

Eugene Borgida and Anita Kim

Our story begins with the fourteenth annual convention of the National Employment Lawyers Association (NELA) held in June 2003. NELA's annual meeting took place in Vail, Colorado, and its geographically apt theme was "Conquering Mountains for Workers' Rights." This chapter's first author had been invited to participate in a panel session on "Stereotyping evidence: The forgotten method of proof" along with Seattle-based attorney, Michael C. Subit, who had prior litigation experience with expert testimony on gender stereotyping. The session was quite well attended, though attendance may have been inflated by NELA members exiting the exhilarating keynote address ("Fighting for Justice") of nationally renowned plaintiffs' attorney, Gerry Spence, from an adjacent ballroom.

During the panel session, which was deemed a great success by NELA, a then anonymous attorney from the audience operated the overhead projector during both presentations on the use of stereotyping evidence in employment discrimination cases. It turns out, however, that this attorney was paying very close attention to the content of the overhead slides that she was so graciously flipping. Later that summer the attorney, from the Seattle law firm representing female plaintiffs in a class action case against The Boeing Company, stepped out of the shadow of anonymity, contacted the chapter's first author, and retained him as the plaintiffs' expert witness on gender stereotyping and prejudice. On February 25, 2000, a group of non-management female plaintiffs had filed a class action suit against The Boeing Company.[1] Many of the plaintiffs claimed they were paid less than similarly situated males for doing the same job, or were not granted opportunities for training, overtime, or promotion which advantaged their male counterparts. Some plaintiffs also complained they were subjected to unwelcome sexual overtures or comments about their bodies. When these women complained about the harassment or unequal treatment to Boeing officials, some were relocated to less desirable job sites or to work less desirable shifts, some were ostracized by their co-workers, and some were denied even more gainful job opportunities; in short, they alleged they suffered retaliation by their employers for complaining. In its defense, Boeing denied all allegations of misconduct, including the plaintiffs' claims they were treated differently than their male counterparts based on their sex. After a four-year legal battle, the litigation was settled in May 2004, though the terms of the settlement were not disclosed.

The purpose of this chapter is to review the challenges to the first author's expert testimony in this case, and to highlight some important lessons learned. We first generally review the expert's psychological testimony on gender stereotyping and prejudice as it was presented in the first step of his testimony, the expert report. Next, we review and discuss his deposition and, in particular, the specific defense challenges to the expert's report and opinions. We describe the exchange in greater detail because it is diagnostic of the set of key challenges to expert psychological testimony that are common in class action sex discrimination cases. We argue that there are important lessons to be learned from these challenges and (perhaps more importantly) from the defense motions to exclude the expert's testimony. Although the federal judge in the case ultimately denied the defense motion to exclude the testimony, there is every reason to believe that these issues will resurface in future class action and single plaintiff litigation in this legal arena.

Borgida's Experiences in the Case

The plaintiffs in *Beck et al. v. The Boeing Company* claimed to have been denied, based on their gender, competitive promotions (for non-management female employees), annual compensation adjustments for salaried women, and overtime opportunities at Boeing's Puget Sound facilities between late February 1997 and November 2003. Plaintiffs' counsel asked Borgida to review all available case materials and address the extent to which gender stereotyping may (or may not) have played a role in understanding these claims. Plaintiffs' counsel also asked if the report would address whether women would likely be disadvantaged by various Boeing employment practices.

A general opinion was proffered in the report: that the social scientific research literature on gender stereotyping and prejudice played an important explanatory role in understanding how gender stereotypes affected pay and promotion and overtime practices at Boeing. Several related and more specific opinions were also offered (e.g., that under various conditions, people make decisions based on gender stereotypes, whether or not they are aware that such generalizations about women can result in faulty judgments about specific individuals; in the absence of specific, accurate evidence of competent performance, there is an increased likelihood that gender stereotypes will bias managers' compensation decisions and managers will be more inclined to rely on the opinions of fellow managers who are usually male).

The opinion offered in this case reflected the application of a social framework analysis. This approach to expert scientific testimony represents a scientifically known and established approach to using social science evidence in litigation.[2] It is an approach that has increasingly been accepted in the courts over the past decade or more in cases involving, for example, employment discrimination, eyewitness identification, and sexual victimization. This approach has been written about most extensively by Monahan and Walker who have discussed the social framework approach in their law review writings,[3] but others also have written about the approach.[4]

A social framework analysis uses general conclusions from tested, reliable, and peer-reviewed social science research and applies them to the case at hand. It provides an assessment of general causation in a research area in order to inform fact finders about more specific causation issues associated with a particular case.[5] General causation refers to whether causality between two factors exists at all. For example, an expert who testifies that smoking can cause lung cancer is addressing general causation because the testimony is designed to establish that the phenomenon occurs. Specific causation, in contrast, refers to whether the phenomenon of interest occurred in a particular context. It refers to whether causality between two factors actually did exist in the case at hand. In our smoking and lung cancer example, an expert who testifies that smoking a particular brand of cigarettes caused a specific patient's lung cancer is addressing specific causation.[6]

How exactly does the expert present a social framework analysis? In this instance, Borgida drew on his knowledge of social psychology and the established, peer-reviewed scientific research literature on gender stereotyping and gender prejudice, including his own contributions to this body of social scientific knowledge, to review the set of case documents provided by plaintiffs' or defense counsel. Specific examples were then drawn from the case materials to illustrate and highlight the pertinent scientific conclusions drawn from the social scientific research literature. De facto, this was the approach taken in the American Psychological Association's (APA's) amicus curiae brief submitted to the U.S. Supreme Court in *Price Waterhouse v. Hopkins*.[7]

This use of a social framework to present social science evidence has generally served to educate fact finders about the conditions under which gender stereotypes and gender prejudice are likely to influence impressions, evaluations, and behavior in social and organizational settings.

In fact, a considerable body of theory and research in psychology and other social sciences on the nature and consequences of gender stereotyping has accumulated over the past several decades, and was recently reviewed by Hunt, Borgida, Kelly, and Burgess.[8] Several areas of general scientific consensus emerged from this analysis.

First, there seems to be general agreement about the content of gender stereotypes (e.g., communal attributes, agentic attributes) as well as the existence of various subcategories of women (e.g., "career women," "feminists," or "housewives"). Second, gender stereotypes have small to modest but consistent effects on judgments of women and men (including in the context of employment decisions), particularly when men and women behave in stereotype-inconsistent ways. For example, when women are confrontational and assertive, and not passive, submissive, and relational, stereotypes are activated and the women are more likely to be seen as "gender nonconformists" by men and even by other women.[9] Third, gender stereotypes are more likely to be used in certain circumstances, such as when gender is salient (e.g., few women in a particular workforce or organization) and when decision makers are not motivated to make accurate judgments. Finally, Hunt et al. concluded that there also was general agreement about certain psychological processes associated with gender stereotyping: that people automatically categorize others according to their memberships in social groups; that gender is a fundamental dimension of categorization; that categorization can lead to stereotype activation, of which individuals may be unaware; and that certain individual differences can influence the use of gender stereotypes. It is also the case that the strength of learned associations and different goals (e.g., knowledge or self-enhancement goals) can influence the activation and application of stereotypes when judging individuals.

Expert report

In Borgida's expert report submitted in *Beck*, several areas of the research literature on gender stereotypes,[10] in conjunction with the various conditions previously reviewed in Fiske et al.[11] and others, provided the basis for examining the plaintiffs' claims about adverse employment decisions at Boeing's Puget Sound facilities. In particular, the content of gender stereotypes, the consequences of not meeting prescriptive expectations, and the problematic role of unchecked subjectivity in making pay and promotion decisions were chosen as themes that could be illustrated with selected case material from *Beck*. However, as discussed in the next section, Borgida's approach and the conclusions that he drew from the research literature were challenged by defense counsel in the deposition.

The deposition

During a deposition, a witness gives testimony that is written down and/or videotaped by a duly qualified officer of the court and sworn to by the deposition. In this case, the defense counsel used the deposition context to challenge the scientific status of Borgida's report in two ways. First, counsel attacked the validity of Borgida's claims, questioning the methodology used to reach his findings and the failure to apply those findings to specific Boeing business practices. Second, counsel also questioned the utility of the general body of gender stereotyping research, arguing that the primarily experimental findings are not generalizable to the "real world" and therefore had no place in this litigation.

At the crux of Boeing's challenges to Borgida's expert report, both about the validity of his claims and the utility of the body of gender stereotyping research, was the belief that Borgida should have addressed specific causation. In other words, defense counsel suggested that unless the science was applied specifically to The Boeing Company, it wasn't science at all. Although the social framework analysis that Borgida provided in his report was geared to general causation, Boeing charged that general causation was not sufficient, and that Borgida's report should have addressed specific employment practices at Boeing.

Consistent with this critique, Boeing's attorney first questioned the overall opinion proffered, indicating his belief that Borgida should have supported his opinion by analyzing actual employment decisions at Boeing. Then he was critical of the non-random process used to select documents that constituted the basis for Borgida's opinions in the case, "If you were attempting to obtain data for . . . peer-reviewed scientific inquiry, would accepting the evidence . . . of the declarants . . . at face value and using that . . . to base scientific conclusions have been consistent with the scientific method?"[12] As he continued, defense counsel implied that Borgida's review of the documents was not comprehensive and that he should have asked for additional (though unspecified) defense documents that would have provided a more balanced view of the case.

Boeing also questioned the scientific standing of Borgida's findings, pointing out that the expert report did not assert a specific and quantifiable confidence level for the claims made in the report. Because Borgida did not conduct any statistical analyses of original data collected at Boeing, the defense questioned how it was even possible to test the falsifiability of Borgida's conclusions.[13] This exchange culminated in the defense attorney commenting, ". . . but there is no attempt, no visible attempt, to me, to test those hypotheses in any sort of scientifically valid, methodologically rigorous way."[14]

During the deposition, the Boeing attorney repeatedly asked whether Borgida had specifically applied his findings to Boeing. For example, when discussing organizational remedies for monitoring and reducing the effects of stereotypes that were described in Borgida's expert report, Boeing asked whether Borgida was aware if these remedies already existed at Boeing. When considering the role of adequate information in employment decisions, for example, defense counsel asked, "Have you done any systematic examination of the record to determine whether, in fact, Boeing managers do not have access to adequate information when they make employment decisions?"[15]

This line of questioning demonstrates and underscores Boeing's view that Borgida should have been able to testify about the specific conditions at Boeing. Whether through collecting original, primary data from Boeing employees or by reviewing Boeing's specific employment practices, Boeing argued that Borgida should have addressed specific causation issues. And as we will see later, this critique was central to the defense motion to exclude Borgida's testimony.

The defense not only attacked the scientific status and foundation for Borgida's claims, but also attacked the utility of the body of gender stereotyping research described in the expert report, basing much of the challenge on the kinds of arguments developed by Copus,[16] who believes that plaintiffs' expert opinions on the role of gender stereotypes "have no reliable scientific basis" and "constitute junk science." For example, defense counsel questioned Borgida about the effect sizes reported in a meta-analysis described in the expert report, pushing Borgida to characterize the effect size as very small, and implying that the effect sizes would be even smaller in real-world business settings.[17]

Boeing also questioned Borgida about the generalizability of research on gender stereotyping. Defense counsel argued that because experimental studies typically employ college students as participants, the findings cannot be generalized to actual conditions at Boeing, especially with respect to those factors that might reduce the prejudicial effects of stereotypical thinking. "Would it be fair to say . . . the subjects of the experiment have less incentive for being correct, less time, and less diagnostic individuating information than would a manager in a typical employment environment?"[18] In other words, according to Boeing, college students are not motivated to be accurate the way Boeing managers are motivated because Boeing managers know that their judgments have real consequences. In addition, college students do not have adequate, individuating information about the female employee about whom they are making a fictitious decision. As noted before, the issues described here also highlight defense counsel's belief that Borgida's research should have been directly applicable to the employment practices at Boeing.

In summary, the Boeing attorneys challenged the scientific status of the proffered testimony, arguing that the scientific method, which is at the heart of peer-reviewed research, did not characterize Borgida's expert report. They argued that the sampling of documents was not comprehensive and was biased against the defendants; the studies in the research literature were limited in terms of effect size and how generalizable the studies were to "real-world" work settings; and that hypotheses were not tested using original data collected at Boeing facilities. The latter claim was made several times during the deposition.

However, Borgida was not asked to conduct contract research on behalf of the plaintiffs. As he repeated throughout the deposition, he was not asked to do contract research evaluating Boeing's hiring, promotion, and pay decisions. Rather, he was asked to provide a social framework analysis wherein he established the conditions under which gender stereotyping was more likely than not to occur in a workplace setting. Conclusions based on the research literature, in this approach, can be illustrated by drawing on documents and specific case facts. These conclusions also can be construed as hypotheses that can be evaluated by available archival data. For example, Borgida did review an internal study conducted by human resources staff at Boeing. This study showed that when decisions by Boeing managers were monitored, overtime assignments to men and women in fact were fairly distributed and not subject to gender bias compared

to those who were not monitored. The hypothesis, based on the research literature, suggested that managerial monitoring should attenuate, if not eliminate,
gender bias in overtime assignments, and this is precisely what the Boeing study
demonstrated, much to the chagrin of the Boeing defense lawyers.

The defense motion to exclude the expert report and testimony

Given Boeing's challenges to the credibility of the psychological science during
the deposition, it came as no surprise when in April 2004 Boeing filed for the
exclusion of Borgida's expert report on the grounds that it did not satisfy the
requirements outlined in *Daubert v. Merrell Dow Pharmaceuticals, Inc.*[19] Boeing
argued that Borgida's theory could not be, and had not been, tested; that it was
not subject to the peer review process and publication; that there was no known
or potential rate of error; and finally, that his theory had not gained widespread
acceptance within the scientific community. Boeing also charged that the
methodology employed by Borgida did not reflect the scientific rigor characteristic of peer-reviewed research in the field.[20]

In its motion, Boeing also argued that Borgida's report should not be admissible because it was not relevant to the case at hand. Boeing argued that there
was no empirical link between the research on gender stereotypes and Borgida's
opinion that stereotypes specifically, and in a quantifiable way, influenced
decision makers at Boeing. Again, Boeing's belief that Borgida should have
conducted contract research at Boeing was reiterated. In the motion, Boeing
charged that Borgida had not analyzed the extent to which the situation at
Boeing precisely resembled the conditions described in the literature on gender
stereotyping and prejudice: Borgida admitted that, although "it is possible to
generate hypotheses based on the [social science] literature and then examine
the extent to which those hypotheses are supported by the archival [i.e., case
related] data . . . I didn't do a quantitative study of that."[21].

Furthermore, Boeing charged that the research outlined in Borgida's report
illustrates that stereotypes likely have a small impact at Boeing.[22] In this regard,
Boeing raised the argument that the effect sizes typically reported in gender
stereotyping research are small, and that they are smaller still (as opposed to
potentially larger) when one accounts for all of the moderators associated with
the influence of stereotypes; moderators that the defense claimed are present
in "real-world" employment practices at Boeing.

Lastly, in its motion to exclude Borgida's report and testimony from trial,
Boeing argued that establishing general causation would not assist the fact
finder.[23] Because the content of Borgida's report and testimony did not address
specific causation, the report had little added value for fact finders.

In their reply to the defense motion,[24] plaintiffs rebutted the notion that
Borgida needed to address specific causation. In pattern and practice discrimination cases, they argued, evidence of an employer's general discriminatory
attitude is relevant and admissible to prove discrimination; in other words, the

test is general, not specific, causation.[25] In a pattern and practice case, as defined by the context of Title VII of the 1964 Civil Rights Act, plaintiffs have the burden of showing that unlawful employment practices were the defendant's regular policy or procedure, rather than an unusual practice.

Also, the plaintiffs argued that Borgida's testimony would be helpful in aiding the fact finder in several ways. For example, Borgida's testimony would establish that most people harbor gender stereotypes, whether they are consciously held or not, and that the research literature establishes that these stereotypes often influence the decisions people make even if they are unaware of it. Furthermore, Borgida's testimony would aid the jurors in understanding the actual practices at Boeing because Borgida would describe the effect of working in a male-dominated industry (as was the case with Boeing), and the effect of not having specific, accurate information about female employees, as was often the case at Boeing.[26]

With respect to rebutting Boeing's attack on the scientific validity of Borgida's findings, the plaintiffs clarified the "relevance" standards set by the Federal Rules of Evidence. According to the Federal Rules of Evidence, plaintiffs argued, evidence is relevant if it makes "the determination of the action more probable or less probable than it would be without the evidence." Thus, Borgida did not have to testify about the specific conditions at Boeing in order to qualify under the Federal Rules of Evidence.[27]

Plaintiffs also outlined other cases in which a social framework analysis, the type of analysis that Borgida offered, had been used (explicitly or implicitly) by the courts.[28] As examples, they cited *Robinson v. Jacksonville Shipyards, Inc.*[29] and *Butler v. Home Depot* (1997)[30], both of which were sex discrimination cases that relied upon social framework analyses. With respect to Boeing's claim that Borgida should have conducted an empirical study about the conditions at Boeing, plaintiffs reiterated the argument that such evidence is not necessary in a pattern and practice case, and highlighted the finding in *Butler* that declared this an issue of weight, rather than admissibility.

Finally, the defense argued that Borgida's testimony did not exceed common knowledge and experience in educating the fact finders in the case. Plaintiffs argued that Borgida's testimony would be particularly useful to the fact finders in a pattern and practice case, where the nature of the discrimination is so "pervasive and culturally ingrained that their [i.e., gender stereotypes'] role in perpetuating discrimination is not readily recognizable to the jury or judge."[31] In other words, sex discrimination is often so subtle and pervasive that it often goes unnoticed in our society. Both judges and juries could benefit from the kind of expert testimony offered.

Boeing's reply to the plaintiffs' rebuttal was to reiterate its claim that Borgida's testimony did not address specific conditions at Boeing, and to argue that a social framework analysis has never been used in court. To this end, Boeing argued that the term "social framework analysis" had been mentioned once in a court decision, and that was in *Ray v. Miller Meester Advertising, Inc.*,[32] where the admission of such testimony was overturned on appeal.[33]

On May 14, 2004, just before the case settled out of court, Judge Marsha Pechman denied the defense motion to exclude Borgida's report and testimony. In her order, Judge Pechman denied the defendant's motions on all counts, including the attacks on the scientific validity of the expert report. She outlined the ways in which Borgida qualified to testify as an expert according to the Federal Rules of Evidence and *Daubert*, and ruled that the method by which Borgida reached his conclusions was valid, accepted by the field, and accepted by previous courts in similar cases. Furthermore, she ruled that Boeing's contention that Borgida did not relate enough of the evidence back to the practices at Boeing was indeed a matter of weight, and therefore could be subject to cross-examination.[34]

Lessons

In this chapter, we discussed the expert report and deposition in *Beck* as a case study of the key challenges that confront expert psychological testimony in class action sex discrimination cases. Typically in such cases, there are statistical disparities of at least two standard deviations (often more) across several job-related dimensions (e.g., pay and promotion gaps between men and women). The question in the face of such disparities is: What accounts for these discrepancies between men and women in a given organization? As was the case in *Beck*, different experts were retained to offer different "accounts" for these disparities. Expert psychological testimony in the form of a social framework analysis of gender stereotyping and prejudice research constitutes one such account. The extant research literature provides the foundation on which areas of scientific consensus can be identified, and these conclusions in turn provide the basis for generating hypotheses about the nature of the disparities at issue that the expert can address in the expert report, and then defend in deposition and at trial.

But what is quite clear from the case study offered in this chapter is that this approach is embedded within an adversarial context which virtually ensures that the proffered expertise will be rigorously challenged. The kinds of challenges that are common to litigation in this arena are important to reflect upon. Is the scientific database involved, for example, sufficiently coherent that one can generate testable hypotheses? If so, then how do the findings from the aggregate-level, scientific database apply to the specifics of the case? If they do not, then should new, on-site data be collected to test hypotheses about the gender disparities at the heart of the litigation? On the other hand, do findings from the scientific database provide an account for these disparities that has the potential to educate fact finders in the case?

In *Beck* as well as in some other class action sex discrimination cases, it was determined that there is a body of social scientific knowledge that can be used to generate a scientifically-grounded account of the demonstrable statistical disparities between men and women. In addition, it is important to underscore the extent to which the scientific challenges to the expert testimony in *Beck* are common in the employment discrimination arena, and by no means idiosyncratic to this particular case.[35] Bielby, for example, discusses several of these very same challenges to expert testimony in class action sex discrimination cases.[36] Specifically, the external validity of experimental investigations to "real-world" organizational dynamics can be challenged as an "untested theory" about workplace disparities between men and women. Similarly, an "account" and expert opinions that rest on the pertinent research literature (even with illustrative examples from deposition material and case exhibits) is not considered as scientifically valid an account as an account that is based on contract research conducted to test hypotheses in the specific organizational context. Finally, it is typical to challenge expert testimony on the grounds that the plaintiffs' expert is basing his or her account on a selective and biased interpretation of the database, an interpretation that, for example, overstates the significance of the effect sizes found in the research literature.

From our perspective, it is incumbent on attorneys and the experts they retain in class action sex discrimination cases to be aware of these common challenges to expert psychological testimony. As (if not more) important, it is crucial for social scientists retained in such cases to anticipate these challenges and issues at the outset of their involvement in litigation. The contours of an expert report, the dynamics of a deposition, and ultimately trial testimony will be influenced by the ways in which the expert decides to address these scientific challenges. Moreover, the obvious also needs to be kept in mind. However the expert psychologist decides to take on these challenges, the approach must be consistent with APA's Ethical Principles of Psychologists and Code of Conduct.[37] Psychologists serving as experts should always "seek to promote accuracy, honesty, and truthfulness in science, teaching, and the practice of psychology" and they should base their analyses "upon established scientific and professional knowledge of the discipline."[38] As Brodsky[39] suggests, an expert is obligated to the ethical standards of the field when it comes to representing science in legal (and non-legal) contexts. To do otherwise would unacceptably compromise the integrity and applicability of the scientific knowledge and findings that are intended to educate fact finders and contribute to the overall quality of justice that is dispensed.

Notes

1   Beck v. Boeing Co., 203 F.R.D. 459 (W.D. Wash. 2001).
2   See: Fiske, S., & Borgida, E. (1999). Social framework analysis as expert testimony in sexual harassment suits. In S. Estreicher (Ed.), *Sexual harassment in the workplace* (pp. 575–583). Boston: Kluwer Law International. See also: Hunt, J. S., Borgida, E., Kelly, K. M., & Burgess, D. (2002). Gender stereotyping: Scientific status. In D. L. Faigman, D. J. Kaye, M. J.

Saks, & J. Sanders (Eds.), *Modern scientific evidence: The law and science of expert testimony* (pp. 374–426). St. Paul, MN: West Publishing Co.

3 Faigman, D. L., & Monahan, J. (2005). Psychological evidence at the dawn of the law's scientific age. *Annual Review of Psychology, 56*, 631–660.

4 Bielby, W. T. (2003). Can I get a witness? Challenges of using expert testimony on cognitive bias in employment discrimination. *Employee Rights and Employment Policy Journal, 7*, 377–397. Fiske & Borgida (1999). Gutek, B. A., & Stockdale, M. S. (2005). Sex discrimination in employment. In F. J. Landy (Ed.), *Employment discrimination litigation: Behavioral, quantitative, and legal perspectives* (pp. 229–255). San Francisco: Jossey-Bass. Krieger, L. H. (2004). The intuitive psychologist behind the bench: Models of gender bias in social psychology and employment discrimination law. *Journal of Social Issues, 60*, 835–848. Outtz, J. L., & Landy, F. J. (2005). Concluding thoughts. In F. J. Landy (Ed.), *Employment discrimination litigation: Behavioral, quantitative, and legal perspectives* (pp. 575–590). San Francisco: Jossey-Bass.

5 Faigman, D. L., Kaye, D. H., Saks, M. J., & Sanders, J. (2002). *Modern scientific evidence: The law and science of expert testimony*. St. Paul, MN: West Publishing Co.

6 Faigman & Monahan (2005). Faigman et al. (2002).

7 Price Waterhouse v. Hopkins, 109 S.Ct. 1775 (1989). Fiske, S. T., Bersoff, D. N., Borgida, E., Deaux, K., & Heilman, M. E. (1991). Social science research on trial: Use of sex stereotyping research in Price Waterhouse v. Hopkins. *American Psychologist, 46*, 1049–1060.

8 Hunt et al. (2002). See also: Borgida, E., Hunt, C., & Kim, A. (2005). On the use of gender stereotyping research in sex discrimination litigation. *Journal of Law and Policy, 13*(2), 613–628.

9 Hyde, J. S. (2005). The gender similarities hypothesis. *American Psychologist, 60*(6), 581–592. Heilman, M. E. (2001). Description and prescription: How gender stereotypes prevent women's ascent up the organizational ladder. *Journal of Social Issues, 57*(4), 657–674. Rudman, L .A. (2005). Rejection of women? Beyond prejudice as antipathy. In J. F. Dovidio, P. Glick, & L. A. Rudman (Eds.), *On the nature of prejudice: Fifty years after Allport* (pp. 107–120). Malden, MA: Blackwell.

10 Hunt et al. (2002).

11 Fiske et al. (1991).

12 Videotaped deposition of Eugene Borgida, PhD, at 23, Beck v. Boeing Co., No. C00-301P (W.D. Wash. Dec. 11, 2003).

13 Borgida deposition, p. 57.

14 Borgida deposition, p. 59.

15 Borgida deposition, p. 176.

16 Copus, D. (2005). A lawyer's view: Avoiding junk science. In F. J. Landy (Ed.), *Employment discrimination litigation: Behavioral, quantitative, and legal perspectives* (pp. 450–462). San Francisco: Jossey-Bass.

17   Borgida deposition, pp. 150 and 200.

18   Borgida deposition, p. 201.

19   Daubert v. Merrell Dow Pharmaceuticals, Inc., 113 S. Ct. 2786 (1993).

20   Defendant's motion *in limine* to exclude expert report, opinions, and testimony of plaintiffs' expert Eugene Borgida, Ph.D., Beck v. Boeing Co., No. C00-301P (W.D. Wash. Apr. 12, 2004).

21   Defendant's motion *in limine*, part IIB2a, p. 7 (emphasis added by defense).

22   Defendant's motion *in limine*, part IIB2b, p. 8.

23   Defendant's motion *in limine* part IIC, p. 11.

24   Plaintiffs' opposition to Boeing's motion *in limine* to exclude expert report, opinions, and testimony of plaintiffs' expert Eugene Borgida, Ph.D., Beck v. Boeing Co., No. C00-301P (W.D. Wash. Apr. 26, 2004).

25   See Faigman & Monahan (2005).

26   Plaintiff's opposition to Boeing's motion *in limine*, Part II, pp. 2–3.

27   Plaintiff's opposition to Boeing's motion *in limine*, Part IIIA, p. 5.

28   Plaintiff's opposition to Boeing's motion *in limine*, Part IIIB, p. 6.

29   Robinson v. Jacksonville Shipyards, Inc., 760 F. Supp. 148 (1991).

30   Butler v. Home Depot, 984 F. Supp. 1257 (N.D. Cal. 1997).

31   Plaintiff's opposition to Boeing's motion *in limine*, Part IIIC, p. 9.

32   Ray v. Miller Meester Advertising, Inc. 664 N.W.2d 355 (Minn. 2003). In the Ray v. Miller Meester decision, which Borgida was handed just moments before he gave his 2003 NELA presentation, social framework analysis was rejected because the Minnesota appellate court ruled it did not exceed common knowledge for fact-finders who, according to this opinion, are adequately informed about gender relations and gender stereotyping via television sitcoms and other media coverage. While the Minnesota appellate court was not persuaded by the "added value" of social science, Judge Pechman's opinion in Beck v. Boeing Co. found that the social framework analysis provided by Borgida provided added value in Beck v. Boeing Co. because the jury would have to decide if the *class* of plaintiffs suffered from a pattern of discrimination at Boeing. Thus, an expert who could explain what stereotyping is and the conditions under which it is more likely than not to occur would assist the jury in this task.

33   Boeing's reply on motion to strike expert report, opinion, and testimony of plaintiffs' expert Eugene Borgida, Ph.D., part IIB, p. 3., Beck v. Boeing Co., No. C00-301P (W.D. Wash. Apr. 29, 2004).

34   Order denying defendant's motion to exclude expert report, opinions, and testimony of plaintiffs' expert Eugene Borgida, Ph.D., Beck v. Boeing Co., No. C00-301P (W.D. Wash. May 14, 2004).

35   Gutek, B. A., & Stockdale, M. S. (2005). Sex discrimination in employment. In F. J. Landy (Ed.), *Employment discrimination litigation: Behavioral, quantitative, and legal perspectives* (pp. 229–255). San Francisco: Jossey-Bass.

36   Bielby (2003).

37   American Psychological Association (2002). Ethical principles of psychologists and code of conduct. In D. N. Bersoff (Ed.), *Ethical conflicts in psychology* (pp 28–45). Washington, DC: American Psychological Association.

38   Bersoff, D. N. (Ed.). (2003). *Ethical conflicts in psychology* (3rd ed). Washington, DC: American Psychological Association.

39   Brodsky, S. L. (1999). *The expert witness: More maxims and guidelines for testifying in court.* Washington, DC: American Psychological Association.

10

My Experience as an Expert Witness in Sex Discrimination and Sexual Harassment Litigation

Barbara A. Gutek

I have served as an expert witness for over 25 years. In that time, I have had a variety of experiences. My hope is that others may learn from them.

Early Days

Getting started

My first experience as an expert witness was in the late 1970s and it was not about discrimination or sexual harassment. The attorney who called was looking for an expert in survey research methods. I had never heard the term "expert witness" and had no idea what one did, but since I taught a course on that topic and conducted surveys regularly in my research, he and I thought I qualified. The idea of talking about research in court was intriguing. I had a small amount of material to read and all of my time that was needed was an afternoon in court in San Francisco. At that time I was on the faculty of the Claremont Graduate School and lived in Los Angeles.

The trial was in front of a judge and consisted primarily of the testimony of two experts, one for each side. One company claimed that another company was mailing misleading information to potential customers making it appear as if the suing company was endorsing the other company's product. As part of the lawsuit the plaintiffs hired a well-known survey research firm to do a survey to see if the people thought the suing firm endorsed the sales pitch in the letter. The two companies had come to some agreement in the past and then the

defendant company changed its standard solicitation letter to potential customers. That change was the impetus for the survey and the lawsuit.

Hired by the defense, I was asked by the attorney to sit with him during the
trial so he could ask me about matters as the other expert testified. As the day
went along, the judge announced that he had an appointment and was adjourn-
ing until the next day. I was stunned because I had assumed I would be back
home in the evening. I didn't bring any clothes or other items that I would have
liked had I known I would be testifying over two days. Also, I was expected to
teach the following morning. I reluctantly called to cancel my class.

The next day, I testified on behalf of the defendant that the survey itself was
irrelevant. What was needed was an experimental manipulation to see if the new
format was significantly more misleading than the old format that had been
approved for use. At the end of my testimony, the judge decided in favor of the
company that retained me. The attorney was elated with my testimony and
described to his client in graphic terms (that embarrassed me tremendously at
the time) how I had emasculated the competition. That was my first experience
with an openly adversarial system where facts are used in the service of winning.

All of my subsequent testimony has had to do with sexual harassment and
sex discrimination. I have been asked to testify in age discrimination and race
discrimination cases, but I have always declined given that I have not done
research directly in either of those areas and do not consider myself an expert
in either area.

The second time I was asked to testify, also in San Francisco, was in the mid-
1980s. The case involved treatment of female employees at an airline company.
A number of female flight attendants had appeared in a *Playboy Magazine*
article. None was in uniform, of course, but the airline for which each one
worked was identified. The defendant airline fired the flight attendants, saying
that they had behaved unprofessionally. They argued that their image was sufficiently different – more formal and professional – from other airlines (this was
the era of hot pants for flight attendants) and that they were justified in holding
their employees to a high standard of behavior. I was quite sure that if a random
sample of airline passengers was asked about the image of that airline, few would
differentiate them from other airlines in such a way to justify terminating the
flight attendants when no other airline did so. I do not recall much about the
case, except that I believe it was settled before I had an opportunity to give my
testimony.

I received a lot of kidding about that case because *Playboy Magazine* provided at least some of the funds to support the flight attendants in their lawsuit
against their company. The check I received for my work on the case came from
Playboy, the only check I have ever received from that organization!

In the early 1990s, I started receiving a lot of calls from attorneys for sex discrimination and sexual harassment lawsuits. It seems that it took about ten years
after the EEOC guidelines were passed in 1980 for litigating attorneys to discover the possibility of hiring expert witnesses whose base of expertise was
research on sexual harassment. Perhaps more important than the Guidelines –

which after all are only guidelines and not laws – was the 1993 U.S. Supreme Court acknowledgment that sexual harassment was illegal. That ruling most likely provided attorneys representing victims of sexual harassment with some guidance about what was necessary to prevail in court.[1] A number of plaintiffs' attorneys were aware of at least some of the research that was being done at the time and they felt that the research contradicted some "common sense" notions about who was likely to be harassed and why.

Not surprisingly, most of the calls I received in the 1990s came from plaintiffs' attorneys and most of the plaintiffs' attorneys were employment lawyers interested in feminist employment issues. I received a few calls from attorneys representing defendants, but in most cases once I heard their short version of the facts, I said that my opinions would likely not support their client. That changed gradually as employers became more knowledgeable about sexual harassment. But early on, I was amazed at the behavior employers were willing to defend.

More cases

In the 1990s, many of the attorneys who called me wanted an expert to explain to a jury that someone could be sexually harassed but not file a formal complaint or otherwise notify management about it. Since the late 1970s, I had been doing research on sexual harassment and by 1980 I had done a large-scale study of sexual harassment using random sampling procedures. I was thus able to apply these research findings to sexual harassment proceedings. Our study showed that most people do not complain about behavior that they would define as sexual harassment and they give sensible reasons for not wanting to do so.[2] Of course, other studies subsequently also found that people often do not complain about social-sexual behavior.

In those early years, one case in particular stands out in my mind. The plaintiff worked for a janitorial service in Dallas. She alleged that her supervisor had insisted she come to his house where he subsequently forced her to have sex with him. Some time after the first incident, she said he did the same thing – insisted that she come to his house. She said that she brought a friend who was told by the supervisor to leave the house. The friend said that she subsequently saw the supervisor through the living room window as he pulled the woman by the hair away from the living room. Those were not the only alleged incidents; there was much more of the same kind of behavior. Ultimately, the plaintiff complained to her supervisor's supervisor who promptly fired her for making a false complaint. The harassing supervisor had apparently talked to his supervisor, disparaging the plaintiff and telling his boss that she might make a false allegation against him.

The attorney who called me was looking not only for an expert, but someone who might explain to him why or how someone would put up with such blatantly unethical and illegal behavior. It seemed to me that the attorney was not sure he believed his client, or that perhaps she was exaggerating what actually happened. She was apparently quite overweight and not particularly attractive. Furthermore, he could not imagine someone tolerating that behavior for so long without complaining. Neither could the defense counsel. At first, I had a hard time believing it, too, even though I knew from research that targets of harassment are reluctant to complain. This was a classic, if extreme, case of how people often respond to sexual harassment. The behavior escalated; it didn't start with rape. In addition, the harasser was her supervisor, so she could not complain to him. Furthermore, her supervisor was very friendly with his own boss. I recall that they saw each other socially and went to activities together. Ultimately, it was learned that the plaintiff's former husband, a police officer, was physically abusive to her as was one of her two sons. The plaintiff was uneducated, unskilled, separated from her abusive husband. She left her home in Florida to work for a large janitorial service that cleaned office buildings in downtown Dallas. It was as good a job as she was likely to find. She received regular wages and benefits like health insurance for which she was willing to endure a lot.

By the time my deposition was taken, some additional evidence for her assertions had come to light. First, there were cameras around the building and one of them caught the alleged harasser following the plaintiff into the women's bathroom where he pinned her against the wall. He also followed her into another area of the building where he was not supposed to be working. Second, she was fired the Monday after she had complained. There was a short written note by the manager who, when he received the complaint, dismissed it as an attempt by the plaintiff to disparage her supervisor – based entirely on what the supervisor told his manager. I remember sitting in a hotel room checking dates. In order to find out the days of the week she complained and then was fired, I set the date function on my laptop computer back to the year and date of her termination. Sure enough, she filed the complaint on a Friday according to the documentation and her termination date was the following Monday.

This case settled shortly after my deposition. I felt very bad about the terrible treatment the plaintiff had received from so many people who should have been positive forces in her life. She was psychologically damaged by all of it, but I was glad that at least she was not accused of being a liar and she received some compensation for the misery through which she was put. And two attorneys knew a lot more about sexual harassment than they had before this case started. I was pleased that social science knowledge could make a real difference.

I later encountered another instance of terrible mistreatment at work. In that case, a supervisor who was severely harassing his young female subordinate also reminded her that he was a karate expert. He allegedly told her that he could easily break her neck, for example. The young woman being harassed by the supervisor eventually told another female employee who said she was also being harassed by the same man. The two of them went to an older female employee and talked to her about it. That older employee then reported it to someone "in charge." After that, both young women were coerced into signing written statements listing their allegations and the man was terminated from the company. The alleged harasser then sued the company alleging that the two women made up stories about him that got him fired.

The company would not defend the young woman who had complained, and so she sued the alleged harasser who was suing her. The alleged harasser's case came to court first. As part of it, he asked the jury to determine if the young woman was lying. In fact, the jury decided exactly that and awarded the man a large sum of money. After being harassed, then being forced to file a complaint that she did not want to file – she needed her job and was afraid of her supervisor – she was sued. Her company did not support her and someone who was apparently incompetent or negligent represented her. In fact, the person who called me was yet another attorney who had sued her original attorney. Unfortunately, in this case, the young woman wanted some guarantee that she would not be put through more stress and misery in a second trial. When her attorney could not promise her that, she withdrew her complaint against her first attorney.

If I felt good about the previous case, I felt really bad about this one. Not only in all probability did her supervisor at work harass her, but her employer also abused her and so did the legal system in form of the attorney she and her father had hired to represent her. She spent money she could ill afford to spend on an effort that resulted in more pain and suffering to her.

One other case from the early years stands out. I always thought a certain plaintiff did not really want to file a sexual harassment complaint, but was pushed into doing so by her husband who saw it as a way to make money from a bad situation. The attorney who called me had never worked on a sexual harassment case and that ultimately hurt him and his small law firm as well as the plaintiff. The plaintiff and her husband both worked for a manufacturing company. She was ultimately terminated for poor performance. The defense attorney's strategy seemed to be to disparage the plaintiff and he succeeded. The plaintiff and her husband had been bodybuilders and on their lockers at work, both had posted pictures of themselves in bodybuilding outfits. In addition, when the plaintiff retired from bodybuilding, she had what she called breast reconstructive surgery to make her breasts more traditionally feminine in appearance. The defense attorney claimed she had breast enlargement surgery for the purpose of attracting the attention of men at work. It was also alleged that she had an affair with a co-worker. When I testified in court, I was asked if I was a feminist and the defense attorney tried to imply that I was a lesbian who hated men – all attempts to discredit me along with the plaintiff.[3]

Although it had looked as if the case was a slam-dunk for the plaintiff because some of the alleged offensive behavior, like blatantly offensive posters, were easily verified, she did not win. My understanding was that the jury thought that, given her own behavior, the plaintiff would not have been offended at the behavior she described. Her attorney later said that he did not anticipate the defense's tactics. Some months later, the plaintiff's husband called me to say that she was going to be on a TV talk-show – I forget which one – and he wondered if I would also be on that show. I declined.[4]

Class Actions

At some point, I was asked to serve as an expert in some class action cases. I found these cases interesting for several reasons. For one, dragging an individual plaintiff's reputation through the mud was not an option. It is hard to argue that a company has somehow inadvertently hired hundreds of morally loose women who are sexual predators. Second, it is an interesting challenge to put together enough information to conclude that a whole class of employees has been sexually harassed both because of the sheer number of people in the class and, frequently, the long period of time for which a class action lawsuit applies, up to decade or more. Third, I thought the potential for impact was greater for class actions than for individual lawsuits, that the decisions from class actions were more likely to be known by HR managers and in-house legal staffs.

The most interesting case for me among the class actions was one in which the EEOC was suing the Dial Corporation.[5] I was hired by the defense. I was on sabbatical at the time and therefore had the time the case required. The case was complicated and involved and the defense attorneys made it clear from the start that there had been inappropriate behavior, at least in the past. The lawsuit covered 11 years and focused on one production plant in Illinois. Attorneys at Seyfarth Shaw in Chicago who represented Dial told me that a survey instrument was administered to current and former employees of Dial and that the plaintiff's expert had relied on survey results to form conclusions about sexual harassment. I was asked to evaluate and re-analyze the survey and the conclusions drawn by the plaintiff's expert.[6] The company had data sets and copies of all of the completed surveys, copies of which they sent to me. The survey was 27 pages in length and the respondents who were – or had been – production workers at Dial were told on the cover sheet that the survey would take about 30 minutes to complete, which, even if they only answered half the questions, would mean allocating about 11 seconds to each question.

The survey contained a version of the Sexual Experiences Questionnaire (SEQ), which was used to provide information about the amount of sexual harassment at the Dial plant. A graduate student and I had just completed a book chapter on sexual harassment, including how it is measured.[7] At that time, I discovered there were multiple SEQs but was frustrated by the fact that I could not find a publication that contained any version of it or find any consistent information on how many people reported various SEQ behaviors. Most importantly, I could find nothing in the published data that would allow one to conclude that there was "a lot of" or "a little" sexual harassment in the organization, which is typically of great interest to both plaintiff and defendant, and a prime reason, if not *the* reason, for doing a survey of the relevant population. Indeed, the plaintiff's expert used the survey to conclude that a "high level of hostile and degrading sexualized behavior" was directed toward women. In addition, based on the publications using the SEQ, it was not clear what definition of sexual harassment the SEQ intends to measure. For these and many

other reasons, my report was critical of the use of the SEQ to draw any conclusions about the amount of sexual harassment at the relevant Dial plant, and
in the end, the court agreed.[8] Later Bambi Douma, Ryan Murphy, and I
published a critique of the SEQ.[9]

Although in principle it might be feasible to conduct a survey in a company
while a lawsuit is ongoing, there are many factors that can affect the survey's
results and such surveys should, I believe, be given close scrutiny, regardless of
which side chooses to conduct one. For example, it is so easy to manipulate
question wording to lead respondents in the direction desired.[10] Furthermore,
because a survey conducted for a particular legal case is not subject to peer
review, it is more vulnerable to challenge by the opposing party.[11]

I can also appreciate the difficulty of organizing the massive amounts of evidence generated in class action suits. In that respect, resorting to a survey can
be appealing.[12] If a survey can summarize the experiences of relevant parties,
then it would seem to be more straightforward, potentially cheaper, and easier
than the alternatives. But given the long time frame of this case and many other
class actions, it is important to find out when relevant behaviors occurred; surely
it makes a difference if all objectionable behavior occurred more than five years
ago or if the amount of potentially harassing behavior increased over time.
Despite its length, the Dial survey had no questions about when any assessed
behavior occurred.

Recently a reporter asked me how I could criticize an instrument purportedly measuring sexual harassment given that I was interested in eradicating
sexual harassment from the workplace. Needless to say, I am interested in seeing
justice done and that means using reliable instruments that measure the relevant construct, and in charges of sexual harassment, that construct is illegal
sexual harassment. I want our research to be able to stand up in court. In that
regard, it is gratifying to have a law professor use the social science research on
sexual harassment to argue for changes in the law to make it more compatible
with people's behavior.[13]

Objectives and Practices

The passage of The Civil Rights Act of 1991 authorized compensatory and
punitive damages for discriminatory treatment, greatly increasing the opportunities for employees to file discrimination charges against their employers and
greatly increasing the attractiveness of discrimination cases to plaintiffs' attorneys. The number of cases increased dramatically after that. Occasional newspaper and TV stories about large awards to sexual harassment plaintiffs might
have also encouraged more potential plaintiffs to seek the services of an attorney. Training programs and publicity in the media made more employees aware
of potentially actionable behavior. And the confrontation between Anita Hill
and Clarence Thomas at his U.S. Supreme Court confirmation hearings, which
attracted countless viewers, sensitized the general public to the phenomenon of

sexual harassment. All of this means more opportunities than before for social scientists to demonstrate the usefulness of their research, but it also provides a new forum from which research is scrutinized, ultimately, I hope, leading to better research.

Principles

Over the years, I have developed some general practices and principles. All of the work I have done came from people who knew directly of my research or talked to others who did. Word of mouth was and is the way I have become an expert witness. On several occasions, the person who was on the other side ultimately called me or referred me to other attorneys. I tried to work for both plaintiffs and defendants once I realized that when one works for only one side, the other side quickly tries to disparage the expert as biased; why else would they work on only one side? The fact is, of course, that one's area of expertise may be more relevant to one side than the other.

In the 1980s, it was rare that I heard from a defense attorney and if I did, it was even rarer that I thought my research would be useful to them. I also recall one case in which attorneys on both sides called me. The second attorney made the pitch that it would be more interesting for me to be on the side he represented. I wasn't sure what the correct thing to do was under the circumstances, so I turned him down and the case settled before I learned about many of the facts or allegations.

As employers became more sophisticated about sexual harassment and put forth more effort to deal with it, I began doing work for the defense. The *Dial* case discussed above is an example. In several cases, I had read an expert report critiquing the organization's sexual harassment policy. These critiques were uniformly negative with experts generally concluding that the policy was ineffective because the plaintiff alleged that she or he had been harassed. If the policy was effective, no allegations should be forthcoming. Curiously, I also encountered an expert's report that made the opposite claim: because no one (or almost no one) had complained, the policy was ineffective. The rationale was that if it was effective, more people would have come forward to complain.

Of course, the defense can use the same arguments, too. It seems just as plausible that if no one complains, it is because there is no serious sexual harassment. And if people do complain, that indicates the policy is effective in bringing the matter to management's attention. Then management has to do something about the complaints.

Policies

Asked to write a chapter for a book on sexual harassment, I decided to focus on sexual harassment policies because I found the various expert reports confusing or illogical. Because they did not cite any research, I ultimately did some research on what constitutes an effective sexual harassment policy.[14] I used three policies that were in use in companies and modified them so that we manipulated two features frequently recommended for inclusion in sexual harassment policies – a list of potentially harassing behaviors and a non-retaliation statement – to see whether their presence affects evaluations of policy effectiveness. We found little support for the argument that a sexual harassment policy is perceived to be more effective with either of these features than without them.[15]

In the results, perceived effectiveness of sexual harassment policies consisted of three components: a global assessment of effectiveness including protecting the complaining party, protecting the firm and the individual alleged perpetrator, and educating employees and managers. Although this set of components of perceived effectiveness is a function of the questions we asked, it includes most of the goals I had identified for effective policies.[16] For example, making the company's stance public, deterring potential harassers, and providing guidelines for dealing with sexual harassment formed one factor, which we labeled protection for the complainant. Educating people about sexual harassment formed a second factor. Protecting the company in the event of a lawsuit loaded on the third factor, protection for the accused.[17]

When I started doing expert witness work, I had the idea that research findings would be useful in the courtroom. I later realized that my experience in the courtroom was also useful in my research.

How to Be a Good Expert

My advice: know the facts of the case; know the research; do not get rattled; do not get into an argument with an attorney in deposition or in the courtroom. Also, try to think one step ahead and expect to be attacked. Think of the most critical review you have ever received in response to sending your manuscript to a journal and expect something much worse. The legal system is an adversarial system.

Working with lawyers can be fun or frustrating. Although some are very organized, others are disorganized. Many are overworked, just like professors. Many have piles of work on their desks, reminiscent of the desks of professors. They may have relatively little control over when a trial will actually start. Most commonly, consistent with the legal process that "everything takes longer than initially expected," depositions get postponed, trial dates get postponed and then get postponed again. Expect to be called when you are on vacation or at a conference in Europe. I remember vividly once trying to find the equivalent of a notary in Stockholm and then exploring the best way to get an affidavit back to the U.S. as quickly as possible.

Like expert witnesses, attorneys vary in their ethical behavior. I remember an early case in which a woman who worked in construction charged sexual harassment. After I had agreed to work on the case, I found out that the attorney who hired me knew nothing about the area and only took the case as a way of learning about employment litigation in general, and sexual harassment in particular. I realized he talked his client into hiring me primarily so that he

could learn enough to decide whether he wanted to do more employment litigation. I'm quite sure his client was not well represented. She lost her case.

When I sent the attorney my bill, he merely forwarded it to his client telling
her to send me a check and copied me on it. I knew she could not afford to
pay me, as she was unemployed. What I did not realize at the time was that it
was his responsibility to pay me if his client could not. On other occasions, I
had to send multiple invoices that were either misplaced or just did not get
processed without multiple reminders. Much later, I worked for someone who
kept telling me a check was in the mail, that her partner was bringing a check
to the deposition, and the like. None of it was true and ultimately, I collected
only a small fraction of what I had billed. Although most lawyers and law firms
treat experts with courtesy and respect, it behooves experts to set up a clear
system for payment with all the rules agreed in advance.

Why I do expert witness work

I have always wanted to do work that was fun and interesting to me *and* that
would also be useful in the sense that it might help make people's lives better,
more productive, more fair and just. I was intrigued by the possibility that social
science research could help to bring about just decisions in the courtroom. Over
the years, I learned some about the law, but it is specific to the kinds of cases
in which I've been involved.

A bonus of serving as an expert witness is the interesting information I
learned about how organizations operate, information that is not in textbooks,
but that is useful to me in the classroom as well. For a professor in a business
school, it is helpful to know, for example, how bananas are shipped, stored, and
"ripened" in storage facilities; what flight attendants generally think of passengers, which is not very positive; what it is like to be a police officer on patrol;
what it is like to work in a morgue; why an attorney would sue her law firm for
sexual harassment; what it is like to be a female airplane pilot working almost
exclusively with male pilots. I was surprised to find out that in at least one
company, being an ambulance driver is a very macho occupation, and that in
another company managers of fast food restaurants have written instructions
saying that they are expected to work over 60 hours per week when their
employment forms say a fulltime job is 40 hours per week. Because I teach business students, there were numerous opportunities to bring into the classroom
information I had learned from being an expert witness. In addition, Maureen
O'Connor and I used the case of the bodybuilder who had breast reconstructive surgery in research. We created multiple versions of a videotrial based on
the fact pattern from that case.[18]

Final thought

I always hoped companies would call me to explain to their managers how
sexual harassment happens. Then they could make changes that would decrease
the probability of someone being sexually harassed in their organization. But

that never happened. Companies hire lawyers or law firms to write sexual harassment policies and do sexual harassment training and they specialize, not surprisingly, on how to avoid breaking the law and, if the law may have been broken, how to handle the matter to minimize losing a lawsuit. Only twice have I had the opportunity to educate employers and employees. Once was when a law firm asked me to give a talk as part of their sexual harassment training for managers. The second time was when Peggy Stockdale and I provided training for a company's managers in exchange for allowing us to conduct research with them. I expect I will have to be content with trying to make sure that social science research contributes to just decisions in court.

Notes

1   Harris v. Forklift Systems, Inc., 510 U.S. 17 (1993).
2   I published the descriptive research findings as a research monograph: Gutek, B. A. (1985). *Sex and the workplace: Impact of sexual behavior and harassment on women, men and organizations.* San Francisco: Jossey-Bass. The book has been cited quite widely by law professors and in legal proceedings. The earliest citation I know is the First Circuit Court of Appeals (Lipsett v. University of Puerto Rico, 864 F.2d 881, 889, n.19, 1st Cir, 1988). Had I only published journal articles, I am not sure lawyers and law professors would have noticed my research so quickly.
3   I defined feminist as someone who believes that women are equally deserving of the same rights and privileges as men and said I assumed that the defense attorney was also a feminist by that definition. I also managed to bring my family into my testimony.
4   I had already appeared on TV twice to talk about sexual harassment, on the assumption that I could be a voice of reason and knowledge. The first time, an interview on the Christian Broadcasting Network, I thought that I was a successful voice of reason and knowledge. But I vowed never again after I agreed to be on the Montel Williams show – not knowing who he was – when they were devoting their show to sexual harassment. Several people were there to tell their stories and then I was asked to make some comments – in one minute or less. The stories were highly implausible, the women were portrayed as foolish philanderers or sexual predators and the men were portrayed as victims. I came away convinced that the people on the show were actors playing a role that someone else had designed for them, all in the service of entertaining the audience.
5   Equal Employment Opportunity Commission v. Dial Corporation (Sept. 17, 2002) WL 31061088, N. D. Ill.; Equal Employment Opportunity Commission v. Dial Corporation (Nov. 17, 2002). Northern District, Ill., No. 99 C 3356.
6   I had undertaken a similar re-evaluation project several years earlier when The California Institute of Technology asked me to re-analyze a survey

that a consultant had given to faculty there. I have taught courses in survey research methods off and on since I was a graduate student working at the Institute for Social Research at the University of Michigan.

7   Gutek, B. A., & Done, R. (2001). Sexual harassment. In R. K. Unger (Ed.), *Handbook of the psychology of women and gender* (pp. 367–387). New York: Wiley.

8   EEOC v. Dial (2002).

9   Gutek, B. A., Murphy, R. O. & Douma, B. (2004). A review and critique of the Sexual Experiences Questionnaire (SEQ). *Law and Human Behavior, 28,* 457–482.

10 See, Gutek, B. A., & Stockdale, M. S. (2005). Sex discrimination in employment. In F. J. Landy (Ed.), *Employment discrimination litigation: Behavioral, quantitative, and legal perspectives* (p. 229–255). San Francisco: Jossey-Bass.

11 See also Daubert v. Merrell Dow Pharmaceuticals, Inc., 113 S. Ct. 2786 (1993).

12 I later worked on another case in which the EEOC had conducted their own survey, apparently without any survey research expertise or consultation with survey experts.

13 Beiner, T. M. (2005). *Gender myths v. working realities: Using social science to reformulate sexual harassment law.* New York: New York University Press.

14 Gutek, B. A. (1997). Sexual harassment policy initiatives. In W. O'Donohue (Ed.), *Sexual harassment: Theory, research, treatment* (pp. 185–198). New York: Allyn & Bacon.

15 Gutek, B. A., & Done, R. (2005). What influences evaluations of sexual harassment policy effectiveness? University of Arizona, unpublished manuscript.

16 Gutek (1997).

17 Gutek & Done (2005).

18 O'Connor, M., Gutek, B. A., Stockdale, M., Geer, T. M., & Melançon, R. (2004). Explaining sexual harassment judgments: Looking beyond gender of the rater. *Law and Human Behavior, 28*(1), 9–27; and Gutek, B. A., O'Connor, M., Melançon, R., Stockdale, M., Geer, T. M., & Done, R. S. (1999). The utility of the reasonable woman standard in hostile environment sexual harassment cases: A multimethod, multistudy examination. *Psychology, Public Policy and the Law, 5*(3), 596–629.

11

Sex Discrimination in the Workplace: Lessons from Two High-Profile Cases

Wayne F. Cascio

In an ideal world, expert witnesses accept cases because they are convinced that the cause in question is just, and that they represent the side that is "right." After three decades of serving as a testifying expert in a number of high-profile cases, I can say unequivocally that there is no absolute standard of truth, and that advocates on both sides can identify important issues to contest. I can also say that it is hard to argue convincingly and passionately to a judge or jury about a cause unless you believe in your heart that what you claim is "right."

In this chapter I will describe two cases that I testified in as an expert witness in the field of industrial and organizational psychology, and that I believed in strongly. The first is *Berkman et al. v. City of New York et al.*, argued in 1981 and decided on March 4, 1982.[1] The second is *Beck v. Boeing*, a long-running case that was settled out of court in 2004.

Berkman et al. v. City of New York et al. (1981–1982)

Brenda Berkman wanted to do a "man's job" – to be a firefighter. As of 1977, when she first applied for that job in New York City, there were no female firefighters. After she and a small group of women applied, the Fire Department of New York (FDNY) unveiled a new firefighter entrance examination, one that the New York City Assistant Personnel Director described as the "most arduous test we have ever given to anyone." When 90 out of 400 eligible women took the new physical abilities test, all of them failed (along with 50 percent of the male applicants). Brenda Berkman, a marathon runner and a law student at

New York University, was among them. Rather than walk away quietly, however, Berkman sued New York City and the FDNY in 1979 for gender discrimination. As she noted, "Prior to 1977, New York City had a quota for women firefighters. The quota was zero."[2]

The federal Uniform Guidelines on Employee Selection Procedures, adopted in 1978,[3] specified clearly that adverse impact was the triggering mechanism for enforcement of Title VII of the 1964 Civil Rights Act, which had outlawed sex discrimination in the workplace. Adverse impact was defined operationally as a selection rate for any racial, ethnic, or sex group that was less than four-fifths or 80 percent of the selection rate of the group with the highest rate. Adverse impact occurs when identical standards or procedures are applied to everyone, despite the fact that they lead to a substantial difference in employment outcomes (selection, promotion, layoffs) for members of a particular group *and* when the standards are unrelated to success on the job.[4]

The fact that no women passed the FDNY physical abilities test constituted "the inexorable zero" in adverse impact calculations. Clearly the test produced an adverse impact against women. The remaining question for the court to decide was whether or not the test was job-related and consistent with business necessity. Plaintiffs' testifying experts, exercise physiologist Dr. William McArdle, and myself (an industrial and organizational psychologist), argued that it was not.

There were multiple events in the physical abilities test, all of which were scored on the basis of speed. One such event was the dummy carry, which was designed to simulate the rescue of a victim at an emergency scene. A candidate had to lift a duffel bag that contained two 60-pound bags of cement, and then toss it over his or her shoulder in a "fireman's" carry. Then the candidate had to carry the duffel bag up one flight of stairs, walk around the marked lines of the upper-stair landing, return down the stairs, bend down on one knee, then place the dummy back on the mat under control. A candidate's score was based on time to completion.

At the trial, plaintiffs' attorney Bob King (of law firm Debevoise & Plimpton, which took the case on a *pro bono* basis) brought in a female firefighter from Chicago who had received excellent performance reviews on the job. At one point he asked her to come down from the witness stand and to put him in a fireman's carry. He was about six feet tall, and about 180 pounds. She had no problem doing so, and in fact walked around the courtroom carrying him while he was asking her questions! He then asked her to put both a gentleman and a lady in the courtroom in the same fireman's carry, and again she had no problem completing the task.

Then, in a very dramatic moment in the trial, he asked her to lift the "dummy" with the two 60-pound cement bags inside. She couldn't do it! The lesson was obvious to everyone in the courtroom: even an unconscious person doesn't have all of his or her weight in the heels. A test item should reflect accurately the aspect of the job that it is designed to assess, but unless one uses an articulated dummy whose weight distribution is similar to a human's, it is not possible to develop a high-fidelity, content-valid simulation of a victim-rescue operation.

Actually, there was one additional problem with that test item. I had gone to New York City to observe actual victim rescues at emergency scenes. What I found was that firefighters only sometimes used the fireman's carry to rescue victims. At a fire scene choked with smoke, for example, firefighters often crawled on their hands and knees. When they encountered a victim, they dragged him or her out. They did not stand up and place the victim in a fireman's carry, and then walk out of a building. Often they dragged victims out by grasping them under their arms, by the backs of their shirts, even by the belts around their waists. There was one more important detail, namely, that most of the time they were bringing the victims *down* stairs, not climbing *up* stairs while carrying a victim. At the trial, I testified to that fact.

In terms of content-oriented evidence of validity, therefore, the test item used by FDNY that simulated the "victim rescue" was deeply flawed in that it did not represent accurately how that aspect of the job actually was performed. I made similar arguments with respect to the use of speed as a valid indicator of performance on the job. For example, in extending a wooden ladder fully, and then placing it against a wall, it is not only speed that is important; one must also ensure that the ladder is not propped against a window. Indeed, a great deal of job analysis evidence indicated that pacing also matters. When descending from an aerial ladder onto the roof of a building, for example, it is not prudent simply to jump off without first looking carefully to see if the tar on the roof is bubbling, and probing with a pike pole to ensure that the roof is stable and not likely to collapse.

In addition to arguing that at least some items on the test were not representative of the way the job was performed in practice, I also challenged opposing experts' claims that New York City would realize approximately $11 million per year (in 1982 dollars) in improved productivity by using FDNY's new physical ability test. The FDNY had argued that the economic utility of the new test was approximately $11 million per year. An important parameter in their calculation was the incremental validity of the new test relative to the previous test. Yet if there were serious questions about the content-oriented evidence of validity of the new test, then how could any statistical relationship, even an assumed one, between test performance and job performance be relied upon to produce an accurate estimate of the annual payoff of the new test?

I was only one of several experts and trial attorneys involved in this case on behalf of the female plaintiffs. Laura Sager, a law professor at New York University and representing the Women's Rights Clinic of Washington Square Legal Services, Inc., worked incredibly hard on the case and at trial. On March 5, 1982 the federal judge hearing the case, Judge Charles Sifton, ruled in favor of the plaintiffs, although that was only the beginning of appeals and legal challenges to his ruling. In 1987, for example, an Appeals Court overturned some parts of Judge Sifton's 1982 ruling, and ordered that henceforth the physical ability test would be scored in terms of speed to perform the various items on the test.[5]

Brenda Berkman gave up her job as an attorney to pursue her dream – to join one of the most celebrated – and macho – lifesaving organizations in the world: the New York City Fire Department. Subsequently I lost track of Brenda for the next 20 years, and knew very little about the ensuing legal wrangling and the harassment that Brenda and her fellow female firefighters endured.

According to the 2006 documentary by Bann Roy that aired on PBS, "Taking the Heat: The First Women Firefighters of New York City":

> Berkman and the other women became instant targets for derision and anger from city officials, residents, and even co-workers. Male firefighters allegedly tampered with the women's safety equipment, sometimes even bleeding the oxygen out of their air tanks. There were allegations of women being unwelcome at meals, and being subjected to obscenities and other verbal abuse, physical violence, and even sexual molestation. More often than not, only one or two persons in each firehouse harassed and intimidated the women, but other firefighters did nothing to stop them. In short, the women endured loneliness, violence, and even sexual abuse to serve their communities.[6]

Fast forward now to 9/11/2001, and the tragedy of the World Trade Center. A week later, NBC News broadcast a television special on the female heroes of 9/11. One of the women highlighted was Lieutenant Brenda Berkman, who raced into the World Trade Center to rescue victims, while carrying a full load of gear. Twenty years earlier she was almost rejected for the job of firefighter because she couldn't carry a duffel bag filled with two 60-pound bags of cement up one flight of stairs! I wrote to Brenda to tell her that her actions on 9/11 had validated my life's work.

In July, 2002 Brenda Berkman was promoted to the rank of Captain. As of 2006, she continues to serve the FDNY and to encourage young women to join that organization.

Beck v. Boeing (2004)

On March 14, 2000, Mary Beck and 37 other female employees of The Boeing Company and its subsidiaries and divisions filed a class action complaint alleging that they were discriminated against unfairly on the basis of their gender. The complaint alleged that female employees were treated differently from similarly situated male employees. It alleged that the plaintiffs and the class they represent (as many as 29,000 women) were denied, based on their gender, desirable job assignments, promotional opportunities, management positions, training, equal pay, overtime, tenure, comparable retention ratings, bonuses, and other benefits and conditions of employment. It also alleged that Boeing failed effectively to enforce policies prohibiting sexual harassment and gender discrimination, and retaliated against females who protested such practices. Finally, it alleged that Boeing's own internal surveys and the studies of its hired consultants showed gender bias in Boeing's promotion and pay practices, and that the United States government, through its Department of Labor, had informed Boeing, based on an audit of Boeing's practices, that it had not paid many of its female workers fairly.

In short, the complaint raised important issues in three areas:

1 *Pay discrimination* – the lawsuit claimed that Boeing systematically paid women less than men.
2 *Hostile work environment* – multiple sworn depositions from female employees described groping, fondling, and offensive language on the part of male colleagues and bosses. Boeing's response said that it strives for a workplace where everyone is treated fairly, with trust and respect.
3 *Suppression of evidence* – Boeing went to extraordinary lengths to hide evidence of years of unfair pay practices.

To be sure, many of the alleged problems could be traced to the culture of the company. I argued in my report as an expert witness for the plaintiffs that organizational culture is an important concept, for it describes the environment within which employment decisions are made and the environment within which employees work on a day-to-day basis. Organizational culture has been described as the DNA of an organization – invisible to the naked eye, but critical in shaping the character of the workplace.[7] Culture is the pattern of basic assumptions that a given group has invented, discovered, or developed in learning to cope with its problems of adapting to its external environment and to integrating its internal processes. The pattern of assumptions has worked well enough to be considered valid and, therefore, to be taught to new members as the correct way to perceive, think, and feel.[8]

Some key aspects of organizational culture include questions such as the following.[9] What does the company value? What does it stand for? What should one look for to see what it's about? Who are the company's heroes and heroines? What are its mottos and slogans? What gets celebrated? What gets rewarded? How is leadership expressed? How does the company handle conflict? How does it handle decision making? How do people communicate there? What are interactions like? What are the staff's perceptions, attitudes, expectations, and needs? How is work monitored? How are people held accountable?

In *Beck v. Boeing* I argued that when individuals (in this case, females) perceive that aspects of their organization's culture are negative, those perceptions affect their attitudes, their behavior, and their job performance. A wide variety of information that I examined supported my conclusion that, at least during the time period of this case, 1997–2004, the organizational culture at Boeing did not support female employees as a group. Independent sources of evidence overlapped and intersected in their conclusions on this issue. These sources included reports of Boeing's own outside consultants, Boeing's internal audits of its various sites, and the sworn deposition testimony of the plaintiffs.

With respect to salary discrepancies between similarly situated men and women, in 1997 Boeing created a Diversity Salary Assessment (DSA) Team to study its compensation and promotion practices.[10] In a 1998 presentation summarizing the team's conclusions, the team wrote that "females . . . are paid less" and "gender differences in starting salaries generally continue and often increase as a result of salary-planning decisions." On the plaintiffs' side, we called that phenomenon, "start low, stay low."

The DSA Team concluded that, to a large extent, the significant gender differences in starting salaries could be explained by initial level and type of work and that the differences were most pronounced for experienced hires. Women and minorities were placed in lower grades/levels and lower-paying functions than similarly situated males. Thus among entry-level managers, the male–female pay gap was, on average, $3,741.04.

The Labor Department's Office of Federal Contract Compliance Programs (OFCCP), which may conduct routine audits of federal contractors, launched a probe in 1998 after finding potential "systemic discrimination concerning the compensation of females and minorities." Boeing acted aggressively to limit the investigation, refusing to reveal its internal studies, which might have corroborated the government's findings. It hired a Washington law firm to put pressure on the Labor Department. In 1999 Boeing got the OFCCP to agree that Boeing should pay $4.5 million and also to agree that OFCCP would do no on-site audits for four years.

While under pressure from the OFCCP, Boeing was considering how to reduce the pay disparities without attracting attention. Frank Marshall, a former senior compensation manager for Boeing, testified that he created a "stealth" compensation plan in an effort "to minimize our legal risks." Any fixes would be embedded in the salary-planning process so that "even senior managers were not aware of them."

Boeing went to extreme lengths to keep its salary studies secret. In an email dated August 27, 2001, compensation manager Paul A. Wells advised colleagues to get rid of drafts of documents related to pay discrimination from the company's Salary Administration server because "that which is retained can potentially be subpoenaed and . . . those with access to the files can be called on to testify about the content."

A ferocious battle by Boeing lawyers to avoid disclosure of the salary studies ensued. However, two rulings on document discovery in March and May, 2004 by Judge Marsha Pechman forced Boeing to hand over the series of salary analyses it had fought hardest to withhold. Because lawyers attended nearly all meetings involving discussions of salary disparities, Boeing had withheld many critical documents from plaintiffs' attorneys. In her ruling, Judge Pechman chided Boeing for stretching the attorney–client privilege "beyond the boundaries" of what it was intended to protect.[11] Boeing subsequently produced more than 12,000 pages of documents.

Those documents revealed that Boeing was aware of the pay disparities for more than ten years – since 1994. Starting that year, attorneys and human resources managers started conducting annual compensation studies. In 1999, an analysis included in the unsealed documents showed that Boeing needed to allocate about $30 million *per year* in salary adjustments to partially eliminate gender-based pay disparities. The company allocated only $10 million, and, thus, the disparities persisted.

What factors contributed to the gender-based pay disparities? Boeing's own Director of Employee Relations, Marcella Fleming, identified a number of possible causes in the course of her deposition:

1 Paying women less than men at the time of hiring because women tend to be paid less than men in the external marketplace for similarly situated work.

2 Red-circling, that is, downgrading someone into another job because of surplus activity, but not taking money away. Red-circling may have operated to the detriment of women because most of the employees being downgraded at Boeing were men. As higher-paid males moved back into lower-paying non-management jobs, many of which included substantial numbers of women, the male–female disparity in pay in those jobs became larger than it was previously.

3 Following the rule that any promotions made internal to the company come out of a manager's merit fund. As a result, managers were generally less inclined to pay people what the job might ultimately be worth because to do so they had to take money from everybody else in the merit pool. If the new person moving in was a lower-paid female, then the common promotion/merit fund would have the potential to affect women adversely.

4 Following the general guideline that you never give anybody more than a 15 percent raise. As a result, pay disparities between higher-paid men and lower-paid women tended to widen over time.

5 Following the principle of "uniform fund generation." Under "uniform fund generation," all salary review groups receive identical base allocations for salary adjustment purposes (for example, 4 percent). This had the effect of giving salary review groups comprised of many high rate-range individuals (predominately males) more in actual dollars than salary review groups comprised of many low rate-range individuals (predominately females). If the average salary in the high-rate range is $100,000, and the average in the low-rate range is $40,000, the same 4 percent allocation means that the average increase available in the high rate-range group is $4,000. However, in the low rate-range group, the average increase available is only $1,600.

6 Allowing one's prior work history at Boeing to affect the level of pay. Because the hourly workers (predominately male) are generally paid more on an annual basis than the salaried workers, when an hourly employee transfers to a salaried job, the company doesn't usually take money away and it might even give a raise if it wants that person and thinks his or her skills are valuable. Doing so, however, might create a difference in the way that person is paid relative to most of the other people in the group.

7 Managing raises rather than salaries. If two workers come to a salaried job with different levels of pay (e.g., one from the higher-paid hourly workforce,

and the other from the lower-paid administrative workforce), managing raises means the disparity may continue to grow. This practice caused the dollar value of the difference to become greater over time.

In its assessment of the *Beck v. Boeing* case, *Business Week* noted:

> It's a classic scenario – the type of confrontation that has served as dramatic fodder for countless movies: A big, powerful company bullies small, weak individuals. *Erin Brockovich*, *A Civil Action*, and many other legal thrillers tell this tale from the point of view of the victims. But *Business Week* has obtained a rare view of the other side of the story: what takes place at the company . . . This hidden corporate history raises questions as to whether the company and its lawyers engaged in a systematic campaign to hide evidence and take advantage of attorney–client privilege.[12]

Faced with the prospect of telling jurors why its own internal documents seemingly contradicted its legal theory that company policies were proper and were implemented properly, Boeing became accommodating, and proposed a settlement offer, two days before it was scheduled to go to trial. The company agreed to change its employment, promotion, and compensation practices, and to pay as much as $72.5 million to as many as 29,000 current and former female workers at its Seattle-area aircraft plants.

At the time the *Beck v. Boeing* case was settled in 2004, Boeing was embroiled in several ethics scandals, from possessing 35,000 pages of stolen Lockheed Martin Corporation documents involving a rocket-launch contract, to criminal probes into its controversial $23.5 billion Pentagon air tanker deal. As if that were not enough, in March, 2005 the firm's Chief Executive Officer, Harry Stonecipher, was forced to resign over a sexual affair with a female executive.[13] The good news is that the company has made a remarkable turnaround since the hiring of its current Chairman, President, and CEO, Jim McNerney, from 3M Company, on June 30, 2005.[14] In May, 2006 it agreed to pay a $615 million fine to settle the procurement scandals, the largest fine ever by a government contractor.[15]

Conclusion

From an expert-witness perspective, having testified on both sides of the aisle, I can say unequivocally that the main difference between testifying for defendants versus testifying for plaintiffs is in access to information. Testifying for a defendant organization opens doors to company facilities, data, internal studies, and relevant information, and it provides access to key decision makers who are central to the case. When one testifies for the plaintiff side, however, many of those same portals are closed or difficult to gain access to.

Having said that, it has been my experience that most companies want to do the right thing, not to discriminate on the basis of gender or any other protected characteristic, and their written policies reflect that intent. What often gets them into trouble, at least in my experience, is the implementation of those policies. Experts, whether working for the plaintiff or for the defendant, need to work diligently to ferret out information that can shed light on the actual implementation of organizational policies.

With respect specifically to the *Berkman* and *Beck* cases, there are some important lessons to be drawn. The first is that it took incredible courage for Brenda Berkman and Mary Beck to step forward as lead plaintiffs in these cases. They did so at great personal cost, even though they did ultimately prevail. Their tenacity and persistence were remarkable.

Second, their lawsuits accomplished what legions of internal managers and external consultants could not, namely, the imposition of social justice and fair working conditions on their organizations. The legal system can change employment practices overnight, but the legal system itself moves slowly and deliberately, and plaintiffs need to understand that the race is a marathon, not a sprint.

Third, I began this chapter by noting that in an ideal world, expert witnesses accept cases because they are convinced that the cause in question is just, and that they represent the side that is "right." In other cases, however, "right" is not so obvious, especially when opposing experts differ about the findings and practical implications of a body of empirical research, for example, in job analysis, pre-employment interviews, validation, meta-analysis, or performance management. Unpublished, internal organizational research findings ("company studies") are even more contentious.

In the two cases described here, "right" was reasonably clear, especially from the perspective of the plaintiffs, and, ultimately, in the resolution of the cases. In *Berkman*, many members of the FDNY and its management, as well as much of the public, sincerely believed that women simply did not belong in firehouses. In *Beck*, the company argued strenuously that its policies were lawful. In both of these cases there were many high-stress, nasty depositions and courtroom battles. In the end, however, I believe that "right" prevailed and that the cases resulted in significant gains for women's rights and economic opportunities. In addition to the plaintiffs, many incredibly dedicated attorneys and other experts devoted countless hours to these cases. As a group, they embody what anthropologist Margaret Mead once said:[16] "A small group of thoughtful people can change the world. Indeed, it's the only thing that ever has."

Notes

1   Berkman v. New York, No. 79 C 1813, United States District Court for the Eastern District of New York, 536 F. Supp. 177; 1982 U.S. Dist. LEXIS 12396; 28 Fair Empl. Prac. Cas. (BNA) 856; 30 Empl. Prac. Dec. (CCH) P33, 320, March 4, 1982.
2   Roy, B. (Producer). (2006, March 28). *Taking the heat: The first women firefighters of New York City.* New York: Public Broadcasting Service.

3   Uniform guidelines on employee selection procedures (1978). *Federal Register, 43*, 38290–38315.

4   Cascio, W. F., & Aguinis, H. (2005). *Applied psychology in human resource management* (6th ed.). Upper Saddle River, NJ: Prentice-Hall.

5   Berkman v. New York, Nos. 86–7157, 86–7159, 86–7167, 86–7201, United States Court of Appeals for the Second Circuit, 812 F.2d 52; 1987 U.S. App. LEXIS 2329; 43 Fair Empl. Prac. Cas. (BNA) 318; 42 Empl. Prac. Dec. (CCH) P36, 902, argued May 28, 1986; decided February 17, 1987.

6   Roy (2006). Description downloaded from www.pbs.org/independentlens/takingtheheat/film.html on March 29, 2006.

7   Tetenbaum, T. (1999, Autumn). Beating the odds of merger & acquisition failure. *Organizational Dynamics*, 22–36.

8   Schein, E. H. (1983). The role of the founder in creating organization culture. *Organization Dynamics*, 11, 13–28. See also Schein, E. H. (1985). *Organizational culture and leadership*. San Francisco: Jossey-Bass. See also Schneider, B. (Ed.). (1990). *Organizational climate and culture*. San Francisco: Jossey-Bass.

9   Tetenbaum, 1999. See also Kotter, J., & Heskett, J. (1992). *Corporate culture and performance*. New York: The Free Press.

10 Information about the Boeing case comes from my own expert-witness reports, as well as from public sources. See, for example, Holmes, S. (2004, April 26). A new black eye for Boeing? *Business Week*, pp. 90–92. Holmes, S., & France, M. (2004, June 28). Coverup at Boeing? *Business Week*, Retrieved June 10, 2006, from www.businessweek.com/print/magazine/content/04_26/b3889088.htm. See also Lunsford, J. L. (2004, July 19). Boeing to change pay plan to settle sex-bias lawsuit. *The Wall Street Journal*, p. B2.

11 Attorney–client privilege is a legal doctrine that shields confidential communications between executives and their attorneys from public disclosure. It is intended to allow managers to be candid with their legal counselors (Holmes & France, 2004).

12 Holmes & France (2004).

13 Merle, R. (2005, March 8). Boeing CEO resigns over affair with subordinate. *The Washington Post*, p. A1.

14 Carpenter, D. (2006, July 5). Boeing's chief ethics champ. *The Denver Post*, p. 2C.

15 Boeing pays a biggie. (2006, May 29). *Business Week*, p. 30.

16 Downloaded from www.brainyquote.com/quotes/authors/m/margaret_mead.html on June 30, 2006.

Part III

Disciplinary Perspectives

12

Sex Discrimination: The Psychological Approach

Peter Glick and Susan T. Fiske

The psychological approach to sex discrimination is complementary to approaches that use a broader level of analysis such as economics and sociology. Psychology, however, adds a crucial piece to solving the puzzle of discrimination. Discrimination can be embedded in the structure of an organization, in what is known as institutional racism or sexism, but discriminatory acts are ultimately carried out by individuals who both accommodate themselves to and shape the culture and practices of a workplace. Not only does psychology look at discrimination, defined in psychology as behavior, it also looks at how such behavior is mediated through individuals' perceptions, beliefs, and feelings.

What are people thinking or feeling when they discriminate? What triggers discriminatory behavior? Research psychologists have tested and refined a set of psychological theories that paint a complex but coherent picture of how, when, why, and toward whom sex discrimination is likely to occur, as well as the consequences for women who are victims of discrimination.[1] Both in terms of the causes of discrimination and its consequences, what psychologists have found is not always in concert with people's commonsense notions.[2] Indeed, one of the major benefits of systematic research on sex discrimination is that it illuminates faults in how people "normally" think about sex discrimination and thus clears the path to reducing discrimination.

The Psychology of Discrimination

Misconceptions about the psychology of discrimination follow from the general assumption that people's actions stem directly and almost exclusively from their underlying dispositions, which generate motives and intentions of which the individual is fully cognizant.[3] In other words, the popular belief is that people act in specific ways solely because of "who they are" (i.e., their personality traits, beliefs, values) and that they are fully aware of why they behave as they do. These assumptions are contradicted by psychological research on the influence of situations and of automatic and nonconscious processes (both to be reviewed).

Social context matters

The popular belief that behavior primarily follows (in a stable, consistent, predictable pattern) from individuals' dispositions implies that, for example, a male supervisor who discriminates against a female employee must have overtly hostile and discriminatory attitudes toward women. Early research on the psychology of prejudice embraced this personality-driven view of behavior,[4] but quickly progressed (along with the rest of the field of social psychology) to a more contextualized understanding, as research clarified the impressive degree to which people's behavior is influenced by the situation.

The psychological approach to discrimination is *social* psychological, meaning that it considers not only what goes on inside the individual's mind, but how the individual is affected by and adapts to social contexts, ranging from proximal influences (e.g., the norms of one's immediate work group) to more distal influences (e.g., the division of male and female roles in society). Individuals' traits and beliefs are important, but a psychological approach that focused solely on the individual and ignored the larger context in which discrimination occurs would be misleading. Individuals do not exist in a vacuum, but in organizational and social contexts that influence their behavior much more than most people realize.

For example, Milgram[5] showed that ordinary Americans could be induced to participate in delivering what they believed to be dangerous (perhaps lethal) electric shocks to an innocent victim (as part of an experiment, ostensibly about the effects of punishment on learning). Importantly, Milgram's studies demonstrated that manipulations of the situation (such as the proximity of an authority figure and the nature of the task) strongly influenced people's actions. Depending on the situation, the obedience of participants in proceeding to the highest levels of shock ranged from 0 (when two authority figures disagreed about continuing) to over 90 percent (when participants were asked to be a cog in the system, but did not personally deliver the shocks). Besides obeying authorities, people conform to their peers far more than they (or others) realize.[6] People will even go against the evidence of their own eyes in order to agree with their peers.[7]

The fact that one can construct situations in which most people can apparently be led to harm an innocent victim or to mimic others rather than to trust their own senses suggests that people's behavior is highly malleable. Acts of harm toward others are not confined to a well-defined subset of aggressive or irrational individuals, nor is blind conformity the exclusive province of weak-willed doormats. Similarly, acts of discrimination are not committed only by obvious bigots. Decades of research on prejudice confirm that discrimination (like aggression and irrational conformity) is a situation-dependent social phenomenon.[8]

That situations can exert such strong control over behavior might appear to contradict the claim that individuals' thoughts and emotions are crucial mediators of behavior. If the situations are so powerful, why do we need to understand what people are thinking or feeling? The answer is twofold. First, situations are interpreted by individuals, so to understand how and why situations affect people's behavior it is necessary to understand what goes on inside people's minds. The effect of the situation is dependent on how the individual perceives it, a phenomenon called construal.[9] For example, people obey only an authority figure whom they perceive to be legitimate[10] and conform only to groups of others perceived to be similar to themselves.[11]

Second, people's beliefs and values are important underlying sources of discrimination even though they may be suppressed or "released" depending upon the situation.[12] Prejudiced beliefs result in discriminatory behavior when they are not suppressed.[13] Suppression can occur due to other beliefs the individual holds (e.g., a desire to be egalitarian) or due to situational forces (e.g., social norms).[14] Discrimination is likely to occur when the situation does not suppress (or actively supports) the expression of an individual's prejudices and the individual feels that discriminatory behavior is justified.

In the case of sex discrimination, suppression due to self-image concerns, such as the American value on being fair-minded and unprejudiced, are relatively weak in comparison to the other most studied form of prejudice, racism. People are much more likely to react to accusations that they have acted in a sexist manner with amusement, rather than with concern, guilt, and self-doubt.[15] As a result, sexism may be less suppressed and also easier to justify, making sex discrimination more frequent.[16] Thus, sexism must be mitigated through effective forms of external suppression, such as well-enforced policies of nondiscrimination, peer pressure, and authority sanctions.

Not every decision is conscious

A second popular misconception about human behavior that follows from the general belief in individual autonomy is the notion that people are fully aware of the reasons for their actions. Krieger notes that this belief is strongly embedded in legal notions of "intent" and "motive" that inform decisions about a defendant's guilt or innocence.[17] Research, however, has firmly established that: (1) people fail to accurately detect the causes of their own behavior and (2) behavior often occurs as a result of automatic, nonconscious processes.[18] Especially relevant to understanding discrimination is research on how stereotypes of groups can influence treatment of members of those groups even among individuals who do not want to act in a discriminatory way.

Well-intentioned individuals, even those who score low on questionnaire measures of prejudice, are influenced by ambient cultural stereotypes that they do not personally and consciously endorse.[19] Spontaneous associations between a group and stereotypic traits come to mind and influence subsequent reactions. Implicit stereotypes, as they are sometimes called, definitely influence nonverbal behavior, which is less controllable than verbal behavior.[20] A recent meta-analysis indicates even wider applicability for subtle measures to discriminatory behaviors, whether nonverbal or otherwise.[21] Granted, the implicit/explicit contrast has been drawn most often with regard to racial prejudice, rather than gender prejudice. Nevertheless, subtle forms of gender prejudice are also clear.[22] Moreover, they predict backlash against women who display stereotypically masculine personality traits (e.g., ambition) better than do explicit measures.[23]

Psychological Framework for Understanding Sex Discrimination

Sex discrimination differs from other forms of discrimination

Although discrimination toward different groups can take similar forms, these forms also exhibit what Allport referred to as "curious patterns" specific to each targeted group.[24] Discrimination against women, which Allport ignored in his classic treatise on prejudice, is especially "curious." Women quite clearly are targets of discrimination at work, both in terms of earnings and promotions to positions of power, such as executive positions in corporations.[25] Yet men and women interact more frequently with each other than do members of other groups, such as those that are differentiated by ethnicity, religion, and age. Further, interaction between men and women occurs in the most intimate realms of life, in heterosexual sexuality and romance, marriage, and the family. In contemporary American society, marriage (between a man and a woman) is commonly viewed as one of the closest and most important of all adult relationships.

Clearly, then, sex discrimination is likely to be complex. Indeed, cross-sex interactions appear to involve strangely polarized behavior. For instance, the same men who exclude, demean, and harass women at work may, at the end of the day, go home to wives and daughters whom they cherish. In contrast, a white person who is overtly racist at work is unlikely to choose to interact with blacks on weekends. Contemporary race relations have their own ambiguities and ambivalences,[26] but nevertheless fit a much clearer pattern of hostility, segregation, and discrimination. In contrast, the patterning of men's behavior toward women appears, at first blush, to be incoherent, unpredictable, and arbitrary.

Understanding the regularities that lie beneath the apparent inconsistencies in how women are treated is of critical importance to understanding workplace discrimination. Commonsense notions of what kinds of people discriminate or when, how, and why they do so are insufficient. As a consequence, it is all too easy for jurors and judges who are confronted by these complexities and subtleties to doubt (in all but the most clear-cut cases) whether a given behavior entailed sex discrimination. A defense attorney might ask: How can my client, a man who loves his wife, sister, daughter, and mother, be "sexist"? If my client is hostile toward women, why does he always hire a female secretary? My client may have been hostile to the plaintiff, Ms. A, but he consistently praised Ms. B's work – doesn't this suggest that Ms. A's aggressive personality (not my client's allegedly sexist beliefs) caused the problem?

The social psychological approach makes sense of these otherwise curious patterns. In particular, social psychological theories and research illuminate how the structure of male–female relations within society creates complex and polarized, but predictable, patterns of discrimination. This approach links the sociological level of analysis with the thoughts, emotions, and (consequent) behavior of individuals. Further, it explains how and why discriminatory treatment of women depends not only on an individual's personal traits (e.g., sexist beliefs), but also on the situational (e.g., organizational) context.

Gender stereotypes and ideologies mediate discrimination

The patterns and circumstances of sex discrimination must be understood against the broader social context of male–female relations. Prejudice researchers have long focused on differences in power and status as causes of discriminatory behavior. Men's greater (and women's lesser) power is one of the most important determinants of the tenor of gender stereotypes and, consequently, of sex discrimination. (Indeed, many of the similarities between discrimination toward women and disadvantaged minorities reflect commonalities in how low-power groups are treated).[27] To account for the unique aspects and patterning of discrimination toward women, however, it is necessary to understand how male–female relations differ from relations between other high- and low-power groups. The most important difference is that heterosexual reproduction ensures an intimate interdependence between the sexes – centered around heterosexual romance, domestic life, and child rearing.[28] This interdependence is instantiated in traditional, complementary (though differently rewarded) gender roles (primarily breadwinner and homemaker) that arguably shape gender stereotypes and sex discrimination at least as strongly as do power differences between the sexes.[29]

The more general social context of gender relations affects how women are treated in the workplace, by fostering socially-shared *gender stereotypes* and *gender ideologies*. Stereotypes associate various attributes (such as personality traits) with social categories. Psychologists distinguish stereotypes that are purely *descriptive* (expectations about what traits are likely to be associated with members of a group) and those that are *prescriptive* (beliefs about what individual members of the category *ought* to or *should* be like).[30] *Gender ideologies* are more general prescriptive beliefs that include gender stereotypes as well as broader beliefs about men's and women's proper roles in society.[31]

Gender stereotypes and ideologies are socially shared beliefs. Though the degree to which individuals endorse prescriptive gender beliefs varies, descriptive stereotypes about men and women exhibit a high degree of social consensus.[32] These stereotypes are shaped by a lifetime of experiences, including socialization through exposure to others' attitudes and the media's often stereotypical portrayal of men and women. Because descriptive gender stereotypes are learned early in life and entrenched through repeated exposure, they become over-learned and automatic.[33] Descriptive stereotypes can therefore color how perceivers view and treat individual men and women, even without conscious awareness that they are discriminating. Women may therefore be as likely as men to engage in nonconscious and automatic stereotyping (to be reviewed in more detail) that can have discriminatory consequences in the workplace. Descriptive stereotypes affect such outcomes as how people are assessed in hiring and promotion (e.g., perceived "fit" with the job),[34] the subtle (dominant versus deferent) behaviors that communicate and reinforce sex-based status differences,[35] and the degree to which people are open to influence by women as compared to men.[36]

Prescriptive gender stereotypes create distinct subtypes of women, mainly dividing those who conform from those who do not conform to gender prescriptions. Generally speaking, popularly perceived subtypes of women include clusters who are loyal, dependable helpmates (housewives, secretaries) versus those who fail to conform to traditional roles (feminists, lesbians, female professionals).[37] The risk of being moved from the approved (though underpaid) cluster to the disapproved, disliked cluster doubtless keeps many women behaving in line with societal norms.

While prescriptive gender beliefs are also cultural ideologies, cultures and individuals vary considerably in endorsing such beliefs.[38] Two factors – the extent to which the norms of a culture (or an organization) communicate sexist prescriptions and the degree to which individuals within organizations endorse them – both affect the likelihood of discrimination. The type of discrimination that stems from prescriptive beliefs about "a woman's proper place" is more overtly hostile and intentional (e.g., harassing or sabotaging a co-worker) than is discrimination due to automatic, over-learned descriptive stereotypes.[39] Such overt discrimination occurs when a woman (or man) violates gender prescriptions endorsed by co-workers.[40]

In sum, the distinction between descriptive and prescriptive gender beliefs maps onto different types of discrimination. Over-learned, automatic descriptive stereotypes are more likely to yield discrimination that is relatively cognitive (or "cold"), a result of (often unintentional) processes of categorization and stereotyping. In contrast, conscious prescriptive beliefs are more likely to provoke "hot" discrimination based on negative emotional reactions toward targets who violate those prescriptions. Observers are likely to feel surprise when a woman fails to conform to descriptive expectations, but they will generally feel anger or hostility when she violates prescriptive expectations. And while the effects of descriptive stereotyping can often be overcome by information that an individual does not possess stereotypical traits, prescriptive stereotypes (e.g., that a specific occupational role is a "man's job") can continue to drive discriminatory behavior.[41]

Sources of Stereotypes and Gender Ideologies

Social roles create stereotypes

How and why do gender stereotypes and ideologies develop? Social structural theories such as *social role theory* explain how the relative positions and roles of men and women in society generate shared gender stereotypes and prescriptive gender ideologies.[42] Social role theory focuses on the effects of the traditional division of labor, with women confined more to domestic tasks and men engaging in paid work outside the home. These role divisions by themselves are sufficient to produce stereotypes that members of each sex have the traits suited to their respective roles.[43] Because successful performance of work outside the home typically requires *agentic* traits (e.g., competence, ambition, leadership abilities, independence), these traits (associated more generally with competence) are stereotypically masculine. In contrast, because successful child rearing and homemaking requires *communal* traits (warmth, nurturance, kindness, empathy), these traits (associated more generally with warmth) are stereotypically feminine.

Experiments demonstrate that typical gender stereotypes can be recreated simply by making reference to fictional groups that are associated with either child rearing or work outside the home. In one study, participants read descriptions of individuals from two imaginary groups. Each description included an individual's group membership (*Orinthian* or *Ackmian*), role ("city worker" or "child raiser") and three personality traits (in each case, one agentic, one communal, and one gender-neutral trait). Most (80%) of the Orinthians were said to be "city workers' and a minority (20%) to be "child raisers," with the reverse ratio for the *Ackmians*. Even though the individual *Orinthians'* and *Ackmians'* personalities were described as equally "masculine" and "feminine," the group that consisted mostly of city workers was rated as relatively more agentic and the group that consisted mostly of child raisers as more communal. The traits associated with the roles typically performed by the group became associated with the group despite explicit information suggesting no personality differences between the groups.[44]

Social role theory also posits that overall power differences between men and women (gender hierarchy) reinforce gender stereotypes because the agentic traits associated with work outside the home are also high power, high status traits.[45] In complementary fashion, the communal traits associated with domestic life are low power, low status traits. In fact, status manipulations (independent of role manipulations) using fictional groups also generate agentic (masculine) stereotypes of high-status groups and communal (feminine) stereotypes of low-status groups.[46] Agentic traits are associated with status because they are self-profitable; enacting these traits facilitates garnering power and resources. Having power, in turn, elicits greater self-assertion. In contrast, communal traits are deferent and other-profitable because they involve putting the needs of others before oneself and discouraging self-assertion.[47]

Importantly, role and status differentiation not only create stereotypes, but a reality that corresponds to them. Different roles demand different kinds of behavior. When society relies upon a group-based division of labor, stereotypes are not merely descriptive, but prescriptive because efficient social functioning requires individuals to be socialized to possess the traits required for successful performance of their group's role.[48] Therefore, women are punished when they violate the prescription to be warm or communal. Acts of self-promotion or assertiveness by women, which contradict prescriptions for feminine niceness, are strongly disliked, and can result in discrimination in hiring or promotion.[49] In contrast, because men are not particularly expected to be nice (and are definitely expected to be assertive), they do not get punished for such behavior. Prescriptive gender norms create a dilemma for women at work as they tread the fine line between exhibiting the stereotypically masculine traits that are generally associated with the work world and appearing to be too assertive (and therefore not "nice").

Another social structural approach, ambivalent sexism theory,[50] is complementary to social role theory, but focuses on how the combination of male dominance and intimate interdependence generates polarized attitudes and behavior toward women. This approach views gender roles as one aspect of a more general intimate interdependence between men and women that occurs in the context of romantic and family relationships. Male dominance generates hostility toward women, whereas the sexes' intimate independence fosters benevolent attitudes and behavior toward women. These two sets of attitudes together constitute ambivalent (both subjectively positive and negative) attitudes about women. Although ambivalent, these attitudes are not psychologically inconsistent, but (for reasons explained below) act in concert to justify gender inequality.

Hostile sexism views women as adversaries in a power struggle, expressing resentment toward women who are perceived as seeking to control men. In contrast, *benevolent sexism* is a paternalistic attitude that views women as wonderful but fragile creatures who are necessary to "complete" a man. Although it is a subjectively positive orientation toward women, benevolent sexism reflects and reinforces assumptions of women's lesser competence.

Both benevolent and hostile sexism are prescriptive gender ideologies, but differentially associated with positive and negative stereotypes of women. As the dominant group, men are motivated to maintain their power and status. To do so, not only must they display agentic competence, but women must defer by behaving in a less self-assertive, more communal manner. Men's dependence on women (to fulfill their needs in familial and romantic relationships) also motivates prescriptions for women to enact low-status, communal traits that suit them to domestic roles and to being faithful, supportive romantic partners upon whom men can rely.

Social role theory and ambivalent sexism theory help to explain an otherwise puzzling aspect of gender stereotypes, namely that stereotypes of women are more favorable than stereotypes of men (not just for female but also for male perceivers).[51] From the older perspective of prejudice as pure antipathy, this is a paradox. How can stereotypes of a disadvantaged group be more favorable than those of a group with greater status and power? From the perspective of the social structural theories outlined here, however, gender prejudice can be defined by the reinforcement of traditional gender roles and power differentials. In other words, the relatively greater favorability or likability of stereotypically feminine as opposed to masculine traits is secondary to considerations of how these stereotypes reinforce traditional role divisions and gender hierarchy. Agentic traits (e.g., ambition, competitiveness, arrogance) are not necessarily likable, precisely because they are self-profitable and associated with dominance over others. In contrast, communal traits (e.g., being accommodating, helpful, putting others' needs before one's own) are extremely likable because they are other-profitable (making it pleasant to interact with others who enact these traits), but are associated with deference and lower status.[52]

Ambivalent sexism theory highlights how subjectively favorable attitudes toward women reinforce and maintain their subordination. Benevolent and hostile sexism act as the "carrot" and "stick" (respectively) of gender prescription. What's more, they are positively correlated (that is, people who endorse hostile sexism are likely to endorse benevolent sexism as well). Women who act consistently with traditional gender roles and who defer to men are rewarded with paternalistic affection, whereas women who violate these prescriptions, by seeking high-status or high-power roles, are punished with hostile discrimination.[53] Although sexism research (like prejudice research more generally) has focused on hostile forms of discrimination, more recent work illustrates how seemingly benevolent, but patronizing behaviors can be discriminatory and damaging.

Hostile discrimination differs from patronizing sex discrimination

Hostile discrimination is behavior that overtly and actively aims to harm the target toward whom it is directed. It encompasses the kinds of actions that most easily come to mind when thinking of discrimination, such as segregation, exclusion, demeaning comments, harassment, and attack. Patronizing discrimination is behavior that is ostensibly benevolent, but demeans and excludes by reinforcing assumptions that the target is incompetent and low-status. Such behaviors may appear to be "nice," and the people who enact them may truly believe that they are helpful, but the outcomes can be harmful and discriminatory. Examples include over-helping (e.g., taking over a co-worker's task on the presumption that she is incapable of completing it herself), praising minor accomplishments (implying that one held low expectations of her performance), substituting praise for tangible rewards such as promotion or important assignments ("atta girls," but no pay raises), and imposing limits on women's autonomy or responsibilities "for their own good." Besides women, people with disabilities and older people receive patronizing discrimination.[54] Importantly, patronized groups are typically denied control over resources, power, or tangible rewards (e.g., training, promotion, compensation).

In daily life, patronizing discrimination can be extremely difficult to distinguish from "prosocial" or beneficent acts. We do not mean to imply that helping another person who is truly in need is patronizing or discriminatory. A male supervisor who spends time teaching a new task to a female subordinate is not being patronizing if he does so in a way that increases her skills and autonomy. Most importantly, if his actions toward male subordinates are similar, his behavior cannot be considered to indicate sex discrimination. If, however, a male supervisor explains tasks more slowly and repetitively, is more likely to simply "take over" their completion, and offers more praise but less autonomy when dealing with female as compared to male subordinates, his behavior can be classified as paternalistic sex discrimination. Patronizing discrimination is perfectly illustrated by recent research showing that male supervisors are more likely to lavish female (in comparison to male) subordinates with patronizing praise, but less likely to allocate tangible resources (e.g., valued tasks) to them.[55]

Hostile discrimination is more obviously damaging, but paternalistic discrimination can also cause significant harm. This can be true even when the target of paternalistic discrimination tolerates or even welcomes the behavior. For instance, an individual woman might not object to and could profit from a man's patronizing help; however, this kind of interaction can strengthen group-based status differences, both for the people involved in the interaction and onlookers, by reinforcing the perceived legitimacy of gender hierarchy.[56] Patronizing behavior can be especially insidious because both perpetrators and even victims may not view such acts as "discrimination."

Although hostile and patronizing discrimination have opposing affective qualities in terms of the discriminating actor's subjective orientation toward the target of discrimination, they are complementary in another sense – they work in concert to reinforce traditional gender roles and power differences. Hostile discrimination follows perceived transgressions of gender boundaries.[57] In some male-dominated occupations, women's mere presence violates gender prescriptions. Even for other occupations, women may be penalized when they behave in ways that, though appropriate for the job, contradict prescriptions for feminine niceness. In contrast, patronizing discrimination toward women is likely to occur when gender roles and boundaries are well entrenched and appear to be accepted by women as well as men (e.g., a workplace in which jobs are sex segregated, with women in "helper" support roles, or toward women who appear to possess traditionally feminine characteristics).

It would not, therefore, be inconsistent for the same individual to treat some female co-workers in a patronizing and others in a hostile fashion. For example, female subordinates in low-status and supportive roles might be patronized, whereas female colleagues with higher status might be treated with hostile resentment. Individual women might experience both forms of discrimination, depending on changes in their status (e.g., upon being promoted to a super-visory role, women might find that formerly friendly male co-workers exhibit hostile resentment).[58]

Hostile and patronizing discrimination can also occur independently. Although the hostile and benevolently sexist attitudes that underpin the two forms of discrimination are positively correlated, the correlation is far from perfect. This means that a specific individual might, for example, endorse bene-volent, but not hostile, sexism. Further, these benevolently sexist attitudes may be context-dependent. Benevolent sexism is most likely to manifest itself in domestic and romantic contexts (e.g., attitudes about male and female roles in marriage). A man who is a benevolent, but not a hostile, sexist might exhibit protective, paternalistic behavior toward female romantic partners, preferring them to be demure and submissive. At the same time, however, he might be tolerant of assertive women at work because he views the workplace as a social context with different norms and expectations.

To further complicate the lay understanding of discrimination, some patron-izing or hostile responses may be relatively automatic and rapidly triggered by the mere presence of another person in the out-group category. This has been demonstrated for face and age, though not for gender. That is, white people subliminally exposed to photos of young black men responded more hostilely to an experimenter's provocation than people exposed to white faces, and young people exposed to words stereotypically associated with elderly people walked more slowly than people exposed to unrelated words.[59] Both the potential automaticity and the patronizing–hostile bipolarity make sex discrimination a more subtle and often unexamined matter than commonsense hunches would have it.

Sex Segregation, Stereotyping, and Sex-Role Spillover

The American workforce is sex segregated

The paid workforce is still highly segregated by gender. In the United States, approximately 50 percent of all workers would need to switch to different occu-pational categories to achieve the even distribution of men and women across occupations.[60] Furthermore, in terms of salaries and prestige, separate is not equal when it comes to the sex-segregated workforce. Female-dominated jobs tend to replicate women's generally lower status in society, garner less pay, and have less prestige than male-dominated jobs.[61] Occupations held primarily by women tend to be viewed as requiring stereotypically feminine traits and to involve duties that are similar to (or represent the professionalization of) women's traditional role. The most female-dominated jobs involve domestic work (e.g., house cleaning), nurturing or educating young children (e.g., day-care workers, elementary school teachers), taking care of the sick and elderly (e.g., nursing), or serving in supporting roles (e.g., receptionist, secretary) to (more often than not) male superiors. In contrast, the most male-dominated occupations are blue-collar jobs that emphasize masculine physical traits and high-status leadership roles viewed as requiring masculine personality traits.[62]

The segregation of work roles means that a company employing an equal number of men and women can nevertheless have considerable gender segregation in terms of the jobs each sex typically performs. Such gender segregation, which stems partly from individuals' occupational choices and partly from discrimination,[63] both reflects and reinforces traditional gender roles. If most of the lower-status supporting roles in a company are held by women, while most of the higher-status, decision-making roles are held by men, gender stereotypes are reinforced rather than challenged, and sex discrimination is likely to be perpetuated.

Gendered images of occupations influence who seems to "fit" different jobs

The sex segregation of jobs creates gender-typed occupational images that, in turn, foster sex discrimination. These images not only include whether the job is viewed as requiring masculine or feminine traits (gender-typing), but also whether the typical job-holder is male or female (sex-typing). Both of these aspects of occupational images can affect hiring decisions. First, job candidates are judged on how well their perceived personality traits match those associated with the job, allowing gender stereotyping of candidates to creep into hiring decisions.[64] Because managerial jobs are characterized as requiring agentic personality traits, discrimination occurs when evaluators assume that men are more and women are less likely to possess these stereotypically masculine traits: a perceived "lack of fit" between women's stereotypical traits and managerial or leadership positions puts women at a disadvantage relative to men for these jobs.[65]

To some extent, the effects of gender stereotypes about men's and women's personality traits can be mitigated by information about the individual that contradicts the stereotypes.[66] Women's perceived lack of personality fit with high-status roles, however, is only part of the story. Occupations are not only typed as masculine or feminine (in terms of traits that are required), but as male or female simply by virtue of the sex of typical job-holder.[67] For instance, most people find the image of a male receptionist incongruent with their image of the typical person in the job. Thus, even when the effects of gender stereotypes are removed by providing unambiguous information that a job candidate has the right personality traits for the job (e.g., a male candidate had the personality traits desired for a receptionist), discrimination still occurs, such that women are preferred for female-dominated jobs and men for male-dominated jobs. So, for example, an individual female candidate who presents convincing evidence that she is assertive, ambitious, and has leadership abilities is still less likely to be hired than a man who is perceived to have the same traits for a job that is associated with men (and not women).[68]

The gender-typing and sex-typing of occupational images go hand in hand: Male-dominated jobs are associated with masculine traits and with men, female-dominated jobs with feminine traits and with women.[69] Thus, in a sex-segregated job market, both forms of matching (based on stereotypical personality traits and on sex category) act together to reinforce gender-congruent hiring preferences – a greater likelihood of hiring men (over women) for male-dominated occupations and women (over men) for female-dominated occupations.[70] Although sex segregation results in discrimination against men (for feminine/female jobs) as well as against women (for masculine/male jobs), the overall effect is more severe for women, given that the most prestigious and high-paying jobs are both masculine (in terms of traits that are perceived to be required) and male-dominated.[71] Furthermore, even though men may be less likely than women to be hired in female-dominated occupations, the exceptional male hires are at least as (or more) likely to attain positions of authority (e.g., head librarian).[72] Most likely, this occurs because leadership positions stereotypically require masculine traits and because simply being male is associated with status and authority.[73]

Gender stereotypes create shifting standards

In addition to assessments of candidates' "fit" to jobs, gender stereotypes create "shifting standards" by which men's and women's behavior is subjectively assessed.[74] For instance, consider asking someone to rate the "assertiveness" of a target using a 5-point rating scale, from "not at all" to "extremely" (frequently used by stereotyping researchers), based on a description of the target's behavior. Because assertiveness is a stereotypically male and not a stereotypical female trait, different standards apply to male and female targets. The same behavior might be described as "very assertive" for a woman and "not very assertive" for a man, just as 50-degree weather in February might be described as "very warm" by a Minnesotan, but "not very warm" by a Floridian.

Shifting standards due to gender categorization can lead to patronizing behavior toward women in jobs seen as requiring masculine or agentic traits. Gender stereotypes foster lower expectations for women's performance, and women who exceed them are praised for "doing well" (whereas a man who performed similarly would not be praised because he was expected to perform well). Thus, on subjective measures, stereotyping creates *contrast* effects: When a woman exceeds stereotyped expectations, such as by being assertive, she is likely to be contrasted with the general stereotype (seen as unlike most women) rather than assimilated into it.

Such contrast effects do not ultimately benefit women. Although they can lead to praise or other forms of patronage when women defy low expectations, they do not lessen (and may even reinforce) discrimination in the allocation of tangible resources. People are attuned to the qualification "for a woman" that is implicit (if not explicit) in patronizing praise. The implication is that the performance was not excellent in terms of absolute standards or in comparison to how well men are expected to perform. Such absolute standards, however, do apply when it comes not to subjective characterizations of performance but to the allocation of resources and rewards (i.e., in hiring and promotion decisions, when allocating salary and benefits). By implying that lower standards were used to assess women's performance, patronizing praise reinforces gender stereotypes and the likelihood of discrimination on personnel decisions.

For example, while participants who role-played managing a co-ed softball team more highly praised female as compared to male players who had similar statistics (e.g., batting averages), they nevertheless discriminated against women in assignment to field positions and batting order placement.[75] Similarly, because the most important decisions, such as which of two equally qualified candidates to hire, are made on the basis of absolute (not within-gender) standards, an equally qualified man stands a better chance than his female counterpart. For example, a female applicant for a "masculine" executive position was judged *more* favorably than a similarly qualified male candidate on subjective scales (e.g., rating "How good is this candidate?" on a "not at all" to "extremely" scale). The male candidate, however, was rated higher on scales that invoked absolute standards (e.g., "How would this person score on a standardized intelligence test?") and was preferred when it came down to deciding who to hire.[76]

Shifting criteria define the most important job qualifications

In addition to shifting standards of subjective evaluations of men and women, the criteria considered to be most important for successful job performance can shift for male and female candidates. Comparisons across job candidates often involve trade-offs, with candidates exhibiting different strengths and weaknesses. Such differences create considerable room to allow evaluators to rationalize discrimination by shifting which characteristics evaluators consider most important for the job.

In a recent study, participants who evaluated candidates for a male-dominated job (police chief) shifted the criteria they thought were most important for the job (being "streetwise" versus "formally educated") so that a male (rather than a female) candidate was preferred. That is, when the job candidates were a streetwise man and an educated woman, evaluators viewed being streetwise as particularly important. In contrast, when the finalists were an educated man and a streetwise woman, education was viewed as more important. Thus, even though the candidates themselves were not stereotyped (e.g., the streetwise female candidate was perceived similarly to the streetwise male candidate), job criteria shifted to prefer the male candidate.[77]

The opposite effect occurred for a stereotypically female job. A female candidate was preferred over a male candidate as a "women's studies professor," with the importance of different criteria (being more of an "academic" or an "activist") shifting to favor the female candidate's strength. Thus, this type of discrimination (shifting criteria for most important job qualifications) is also linked to the sex-typing of a job, acting to preserve the existing sex segregation of the workforce. As noted earlier, by maintaining the sex-segregated status quo, such discrimination ultimately favors men as a group over women because the most high-paying and high-status jobs are male dominated.

Importantly, all of the forms of discrimination described above (gender-matching, sex-matching, shifting standards, and shifting job criteria) occur for female as well as male evaluators. These types of discrimination may be relatively automatic, unintentional, and nonconscious, based on descriptive stereotypes of occupations as well as stereotypes of men and women. Thus, these forms of discrimination can occur even if evaluators do not themselves hold sexist or prescriptive beliefs (i.e., even among people who endorse equal rights and roles for women and men). For example, sexist beliefs do not predict the degree to which evaluators discriminate by shifting criteria for job qualifications – people with egalitarian attitudes were just as likely as those with sexist attitudes to shift how they weight job criteria to favor a male candidate's strengths for a male-dominated job and a female candidate's strengths for a female-dominated job.[78] Thus, even well-meaning individuals are prone to making discriminatory decisions by weighting criteria to reach a desired outcome.[79]

Because these forms of discrimination are primarily due to automatic cognitive tendencies and are not necessarily intentional, they can be addressed to some extent by providing more information or changing the nature of the task. Shifts in the criteria viewed as most important for a job can be prevented by having evaluators rate the importance of the criteria before seeing information about male and female candidates. Additionally, individuating information about a specific woman that contradicts sex stereotypes can reduce or eliminate a perceived lack of fit to a managerial job based on personality trait inferences.

Recall, however, that several processes can lead to automatic, unintentional sex discrimination. Thus, while individuating information can eliminate stereotypic personality inferences about a job candidate, this does not eradicate discrimination. The finding that stereotyped personality inferences were easily overcome by providing individuating information[80] was initially over-interpreted. Research showed that when perceivers hear that "Jane always dominates class discussion," they rate Jane as being just as assertive as a similarly described man; this result was taken to indicate that Jane would be treated the same way as John. This is not the case. The research described in this section reveals that even if Jane and John are viewed as having similar personality traits, she is comparatively less likely to be hired for a male-dominated job (and he for a female-dominated job) simply because of a mismatch between the sex of the candidate and the sex-type of the job. Moreover, shifting standards research has shown that while Jane and John may be rated similarly on subjective rating scales, they are likely to be treated differently when it comes to "zero-sum" decisions such as hiring or the allocation of resources.

Finally, it is important to keep in mind that not all discrimination is unintentional and automatic. For reasons to be elaborated next, intentional discrimination that is based on *prescriptive* beliefs may be unaffected or even exacerbated by information or procedures designed to mitigate discrimination due to the automatic application of descriptive stereotypes.

Gender roles spill over at work

While shifting standards can result in different *descriptions* of the same work behaviors if performed by a woman as compared to a man, gender *prescriptions* can result in different emotional and social reactions to the same behavior depending on the sex of the person who performs it. Because prescriptive gender stereotypes or norms are so pervasive and accepted in the wider society, it is not particularly surprising that they affect how men and women are treated at work. *Sex-role spillover* refers to the tendency for gender roles to be replicated in the workplace.[81] For example, women may be more likely to be expected to perform "housekeeping" tasks, such as making coffee or setting up birthday celebrations. Similarly, female employees may be encouraged to adopt a "mothering" role or to be the "little sister" (or mascot) whose role is to provide social support for others.[82] These gendered social roles can subtly but powerfully reinforce sex-based status distinctions, even among co-workers whose official positions ostensibly have equal status. Such interactions not only affect those who are directly involved, but can influence onlookers by reinforcing gender-linked norms of behavior and status differences.[83]

For men, prescriptions about masculinity are congruent with their work roles. For women, however, gender prescriptions can create a variety of dilemmas at work. Women acting in concert with gendered expectations may be liked, but also subject to patronizing discrimination that casts them as low-status, incompetent, and unworthy of promotion. In contrast, in some work contexts, women classified as conforming to a traditional female type may elicit overtly hostile discrimination (e.g., co-workers may view it as inappropriate for a pregnant woman or mother of young children to be working outside the home). For women in jobs that require stereotypically masculine traits, conflict between their work and gender roles is especially likely; to be successful on the job, they must exhibit stereotypically masculine traits (e.g., by being assertive, competitive, and ambitious), but this can generate hostile discrimination or backlash because assertive women are perceived as violating norms of feminine niceness. These various dilemmas (to be reviewed in more detail) force women into a delicate balancing act to deal with competing and contradictory expectations that shift depending on the job, the situation, and co-workers' attitudes.

Sex-role spillover is most likely to occur when targets of discrimination exhibit characteristics that invoke women's child-rearing role or their sexuality. Pregnancy is a powerful and salient reminder of the traditional female role. Pregnant workers are more likely to be subjected to both patronizing and hostile discrimination. For instance, pregnant women are more likely to be helped on tasks, whether or not they seek assistance, to elicit affectionate touching, and to be addressed with diminutive labels (e.g., "honey").[84] These patronizing behaviors reflect the assumption that pregnant women are less competent.

Assumptions of incompetence are even more clearly reflected in personnel evaluations of pregnant workers. People who viewed a videotape of a female worker rated her as less competent and less suitable for a promotion when she performed tasks while wearing (as opposed to not wearing) a pregnancy prosthesis. Similarly, a manager described as recently having become a mother was presumed to be warmer, but less competent (as compared to a father or to a female manager not said to be a mother). This, in turn, predicted discriminatory treatment: less likelihood of hiring, promoting, or training.[85]

In short, when a woman's characteristics remind perceivers of traditional female roles (e.g., mother and homemaker), they are assimilated into the traditional stereotype of women as communal or warm, but not agentic or competent. This, in turn, can elicit patronizing discrimination that may appear to be affectionate and helpful (e.g., offers of help with work) but also presumes incompetence, leading to poorer work outcomes (e.g., less likelihood of promotion, lower pay, etc.).

Pregnant women and mothers of young children sometimes also face overt hostility from co-workers and supervisors who hold traditional gender prescriptions about motherhood. Many Americans expressly disapprove of pregnant women or mothers working full time, which they see as conflicting with a mother's child-rearing role.[86] Thus, pregnant women may elicit patronizing benevolence when they enact a traditional role, but hostility at work or when seeking to be employed. Indeed, pregnant women tend to be viewed as ill-suited for most jobs, especially for management positions.[87] The context-dependent nature of these reactions is illustrated by a field study that sent women into mall stores while (1) either wearing or not wearing a pregnancy prosthesis and (2) posing as a customer (congruent with traditional roles) or as a job seeker (incongruent with traditional roles).[88] Apparently pregnant (as compared to nonpregnant) women were treated in a more benevolently patronizing manner when they posed as customers (eliciting more smiling, nodding, touching, diminutive names, over-helping), but in a more hostile manner (frowning, rudeness, attempts to end the interaction) when they asked about job openings.

A woman's mere physical attractiveness or sexuality can also trigger feminine stereotypes of lesser competence. The findings on the effects of physical attractiveness generally suggest that attractiveness benefits both men and women in the workplace,[89] due to a general tendency for people to attribute both greater warmth and competence to attractive others.[90] Attractive women, however, are also more likely to be assumed to have feminine rather than masculine personality traits; as a result, some studies suggest that attractive women are viewed as a poorer match for managerial jobs.[91]

Attractiveness may be particularly problematic when men are primed to view women as sexual objects. When men viewed television commercials that depicted sexy women as part of an ostensibly unrelated advertising study, they subsequently were more likely to view a female candidate for a research assistant job as less competent.[92] Just as with reactions to pregnant women, however, responses to sexy women are complex – even though men primed for sexuality rated the attractive female applicant as less competent, they also were more likely to recommend that she be hired. Although such behavior may benefit attractive women materially, hiring for looks rather than competence is a patronizing form of discrimination that harms women who are not considered attractive and reinforces the idea that women gain power in the workplace through sexuality rather than competence.

A related type of response to women perceived as sexual objects in the workplace also results in inappropriate favoritism and ultimate disadvantage. Evaluators who hope for a romantic relationship with someone being evaluated on task performance exhibit clouded judgment: Such evaluators fail to distinguish bad performance from good performance on a task.[93] Such poor judgment harms everyone: judge, target, peers, and the organization.

Favoritism toward sexy women may also be limited to low-status, feminine jobs. The images of some stereotypically feminine occupations, such as flight attendant or receptionist, evoke the sexy woman subtype (i.e., sexy women match the image of the job). In contrast, because the "sexy woman" subtype is viewed as particularly feminine and as extremely different from the "career woman" type,[94] sexiness may be viewed unfavorably for women in management or in other high-status jobs. In a study that manipulated the sexiness of a female worker's appearance (e.g., conservative versus low-cut blouse) while keeping her overall attractiveness constant, sexiness led to hostility toward and lower competence ratings of the female target when she was said to be a manager, but did not create any hostile discrimination if she was said to be a receptionist.[95]

Nontraditional women provoke backlash

High-status jobs typically are viewed as requiring stereotypically masculine personality traits, which are associated with competence and leadership. Although prescriptions that women ought not to be too competent may, in the United States, largely be a thing of the past, women who exhibit a high degree of competence and leadership risk being viewed as violating norms of feminine niceness (i.e., as not being sufficiently nurturing, warm, concerned with others). Recall that whereas stereotypically masculine behaviors and traits are self-profitable and communicate high status, stereotypically feminine traits and behaviors are other-profitable, low-status, and deferent. Thus, even if a woman is encouraged to exhibit competence, by doing so she may be seen as not being sufficiently "feminine" and experience backlash – negative social reactions and punishment.

As a result, women are forced to tread much more carefully than men when it comes to exhibiting leadership and competence. For instance, when women engage in self-promoting behavior, they are viewed as being just as competent as a similarly self-promoting man, but are seen as less warm and, consequently, are disliked.[96] On the one hand, women may be encouraged to be competent, but on the other hand, they need to do so without appearing to be too aggressive or too willing to step on others' toes lest they be rejected by co-workers. In contrast, men do not seem to experience the same restrictions.

Women in powerful roles may not always be able to tread the fine line between the need to demonstrate work-related competence while avoiding violations of prescriptions for feminine niceness. For instance, people in positions of authority are typically required to provide critical feedback and evaluations of subordinates. Negative feedback from male superiors is tolerated, whereas the same critical feedback from female superiors leads to backlash, in this case dismissing the superior as incompetent. In both a field study of attitudes toward instructors and a laboratory study in which precisely the same feedback was given by a female or a male evaluator, women who gave negative feedback were rated as less competent than men. This effect occurred only when the feedback was critical, not when participants' work was praised.[97] Thus, female (in comparison to male) superiors may be tolerated or viewed favorably so long as they remain uncritical, but evoke hostile reactions if they criticize subordinates.

The contingent nature of backlash is further illustrated by work showing that how a job is described can have ironic effects on evaluations of agentic women. This research also reinforces the need to recognize that sex discrimination is a complex phenomenon that cannot be "fixed" with a single cure. One such cure, for discrimination based on stereotype matching (of the presumed gender-typed traits of applicants to the gender-typed traits associated with a job), has been to "feminize" managerial job descriptions by including social and interpersonal skills (which are stereotypically feminine). If a managerial job is described as requiring both (male) agentic and (female) communal traits, it seems reasonable to assume that female (as compared to male) applicants would no longer be presumed to be a poorer fit to the job.

This solution would work well if stereotype matching were the only form of sex discrimination at work. Unfortunately, it is not. When managerial jobs are described as requiring both agentic and communal traits, backlash effects cause highly agentic female candidates to experience more sex discrimination than when the job is described only in agentic terms.[98] When candidates are explicitly required to have strong social skills (e.g., to be understanding and empathetic), the job's requirements legitimize or justify excluding candidates who are viewed as not being sufficiently socially skilled. Prescriptive gender stereotypes create a higher standard for a woman (in comparison to a man) to be considered to have good social skills (i.e., the bar for demonstrating good social skills is set higher for women than for men). Unfortunately, when women attempt to demonstrate their competence, they tend to be seen as insufficiently warm (whereas men, who are held to lower standards of niceness, are not penalized in this way).

When it comes to backlash in response to a woman's failure to conform to prescriptions of feminine niceness, moreover, female perceivers tend to exhibit just as much hostility as male perceivers. Because feminine warmth is perceived positively, women are more likely to embrace this prescription for their own sex than they are to endorse overtly restrictive prescriptions (e.g., that women ought to be restricted from traditionally male roles). In general, however, because men tend to endorse prescriptive gender ideologies more than do women, men are more likely than women to commit many forms of hostile discrimination, especially sexual harassment, which combine power and sexuality motives.

Sexual harassment occurs to re-assert traditional hierarchies

Research on sexual harassment has emphasized the importance of the workplace environment – its norms, structure, and "culture" – which can foster or inhibit harassment by those who are prone to engage in such behavior.[99] Sexual harassment predominantly targets women and is typically committed by men, even in those (less frequent) cases where men are the victims.[100] Like other forms of sex discrimination, sexual harassment can take both patronizing and hostile forms, which can be characterized (respectively) as reflecting approach and rejection motivations.[101] In the former case, the harasser's motives may primarily be sexual, perhaps coupled with a desire for a longer-term intimate relationship. Hostile harassment is more likely to reflect motives to exclude and demean women in an attempt to drive them out of male-dominated jobs.[102] Such hostile harassment sometimes targets men who do not live up to prescriptions for masculinity in terms of appearance and physical strength, behaviors (e.g., "toughing out" difficulties without complaint), or traits such as assertiveness.[103] Thus, hostile harassment of "weak" men, who are castigated for being "like a woman" (e.g., a "girly-man" or "pussy") serve a similar function to hostile harassment of women by reinforcing the masculinity of the job or workplace.[104] Punishing "gender deviants" effectively discourages women from pursuing masculine domains.[105]

The presence of sexualized images of women (ranging from explicit photographs on calendars and internet pornography shared via email to milder images of sexy celebrities) "primes" men to view women as sexual objects. Once primed to view women in this manner, men are more likely to engage in sexualized behaviors, such as standing too close to or touching female co-workers.[106] Therefore, workplace environments in which such images are frequently seen are likely to show an increased incidence of sexual harassment.

Similarly, workplaces in which the norms of behavior do not stress professionalism foster sexual harassment. Lack of professionalism includes a general tolerance for disrespectful treatment of others, frequent use of obscenities, and expectations for employees to perform tasks not formally required by the job. Such informal atmospheres can encourage sex-role spillover and the sexualization of the workplace. Consistent with the general complementarity of hostile and patronizing forms of discrimination, in workplaces where women report that they receive generally disrespectful treatment, 67 percent also had received sexual comments intended to be complimentary, whereas this figure was 38 percent for women who reported never having been treated disrespectfully at work.[107]

Power differences between the sexes also exacerbate the problem. In organizations in which men generally have greater status and power by virtue of their positions within the organization, women are at greater risk of sexual harassment. Power makes individuals more likely to act on their motives and impulses, for good or for ill.[108] For some men, having power over a woman is automatically linked to viewing women in a sexual manner,[109] and power manipulations have been shown to increase the likelihood that men who are prone to sexually harass will engage in this behavior.[110] The fact that men tend to monopolize the most powerful positions in many companies therefore puts women at greater risk for harassment. Leaders have a significant amount of influence over organizational norms, which can suppress harassment or permit it. When management is believed to tolerate harassment in an organization, women are more likely to report having been harassed.[111]

The ratio of men to women in an organization also affects the likelihood of sexual harassment. Women in traditionally male jobs are more likely to experience both patronizing and hostile forms of sexual harassment, ranging from ostensibly complimentary comments about female workers' appearances to uninvited sexual touching and overt sexual coercion. Overall, the combination of a male-dominated workplace, in terms of numbers and power, with an informal work environment that permits or encourages sex-role spillover, puts women at much higher risk of harassment.[112]

Changing Organizational Culture and Work Group Norms

Groups of people invariably develop norms of appropriate behavior that are reinforced through social rewards and punishments. Most individuals quickly adapt to situational norms, which is an important reason why human behavior is so malleable and situation-specific. As a result, "local norms" (e.g., shared norms of behavior among a work group) can have substantial effects on inhibiting or encouraging discriminatory behavior. This occurs directly through conformity pressures that may lead individuals who do not personally hold prejudiced beliefs nevertheless to discriminate as a way of gaining the approval of co-workers or of fostering a group identity.[113] Work group norms also affect the likelihood of discriminatory behavior by either suppressing or failing to suppress expressions of individuals' gender prejudices. When co-workers tolerate discriminatory behavior, individuals who subscribe to traditional gender beliefs feel permitted to express these views and to enact these biases through discrimination.

Most companies have official policies that forbid discrimination based on sex and other prominent social categories (e.g., ethnicity). Although such policies can act to suppress the expression of individual employees' prejudices, there is considerable variation on how vigorously these policies are enforced or whether they are even well publicized within an organization. Furthermore, norms within a work group or the organization as a whole (i.e., the "unwritten rules" regarding what behavior is actually tolerated or encouraged in the organization, in a branch office, or in a specific work group) can be at odds with formal nondiscrimination policies. Because proximal social influences exert more social pressure than distal or more pallid influences,[114] whether individuals feel empowered to discriminate can be more strongly influenced by unwritten norms than by official nondiscrimination policies.

In sum, the dynamics of gender discrimination are influenced by organizational context, culture, and policies (so long as the latter are well enforced). Indeed, given that individuals may not be aware of their own subtle, benevolent, or automatic forms of prejudice, the organization as a whole may be the only entity in a position to avert tainted judgments by the contexts and culture that it establishes or fails to establish.[115] Several factors can influence the atmosphere in the organization, to encourage fair or unfair judgments.

A hyper-masculine culture at work impedes gender equality

Occupations numerically dominated by men come to be seen as "male" jobs and gender roles can easily spill over to those contexts, as noted earlier, so the few women in those settings are expected to perform gender stereotypic roles.[116] When women are relegated to subordinate, service-oriented roles, the masculine culture thrives. The context easily primes stereotypic prejudices and behavior, encouraging sexual harassment and underrepresentation of women in significant roles.

Remedies include reframing perceptions of the job duties (e.g. from "secretary" to "administrative assistant"); removing gratuitous, stereotype-priming cues (e.g., heavily gendered uniforms, sexually explicit photographs, gender-biased exemplars in website images); and creating a professional, task-focused atmosphere (e.g., discouraging inappropriate informality, sexual joking, presumed intimacy). Organizational culture matters.

Solo status impedes gender equality

Any individual from a numerically rare category is bound to stand out. The consequences of standing out include being relegated to gender-typed roles,[117] suffering polarized judgments,[118] self-consciousness,[119] being distracted by others' scrutiny,[120] and no doubt other effects not yet documented. Tokens from an outside group, such as women seen as invading a previously male domain, provoke resistance and hostility because they are perceived as interfering with the group's previously comfortable, homogeneous norms.[121] The remedy for solos is proportionate representation, relative to the talent pool. A critical mass of 20–30 percent seems to undercut such dynamics.

Lack of information impedes gender equality

Stereotypes thrive in informational vacuums, when people know little about the individuals in question.[122] Stereotypes are category-based perceptions that function as baseline expectations until or unless the perceiver seeks and uses additional individuating information. Stereotypes are limiting; first, because they anchor perceptions in a biased fashion, and adjustment away from that anchor is notoriously inadequate.[123] Thus, they act as a millstone around the target's neck. Second, stereotypes are limiting because they create boundaries, fencing targets within confined roles prescribed by (e.g.) gender norms. Between the millstone and the fence, it's a wonder stereotyped targets get anywhere at all. The antidote to paucity of information, of course, is openness: providing useful, pertinent, individuating information.

Power asymmetries

Subordinates attend to those who control their outcomes: students attend to faculty, employees attend to managers, and players attend to coaches. Outcome dependency reduces prejudice.[124] Conversely, lack of outcome dependency characterizes positions of power.[125] Because they can afford to be inattentive, powerful decision makers are more vulnerable than their subordinates to relying on convenient stereotypes. Their own incentives need to depend on their ability to grow and sustain a gender-balanced, diverse workforce, one that likely reflects the organization's client base and in fact makes economic sense.

Conclusion: The Cost of Sex Discrimination

This chapter has focused primarily on the causes and patterns of sex discrimination. Remember, however, that sex discrimination also has psychological consequences, both emotional and cognitive, for the individuals whom it targets. To protect themselves from these consequences, women and other targeted groups often deny evidence of personal discrimination as a form of psychological protection.[126] This is especially true in terms of self-presentation to others – people do not want to be labeled as "complainers."[127] For those who are sensitive to perceiving discrimination (or in those cases where discrimination is sufficiently obvious that most women perceive it), the predominant emotional reactions include feelings of threat, uncertainty, depression, fear, and anger.[128] These negative feelings are not only experienced by victims of hostile discrimination, but also when patronizing praise is combined with discriminatory treatment in terms of work assignments and tangible rewards.[129] It even occurs when patronizing discrimination occurs in isolation and is interpreted as intrinsically demeaning. The experience or even the threat of potential discrimination takes an emotional toll, putting women under stress that can endanger emotional and physical well-being.[130]

Although outrage in response to discrimination can potentially lead women to take constructive action, research suggests that people generally do not realize how difficult it is for actual victims of discrimination and harassment to respond in an assertive manner. For instance, although most women believe that they would confront a sexually-harassing job interviewer and walk out of the interview, very few women placed in such a situation actually did so (and the few who did confront the harasser did so in a polite, respectful manner).[131] In real-life situations, people (men as well as women) generally have difficulty confronting authorities or even peers. Thus, discrimination and harassment in organizations is likely to be grossly underreported by employees, especially if management is not viewed to be sympathetic to such concerns.[132] When organizations are not supportive of women who complain about sexual harassment, women who report harassment actually have worse outcomes – occupationally, psychologically, and in terms of their physical health – than women who do not.[133]

The cognitive toll (e.g., reduced ability to focus) that sex discrimination has on its targets is also highly significant and potentially damaging to performance on the job. The threat of being stereotyped negatively can lead to anxiety that diminishes task performance.[134] Stereotype threat occurs in situations where group identity is salient, one group is viewed as less competent, and others (e.g., co-workers) are suspected to be likely to use such stereotypes. Thus, women in male-dominated occupations, which are stereotyped as requiring masculine and not feminine traits, are at risk of not performing as well as they are capable because of stereotype threat.[135]

Individuals face difficulties when they try to change systems. Fortunately, organizations have an economic interest in fighting sex discrimination. First, they are underusing the available talent pool if they allow employees' and managers' unexamined biases to exclude or impede women. Second, potential lawsuits are expensive. Third, client bases are increasingly gender-balanced, and a gender-balanced workforce will better serve them.

Organizations cannot fight discrimination superficially. Workshops alone, though potentially useful for raising awareness and defining the norms of what is considered to be discriminatory or harassing, are insufficient. Rather, for sex discrimination to be diminished, more extensive steps are necessary. Organizations not only need to have nondiscrimination policies, but to enforce them. This means being willing to make structural changes in people's roles, incentives, and numbers. It also means taking the time to understand better the sources and subtleties of sex discrimination.

Notes

1 Deaux, K., & LaFrance, M. (1998). Gender. In D. T. Gilbert, S. T. Fiske, & G. Lindzey, (Eds.), *The handbook of social psychology* (4th ed., Vol. 2, pp. 788–827). New York: McGraw-Hill. Fiske, S. T. (1998). Stereotyping. prejudice, and discrimination. In D. T. Gilbert, S. T. Fiske, & G. Lindzey (Eds.), *The handbook of social psychology* (4th ed., Vol. 2, pp. 357–411). New York: McGraw-Hill.

2 Krieger, L. H. (2004). The intuitive psychologist behind the bench: Models of gender bias in social psychology and employment discrimination law. *Journal of Social Issues, 60,* 835–848.

3 Ross, L. (1977). The intuitive psychologist and his shortcomings: Distortions in the attribution process. In L. Berkowitz (Ed.). *Advances in experimental social psychology* (Vol. 10, pp. 174–221). New York: Academic Press. See also Krieger (2004) concerning how this applies to the courtroom.

4 Dovidio, J. F. (2001). On the nature of contemporary prejudice: The third wave. *Journal of Social Issues, 57,* 829–849.

5 Milgram, S. (1974). *Obedience to authority.* New York: Harper Perennial.

6 Cialdini, R. B., & Trost, M. R. (1998). Social influence: Social norms, conformity, and compliance. In D. T. Gilbert, S. T. Fiske, & G. Lindzey. *The handbook of social psychology* (4th ed., Vol. 2, pp. 151–192), New York: McGraw Hill.

7 Asch, S. E. (1955). Opinions and social pressure. *Scientific American,* 31–35.

8 Fiske (1998).

9 Ross, L., & Nisbett, R. E. (1991). *The person and the situation: Perspectives of social psychology.* New York: McGraw-Hill.

10 Milgram (1974).

11 Cialdini & Trost (1998).

12 Devine, P. G., Plant, E. A., Amodio, D. M., Harmon-Jones, E., & Vance, S. L. (2002). The regulation of explicit and implicit race bias: The role of motivations to respond without prejudice. *Journal of Personality and Social Psychology, 82,* 835–848.

13 Crandall, C. S., & Eshleman, A. (2003). A justification-suppression model of the expression and experience of prejudice. *Psychological Bulletin, 129,* 414–446.

14 Devine et al. (2002).

15 Czopp, A. M., & Monteith, M. J. (2003). Confronting prejudice (literally): Reactions to confrontations of racial and gender bias. *Personality and Social Psychology Bulletin, 29,* 532–544.

16 Swim, J. K., Hyers, L. L., Cohen, L. L., & Ferguson, M. J. (2001). Everyday sexism: Evidence for its incidence, nature and everyday impact from three daily diary studies. *Journal of Social Issues, 57,* 31–53.

17 Krieger (2004).

18 Nisbett, R. E., & Wilson, T. D. (1977). Telling more than we can know: Verbal reports on mental processes. *Psychological Review, 84*, 231–259. See also Wegner, D. M., & Bargh, J. A. (1998). Control and automaticity in social life. In D. T. Gilbert, S. T. Fiske, & G. Lindzey, *The handbook of social psychology* (4th ed., Vol 2, pp. 446–496). New York: McGraw Hill.

19 Devine, P. G. (1989). Stereotypes and prejudice: Their automatic and controlled components. *Journal of Personality and Social Psychology, 56*, 5–18.

20 Dovidio, J. F., Kawakami, K., & Gaertner, S. L. (2002). Implicit and explicit prejudice and interracial interaction. *Journal of Personality and Social Psychology, 82*, 62–68.

21 Poehlman, T. A., Uhlmann, E., Greenwald, A. G., & Banaji, M. R. (submitted). Understanding and using the Implicit Association Test: III. Meta-analysis of predictive validity.

22 Banaji, M. R., & Greenwald, A. G. (1995). Implicit gender stereotyping in judgments of fame. *Journal of Personality and Social Psychology, 68*, 181–198. See also Banaji, M. R., & Hardin, C. D. (1996). Automatic stereotyping. *Psychological Science, 7*, 136–141.

23 Rudman, L. A., & Glick, P. (2001). Prescriptive gender stereotypes and backlash toward agentic women. *Journal of Social Issues*, 57, 743–762.

24 Allport, G. W. (1954). *The nature of prejudice*. Reading, MA: Addison-Wesley. See also Fiske, S. T., Cuddy, A. J. C., Glick, P., & Xu, J. (2002). A model of (often mixed) stereotype content: Competence and warmth respectively follow from perceived status and competition. *Journal of Personality and Social Psychology, 82*, 878–902.

25 Reskin, I., & Padavic, B. (2002). *Women and men at work* (2nd ed.). Thousand Oaks, CA: Pine Forge Press.

26 Gaertner, S. L., & Dovidio, J. F. (1986). The aversive form of racism. In J. F. Dovidio, & S. L. Gaertner (Eds.). *Prejudice, discrimination, and racism* (pp. 61–89). San Diego: Academic Press.

27 Fiske et al. (2002).

28 Glick, P., & Fiske, S. T. (1996). The Ambivalent Sexism Inventory: Differentiating hostile and benevolent sexism. *Journal of Personality and Social Psychology, 70*, 491–512.

29 Eagly, A. H. (1987). *Sex differences in social behavior: A social role interpretation*. Hillsdale, NJ: Erlbaum.

30 Burgess, D., & Borgida, E. (1999). Who women are, who women should be: Descriptive and prescriptive gender stereotyping in sex discrimination. *Psychology, Public Policy, and Law, 5*, 665–692. See also Fiske, S. T., & Stevens, L. E. (1993). What's so special about sex? Gender stereotyping and discrimination. In S. Oskamp & M. Costanzo (Eds.), *Gender issues in contemporary society: Applied social psychology annual* (pp. 173–196). Newbury Park, CA: Sage.

31 Spence, J. T., & Helmreich, R. (1972). The Attitudes Toward Women Scale. *JSAS Catalog of Selected Documents in Psychology, 2*, ms. #153.

32   Spence, J. T., & Buckner, C. E. (2000). Instrumental and expressive traits, trait stereotypes, and sexist attitudes. *Psychology of Women Quarterly, 24,* 44–62.

33   Banaji & Hardin (1996). See also Blair, I. V., & Banaji, M. R. (1996). Automatic and controlled processes in stereotype priming. *Journal of Personality and Social Psychology, 70,* 1142–1163.

34   Heilman, M. E. (1983). Sex bias in work settings: The lack of fit model. *Research in Organizational Behavior, 5,* 269–298.

35   Ridgeway, C. L. (2001). Gender, status, and leadership. *Journal of Social Issues, 57*(4), 627–655.

36   Carli, L. L. (2001) Gender and social influence. *Journal of Social Issues, 57,* 725–741.

37   Eckes, T. (2002). Paternalistic and envious gender stereotypes: Testing predictions from the stereotype content model. *Sex Roles, 47,* 99–114. See also Six, B., & Eckes, T. (1991). A closer look at the complex structure of gender stereotypes. *Sex Roles, 24,* 57–71.

38   Glick, P., Fiske, S. T., et al. (2000). Beyond prejudice as simple antipathy: Hostile and benevolent sexism across cultures. *Journal of Personality and Social Psychology, 79,* 763–775.

39   Burgess & Borgida (1999).

40   Rudman, L. A., & Fairchild, K. (2004). Reactions to counterstereotypic behavior: The role of backlash in cultural stereotype maintenance. *Journal of Personality and Social Psychology, 87,* 157–176.

41   Gill, M. J. (2004). When information does not deter stereotyping: Prescriptive stereotypes foster bias under conditions that deter descriptive stereotyping. *Journal of Experimental Social Psychology, 40,* 619–632.

42   Eagly (1987).

43   Eagly, A. H., & Steffen, V. J. (1984). Gender stereotypes stem from the distribution of women and men into social roles. *Journal of Personality and Social Psychology, 46,* 735–754.

44   Hoffman, C., & Hurst, N. (1990). Gender stereotypes: Perception or rationalization? *Journal of Personality and Social Psychology, 58,* 197–208.

45   Eagly & Steffen (1984).

46   Conway, M., Pizzamiglio, M. T., & Mount, L. (1996). Status, communality, and agency: Implications for stereotypes of gender and other groups. *Journal of Personality and Social Psychology, 71,* 25–38.

47   Peeters, G. (2002). From good and bad to can and must: Subjective necessity of acts associated with positively and negatively valued stimuli. *European Journal of Social Psychology, 32,* 125–136.

48   Eagly (1987).

49   Rudman, L. A. (1998). Self-promotion as a risk factor for women: The costs and benefits of counterstereotypical impression management. *Journal of Personality and Social Psychology, 74,* 629–645; Rudman, L. A., & Glick, P. (1999). Feminized management and backlash toward agentic women: The hidden costs to women of a kinder, gentler image of

middle-managers. *Journal of Personality and Social Psychology*, 77, 1004–1010.

50 Glick & Fiske (1996).

51 Eagly, A. H., & Mladinic, A. (1993). Are people prejudiced against women? Some answers from research on attitudes, gender stereotypes, and judgments of competence. In W. Strobe, & M. Hewstone (Eds.) *European review of social psychology* (Vol. 5, pp. 1–35). New York: Wiley.

52 Peeters (2002). See also Wojciszke, B. (1994). Multiple meanings of behavior: Construing actions in terms of competence or morality. *Journal of Personality and Social Psychology*, 67, 222–232.

53 Glick, P., Diebold, J., Bailey-Werner, B., & Zhu, L. (1997). The two faces of Adam: Ambivalent sexism and polarized attitudes toward women. *Personality and Social Psychology Bulletin*, 23, 1323–1334.

54 Cuddy, A. J. C., Fiske, S. T., & Glick, P. (In press). The BIAS map: Behaviors from intergroup affect and stereotypes. *Journal of Personality and Social Psychology*.

55 Vescio, T. K., Gervais, S. J., Snyder, M., & Hoover, A. (2005). Power and the creation of patronizing environments: The stereotype-based behaviors of the powerful and their effects on female performance in masculine domains. *Journal of Personality and Social Psychology*, 88, 658–672.

56 Ridgeway (2001).

57 Rudman & Fairchild (2004).

58 Reskin & Padavic (2002).

59 Bargh, J. A., Chen, M., & Burrows, L. (1996). Automaticity of social behavior: Direct effects of trait construct and stereotype activation on action. *Journal of Personality and Social Psychology*, 71, 230–244.

60 Reskin & Padavic (2002).

61 Glick, P., Wilk, K., & Perreault, M. (1995). Images of occupations: Components of gender and status in occupational stereotypes. *Sex Roles*, 32, 564–582.

62 Reskin & Padavic (2002).

63 Pratto, F., Stallworth. L. M., Sidanius, J., & Siers, B. (1997). The gender gap in occupational role attainment: A social dominance approach. *Journal of Personality and Social Psychology*, 72, 37–53.

64 Heilman (1983). See also Glick, P. (1991). Trait-based and sex-based discrimination in occupational prestige, occupational salary, and hiring. *Sex Roles*, 25, 351–378.

65 Eagly, A. H., Makhijani, M. G., & Klonsky, B. G. (1992). Gender and evaluation of leaders: A meta-analysis. *Psychological Bulletin*, 111, 3–22. See also Eagly, A. H., & Karau, S. J. (2002). Role congruity theory of prejudice toward female leaders. *Psychological Review*, 109, 573–598.

66 Heilman, M. E. (1984). Information as a deterrent against sex discrimination: The effects of sex and information type on preliminary employment decisions. *Organizational Behavior and Human Performance*, 33, 174–186.

67 Glick et al. (1995).

68 Glick, P., Zion, C., & Nelson, C. (1988). What mediates sex discrimination in hiring decisions? *Journal of Personality and Social Psychology, 55,* 178–186.

69 Glick et al. (1995).

70 Davison, H. K., & Burke, M. J. (2000). Sex discrimination in simulated employment contexts: A meta-analytic investigation. *Journal of Vocational Behavior, 56,* 225–248.

71 Cejka, M. A., & Eagly, A. H. (1999). Gender-stereotypic images of occupations correspond to the sex segregation of employment. *Personality and Social Psychology Bulletin, 25,* 413–423.

72 Maume, D. J., Jr. (1999). Glass ceilings and glass escalators: Occupational segregation and race and sex differences in managerial promotions. *Work and Occupations, 26,* 483–509.

73 Ridgeway (2001). See also Rudman, L. A., & Kilianski, S. E. (2000). Implicit and explicit attitudes toward female authority. *Personality and Social Psychology Bulletin, 26,* 1315–1328.

74 Biernat, M., & Manis, M. (1994). Shifting standards and stereotype-based judgments. *Journal of Personality and Social Psychology, 66,* 5–20.

75 Biernat, M., & Vescio, T. K. (2002). She swings, she hits, she's great, she's benched: Implications of gender-based shifting standards for judgment and behavior. *Personality and Social Psychology Bulletin, 28,* 66–77.

76 Biernat, M., & Kobrynowicz, D. (1997). Gender- and race-based standards of competence: Lower minimum standards but higher ability standards for devalued groups. *Journal of Personality and Social Psychology, 72,* 544–557.

77 Uhlmann, E. L., & Cohen, G. L. (2005). Constructed criteria: Redefining merit to justify discrimination. *Psychological Science, 16,* 474–480.

78 Uhlmann & Cohen (2005).

79 Norton, M. I., Vandello, J. A., & Darley, J. M. (2004). Casuistry and social category bias. *Journal of Personality and Social Psychology, 87,* 817–831.

80 Locksley, A., Borgida, E., Brekke, N., & Hepburn, C. (1980). Sex stereotypes and social judgment. *Journal of Personality and Social Psychology, 39,* 821–831.

81 Nieva, V. F., & Gutek, B. A. (1981). *Women and work: A psychological perspective.* New York: Praeger.

82 Kanter, R. M. (1977). *Men and women of the corporation.* New York: Basic Books. See also Eckes (2002).

83 Ridgeway (2001).

84 Walton, M. D., Sachs, D., Ellington, R., Hazlewood, A., Griffin, S., & Bass, D. (1988). Physical stigma and the pregnancy role: Receiving help from strangers. *Sex Roles, 18,* 323–331. See also Wolkind, S., & Zajicek, E. (Eds.). (1981). *Pregnancy: A psychological and social study.* New York: Grune & Stratton.

85 Cuddy, A. J. C., Fiske, S. T., & Glick, P. (2004). When professionals become mothers, warmth doesn't cut the ice. *Journal of Social Issues, 60*(4), 701–718.

86 Crosby, F. J., Williams, J., & Biernat, M. (2004). The maternal wall. *Journal of Social Issues, 60,* 675–682.

87 Halpert, J. A., & Burg, J. H., (1997). Mixed messages: Co-worker responses to the pregnant employee. *Journal of Business and Psychology, 12,* 241–253.

88 Hebl, M. R., King, E., Glick, P., Singletary, S. L., & Kazama, S. M. (Accepted pending revisions). Hostile and benevolent discrimination toward pregnant women: Complementary interpersonal punishments and rewards that maintain traditional roles. *Journal of Applied Psychology.*

89 Frieze, I. H., Olson, J. E., & Russell, J. (1991). Attractiveness and income for men and women in management. *Journal of Applied Social Psychology, 21,* 1039–1057.

90 Eagly, A. H., Ashmore, R. D., Makhijani, M. G., & Longo, L. C. (1991). What is beautiful is good, but . . . A meta-analytic review of research on the physical attractiveness stereotype. *Psychological Bulletin, 110,* 109–128. See also Langlois, J. H., Kalakanis, L., Rubenstein, A. J., Larson, A., Hallam, M., & Smoot, M. (2000). Maxims or myths of beauty: A meta-analysis and theoretical review. *Psychological Bulletin, 26,* 390–423.

91 Heilman, M. E., & Stopek, M. H. (1985). Being attractive, advantage or disadvantage? Performance-based evaluations and recommended personnel actions as a function of appearance, sex, and job type. *Organizational Behavior and Human Decision Processes, 35,* 202–215.

92 Rudman, L. A., & Borgida, E. (1995). The afterglow of construct accessibility: The behavioral consequences of priming men to view women as sexual objects. *Journal of Experimental Social Psychology, 6,* 493–517.

93 Goodwin, S. A., Fiske, S. T., Rosen, L. D., & Rosenthal, A. M. (2002). The eye of the beholder: Romantic goals and impression biases. *Journal of Experimental Social Psychology, 38,* 232–241.

94 Six & Eckes (1991).

95 Glick, P., Larsen, S., Johnson, C., & Branstiter, H. (2005). Evaluations of sexy women in low and high status jobs. *Psychology of Women Quarterly, 29,* 389–395.

96 Rudman (1998).

97 Sinclair, L., & Kunda, Z. (2000). Motivated stereotyping of women: She's fine if she praised me but incompetent if she criticized me. *Personality and Social Psychology Bulletin, 26,* 1329–1342.

98 Rudman & Glick (1999).

99 Gutek, B. A. (1985). *Sex and the workplace: The impact of sexual behavior and harassment on women, men, and organizations.* San Francisco: Jossey-Bass. See also Pryor, J. B, Giedd, J. L., & Williams, K. B. (1995). A social

psychological model for predicting sexual harassment. *Journal of Social Issues, 51*, 69–84.

100 Stockdale, M. S., Visio, M., & Batra, L. (1999). The sexual harassment of men: Evidence for a broader theory of sexual harassment and sex discrimination. *Psychology, Public Policy, and Law, 5*, 630–664.

101 Stockdale et al. (1999). See also Fiske, S. T. & Glick, P. (1995). Ambivalence and stereotypes cause sexual harassment: A theory with implications for organizational change. *Journal of Social Issues, 51*, 97–115.

102 Gutek (1985).

103 Stockdale et al. (1999).

104 Franke, K. M. (1997). What's wrong with sexual harassment? *Stanford Law Review, 49*, 691–772. See also Maass, A., Cadinu, M., Guarnieri, G., & Grasselli, A. (2003). Sexual harassment under social identity threat: The computer harassment paradigm. *Journal of Personality and Social Psychology, 85*, 853–870.

105 Rudman & Fairchild (2004).

106 Rudman & Borgida (1995). See also McKenzie-Mohr, D., & Zanna, M. P. (1990). Treating women as sexual objects: Look to the (gender schematic) male who has viewed pornography. *Personality and Social Psychology Bulletin, 16*, 296–308.

107 Gutek (1985).

108 Galinsky, A. D., Gruenfeld, D. H., & Magee, J. C. (2003). From power to action. *Journal of Personality and Social Psychology, 85*, 453–466.

109 Bargh, J. A., & Raymond, P. (1995). The naïve misuse of power: Nonconscious sources of sexual harassment. *Journal of Social Issues, 51*, 85–96.

110 Rudman & Borgida (1995).

111 Pryor, J. B., LaVite, C., & Stoller, L. (1993). A social psychological analysis of sexual harassment: The person/situation interaction. *Journal of Vocational Behavior, 42*, 68–83.

112 Gutek (1985).

113 Tajfel, H. (1981). *Social identity and intergroup relations*. Cambridge: Cambridge University Press. See also Maass et al. (2003).

114 Latanè, B. (1981). The psychology of social impact. *American Psychologist, 36*, 343–356.

115 Fiske, S. T., Bersoff, D. N., Borgida, E., Deaux, K., & Heilman, M. E. (1991). Social science research on trial: Use of sex stereotyping research in Price Waterhouse v. Hopkins. *American Psychologist, 46*, 1049–1060.

116 Gutek (1985). Nieva & Gutek (1981).

117 Kanter (1977).

118 Taylor, S. E. (1981). A categorization approach to stereotyping. In D. L. Hamilton (Ed.), *Cognitive processes in stereotyping and intergroup behavior* (pp. 83–114). Mahwah, NJ: Erlbaum.

119 Mullen, B. (1983). Operationalizing the effect of the group on the individual: A self-attention perspective. *Journal of Experimental Social Psychology, 19*, 295–322.

120   Lord, C. G., Saenz, D. S., & Godfrey, D. K. (1987). Effects of perceived scrutiny on participant memory for social interactions. *Journal of Experimental Social Psychology, 23,* 498–517.

121   Fiske, S. T., & Ruscher, J. B. (1993). Negative interdependence and prejudice: Whence the affect? In D. M. Mackie, & D. L. Hamilton (Eds.), *Affect, cognition, and stereotyping: Interactive processes in group perception* (pp. 239–268). San Diego CA: Academic Press.

122   Borgida, E., Rudman, L. A., & Manteufel, L. L. (1995). On the courtroom use and misuse of gender stereotyping research. *Journal of Social Issues, 51,* 181–192. Fiske, S. T., & Neuberg, S. L. (1990). A continuum of impression formation, from category-based to individuating processes: Influences of information and motivation on attention and interpretation. In M. P. Zanna (Ed.), *Advances in experimental social psychology* (Vol. 23, pp 1–74). New York: Academic Press.

123   Tversky, A., & Kahneman, D. (1974). Judgment under uncertainty: Heuristics and biases. *Science, 185,* 1124–1131.

124   Fiske, S. T. (2000). Interdependence and the reduction of prejudice. In S. Oskamp (Ed.) *Reducing prejudice and discrimination* (pp. 115–135). Mahwah, NJ: Erlbaum.

125   Fiske, S. T. (1993). Controlling other people: The impact of power on stereotyping. *American Psychologist, 48,* 621–628.

126   Major, B., & Vick, S. B. (2005). The psychological impact of prejudice. In J. F. Dovidio, P. Glick, & L. A. Rudman (Eds.). *On the nature of prejudice: Fifty years after Allport* (pp. 244–261). Malden, MA: Blackwell.

127   Sechrist, G. B., Swim, J. K., & Stangor, C. (2004). When do the stigmatized make attributions to discrimination occurring to the self and others: The roles of self-presentation and need for control. *Journal of Personality and Social Psychology, 87,* 111–122. See also Kaiser, C. R., & Miller, C. T. (2001b). Stop complaining! The social costs of making attributions to discrimination. *Personality and Social Psychology Bulletin, 27,* 254–263. Kaiser, C. R., & Miller, C. T. (2003). Derogating the victim: The interpersonal consequences of blaming events on discrimination. *Group Processes and Intergroup Relations, 6,* 227–237.

128   Fitzgerald, L. F. (1993). Sexual harassment: Violence against women in the workplace. *American Psychologist, 48,* 1070–1076.

129   Vescio et al. (2005).

130   Dansky, B. S., & Kilpatrick, D. G. (1997). Effects of sexual harassment. In W. O'Donohue (Ed.), *Sexual harassment: Theory, research, and treatment* (pp. 152–174). Needham Heights, MA: Allyn & Bacon.

131   Woodzicka, J., & LaFrance, M. (2001). Real versus imagined gender harassment. *Journal of Social Issues, 57,* 15–30.

132   Fitzgerald, L. F., Swan, S., & Fischer, K. (1995). Why didn't she just report him? The psychological and legal implications of women's responses to sexual harassment. *Journal of Social Issues, 51,* 117–138. See

also Munson, L. J., Miner, A. G., & Hulin, C. (2001). Labeling sexual harassment in the military: An extension and replication. *Journal of Applied Psychology, 86,* 293–303.

133 Bergman, M. E., Langhout, R. D., Palmieri, P. A., Cortina, L. M., & Fitzgerald, L. F. (2002). The (un)reasonableness of reporting: Antecedents and consequences of reporting sexual harassment. *Journal of Applied Psychology, 87,* 230–242.

134 Schmader, T., & Johns, M. (2003). Converging evidence that stereotype threat reduces working memory capacity. *Journal of Personality and Social Psychology, 85,* 440–452.

135 Steele, C. M., Spencer, S. J., & Aronson, J. (2002). Contending with group image: The psychology of stereotype and social identity threat. In M. P. Zanna (Ed.), *Advances in experimental social psychology* (Vol. 34, pp. 379–440). San Diego, CA: Academic Press.

13

Sociological Approaches to Sex Discrimination in Employment

Cecilia L. Ridgeway and Paula England

Sociologists who study sex discrimination focus on two questions. First, we ask about the extent of gender disparities in employment, and particularly in pay and authority, sometimes tracking changes over time and location. Second, we focus on finding the causes for inequalities between men's and women's work and especially for the inequalities in rewards reaped from work.

In the present chapter, we review sociological approaches to sex discrimination. After a brief section on definitions, we present a general overview of contemporary patterns of gender inequality in employment in the United States. This overview helps to delineate the contexts in which sex discrimination might plausibly play a role in the inequalities we see. We then turn to a consideration of the causes of sex discrimination in the workplace. Two general types of causes are important. Primary causes of discrimination begin at the interpersonal level of individuals in the workplace and involve people's expectancies and in-group networking. Secondary causes of discrimination occur at the institutional level of the employment organization and involve organizational arrangements and procedures that have a discriminatory impact on workers due to their sex. As we shall see, the two types of causes are related because interpersonal expectancies and in-group networking play a role in the development of discriminatory organizational practices. Finally, we note the importance of other organizational practices that, while not directly discriminatory themselves, nevertheless can augment or diminish the effects of interpersonal expectancies and networks.

Definitions

Not all inequalities qualify as discrimination. Borrowing terms from economists, sociologists often classify causes of employment inequality as occurring on the "supply" side or the "demand" side of the labor market process. The supply side of labor markets refers to characteristics of those supplying their labor. Gender differences in interests in, preparation for, and willingness to participate in various jobs are supply-side explanations of inequality.

In contrast to the supply side is the demand side, which is the behavior of employers. When sociologists use the term "discrimination" we generally refer to employers' behavior, which is on the demand side of labor markets. Employment discrimination occurs when employers treat women and men differently because of their sex or when employers have policies that affect one sex adversely relative to the other.[1] If employers treat men and women differently in response to the gender biases of co-workers and customers rather than in response to their own biases, the differential treatment is still seen as discrimination. As sociologists use the term, then, sex discrimination in employment covers events that occur in the workplace or in the immediate process of getting a job rather than in the more extended path that leads men and women to the workplace. Sex discrimination can come about through the direct actions of employers and others in the workplace as well as through the indirect effects of institutionalized procedures and arrangements in the employment organization.

Sociologists are careful to note that some demand-side factors influence gender disparities, but not through the working of discrimination. For example, the decline of manufacturing jobs has hurt men's more than women's earnings, because more men than women worked in such jobs. This has contributed to the erosion of the sex gap in pay, but through a process other than a decline in discrimination.

Sociologists also note that many supply-side processes are shaped by biases embedded in cultural beliefs about gender. For instance, like the psychologist Eccles,[2] the sociologist Correll[3] has shown that the widely held cultural belief that males are better at math than females leads women to attribute less math ability to themselves than men do even when they have exactly the same test scores and grades. She shows that how much ability students attribute to themselves, in turn, shapes their willingness to take more courses in the area and to pursue a science and engineering major in college. Although shaped by cultural assumptions, supply-side processes are not classified as discrimination.

Demand-side patterns of behavior suggest three types of sex discrimination that might logically occur, each operating in a slightly different context.[4] *Within job discrimination* is unequal treatment on the basis of the sex of the workers with the same job title and rank. This is the classic case of unequal pay for equal work in the same job. *Valuative discrimination* refers to unequal treatment of men's jobs and women's jobs in terms of the wages and authority associated with them independent of the education, experience, and specialized skill levels that they require. The "devaluation" of women's jobs at issue here is the focus of calls for comparable worth policies designed to pay similarly skilled jobs comparably. Finally, *allocative discrimination* is sex discrimination in hiring, job assignment, promotion, and dismissal.

Allocative and valuative discrimination are related. Allocative discrimination leads to inequality in men's and women's wages and authority even if no valuative discrimination occurs. But if valuative discrimination does exist, such that predominantly female jobs are paid less than male jobs requiring the same amount of education, then the gender gap in pay and authority widens.[5]

Allocative discrimination, which keeps women (or men) out of certain jobs, may involve "error" or "statistical" discrimination. Error discrimination occurs when employers, perhaps on the basis of gender stereotypes, incorrectly assume that men and women, on average, differ in their ability to be productive at a certain type of work and hire accordingly when choosing between men and women with similar resumes.[6] Statistical discrimination occurs when there really are differences, on average, in the skills or productivity of men and women for a particular type of job. Knowing these average differences, employers engage in statistical discrimination when they use sex as an inexpensive substitute for actual, specific information about the particular job candidate's likely productivity, and, say, hire the man over the woman with a similar resume. This behavior is discriminatory if the actual individual woman would be as good or better on the job than the particular man hired, but it is resistant to the leveling forces of the market because on average, over lots of hires, the employer is right more often than wrong in his or her hiring decisions since they are based on correctly perceived average gender differences. (Of course, the gender differences in skills themselves may have been generated by past regimes of discrimination.)[7]

The Gendered Structure of Employment

In the past several decades, women have moved rapidly into the paid labor force. Only 33% of women were in the labor force in 1950, but the figure grew to 49% by 1970, and 74% by 1990. It remained 74% in 2000. By comparison, 94% of men were in the labor force in 1950, and the percentage dropped to 86% in 2000.[8] Thus, women's experience is converging with men, although there has been a slow-down since 1990. Over this same time period, women have also increasingly pursued college education and now receive more than half of bachelor's degrees.[9]

Despite these important changes, substantial inequality in employment persists. Although the gender gap in wages has narrowed in recent decades, women's wages for full-time, year-round work were still only 77% of men's in 2005.[10] Furthermore, there is also a gender gap in authority in the workplace. Women are less likely to be in managerial or supervisory positions in the workplace and when they are, the positions they are in carry less power and authority than those of men.[11] Women hold only 8% of top-level executive positions in Fortune 500 companies.

Perhaps the most striking gender disparity in the contemporary world of paid work is the sex segregation of occupations. An occupation is sex segregated when it is disproportionately occupied by one sex or the other. Nurses, for instance, are overwhelmingly women; engineers are overwhelmingly men. The striking point is that most people work in jobs or occupations that are filled predominately with members of their own sex.[12] Sometimes an occupation as a whole, for instance, physician, contains a mix of men and women; but the men and women are nevertheless located in sex segregated specialties within the occupation, such as pediatrician versus surgeon.[13] In order to eliminate the present level of occupational sex segregation, about half of all women in the workforce would have to change occupations.[14] If we use more detailed occupational categories, or specific jobs within firms, the figure is much higher. In 1960, to achieve gender integration, 62% of women or men would have had to change occupations. While occupational sex segregation has declined, mainly through women entering predominantly male or mixed fields, the decline slowed in the 1990s.[15] Segregation has decreased more slowly than either the gender gap in participation in the labor force or in college education.[16]

The sex segregation of jobs and occupations not only means that men and women have rather different experiences in the workplace. It also provides the framework within which much of the gender inequality in wages and authority occurs. Studies have shown that wage differences between men and women in exactly the same job title and rank account for only a small proportion of the overall gender gap in wages.[17] Most of the wage gap is due to the fact that jobs that are predominantly occupied by women pay less than jobs primarily filled by men. Studies show that this is true even when the female-dominated jobs require as much education and skill as the male jobs, and the incumbents of the two types of jobs are matched on education and experience.[18] The greater the percentage of women in a job, the lower its relative wages, net of skill demands. These are the findings that have raised the "comparable worth" debate in which arguments are made that wages should be adjusted to pay similarly demanding jobs similarly regardless of sex composition.[19]

The sex segregation of jobs and occupations also plays a role in the authority gap between men and women workers. Although employers have a tendency to match the sex (and the race) of supervisors to that of subordinates, jobs filled largely by women are less likely to be on the ladder to middle or top management.[20] In most organizations, for instance, the human relations department is predominantly female, while the finance department is predominantly male; and it is usually more difficult to progress from director of human relations to CEO than it is to progress to CEO from director of finance.

Primary Causes of Sex Discrimination in Employment

The world of paid employment is enacted through multiple, repeating interpersonal contacts among job seekers, employers, employees, co-workers, clients and customers, and so on carried out in varying institutional situations. From examinations of how the world of work is actually carried out, sociologists have generally come to see that the primary causes of sex discrimination in employment lie in widely shared cultural beliefs about men, women and their appropriate relation to one another.[21] People's implicit, taken-for-granted beliefs about "who" men and women "are" – what their typical traits are and how they are likely to behave – exert a powerful effect on the American workplace. Old-fashioned sexist beliefs have given way to espoused egalitarianism,[22] but Americans continue in their widespread knowledge of and agreement about what to expect from the typical man and the typical woman.[23] Even when people do not fully endorse gender stereotypes, they are likely to be both aware of them and unconsciously influenced by them.[24]

If widely shared gender stereotypes tell us what most people expect, then they also tell us how others are likely to judge us. Widely shared gender stereotypes tell us the "rules of the game" of gender in our society.[25] At some level, people reckon with the costs they may encounter for violating the rules.

Cultural beliefs about gender are linked to the workplace through the everyday process of *sex categorization*.[26] Psychologists have shown that we cannot consider ourselves in relation to another, concrete person – be it in person, on paper, on a cell phone, or over the internet – without first sex categorizing that other (and, by implication, ourselves) as male or female.[27] Although we tend to think of sex categorization as "natural," it is worth keeping in mind that in everyday workplace relations, sex categorization is a thoroughly social process that relies on cues of behavior and appearance that are culturally presumed to stand for physical sex differences.[28]

Everyday sex categorization of actors in the workplace, from job applicants to co-workers to managers, sets in motion two processes that create the underlying conditions for sex discrimination. First, sex categorization of another or of the self automatically and unconsciously activates gender stereotypes that affect judgments and behavior. Second, sex categorization of self and others as men and women rather than just workers makes sex a salient basis for in-group and out-group dynamics in the workplace. How stereotyping and in-group bias play out in any given situation, however, depends importantly on workplace context. Understanding the basic mechanisms of both stereotyping and in-group bias as well as how they vary by context limitations has been a concern for sociologists studying gender and the workplace.

Stereotypes and gender status beliefs

Examining how gender affects interpersonal relations in the workplace and elsewhere has been a particular focus of the sociological theory known as "expectation states theory."[29] The theory argues that like race, education, occupation, and a number of other attributes, sex is a status characteristic in society because widely shared gender stereotypes contain not merely beliefs about gender difference, but beliefs about status as well. Gender status beliefs associate greater worthiness and overall competence with men and link men to more

respected specialized skills like instrumental competence while women are associated with less respected communal skills.[30] Although automatic sex categorization makes gender stereotypes available to people in virtually all work
contexts, expectation states theory argues that the status and competence implications of these stereotypes are only effectively salient (i.e., sufficiently salient
to measurably affect behavior and judgments) when a workplace setting has
both men and women in it or is known to require the skills that are culturally
linked to a particular sex.

Expectation states theory argues that in any workplace setting, roles (e.g.,
supervisor, assistant) and salient characteristics of actors (e.g., gender, race,
education) provoke cultural assumptions about status and competence which,
in turn, influence judgments and behaviors. Expectation states theory argues
that people combine the positive and negative status and competence implications of each salient characteristic of an actor, weighted by their relevance to
the task at hand, to form an aggregate expectation for the actor's performance
and suitability for authority compared to another. In the process, roles and identities closely linked to the workplace, like boss and employee, have the most
powerful impact on performance and competence expectations, but other characteristics like gender and race also influence actions and reactions. Specifically,
when people work together in task-oriented settings like the workplace and
gender stereotypes become effectively salient, these gender status and competence beliefs shape expectations for men's and women's performance. The more
gender-typed the setting or the more uncertain the criteria for evaluating competence, the more powerful the impact of gender status beliefs on people's
expectations about performance.

Expectations for performance are important because they bias judgments of
actual competence by making the same accomplishment seem "better" and to
be a stronger sign of genuine ability when coming from a person of the expected
rather than the unexpected sex. Not only do gender status beliefs bias performance expectations, they also make men seem like more legitimate candidates
for authority than similar women.[31]

Employers and others involved in the hiring, salary setting, task assignment,
and promotion processes play a key role in deciding which workers end up
where in the work organization and with what pay and opportunities for promotion. As employers read resumes and interview applicants, routine sex categorization of job seekers is likely to prime gender stereotypes, and in many
situations the mixed-sex or gendered task nature of the context will make gender
status and competence beliefs implicitly salient for the employers. Other things
being equal, the implicit but salient gender beliefs will make male applicants
seem slightly better suited to male-typed and gender-neutral jobs and to positions of authority and women slightly more able for female-typed jobs and jobs
of lesser authority. The size and impact on actual hiring and assignment will
depend on contextual factors that suppress or enhance these implicit cognitive
biases among those making the decisions and consequently vary greatly from
one organization to the next.

Reskin and Roos[32] have studied a series of jobs that increased in female workers by at least 10 percentage points during the 1970s. The patterns of changes that Reskin and Roos found suggested to them that employers implicitly rank workers in a gendered queue in which men are preferred over women, but in which employers turn to women when qualified men become unavailable. The better the job, the stronger the preference for men over women.

Subsequent studies of sex segregation in the contemporary occupational structure have prompted some modifications in the conclusions of Reskin and Roos. According to Charles and Grusky,[33] who have examined the sex composition of occupations in a number of affluent nations, employer biases are more likely to be for men for jobs associated with masculine skills (which include manual jobs), for women for jobs associated with feminine skills (which include many service jobs), and for men for top jobs in any occupational area. Note that this pattern is just what we would expect if gender stereotypes were subtly biasing employer hiring in the manner described by expectation states theory.

More direct evidence that stereotype biases are sometimes at work in hiring and promotion processes comes from recent studies. Fernandez and Sosa[34] compared the applicant pool for telephone customer service jobs at a large bank to those eventually hired. Despite hiring managers' explicit statements that they had no gender preference for the job, they hired a disproportionate number of women and this was related to their image of the job as requiring stereotypically feminine emotional skills as well as to uncertainty in the criteria for judging applicants' actual abilities for the job.

In a study of large U.S. legal firms, Gorman,[35] as well, compared the characteristics that firms listed for the ideal job applicant with the proportion of women they eventually hired, controlling for the potential pool of women applicants and other factors. She found that the greater the number of stereotypically masculine characteristics the firm used to describe what they were looking for, the lower the proportion of women they hired. The greater the number of stereotypically feminine characteristics listed, the greater the proportion of women hired at the entry level but not at higher levels. Gorman's results suggest that employers prefer men for male-typed jobs and women for female-typed, lower-level jobs. However, women are seen as less appropriate for higher-status positions regardless of the gender typing of the job description. These findings are consistent with what we would predict on the basis of expectation states theory.

In a second study, Gorman[36] examined gender differences in promotions in the same large law firms. Consistent with expectation states theory and other accounts of stereotype bias, she found that the greater the uncertainty involved in judging performance and ability for the professional or managerial job at stake, the more likely the promotion was to go to a man rather than a woman.

Expectation states theory suggests that widely shared stereotypes about men's greater status, overall competence, and about each sex's specialized skills, acting in the workplace, may not only bias employers' preferences. They may also facilitate or undermine men and women's actual performance, independent of their skills, at tasks for which they are expected to do better or worse based on their gender. The expectations people form for one person's performance in a situation compared to another's often have self-fulfilling effects on behavior. Recognizing that others expect you to perform poorly can arouse distracting anxiety that makes it difficult to perform your best. Positive expectations for your success, on the other hand can boost confidence and improve performance, much like a home team advantage.[37]

To the extent that gender biased performance expectations do modify employees' actual workplace performances, they create the basis for what we described earlier as statistical discrimination. Statistical discrimination by employers is most likely to occur in hiring since, at promotion, more detailed information about the candidate's performance capacity is usually available. However, small biases at the entry level to large firms can have accumulating long-term effects on employees because such firms often fill higher-level jobs with those who are already working for the firm.

All the above predictions of expectation states theory turn on the fact that the cultural beliefs about status and competence embedded in gender stereotypes provide workplace actors with implicit assumptions about men and women's relative capacity to perform well at various workplace tasks. Logically, the capacity to perform well at a task involves not only ability, but effort. In recent years, as women have entered many jobs, there is some evidence that stereotypes may be shifting to reflect a narrowing of the gender gap in presumed overall competence.[38] If the gender gap in presumed overall competence continues to narrow, sex discrimination in employment may increasingly turn on stereotypic assumptions about women's relative commitment to paid employment and the effort they are therefore expected to put into their job.

Women in the United States are seen as more expressive and communal than men while men are seen as more agentic and instrumental.[39] Gender stereotypes about women's communal nature imply that they will be more committed to relationships than men and, in mainstream U.S. culture, this is often seen to imply putting family first, over paid work. There is little evidence that women who work are actually any less committed or hardworking on the job than men in similar work situations,[40] but stereotypic assumptions may still create unconscious biases about how much effort women put into their paid jobs.

The tension between assumptions concerning women's communal skills, on the one hand, and, on the other, their commitment to work plays out most dramatically with mothers. Contemporary ideas that mothers should "always be there" for their children clash with similar ideas that the ideal worker is devoted to and ever available for work.[41] Ridgeway and Correll[42] argue that this clash causes motherhood to be seen as an additional, gender-related status characteristic that is even more relevant to their work performance than simply being female rather than male. Motherhood, in other words, has a more powerful impact on expectations for performance and competence in the workplace than does sex alone. Except in work settings associated with nurturance skills (e.g., elementary teacher), mothers will be disadvantaged not only relative to men but also relative to women who are not mothers. In support of Ridgeway and Correll's argument, experiments have shown that just adding "parent" to a woman's job application produces a drop in ratings of competence, commitment, and likelihood to be promoted. Mothers are recommended for hiring less often than non-mothers and are offered a significantly lower starting salary. Interestingly, adding parent to a man's application causes him to be recommended more often for hire and to be offered a higher starting salary than a similar non-father, presumably because fathers are culturally seen as hardworking "providers" rather than the one who must always be there for their children.[43] Such implicit bias against mothers may well contribute to the 5 percent wage penalty per child that employed mothers in the US suffer on average compared to non-mothers even after controlling for other factors that affect wages.[44] Because the great majority of women are mothers at some point in their lives, discrimination against mothers in wages and promotion represents a major obstacle to gender equality in the workplace.

In-group biases

People's routine sex categorization of one another in the workplace not only primes gender stereotypes, it also sets in motion in-group–out-group, "us" and "them" dynamics. Salient group distinctions prime people's unconscious cognitive bias to favor their own group.[45] Sex discrimination can come about simply by one sex acting preferentially toward "people like us" with no actual intention to treat the other sex negatively. This is the sort of sex discrimination that in-group biases potentially give rise to, although, again, the extent to which they do so depends importantly on the context.

Rosabeth Kanter[46] has described how in-group biases can play out in the workplace to create a process that she called "homosocial reproduction" in which those in power preferentially promote people like themselves. The inherent uncertainty of management causes authorities to look for subordinates they can trust and "count on" to sponsor for promotions, Kanter argues. According to Kanter, the extent to which sex (or race) determines whom those in power consider to be "like them" and therefore trustworthy depends on the sex (or race) ratio in the organization. When one sex is a distinct minority (under 15%) in the workplace, they have heightened visibility. With heightened visibility, sex is likely to become a significant basis of in-group–out-group dynamics. The visibility of those in the minority also subjects them to stereotyping by the majority and increased performance pressure which may undermine their actual performance.[47]

Meanwhile the visibility of the minority heightens the boundary between the sexes for the majority too, so that the majority sex begins thinking of itself more as a group. With sex a more salient part of their workplace identity, majority members may begin to introduce gendered jokes, interests, and comments into their behavior on the job so a gendered workplace culture begins to emerge among the majority. This gendered culture further isolates those in the minority and makes it even harder for them to be recognized as competent and trustworthy. In the end, it is members of the majority sex that are promoted while those in the minority are trapped in lower-level, lesser-paying positions. The key to minimizing sex-based in-group–out-group dynamics, says Kanter, lies in achieving gender balance in the workplace.

Kanter's description of the development of in-group–out-group dynamics and "homosocial reproduction" has been generally supported by studies of women in male-dominated occupations.[48] For example, Gorman found evidence of in-group bias in her studies of law firms. When the law partner in charge of hiring was a woman, more women were hired. When the law partner in charge of hiring was a man, fewer women were hired. In-group bias in hiring and promotion was especially prevalent in firms with great gender imbalance among their high-ranking members and for jobs in which the criteria for judging performance were more uncertain.

Subsequent research has suggested some revisions to Kanter's underlying argument. Kanter casts her analysis as only a problem of numbers, but later studies have challenged this. What matters is the salience of sex as a group distinction in the workplace. One sex being in a numerical minority does increase the salience of sex[49] but so can other factors such as doing work that is gender-typed for the other sex.[50] Thus, achieving gender balance in the workplace may not always be sufficient to suppress in-group biases based on sex.

Also, and importantly, the effects Kanter describes depend heavily on the status of the minority group.[51] They hold for women in male-dominated occupations, but not for men in female occupations. Evidence suggests that the greater status and cultural appropriateness for authority associated with men actually advantages them compared to women in occupations like nursing and librarian so that, rather than being undermined by heightened visibility, men are sometimes helped by it to rise to the top.[52] Men in women's occupations may, like women in men's occupations, experience a gendered workplace culture dominated by the other sex (e.g., a "girls' club" rather than a "boys' club"), but while this may occasionally isolate them, it does not hold them back.[53] In fact, stereotypic assumptions about their appropriateness for authority may propel them upward on what Williams[54] calls a "glass escalator." Once again, we see how important context is for whether underlying causes of gender bias in employment actually result in sex discrimination.

In-group biases not only affect which job candidates are hired or promoted, they also affect the processes by which employers recruit people to apply for jobs and job seekers learn about jobs for which they can apply. In either process, networks of interpersonal contacts are often involved in addition to more formal procedures such as publication of job advertisements.

Because people are more likely to form ties with similar others, and automatic sex categorization makes sex a salient basis for similarity, most people's social networks overrepresent members of their own sex compared to the pool of possible contacts around them.[55] Because men are more likely than women to be in decision-making positions in regard to hiring and promotion, furthermore, to the extent that decision makers rely on their own informal networks to recruit candidates, they are likely to hire or promote men rather than women. As Reskin and McBrier[56] point out, decision makers often feel the people they know are more trustworthy and competent than candidates from outside their networks. Furthermore, in the more informal process of recruiting though network, stereotypic beliefs about men's greater status, competence, and appropriateness for authority have greater latitude to unconsciously bias decisions than in a standardized recruitment procedure that solicits job applicants more systematically. Consistent with both of these processes, Reskin and McBrier's[57] study of the employment of managers in a national sample of work organizations found that the more decision makers relied on informal networks to recruit managers, the fewer women were placed into those positions.

Sometimes decision makers in organizations do not recruit through their own networks, but through their employees' networks. But this does not guarantee that in-group biases are abated because employees' networks tend to be biased toward their own group as well, which affects who receives leads about which jobs. Given that men are more likely to be in better-paying jobs with more authority, relying on employee networks to recruit is likely to perpetuate gender inequalities in earning and authority and to maintain the sex segregation of jobs.[58]

Studies of how job seekers pass job leads among their networks, however, suggest that the biased transmission of job information is not simply a result of sex segregated networks and in-group biases. As with Kanter's processes of homosocial reproduction, stereotypic beliefs about gender status and competence also appear to be at work. Huffman and Torres[59] found that the sex composition of their networks did not affect their access to job leads or to the quality of those job leads. For women, however, access to high-quality job leads increased with the number of men in their networks. These data suggest that men are more likely to have information on good jobs and both men and women are more likely to pass the high-quality job leads they have on to men rather than women. Consequently, for women to gain access to these high-quality leads they need more men in their networks than men do.

Secondary Institutional Causes of Sex Discrimination in Employment

It is possible to distinguish between what we are calling "primary causes of sex discrimination" and what we are calling "secondary causes." The primary causes of sex discrimination in employment occur in the behaviors and judgments of individuals in organizations, behaviors and judgments that are often driven by widely shared cultural beliefs about gender. Supplementing the primary, interpersonal sources of employment discrimination are secondary causes. Secondary causes include institutional structures and practices.

Organizational rules, structures, and cultural practices govern much of what happens between individuals in the workplace. These institutional arrangements and procedures themselves become instruments of discrimination when they implicitly embody or presume stereotypic assumptions about men and women in such a way that they have an adverse impact on workers due to their sex. Such organizational practices act as independent causes of discrimination because they constrain even individuals in the workplace who are personally unbiased to act in a discriminatory fashion.

Organizational practices that have an adverse impact on women often appear on their face to be unbiased and neutral despite implicitly presuming gender stereotypic assumptions. A classic example is the practice of employers giving extra credit to veterans in hiring. This is discriminatory because women were barred from major military service for many years and because veteran status is not clearly related to an employee's productivity or work performance. Although not necessarily intended to discriminate against women, preferences for veterans were devised by decision makers with an implicitly gendered image of workers they wished to assist, an image of a (male) veteran. As they devised the procedure, the decision makers unintentionally wrote into the procedure cultural assumptions about status and deservingness based on a culturally masculine activity, military service. Once embodied in an organizational practice, the practice itself becomes an agent of stereotypic treatment of men and women independent of the biases of the individual actors who carry out the practice.

As this example shows, discriminatory organizational arrangements and procedures have often developed because the decision makers who devised them at a particular historical period were themselves affected by the primary causes of discrimination, stereotype bias and in-group bias. At time one, institutional decision makers who were "at the table" when rules and arrangements were worked out, who were more likely to be white men, created procedures that represented their own cultural assumptions about gender and their own group interests at the time with less attention to the interests of others such as women and minorities. The implicitly biased new organizational practices then became, at time two, causes of discrimination in their own right. Such practices persist through institutional inertia despite subsequent cultural changes in the organization and the surrounding society.

Sociologists have argued that a wide variety of routine organizational arrangements that structure the contemporary job and workplace, including job ladders and salary structures, embody implicit assumptions about the gender status of the person expected to hold the job.[60] The persistent association between the sex composition of a job and its wages, independent of other factors, has often been assumed to result partly from processes by which the sex of the expected job holder implicitly biases the wage schedules the organization develops.[61] Similar processes have been invoked to explain evidence that the more closely an occupation is associated with nurturance or care, the skills most strongly associated with women, the lower its pay, net of other job requirements that affect wages.[62]

Especially in larger organizations, as new jobs are created, formal procedures are often used to evaluate them in order to assign a salary. The resulting salary structures are often somewhat insulated from direct market forces.[63] One widely used system for job evaluation, the Hay system, was originally developed in the middle of the last century before cultural assumptions were yet established that women should be fully equal participants in the labor force. Steinberg[64] argues that these founding conditions infused gender bias into the evaluation criteria of the Hay system in ways that gave greater attention to job characteristics found in historically male work and more finely differentiated job complexity, which justifies wage increases, in male jobs than women's jobs. These evaluation criteria then became a "standard" that has persisted to the present so that, Steinberg argues, they continue to affect the wages assigned to men's and women's jobs today. Nelson and Bridges[65] describe several additional cases in which organizations' job evaluation systems preserved wage differences between men's and women's jobs by embodying traditional assumptions about the wages appropriate to men's and women's work.

Another study also shows how the founding conditions in which organizational practices develop can have persistent effects on how men and women fare in the organization. Baron and colleagues studied the emerging organizational structures of a set of high-tech firms.[66] They found that the organizational "blueprint" of firms took shape from the assumptions of the firm's founders and persisted despite later leaders. Women employees did worse, in terms of being hired in the firm's core scientific and technical jobs, under some organizational blueprints than others. In contrast to four other organizational models, including bureaucratic and star (i.e., top performer)-oriented systems, women fared least well in "commitment" firms that emphasized "company culture" and "fitting in." Given Kanter's arguments about how in-group dynamics can create gendered workplace cultures, these findings are not surprising. All the high-tech firms in the study specialized in the stereotypically masculine area of science and engineering and were about 80 percent male. In this context, companies whose practices put the emphasis on workers being "our kind of person" heighten the salience of gender in the workplace relations, making them especially unfriendly to women scientists and engineers. In contrast, companies whose procedures focus on professional accomplishments or formal rules provide a somewhat more level playing field for different others like women and minorities.

Organizational practices may play an especially large role in employment discrimination against women who are mothers of dependent children. The traditional structure of work as something that is conducted for eight consecutive hours, five days a week is in itself something of a challenge for those who have primary responsibility for small children.[67] More specifically, however, many skilled jobs, particularly the professions, have a ritual apprentice period when the worker is expected to engage in intensive training and achievement in order to earn a full, more secure position in the field. Examples are completing residencies in medicine, gaining tenure in academe, or earning promotion to partner in law. The timing of these apprentice periods and their accompanying promotion rituals coincide with women's peak child-bearing years, forcing women in these fields to make difficult choices between career or children that their male colleagues do not face in the same way. Perhaps it is not surprising that women who succeed in high-powered business and professional jobs are especially likely to be childless compared to other women.[68]

Contextual Factors that Suppress or Enhance Discrimination

One of the central tenets of the sociological approaches to sex discrimination in the workplace is that contextual factors can enlarge or reduce the effects of gender stereotypes and of in-group bias. Some employment practices, while not direct causes of discrimination in their own right, nevertheless encourage actors in the workplace to make decisions in ways that are especially susceptible to stereotype and in-group biases. Other employment practices constrain actors to behave in ways that tend to interrupt the link between their implicit gender expectations and their decisions. Based on sociological theorizing and empirical research, we have identified three practices that would be likely to produce greater gender equity.

Accountability

Recall that in evaluating workers, workplace actors rely more heavily on gender stereotypes the more uncertainty or subjectivity there is in judging performance. In addition, research shows that when people take the time to evaluate carefully, when they know they will be held accountable, and when they must justify their decisions, they rely less heavily on stereotypes in their judgments.[69]

Accountability through affirmative action is a feature for most large work organizations, especially if the organizations enjoy a contract with the government in excess of $50,000. Although most work organizations are subject to regulation by equal employment opportunity (EEO) laws, studies have shown that organizations have considerable discretion in the extent to which they make serious, substantive efforts to comply rather than simply "go through the motions" with symbolic actions.[70]

To suppress discrimination, organizations must make their members accountable for genuine compliance. Firms that maintain clear records that they use to regularly monitor how women and minorities are faring in the firm and that hold managers accountable for the extent to which their decisions contribute to the firm's EEO goals do better in achieving a more diverse workforce at all levels of the organization.[71]

Petersen and Saporta[72] argue that legal concerns in fact create an "opportunity structure" for discrimination for large work organizations. Essentially, work organizations should be more motivated to avoid discrimination in contexts in which it is more easily proved because victims and interested others have access to information about the process. The opportunity for discrimination is relatively large in recruitment and hiring, for instance, since candidates who are not hired rarely have access to information on the applicant pool that would allow them to formulate a persuasive complaint. Indeed, several studies find that recruitment processes seem to be especially vulnerable to gender biases.[73] The opportunity for discrimination in promotion, at least to mid-level positions, on the other hand, is more constrained. Candidates for promotion typically all work for the organization and there is more information available about their qualifications. Petersen and Saporta did not consider promotion to the highest ranks in organizations, but it is possible that at this level, there is once again a greater opportunity for discrimination. High-ranking positions tend to have a "one of a kind" aspect that increases the subjectivity of performance evaluations and limits comparisons.[74]

Formal personnel procedures

Given the prevalence of cultural stereotypes, it benefits women to work in environments where explicit organizational rules and structures govern much of what happens between actors in the workplace. Research has shown that formal personnel procedures, particularly for recruitment and the evaluation of performance, appear to suppress bias as long as workplace actors actually abide by them. Open recruitment methods, such as job ads, rather than reliance on informal networks increase the numbers of women and minorities that are hired.[75]

In addition, clear, detailed procedures for evaluating performance and close attention to the "bottom line" of productivity suppress bias. They do so both by reducing evaluators' reliance on gender stereotypes and by overwhelming the effects of those stereotypes with more specific, task-relevant information. As we noted above, Gorman[76] demonstrated this effect in her study of gender differences in promotions in large law firms. McIlwee and Robinson[77] found that women engineers were more successful in moving up in organizations in which work was rule based rather than unstructured. Probably related to a focus on actual outcomes, women also tend to do better in organizations and industries that face more direct market competition.[78]

Decreasing the salience of gender in the workplace

Finally, procedures that increase or reduce the salience of gender in the workplace will suppress or enhance the likelihood of discrimination. We have noted gender will be more salient in organizations in which the core work is gender typed (engineering, the military, nursing, elementary teaching) and in which the gender composition of the workplace is skewed. Even in these contexts, however, workplace arrangements can further heighten or reduce the salience of gender. Forming mixed sex work groups of relatively equal status men and women in order to create a shared, overarching in-group identity for them should reduce, although not eliminate, the relative impact of gender on their behavior and evaluations.[79] In contrast, as Baron et al.[80] showed, placing great emphasis on workplace culture and fitting in will further increase gender's salience.

Conclusion

Sociological approaches show us that although the underlying causes of sex discrimination are fairly straightforward, the way these play out to create discriminatory effects in the workplace are complex and context-dependent. The underlying sources of discrimination lie in widely shared cultural beliefs about gender that tell us what "most people" expect from the typical man or woman. Particularly important for workplace discrimination are beliefs about men's greater status, competence, and each sex's specialized skills that are embedded in these widely accepted gender stereotypes. These beliefs are brought into the workplace through the routine process by which workplace actors categorize each other on the basis of sex as they apply for and are considered for jobs and as they work with and evaluate others and themselves. When gender status and competence beliefs are implicitly salient for workplace actors, they create performance expectations that favor men for male-typed and gender-neutral jobs and for positions of authority, but that favor women for female-typed jobs and positions of lesser authority. As this suggests, sex categorization sets the conditions for unconscious stereotype bias and in-group–out-group dynamics based on sex, but the extent to which these shape behavior and judgments in the workplace depends on a number of contextual elements. Furthermore, these underlying biases can create sex discrimination both through the direct actions of employers and others in the workplace and by becoming embedded in organizational arrangements and procedures that have a disparate impact on men and women workers.

Stereotype biases about status and competence work together with in-group–out-group dynamics that create "homosocial reproduction" in the workplace. There is indeed evidence that to the extent that decision makers in the workplace are of one sex, they tend to favor others of that sex in hiring, especially when gender is highly salient in the workplace due to the gendered nature of the work or the skewed gender makeup of the workplace. However, these effects are conditioned by stereotypic assumptions about men's greater status and overall competence.

In addition to biasing the behavior and judgments of workplace actors, cultural beliefs about gender can act as framing assumptions about work and workers that become embedded in the organizational structures, authority lines, job classifications, wage-setting procedures, and administrative rules of employment organizations. When this happens, apparently neutral organizational arrangements such as the procedures by which jobs are assigned to a pay scale can become agents of discrimination because they adversely affect workers of one sex compared to the other. Once such implicitly gendered organizational arrangements develop, they tend to persist through institutional inertia. The persistent association between the sex composition of a job and its wages, the tendency for jobs to pay less the more closely associated they are with stereotypic female skills, appears to be partly a result of such implicitly biased wage-setting procedures.

Although organizational practices can be independent agents of discrimination, such practices can also reduce discrimination by suppressing gender stereotype and in-group biases on the part of workplace actors. In general, sex discrimination is reduced by the existence of accountability and formal personnel procedures for recruitment, hiring, and promotion. Occupations that emphasize sex or gender are more resistant to the reduction of sex discrimination than are other occupations.

A wide variety of contextual factors determine the extent to which sex discrimination occurs in a given workplace. A strength of the sociological approach to sex discrimination is that it systematically examines contextual factors that shape the way the underlying sources of sex discrimination play out in the workplace. The further development of such systematic accounts of the contextual mediation of underlying causes of sex discrimination in employment may offer our greatest potential both for understanding and for constructive change.

Notes

1   Policies that have an adverse impact on women are numerous. They include strength and height requirements for police or firefighter jobs, wage systems that reward seniority or pay full-time workers more per hour than part-time workers, or policies that make promotion conditional on unusually long hours. Some of the adverse impact comes because the rest of society is organized to expect mothers rather than fathers or the state to be responsible for child care. Scholars differ in which of these policies they call discriminatory. One could argue that a policy should only be seen as discriminatory if its origin is rooted in a valuation of a certain kind of behavior not because it is relevant for a job, but because of its link to gender; but of course it is often hard to know the motivation for policies. U.S. federal courts have offered the following distinction. When a policy is shown by plaintiffs to have a disparate impact on a race or sex group, then the burden of proof shifts to defendants to show that the policy really does help them get more productive workers in the job in question. If it does, then it is not seen as illegal discrimination despite the disparate impact. If it does not, it is illegal discrimination. Our reading of the sociological literature suggests there is no clear consensus on how many such policies scholars classify as discriminatory and what criterion they use for inclusion.

2   Eccles, J. S. (1989). Bringing young women to math and science. In M. Crawford & M. Gentry, (Eds.), *Gender and thought: Psychological perspectives*

(pp. 36–58). New York: Springer-Verlag; Jacobs, J. E., Davis-Kean, P., Bleeker, M., Eccles, J. S., & Malanchuck, O. (2005). "I can, but I don't want to": The impact of parents, interests, and activities on gender differences in math. In A. M. Gallagher & J. C. Kaufman, (Eds.), *Gender differences in mathematics* (pp. 246–263). Cambridge: Cambridge University Press.

3   Correll, S. J. (2001). Gender and the career choice process: The role of biased self-assessments. *American Journal of Sociology, 106*, 1691–1730; Correll, S. J. (2004). Constraints into preferences: Gender, status and emerging career aspirations. *American Sociological Review, 69*(1), 93–113.

4   Petersen, T., & Saporta, I. (2004). The opportunity structure for discrimination. *American Journal of Sociology, 109*(4), 852–901.

5   Bielby, W. T., & Baron, J. N. (1986). Men and women at work: Sex segregation and statistical discrimination. *American Journal of Sociology, 91*, 759–799; Petersen, T., & Morgan, L. (1995). Separate and unequal: Occupation, establishment, sex segregation, and the gender wage gap. *American Journal of Sociology, 101*, 329–365.

6   England, P. (1992). *Comparable worth: Theories and evidence*. New York: Aldine.

7   Bergmann in this volume uses the term "statistical discrimination" more broadly than most economists, to include the case where employers are in error about the magnitude or existence of a sex difference in average productivity, as well as the case where they act on the basis of a correct perception of average sex differences in productivity. In either case, it is the fact that productivity is too expensive to measure before hire that motivates the discrimination. In either case it is illegal, and many would view it as unfair. But in the case of what England has called "error discrimination," cultural beliefs are creating biased perceptions so that gender differences are perceived where there are none (or are perceived as bigger than they are), whereas in what most economists mean by statistical discrimination, employers are responding to correctly perceived (though possibly socially created) gender differences. Unfortunately, there is almost no research directly testing between these views.

8   Cotter, D., Hermsen, J. M., & Vanneman, R. (2004). *Gender inequality at work*. New York: Russell Sage Foundation. Note that the figures come from census data and refer to workers aged 25 to 54, thought of by the Department of Labor as the prime working age. Different figures would be found if one looked at statistics covering age 16 to retirement or later, but the basic pattern would remain the same.

9   Cotter et al. (2004). Actually, employed women have had an average level of education as high as men's for decades because, although in previous decades men got more college degrees, more men were also high school dropouts (England, 1992).

10 Institute for Women's Policy Research. (2005). *The gender wage ratio: Women's and men's earnings*. IWPR Fact Sheet #C350. Washington DC: Institute for Women's Policy Research.

11   Reskin, B. F., & McBrier, D. B. (2000). Why not ascription? Organizations' employment of male and female managers. *American Sociological Review*, 65(2), 210–233; Reskin, B. F., & Ross, C. E. (1995). Jobs, authority, and earnings among managers: The continuing significance of sex. In J. A. Jacobs (Ed.), *Gender inequality at work* (pp. 127–151). Thousand Oaks, CA: Sage; Smith, R. (2002). Race, gender, and authority in the workplace: Theory and research. *Annual Review of Sociology*, 509–542.

12   Charles, M., & Grusky, D. B. (2004). *Occupational ghettos: The worldwide segregation of women and men.* Stanford, CA: Stanford University Press; Cotter et al. (2004).

13   Reskin, B. F., & Roos, P. (1990). *Job queues, gender queues.* Philadelphia: Temple University Press.

14   Cotter et al. (2004).

15   Cotter et al. (2004).

16   Charles & Grusky (2004).

17   Petersen & Morgan (1995).

18   England (1992); Kilbourne, B. S., England, P., Farkas, G., Beron, K., & Weir, D. (1994). Returns to skill, compensating differentials, and gender bias: Effects of occupational characteristics on the wages of white women and men. *American Journal of Sociology*, 100, 689–719; Steinberg, R., Haignere, L., Possin, C., Chertos, C. H., and Treiman, D. (1986). The New York State pay equity study: A research report. Albany, NY: Center for Women in Government/SUNY Press.

19   England (1992); Nelson, R., & Bridges, W. (1999). *Legalizing gender inequality: Courts, markets, and unequal pay for women in America.* New York: Cambridge University Press.

20   Padavic, I., & Reskin, B. F. (2002). *Women and men at work.* Thousand Oaks, CA: Pine Forge Press; Reskin & McBrier (2000); Smith (2002).

21   Bielby, W. T. (2000). Minimizing workplace gender and racial bias. *Contemporary Sociology*, 29(1), 120–129; Charles & Grusky (2004); Reskin, B. F. (2000). The proximate causes of employment discrimination. *Contemporary Sociology*, 29(2), 319–328; Ridgeway, C. L. (1997). Interaction and the conservation of gender inequality: Considering employment. *American Sociological Review*, 62(2), 218–235; Ridgeway, C. L., & Correll, S. J. (2004). Unpacking the gender system: A theoretical perspective on gender beliefs and social relations. *Gender and Society*, 18(4), 510–531.

22   Smith, T. W. (1999). *The emerging 21st century American family.* GSS Social Change Report no. 42. Chicago, IL: National Opinion Research Center.

23   Fiske, S., Cuddy, A. J., Glick, P., & Xu, J. (2002). A model of (often mixed) stereotype content: Competence and warmth respectively follow from perceived status and competence. *Journal of Personality and Social Psychology*, 82, 878–902; Spence, J. T., & Buckner, C. E. (2000). Instrumental and expressive traits, trait stereotypes, and sexist attitudes: What do they signify? *Psychology of Women Quarterly*, 24, 44–62.

24 Blair, I. V., & Banaji, M. R. (1996). Automatic and controlled process in stereotype priming. *Journal of Personality and Social Psychology, 70,* 1142–1163; Rudman, L. A., & Kilianski, S. E. (2000). Implicit and explicit attitudes toward female authority. *Personality and Social Psychology Bulletin, 26,* 1315–1328.

25 Ridgeway & Correll (2004).

26 Ridgeway (1997); Ridgeway & Correll (2004).

27 Brewer, M. B., & Lui, L. (1989). The primacy of age and sex in the structure of person categories. *Social Cognition, 7,* 262–274; Stangor, C., Lynch, L., Duan, C., & Glass, B. (1992). Categorization of individuals on the basis of multiple social features. *Journal of Personality and Social Psychology, 62,* 207–218.

28 West, C., & Zimmerman, D. (1987). Doing gender. *Gender and Society, 1,* 125–151.

29 Berger, J., Rosenholtz, S. J., & Zelditch, M., Jr. (1980). Status organizing processes. *Annual Review of Sociology, 6,* 479–508; Ridgeway, C. L. (2001). Gender, status, and leadership. *Journal of Social Issues, 57*(4), 637–655; Wagner, D. G., & Berger, J. (1997). Gender and interpersonal task behaviors: Status expectation accounts. *Sociological Perspectives, 40,* 1–32.

30 Conway, M., Pizzamiglio, M. T., & Mount, L. (1996). Status, communality, and agency: Implications for stereotypes of gender and other groups. *Journal of Personality and Social Psychology, 71,* 25–38; Fiske et al. (2002); Jackson, L. M., Esses, V. M., & Burris, C. T. (2001). Contemporary sexism and discrimination: The importance of respect for men and women. *Personality and Social Psychology Bulletin, 27*(1), 48–61.

31 Berger et al. (1980); Ridgeway (2001); Ridgeway, C. L., & Smith-Lovin, L. (1999). The gender system and interaction. *Annual Review of Sociology, 25,* 191–216; Wagner & Berger (1997).

32 Reskin & Roos (1990).

33 Charles & Grusky (2004).

34 Fernandez, R. M., & Sosa, L. (2005). Gendering the job: Networks and recruitment at a call center. *American Journal of Sociology, 115,* 859–904.

35 Gorman, E. H. (2005). Gender stereotypes, same-gender preferences, and organizational variation in the hiring of women: Evidence from law firms. *American Sociological Review, 70*(4), 702–728.

36 Gorman (2005).

37 Shih, M., Pittinsky, T. L., & Ambady, N. (1999). Stereotype susceptibility: Identity salience and shifts in quantitative performance. *Psychological Science, 10,* 80–83; Spencer, S. J., Steele, C. M., & Quinn, D. M. (1999). Under suspicion of inability: Stereotype threat and women's math performance. *Journal of Experimental Social Psychology, 35,* 4–28; Wagner & Berger (1997).

38 Spence, & Buckner (2000).

39 Eagly, A. H., Wood, W., & Diekman, A. B. (2000). Social role theory of sex differences and similarities: A current appraisal. In T. Eckes & H. M.

Trautner (Eds.), *The developmental social psychology of gender* (pp. 123–174). Mahwah, NJ: Lawrence Erlbaum.

40 Bielby, D., & Bielby, W. T. (1985). She works hard for the money: Household responsibilities and the allocation of work effort. *American Journal of Sociology*, 93, 1031–1059; Bielby, W. T., & Bielby, D. (2002). Telling stories about gender and effort: Social science narratives about who works hard for the money. In M. Guillen, R. Collins, P. England, & M. Meyer (Eds.), *The new economic sociology: Developments in an emerging field* (pp. 193–217). New York: Russell Sage Foundation; Petersen & Saporta (2004).

41 Ridgeway & Correll (2004); Williams, J. (2000). *Unbending gender: Why family and work conflict and what to do about it.* Oxford: Oxford University Press.

42 Ridgeway & Correll (2004).

43 Correll, S. J., & Bernard, S. (2005). *Getting a job: Is there a motherhood penalty?* Paper presented at the American Sociological Association, Philadelphia.

44 Budig, M. J., & England, P. (2001). The wage penalty for motherhood. *American Sociological Review*, 66(2), 204–225.

45 Brewer, M., & Brown, R. J. (1998). Intergroup relations. In D. T. Gilbert, S. T. Fiske, & G. Lindzey (Eds.), *Handbook of social psychology* (4th ed., Vol. 2, pp. 554–594). New York: McGraw-Hill.

46 Kanter, R. M. (1977). *Men and women of the corporation.* New York: Basic Books.

47 Reskin, B. F., McBrier, D. B., & Kmec, J. A. (1999). The determinants and consequences of workplace sex and race composition. *Annual Review of Sociology*, 25, 347–348; Yoder, J. D. (1991). Rethinking tokenism: Looking beyond numbers. *Gender and Society*, 5(2), 178–192.

48 Reskin et al. (1999).

49 Cota, A. A., & Dion, K. L. (1986). Salience of gender and sex composition in ad hoc groups: An experimental test of distinctiveness theory. *Journal of Personality and Social Psychology*, 50, 770–776.

50 Yoder (1991).

51 Yoder (1991).

52 Budig, M. J. (2002). Male advantage and the gender composition of jobs: Who rides the glass escalator? *Social Problems*, 49(2), 258–277; Yoder (1991).

53 Williams, C. (1992). The glass escalator: Hidden advantages for men in the "female" professions. *Social Problems*, 39(3), 253–267.

54 Williams (1992).

55 McPherson, J. M., Smith-Lovin, L., & Cook, J. M. (2001). Birds of a feather: Homphily in social networks. *Annual Review of Sociology*, 27, 415–444.

56 Reskin & McBrier (2000).

57 Reskin & McBrier (2000).

58   Charles & Grusky (2004); Huffman, M. L., & Torres, L. (2002). It's not only "who you know" that matters: Gender, personal contacts and job lead quality. *Gender and Society*, *16*, 793–813.

59   Huffman & Torres (2002); Torres, L., & Huffman, M. L. (2004). Who benefits? Gender differences in returns to social network diversity. *Research in the Sociology of Work*, *14*, 17–33.

60   Acker, J. (1990). Hierarchies, jobs, and bodies: A theory of gendered organizations. *Gender and Society*, *4*, 139–158.

61   Baron, J. N., & Newman, A. E. (1989). Pay the man: Effects of demographic composition on prescribed wage rates in the California civil service. In R. T. Michael, H. I. Hartmann, & B. O'Farrell (Eds.), *Pay equity: Empirical inquiries* (pp. 107–130). Washington, DC: National Academy Press; Baron, J. N., & Pfeffer, J. (1994). The social psychology of organizations and inequality. *Social Psychology Quarterly*, *57*(3), 190–209; Nelson & Bridges (1999); England, P., Hermsen, J. M., & Cotter, D. A. (2000). The devaluation of women's work: A comment on Tam. *American Journal of Sociology*, *105*, 1741–1751.

62   Kilbourne et al. (1994); England, P., Budig, M. J., & Folbre, N. (2002). The wages of virtue: The relative pay of care work. *Social Problems*, *49*, 455–473.

63   Nelson & Bridges (1999).

64   Steinberg, R. J. (1995). Gendered instructions: Cultural lag and gender bias in the hay system of job evaluation. In J. A. Jacobs (Ed.), *Gender inequality at work* (pp. 57–92). Thousand Oaks, CA: Sage.

65   Nelson & Bridges (1999).

66   Baron, J. N., Hannan, M. T., Hsu, G., & Kocak, O. (2002). Gender and the organization-building process in young, high-tech firms. In M. Guillen, R. Collins, P. England, & M. Meyer (Eds.), *The new economic sociology: Developments in an emerging field* (pp. 245–273). New York: Russell Sage Foundation.

67   Williams (2000).

68   Goldin, C. (1995). *Career and family: College women look to the past*. Working Paper 5188. Cambridge, MA: National Bureau of Economic Research.

69   Fiske, S. (1998). Stereotyping, prejudice, and discrimination. In D. T. Gilbert, S. T. Fiske, & G. Lindzey (Eds.), *The handbook of social psychology* (4th ed., Vol. 2, pp. 357–411). Boston: McGraw-Hill; Tetlock, P. E., & Lerner, J. (1999). The social contingency model: Identifying empirical and normative boundary conditions on the error-and-bias portrait of human nature. In S. Chaiken & Y. Trope (Eds.), *Dual process models in social psychology* (pp. 571–585). New York: Guilford Press.

70   Edelman, L. B., & Petterson, S. (1999). Symbols and substance in organizational response to civil rights law. *Research in Social Stratification and Mobility*, *17*, 107–135.

71   Bielby (2000).

72   Petersen & Saporta (2004).

73 Fernandez & Sosa (2005); Reskin & McBrier (2000); Petersen & Saporta (2004).
74 Baron & Pfeffer (1994).
75 Bielby (2000); Reskin & McBrier (2000).
76 Gorman (2005).
77 McIlwee, J. S., & Robinson, J. G. (1992). *Women in engineering: Gender, power, and workplace culture.* Albany, NY: SUNY Press.
78 Reskin & McBrier (2000).
79 Brewer & Brown (1998); Cohen, B. P., & Zhou, X. (1991). Status processes in enduring work groups. *American Sociological Review*, 56(2), 179–188; Reskin (2000).
80 Baron et al. (2002).

14

Discrimination through the Economist's Eye

Barbara R. Bergmann

Women's position in the labor market has two major aspects: their lower average pay as compared to men's, and the sex segregation of occupations. There is a great body of evidence that discrimination – the disadvantageous treatment of women by employers on account of their sex – is an important cause of women's labor market inferiority, needing rectification.

However, economists are far from unified in the way they view this matter. A sizable faction of the profession denies that sex discrimination plays a significant part in causing women's lower pay and occupational exclusions. They adhere to the view that markets, peopled by rational actors, are structured to produce fair results. They attribute the sizable differences in labor market outcomes for women and men to the biological differences between the sexes, and to the social arrangements and choices which, they claim, benignly result from them.

In this review, I will first describe and critique the position of those economists who deny the importance of discrimination. Next, I will review the evidence that discrimination is an important phenomenon. This is followed by a discussion of occupational segregation and its connection to the wage gap between the sexes. Finally, I will briefly trace the progress that has been made in reducing discrimination.

The Deniers

The classical model economists use to explain price setting pictures an impersonal marketplace, peopled by completely rational actors who are single-mindedly alert to do the best they can for themselves through buying and selling. They are "all business." The actors' identities are seen as irrelevant to the analysis; only the price buyers are willing to pay or sellers are willing to accept is what counts. The buyers and sellers compete to get the best deal they can. This process is seen as producing optimal results, and any government intervention is seen as inevitably making things worse.

This model of price setting, which originated in a period before the employment of racial minorities and women had become an issue in economic research, had been designed originally for thinking about how prices would be set in a place like the Chicago wheat exchange. In such a place, the corps of buyers and sellers might with some realism be envisaged as attentive to nothing but business. However, there has been no hesitation in utilizing the same mode of analysis in thinking about a wide range of other price-setting situations, including hiring and wage setting, where the assumptions that might fit well enough for the Chicago wheat market are far less realistic. (I say "might fit" because there is little or no observationally validated evidence that these assumptions actually do fit even in the wheat exchange.[1] Economists are not trained to make direct observations and gather evidence, just to spin theories about what might be going on.)

In this mode of analysis, a rationally operated business enterprise is seen as buying labor at the price set in an impersonal market with the sole aim of using it to produce output. Again, the personal characteristics of the workers and the personal preferences of the employers with regard to race or sex are no part of the analysis. It is only the productivity of a worker that counts. Economists envisage a worker's productivity as deriving from his or her "human capital" – that worker's education and experience. When the concept of human capital was put forth, its author and most other economists immediately attributed all wage differentials to human capital differences among workers.[2]

Competition among market actors is taken to be relentless. Discrimination is viewed as a departure from rational behavior, because it posits that the discriminator is straying from exclusive attention to issues of productivity. It raises the perpetrator's costs, and therefore the price that must be charged for the perpetrator's output. This opens up the perpetrator to being undersold by other producers in the competitive marketplace who don't discriminate.

Becker's analysis of discrimination

The first modern treatment of discrimination by an economist was undertaken by Gary Becker,[3] who fixed his attention almost exclusively on wage differentials by race and sex. If he were to discuss the subject at all, Becker needed to depart from the assumption that the employer paid attention to nothing but a worker's productivity. His solution was to import some elements from the economists' theory of household purchasing decisions, in which idiosyncratic and unaccounted-for individual tastes with respect to various products are assumed to play an important role. He posited a "taste for discrimination," thus conflating employers' racist and sexist behavior with an individual's preference for coffee over tea. Sex discrimination was seen as an aversion to contact (at least in the workplace) with women. But just as a person who would prefer to drink coffee might buy tea if its price were low enough compared to the price of coffee, the aversion to women's presence in the workplace could be overcome if the ratio of women's market wage to men's was low enough.

The difference in the market wages of men and women of equal productivity was thus taken to reflect the taste for discrimination on the demand side of the labor market. The wage differential serves as a kind of bribe to get at least some employers – the ones with the least taste for discrimination – to hire women.

Although Becker had been forced to depart from the characterization of employers as uniformly indifferent to the personal characteristics of their employees, he apparently could not bring himself to abandon the standard model's assumption of relentless competition among economic actors. Becker's book on discrimination contains a short section suggesting that discrimination by race and sex was in actuality absent from the labor market. It argued that if some employers discriminated, there would be other employers who lacked a taste for discrimination, and who could employ lots of women. Since these companies would be getting their labor cheaply, they would have lower costs of production than the discriminators who were paying men their high wages, and could charge lower prices for their product. In the competition for customers, the discriminators would lose out, go bankrupt, and leave the market. So the market would continually be cleansing itself of any discriminators, and any observed wage differentials between men and women or blacks and whites that remained would entirely be due to productivity differences.

Thus we have the curious result that the first (and still influential) treatment of the economics of discrimination maintained that its subject matter was a phenomenon that did not exist, except perhaps occasionally and fleetingly.[4] That short section theorizing away the very possibility that discrimination might be an important phenomenon was the major lesson that many, perhaps most, economists took away from Becker's work. Despite considerable evidence to the contrary, that section continues to be the most quoted part of the book. It was approvingly referred to in 2005 by Lawrence Summers, the distinguished economist then serving as president of Harvard, in his famous address to a session called to discuss the paucity of women on the university's science faculty. As part of his argument that innate lack of talent was a more likely cause of women's absence than was discrimination, Summers said that if there really were Harvard-worthy women scientists that Harvard had discriminated against, some other nondiscriminating school would have snapped them all up, and outshone Harvard. The implication was that, since Harvard continued to reign supreme, Harvard must not be discriminating.

We see thousands of business failures every year in the United States, so firms do make fatal mistakes; but no one has ever reported seeing a firm that discriminated reduced to ruin by a less bigoted competitor. On the other hand, we do know of firms that have discriminated, yet have remained highly successful. In deciding a discrimination case against the Hertz car rental company, the judge, after hearing the evidence, declared the company had had "a long history of discriminating against women."[5] Yet it has famously managed to remain number one in its industry. Wal-Mart, one of the country's and the world's most successful corporations is, at this writing, a defendant in a class action suit alleging discrimination against women. Such firms typically do not fail, at least not for that reason.

The problem with arguments like Becker's was pointed out by John Stuart Mill more than a century and a half ago. Mill observes that the assumption of rigorous competition is needed by economists as a necessary ingredient for the construction of their theories. However, competition is in reality not necessarily always severe enough to accomplish in actuality what armchair theorizing leads us to think it would tend to do – in this case eliminate companies that do not charge rock bottom prices.[6] As a modern illustration of Mill's point, two gas stations across the street from each other can go on selling an identical product at markedly different prices for years.

Moreover, if most employers discriminate, and those who do not discriminate are very few and far between, price competition by the latter is not a big problem for the former. Unfortunately for the science of economics, the acceptance and circulation of an economic theory has never depended on the existence of actual observations that support it. Nor have counterexamples impeded its circulation.

A second peculiar feature of Becker's approach was the small amount of attention he devoted to occupational segregation by race and sex, which was and still is a prominent feature of the labor market. Becker's account of discrimination is compatible with a world where all persons can compete on a fair basis to be hired for any job in any occupation, provided they are willing to accept an appropriately discounted wage if they happen to be of a race or sex that the employer finds distasteful. But that is not, of course, the world we live in.

Explaining away women's inferior position

Those who take the position that there is little or no discrimination have the task of finding alternative "innocent" causes for women's inferior position in the labor market. The first attempts to do that attributed women's lower wages entirely to a deficiency of human capital. Mincer and Polachek[7] argued that a woman on average had spent less time in the labor market than a man of her age, because of dropping out to rear children. She therefore would have less human capital deriving from on-the-job experience. Moreover, since she would spend fewer years in the labor market, she would have fewer years to receive a payoff for any human capital she accumulated in the form of schooling. Therefore women would have less incentive than men to invest their time and money in schooling, which would cause them to invest less.

A further elaboration of the human capital argument was provided by Polachek[8] who addressed the issue of occupational segregation. During their years of withdrawal from the labor market, he suggested that women's human capital "rusted," i.e., became less valuable, because their skills became outdated, and also because the skills declined from lack of use. So a year of education or experience gained by a woman added less to her productivity than that gained by a man who had never dropped out.

He argued that occupations differed in terms of the extent to which the human capital involved rusted. Women would do best, he theorized, if they concentrated in occupations where the rate of rusting was least, and that explained occupational segregation. This argument was demolished by sociologist Paula England,[9] who showed that, even allowing for "rusting" women would do better in men's occupations.

Further, the "rusting" conjecture does not help us much in explaining some of the differences in pay between men and women in the same occupations. A job as driver of a truck is probably easy to drop out of and return to. Very little human capital is likely to rust during the break in service. But it is hard to believe that women coming back to work after having a baby purposely look for the truck-driving jobs that pay $443 rather than the ones that pay $604. Yet it is the lower-paying ones that they end up in.

Evidence that Discrimination is Important

Statistical evidence

Economists' attempts to measure the importance of sex discrimination have focused on the wage gap. They have tried to identify how much of the gap could be accounted for by reasons other than discrimination. Obviously, they have looked for differences between women and men in qualifications – in "human capital." They have also looked for indications that women workers' behavior, particularly the behavior of those who were mothers, might lower their productivity. For example, women workers stay home with sick children more often than fathers do.

But just asserting that "men have more human capital than women," or "women behave in ways that make them less valuable workers than men" is not enough to clinch the argument that none of the wage gap arises from discrimination. We have to look systematically at what the data show about the size of the differences in human capital between women and men and at the evidence about differences in behavior. And when we have done that, we have to look at how much these differences actually affect wages. The technique of multiple regression allows us to estimate how much of the gap between women's and men's wages has an "innocent," i.e., nondiscriminatory, explanation, and how much remains to be explained by discrimination.[10]

A study of men's and women's wages in 1975, when women on average earned 40 percent less than men, found that men had slightly more education and a considerable amount more of experience and training than women.[11] However, such differences accounted for only about a quarter of the wage gap between women and men working full time.[12] The researchers also considered the effect on women's wages of the greater responsibility women undertook for the care of children. Having in the past worked part time or having left the work force for a spell were taken to be indications of a lower level of "labor force attachment." This accounted for another fifth of the gap. In total, 45 percent of the gap was accounted for by these seemingly "innocent" factors, leaving 55 percent of the gap to be explained by other factors. Discrimination, including the discrimination which excludes women from entering male-typical occupations, is the most obvious factor.

A similar calculation on data for 2002 shows that the gap had diminished considerably.[13] Adult women earned 25 percent less than adult men. Workers included in the survey were asked questions about their age, education, weekly salary, race and ethnicity, the number and ages of children in their family, and whether they had worked full time year round in the previous year.

Between 1975 and 2002, women have decisively moved ahead of men in education. Fewer men than women now in the work force had gone on to get some higher education – only 56.6 percent of men compared with 63.1 percent of women. More women than men got BA degrees, and about the same proportion got graduate degrees. At the lower end of the educational scale, having dropped out of high school before graduation was 50 percent more common among men than women. Thus in 2002, unlike what was true in earlier decades, none of the deficiencies in women's pay can be attributed to deficiencies in the length of their formal education. Women and men are about equal in the number of years since leaving school. On the other hand, more men than women had worked full time year round in the year before the survey was taken.[14]

The 2002 Census data set does not give explicit information about previous periods of part-time work or being out of the labor force entirely or being absent from a job to tend to sick family members. All of these factors accounted for some of women's lower pay in the 1979 study.[15] However, we do have information for 2002 on whether or not a woman worker has children at home, and how many she has. It is, after all, the birth and care of children which cause most of the periods out of the labor force and much of the absenteeism that, it is claimed, cause women workers to have justifiably lower pay than men. Of course not all women workers have children under 18; a majority of women who work full time do not. In 2002, 85 percent had no children under 6, and 65 percent had no school-age children.[16]

The most surprising aspect of the 2002 data is that women with children who work full time do not earn less than women who have the same education and are of the same age but have no children under 18 in the home.[17] In fact, they average slightly more.[18] We can draw the important conclusion that in 2002 none of the $210 gap in weekly pay between full-time men and women workers appears to be attributable to the responsibilities women workers currently assume with respect to children.[19]

Race discrimination continued to play a big part in the American labor market in 2002. African Americans earned an average of $105 less per week than other workers with similar education and experience, and Hispanics earned $90 less than non-Hispanics.[20] Adding the penalty for being black to the penalty for being a woman, we can see that an African American woman working full time could expect to earn $336 less than a white male with similar education and age, a discount in pay of almost 40 percent.

In the 1975 study discussed above, 65 percent of the pay gap remained after differences in men's and women's characteristics were accounted for, and could be attributed to discrimination. In 2002, the estimated loss in women's weekly pay due to their sex, after education, age, and the presence of children are taken into account, is $231. The loss is actually larger than the gross difference between women's and men's pay. This suggests that women full-time workers now have better qualifications than men and that the entire pay gap is due to discrimination. *Were it not for discrimination against them, women would be earning as much or even more than men.*

There are some economists who would argue that this type of analysis over-estimates the extent to which discrimination is responsible for the pay gap. They would point out, quite correctly, that some of the worker characteristics that might account in a nondiscriminatory way for the gap were not included in the analysis. For example, the Census data do not tell us anything about what the people they surveyed had studied in school. They tell us nothing about their on-the-job training. Both of these probably do explain some of the wage gap, although previous studies suggest it is only a modest amount. For example, if women had studied engineering and become engineers in proportion to their numbers in professional jobs, that would have erased about four percentage points of the gap.[21] The difference between the sexes in the amount of on-the-job training was found to account for 11 percent of the gap in the 1979 study, and may account for some in 2002. However, in most places of work, the decision as to who gets a training slot is controlled by the employer, and employers' exclusion of women from training opportunities should certainly count as a form of discrimination.

Of course, while we are thinking of the factors that have not been accounted for in the statistical analysis that could legitimately have the effect of pushing women's average wages down relative to men's, we should not (as almost all analysts do) omit to remember that there are factors, also unaccounted for in the analysis, that should have the opposite effect – pushing men's wages down relative to women's. Employed men suffer more from alcoholism than do employed women. Men in charge of a vehicle are more likely than women to have a bad accident. Men are far more likely to have criminal records than women. Alcoholism, a criminal record, and an accident-studded driving record are likely to affect one's ability to get and keep a good job, and one's promotion possibilities as well. So people with those problems would be likely to have less than average earnings. Since the study did not account for any of them, it omitted some important and legitimate factors that should lower men's pay relative to women's.

Analyses of this type do not give precise answers to the question of the extent of discrimination. However, the conclusion that all or close to all of the pay gap is now due to discrimination is unlikely to be far off.

Those economists who deny the importance of discrimination have apparently been frustrated by their inability to demonstrate statistically that the wage gap is caused by women's poor qualifications or measurable lack of devotion to their careers. Some of them have cast around for other explanations. For example Gary Becker argued that,

> . . . women with responsibilities for housework would have less energy available for the market than men would. This would reduce the hourly earnings of married women, affect their jobs and occupations, and even lower their investment in market human capital when they worked the same number of hours as married men.[22]

Becker (who maintains in another of his books that it is rational and therefore right and inevitable for wives to do all the housework) was saying that women are simply too tired to put forward the necessary effort to earn good wages, *and so no blame need be placed on employers*.[23] Becker was just guessing when he wrote that; he had no measurements of the energy level of women workers or men (who also have some energy-draining ways of spending time). Luckily, we do not have to accept Becker's guess on faith. When actual evidence on work effort was examined by sociologists Denise Bielby and William Bielby, they found that women allocate more effort to their work on the job than men do.[24]

Experimental evidence

Experimental methods are coming into more common use among economists, and are being applied to discrimination. Peter Riach and Judith Rich performed an experiment in which they responded to advertisements of job openings for accountants. For each job, they wrote two letters offering very similar credentials, one seeming to come from a male applicant, the other from a female. The "male" applicants got many more responses than the "female" ones.[25] This helps to explain why there are few women applicants for jobs in occupations that don't already employ women. It is difficult for women to enter mostly male occupations and relatively easy to enter mostly female ones. Holding out for a "man's job" means a longer and potentially more frustrating period of unemployment.

Direct evidence

Much direct evidence of discriminatory behavior can be gleaned from the evidence presented in lawsuits. One of the largest recent cases was filed against the Home Depot chain, which sells hardware, housewares, and material for remodeling. At Home Depot the new hires were assigned either to sales jobs or to jobs as cashiers. Those in sales jobs had opportunities to move into positions as department supervisors and assistant store managers, while promotion was unlikely for those given jobs as cashiers. About 77 percent of the newly hired men were assigned to sales jobs, but only about 20 percent of the newly hired women got them. The few women assigned to the sales floor were in home decor or gardening, which were deemed "women's work." The lawyers who brought the suit likened the cashiers' situation to being under a glass ceiling supported by glass walls, because they were kept separate from the kinds of entry-level jobs that could lead upward. The result was that only 20 percent of those considered for promotion to Assistant Manager Trainee were women. Moreover, the few women who did get to be considered had a much smaller chance of actually landing a managerial slot than the men being considered. Only 12 percent of those slots went to women.[26]

The company originally said the allegations were unjustified and that it would fight them, but ended up settling the cases out of court. The company did not admit to wrongdoing, but agreed to pay $104 million dollars to settle the claims.[27] It also agreed to change its promotion procedures, to train managers in equal employment opportunity issues, and to improve its internal procedure of dealing with complaints of gender discrimination. A lawyer for the women employees said of the settlement, "The important thing is that it includes a system where the employees can register their interest in jobs and provides procedures to make sure they are fairly considered whether they are men or women."[28]

Other recent sex discrimination lawsuits against retailers include the supermarket chains Lucky Stores, which paid $107 million in 1997 to settle the case against it, and Publix, which paid $81 million that same year.[29] Home Depot's defense that the sex segregation of jobs reflected men's greater interest in carpentry and plumbing was not available to the supermarkets. Yet the personnel practices in the supermarkets were very similar to those of Home Depot. Women were disproportionately assigned as cashiers, with little or no chance to move up. There were a few other jobs that were considered "women's jobs"; in the supermarkets women were allowed to serve as managers only in the deli and bakery departments. (Remarkably, women managers were restricted to the same departments in a totally unconnected supermarket chain, Giant Foods, in Washington, DC.) They were paid less than the male managers who served in the grocery, produce, or meat departments, and typically did not get a chance to move up into higher management as the managers of those other departments did.

The ongoing suit against Wal-Mart, the nation's largest employer of women, alleges many of the same practices that segregate women into the lowest-level jobs and make it difficult for them to be promoted into better-paying positions. The *New York Times* of February 16, 2003 reported some of the experiences that caused the women to sue. One woman, single with no children, who had made it to assistant store manager, told her superiors of her ambition to become a store manager. The answer she got was that store managers worked long hours and "it was maybe not something for women because it means you have to be away from home a long time each day." Another, a single mother with a child, was told that a man was favored over her for promotion because "he has a family to support." Still another was told that Wal-Mart paid men more than women for the same job because the Bible says God made Adam before Eve.[30]

The Home Depot suit that covered 25,000 women cost that company tens of millions. A successful sex discrimination suit against Wal-Mart, covering 500,000 women employees, could cost billions. One might imagine that the Wal-Mart management might have taken note of the Home Depot suit and made a greater effort to impress on managers that their personnel practices should be nondiscriminatory. The overall statistics by sex on pay and promotion at Wal-Mart that the lawsuit has revealed suggest that sexist attitudes are by no means rare among Wal-Mart managers.

Industries and firms vary considerably in the extent to which women are given a fair chance at management jobs. In the telephone communications industry, which has almost totally excluded women from crafts jobs, women now have 44 percent of the managerial jobs, which is about average for the entire economy. On the other hand, a lawsuit against Texaco in 1991 revealed that of its 54,000 employees in supervisory positions, only four were women.[31]

It's a long, long way from the cashiers at Home Depot and the Lucky Stores supermarkets to the women scientists on the faculty of the Massachusetts Institute of Technology. But those scientists, surely among the best of the best, conducted a study and found that sexist attitudes and behaviors had put them at a severe disadvantage compared to their male colleagues. They found that the number of women scientists given jobs at MIT had not increased in two decades. For the few who had achieved tenured positions there were inequities in salary, teaching assignments, awards and distinctions, inclusion on important committees, and, what is vitally important for scientists, access to laboratory space. "Senior women faculty were 'invisible', excluded from a voice in their departments and from positions of any real power."[32] The chair of the MIT faculty wrote:

> . . . gender discrimination in the 1990s is, and stems largely from unconscious ways of thinking that have been socialized into all of us, men and women alike. This makes the situation better than in previous decades where blatant inequities and sexual assault and intimidation were endured but not spoken of.[33]

He goes on to say that the consequences of such more subtle forms of discrimination are equally serious. The report recommended that the numbers of women faculty be increased, and steps were taken to do that. It was also recommended that administrators who knowingly practice or permit discriminatory practices against women faculty should be replaced. This kind of measure has been notably absent in discrimination cases that have gone through the courts or been settled. And as we have seen, the hundreds of thousands of women employees in retail trade, unlike the handful of women scientists at MIT, have not yet passed from the era of "blatant inequities" into an era of "more subtle forms of discrimination."

How Discrimination Works

Occupational segregation

Discussions of women's inferior position in the labor market, whether by academic experts or in the press, tend to concentrate, as Becker did, on the wage gap. But arguments have been made that occupational segregation is also an important part of the picture.[34] There are some jobs for which an employer will hire either sex. But in most cases, employers will earmark a job for one sex or the other, largely on the basis of tradition. The most common arrangement, even in today's workplaces, is for women to have mostly women as colleagues in their workplace who share the same job title, and for men to have only male colleagues.[35]

The continued existence of occupations that are to all practical purposes closed to women (and that are in many cases closed to African Americans as well) is documented in the Census statistics, but to find out about it doesn't really require the help of the Census Bureau. Examples are easily observable in everyday life. It is on display on every building site or road repair project one passes, on every fire engine that goes by, in every cockpit of the planes one flies on, and in the passenger cabin as well. One can see it whenever a crew comes to paint one's home or office, whenever one delivers one's car to be serviced, and whenever the floor of the New York Stock Exchange, crowded with white men, is shown on TV or in the newspapers.

While everybody is confronted every day by the sex-typing of jobs, very few people seem to consider it a problem. Most people take occupational segregation by sex to be in some sense natural and don't reflect on the reasons for it, or the disadvantages such conditions inflict on women. There is no reason to think that women would be unable to perform adequately in virtually all the jobs currently monopolized by men. They should certainly be willing to do so, given that the pay and working conditions in the alternative employments open to them are considerably worse.

For women and men to have the same distribution among the occupations, nearly 18 million women workers in occupations that are now disproportionately female would have to move into occupations that are now disproportionately male, and the same number of men would have to move into occupations now disproportionately female.[36] The massive changes – 36 million people taking up a different occupation – that would be required to equalize by gender the occupational distribution of the American labor force testifies to the extent of the current segregation in today's labor market.

Occupational segregation affects the demand and supply of labor to each occupation, and therefore affects wage levels in the "women's jobs." Women still have a considerably lower likelihood than men of landing jobs that pay wages that would support more than one person at a decent standard. However, the consequences of occupational segregation go beyond money, important though that is. Having a majority of the job titles effectively off limits to half the population has costs in terms of human expression and human dignity. Some of the means used to enforce occupational segregation, such as sexual harassment, also rob women of their dignity. Jobs earmarked for men tend to allow some independence of action, to be those where the work is not restricted to boring, repetitive duties, and to be those that lead to still better jobs. Not all "men's jobs" have these characteristics, but the jobs men hold are far more likely to have them than the jobs that women hold.

Occupational segregation means that certain talents and aptitudes do not get expressed; that some people have to spend their lives doing things they hate, when a chance to compete for jobs they would have liked better should and could have been open to them. It reinforces the very system of female subordination that motivates it. Women's situation apart from the workplace is made more difficult because of the reduced options that occupational segregation entails.

The segregation of markets affects wages

Because such a high proportion of jobs are open only to people of just one sex, it makes sense to talk of a market for male labor and a substantially separate market for female labor.[37] The markets for workers of each sex set wage levels independently of the other, at least in the short run. The workings of supply and demand in the men's and women's labor markets put very different wages on jobs requiring similar human capital. Those jobs filled in the women's market pay markedly lower wages.

Job segregation is by no means a neutral and benign division of economic functions between the sexes; we are not dealing here with a case of "separate but equal." Rather, there are forces that reserve for men a disproportionate share of the jobs that take talent, and are therefore well paid, that have interesting duties, and that confer power, independence, and status. Women started entering the market for paid work at a time when almost all jobs, except those of servants, were "men's jobs." The opening to women of the kinds of jobs previously occupied only by men is difficult for employers, has been resisted by male workers, and is still far from complete.

As a result, women are fenced off from a disproportionate share of what we might call "labor market turf." The turf assigned to them tends to be relatively overcrowded and low quality, as compared to the male share of the turf. That translates into restricted demand for labor in the women's labor market, and lowers the wage levels in the jobs that are filled there. It makes the wages low in the traditionally female occupations. It also lowers the pay of the jobs that women hold in occupations that are mixed-sex and mostly male, since employers know that those women's best alternative is a job in a low-paid female occupation doing less interesting work under more restrictive supervision.

Economists sometimes speak as though any price set by supply and demand is by definition fair. But the supply and the demand in the markets for men's and women's labor are powerfully affected by discrimination. It is discrimination that keeps the men's and women's labor markets separate from each other. The exclusion of women from a big share of all of the jobs in the economy is what creates two labor markets where there should be only one. So the fact that supply and demand affect wages does not prove that wages are fair, or even economically sensible.

Some writers have argued against the idea that the women's turf is relatively crowded by pointing out that although women are excluded from many men's jobs, so men are excluded from or exclude themselves from women's jobs.[38] The unstated implication of such arguments is that the exclusions on both sides should balance out. To argue this way, however, would be as fallacious as arguing that the tourist-class passengers on a plane have accommodation as roomy as those of the first-class passengers because the first-class passengers don't occupy space in the tourist section of the plane. The idea that there ought to be higher- and lower-class passengers on the plane results in the separation of the classes. It also results in the devotion of a disproportionate amount of the plane's space to the first-class passengers. In the labor market, men's lack of interest in taking low-paying jobs in the women's turf does not balance out the exclusion of women from the male turf.

The wage effects of crowding based on exclusion: A simplified example

At this point in the discussion, we want to explore carefully the connection between wage levels and the segregation of each sex into its own "labor market turf." The crucial point is this: if a group is segregated and furthermore is crowded into a relatively narrow segment of the labor market, its members will as a result be less productive, and their economic rewards will be lower.

The line of argument will be made clearer if we resort to a simplified example. Consider an island inhabited by two tribes of people, the Pinks and the Blues, both of whom make their living gathering berries. We shall assume the gatherers of both tribes to be more or less equal on average in talent and energy. If all gatherers were allowed to range over the whole island, individual gatherers' yields would vary with their talent, energy, and luck. Given our assumption that the two tribes have equal average talents, the average yield per gatherer would be the same in both tribes.

However, suppose the island's territory was partitioned between the tribes, and gatherers were allowed to pick berries only in the territory assigned to their tribe. Were each tribe assigned a share of the territory about proportional to its size, and of equal average quality per acre, then again the yield per gatherer in the two tribes should be about the same. However, consider what would happen if the Blue tribe were to be assigned exclusive possession of a disproportionately large share of territory. In that case, the work of members of the Blue tribe would on average bring in a greater yield than the work of members of the Pink tribe. If the land the Blue tribe got had more berries per acre than the Pinks', the Pink tribe's disadvantage would be greater still.

The Pink and Blue workers in our example have, by assumption, identical productive potential because their personal characteristics and behavior patterns are taken to be identical. However, as a consequence of the uneven division of the territory, the Pink workers would have to exploit their territory more intensively. They would have to work on less accessible and sparser berry patches. This extra difficulty would reduce their per-person take, so the Pinks would have lower productivity than the Blues.

The way things are arranged on our mythical island, no one says to a Pink worker, "Because you are a Pink, we will see to it that you get less than a Blue." The mechanism that arranges for Pinks to get less is a set of rules about who may work where. As long as everyone follows the rules, and all hands keep to their place, the Pinks will average less production per person than the Blues, and will take home less "pay" for their efforts.

In our example, a person's income is the berries they gather, so the low productivity the Pinks suffer because of territorial restrictions translates directly into lower income. In a money economy, people work in "berry patches" owned by others in return for money wages. There, low productivity also results in lower wages. This occurs when workers' low productivity is due to their lack of human capital. But it can also happen when workers are confined to a low-productivity activity, as in the case of our berrying example. In a money economy, the process is somewhat more roundabout than in the case of the simple economy of our example, but the principle at work is the same.

If a boatload of social scientists were to visit the island portrayed in our example, they might hear from economists belonging to the Blue tribe that its success was a sign of innately superior talent and greater attention to business. If, however, these social scientists observed the segregation of the two tribes, and the relative smallness and low quality of the territory assigned to the Pinks (by surveying berry bushes per capita in the two territories), they might very well come to the conclusion that the inequality of rewards was connected to the segregation.

Why occupational segregation persists

Employers may assume that women are on average less reliable, less energetic workers, more likely to quit. An employer who rules out all women for a particular type of job because of a belief that the average male candidate is a better bet than the average female candidate is said to be practicing "statistical discrimination." Thus membership in what is thought to be a low-performing group destroys opportunities for individuals whose behavior may be very different from the average. Whether the perception of difference in averages is true or false, statistical discrimination hurts individuals because of their sex, and is illegal under U.S. law. Yet these practices have not been stamped out. Unfortunately, enforcement of the law against discrimination is quite lax.

One important reason for the continued sex segregation of jobs is that workplaces are not "all business." Employers want high productivity from their work force, and understand that productivity is not just a matter of getting workers capable of doing the job and providing them with good equipment and supervision. The operation of an establishment is crucially affected by the nature of the personal interactions that each employee has with his or her co-workers and supervisor. If these interactions are pleasant and unproblematic, then employees can pay undistracted attention to the details of their work and go at it with a cooperative attitude.

Nothing is more obvious than that people bring with them to their work their ideas about status and respect, and their ideas about when it is right and reasonable for one individual to be subordinated to another. Many bring with them the idea that it is wrong for a man to have to take orders from a woman, and that he is shamed if he does. The managers of an establishment may have liberal attitudes, may have a realistic idea of the capabilities of women workers, and may want to avoid sex discrimination. Yet there may be pressures on them to pay attention to these compatibility issues when hiring, assigning, and promoting workers.

Business suffers if there are time-consuming and disruptive fights. It also suffers if male workers on the job refuse to teach the job to new female workers. Disruptive incidents or a flow of offensive remarks may poison the atmosphere of a workplace and cause breakdowns in the flow of work. When cooperation is called for, it may be refused, degrading performance of duties. Workers may sabotage operations to express spite.

When troubles of this sort arise, an employer has the choice of transferring or firing employees who are causing this kind of trouble, or getting rid of the female workers. The aggressors may be people with considerable experience, special knowledge, and skill, whom it is hard to dispense with. For this reason it may be the innocent victims who are sacrificed. In that case, feelings of injustice are generated, which may have troublesome consequences, including lawsuits. Whatever the case, having to shake up the staffing of a department or a crew is disrupting and potentially difficult and expensive. New people have to be recruited and trained before things are back to normal.

Although managers may have sensible reasons for practicing occupational segregation, those reasons constitute no justification for doing so, either ethically or under the law. If there were rigorous enforcement of antidiscrimination laws, if there were effectively operating affirmative action plans in more workplaces, and if there were strong ethical feelings against giving in to these sexist traditions, then occupational segregation by sex might be less common than it still is. As time went on, the sexist traditions might fade. As it is, in the absence of compulsions requiring change, the easiest thing for managers is to continue to practice occupational segregation. The less liberal among them feel free to indulge their prejudices.

If a woman does manage to land a "man's job," the men who resent her incursion may employ tactics against her designed to dislodge her – to get her fired or get her to quit. Not all men feel or act this way. The strength of the exclusionary sentiment varies from job to job, industry to industry, man to man.

But enough men do feel this way to create a serious barrier to integration in many establishments. In any group of people who have to cooperate on the work, it only takes one man acting obnoxiously to make life very unpleasant for the intruding woman. Regardless of the job, each new worker requires some help from co-workers to get started. She requires help in learning aspects of the work that are undocumented, in dealing with problems that come up in any new job, and she needs to get hints about peculiarities of the work process and the administrative procedures. Where there are multi-person tasks, she needs to be given a chance to learn to cooperate as a team member. If her fellow workers refuse to give that help, and instead surround her with an unrelentingly hostile environment, then her productivity, her morale, and her chance of survival may be low. The low wages for which women can be hired must constitute a continuing temptation to turn over groups of jobs to women whenever that can be done with ease, while maintaining occupational segregation. Any rise in the wage differential may make employers more attentive to niches within their organization where women might substitute for men.[39] However, there are a number of substantial difficulties facing the employer who tries to make the switch in an already existing work group: an awkward period during which males and females have to be mixed, the problems connected with the training of the new women by men who are likely to resent their presence, the uncertainty as to how to recruit suitable women, the lack of experienced women in the applicant pool, the uncertainty as to how relations between the new female employees and males in other kinds of jobs with whom they have to interact in the productive process will go.

Promotional opportunities on the job

Economists have dubbed the structure of promotion opportunities and wages within a workplace the "internal labor market."[40] The internal labor market has formal and informal rules of operation that establish who can make a serious bid for each of the jobs above entry level. In most large work establishments, the possibilities of promotion depend on the job a worker has. From some jobs, relatively long "promotion ladders" lead upwards, with possibilities of promotion to the highest echelon. Still other jobs have either short promotion ladders or are dead-ends. Jobs typically assigned to males tend to have longer ladders than typically female jobs, and at least some of the male jobs lead to the upper echelons, while few female jobs may do so. Even if a woman has a job of the type from which men can be promoted up the ladder, the rules operating in the internal labor market in the place she works may make her ineligible for further advancement.

Up to World War II it was not unusual to read of a man who had reached the headship of a business enterprise after starting work for the company as a clerk. Now it is rare, because clever and ambitious men have not had to take clerical positions in any numbers for decades. A progression from a clerical position to a high executive position has not been available for female employees, because their jobs were and mostly still are considered dead-end in most workplaces. Even in companies in which a policy of promotion from within provides some new hires with long promotion ladders, the men in entry-level positions typically climb those ladders far more often than do the entry-level women.[41]

Some companies allow women to be promoted to low-level supervisory positions where their job is to supervise other women. However their chance to go still higher is poor, and their pay relative to that of male supervisors is low. As a result, the women supervisors will quit more often than their male counterparts. Paradoxically, this kind of setup may sometimes result in a higher rate of promotions for the women than for the men in the company, although the jobs the women are promoted into will be dead-end.[42]

Changing Conditions in the Market for Women's Labor

In 1964, when the Civil Rights Act was passed, the wage of women with full-time jobs averaged about 60 percent of men's. It did not escape notice of some male economists that this ratio was the very same one ordained in the Old Testament: the Book of Leviticus orders that the value of maidservants be counted as three fifths that of manservants. Those who invoked the biblical text did so with obvious relish, and seemed to be hinting that the ratio was one of nature's constants, like pi, and might have been fixed by the Deity Himself.[43]

Indeed, for the next 15 years, that ratio failed to advance significantly. Around about 1979 the Deity apparently relented. Women's pay has since risen slowly but fairly steadily relative to men's. By 2002 women were averaging 78 percent of men's pay.[44] However, at this rate of advance, parity will not arrive until the fifth decade of the twenty-first century. The advantage in pay that men have over women in the American labor market continues to be sizable. A man with a bachelor's degree earns on average $20,521 more a year than a male high school graduate. A woman with a bachelor's degree who works full time earns only $6,758 more than that male high school grad. Outright exclusion and harassment of women workers still occur, and important segments of the labor market remain virtually closed to women.

Women high school graduates still earn less than male high school dropouts, women college graduates earn less than men who have dropped out of college, and women with a doctorate earn less than men with a master's degree. Still, these figures represent a significant improvement over the situation 40 years previously. At the time of the Civil Rights Act, and for many years thereafter, women college graduates working full time were earning less on average than male high school dropouts.

Women are now well represented in management and professional jobs, where significant progress has been made. In large part, this is due to the enactment of Title IX of the Education Act, which required, among other things, colleges to stop discriminating against women applicants to law school, medical school, and business school. However, the clerical and administrative support occupations continue to be a women's ghetto, with women holding 74 percent of the jobs, a figure virtually unchanged since 1972. In 2002, not even 1 percent of women workers had jobs in the skilled crafts, which are relatively high paying, and do not require a college education. The male mechanic's $669 weekly paycheck, as compared with the female clerical worker's average of $512 or the female service worker's average of $366, shows the crucial advantage of men over women in the part of the population that has not been to college. The inability of non-college women to get crafts jobs virtually condemns such a woman to a low standard of living if she finds herself with a child or two and lacks a man who will share his income with her. In this respect, the labor market has not improved since the 1970s.

Only 8% of those selling motor vehicles in 2002 were women, the same percentage as was recorded in the year 1984. Sales representatives, who sell to business firms, were 75% male in 2002; they were 86% male in 1984. A stroll through a department store will verify that the sales occupations found there are still largely segregated. Cashiers are 78% female, and may earn little more than the minimum wage. They were 82% female in 1984. Those selling television and other big-ticket items under more lucrative commission arrangements are 69% male; they were 80% male in 1984. Clearly, much segregation remains. Progress in desegregation has been slow, and in some fields nonexistent.

The destruction by terrorists of the towers of the World Trade Center on 9/11 of 2001 revealed graphic evidence of job segregation by race and sex. The *New York Times* printed several pages full of the portraits of the firefighters who had lost their lives on that day.[45] Out of the 343 who died, only 10 appeared to be African American. Not a single one was a woman. For a considerable time thereafter the sadness for those lost and the respect due to their sacrifice prevented any remark on the near-monopoly for white males that the published collection of the victims' photographs had revealed. However, in 2003 the *New York Times* ran a story that reviewed some of the unsavory history of the Fire Department's personnel practices. Spurred by a lawsuit attacking sex discrimination, the Department had hired 50 women in 1982. However, harassment and ostracism by male colleagues had plagued the women firefighters, and more than half had since left. The hiring of women had been allowed to lapse – of the 5,000 firefighters the New York City Fire Department had hired between 1990 and 2003, only 9 were women.[46]

Conclusion

Part of the improvement of women's labor market situation in the last three decades derives from an improvement in their human capital, and part from a decrease in discrimination in some parts of the labor market. However, sex discrimination remains an important factor in American labor markets.

Under Democratic administrations, ostensibly committed to the achievement of fair employment practices, the agencies charged with fighting employment discrimination have been inept, unimaginative, inefficient, and short of resources. Republican administrations have tended to be openly hostile, if not to the ideal of fair employment practices, then to any and every instrument that might be used by the government to promote that goal.

Women activists have not succeeded in pushing the politicians to do better. Perhaps they have themselves internalized the appropriateness of sex segregation of occupations. The sad truth is that organizations dedicated to women's rights have shown little energy and had little success in pushing measures that would lead toward equality in the workplace. Rather, they seem to concentrate the biggest portion of their energy on issues such as abortion rights and paid parental leave. Yet the importance of conquering employment discrimination for improving women's lives and status can hardly be overestimated, given the continuing decline in the proportion of adult women who are married, and the continuing rise in births to unmarried women. Women who are not living in households where they are sharing the income of a man have a particular need for access to jobs and to pay on the same basis as a man if they and their children are to escape poverty and lead a mainstream lifestyle. But all women deserve such access and have a right to it.

Notes

1   For a disquisition on economists' lack of empirical interface see Bergmann, B. R. (2005a). The state of economics: Needs lots of work. *Annals of the American Academy of Political and Social Science, 600*, 52–67.

2   See Schultz, T. W. (March, 1960). Investment in human capital. *American Economic Review, 51*(1), 1–17. For an extended discussion of gender issues with respect to human capital, see Blau, F. D., Ferber, M. A., & Winkler, A. E. (2006). *The economics of women, men, and work* (5th ed.). Upper Saddle River, NJ: Pearson/Prentice-Hall.

3   Becker, G. S. (1957). *The economics of discrimination*. Chicago: University of Chicago Press.

4   For a review of the curious aspects of Becker's other Nobel Prize-winning work see Bergmann, B. R. (1995). Becker's theory of the family: Preposterous conclusions, *Feminist Economics, 1*(1), 141–150.

5   Morgan v. Hertz Corp. 542 F.Supp. 123 (1981).

6   See Mill, J. S. (2004). *Principles of Political Economy* (1848). Amherst, NY: Prometheus Books. (Original work published 1848.) See Book II, ch. 4.

7   Mincer, J., & Polachek, S. (1974). Family investments in human capital: Earnings of women. *Journal of Political Economy, 82*(2, Part 2), S76–S108.

8   Polachek, S. W. (1981). Occupational self-selection: A human capital approach to sex differences in occupational structure. *Review of Economics and Statistics, 63*(1), 60–69.

9   England, P. (1982). The failure of human capital theory to explain occupational sex segregation. *Journal of Human Resources* (Spring), 358–370.

10 For a fuller discussion see Bergmann, B. R. (2005b). *The economic emergence of women.* New York: Palgrave.

11 Corcoran, M., & Duncan G. J. (1979). Work history, labor force attachment, and earnings differences between the sexes. *Journal of Human Resources, 14*(1, Winter), 3–20.

12 More women than men work part time. But that cannot account for the sex differences in wages noted in the text as unaccounted for by human capital or behavioral differences, since the studies reported there were based on data for full-time workers.

13 These calculations, made by the author, were based on data from the Current Population Survey. See Bergmann (2005b). Ordinary least squares regression on gross weekly wage of all full-time workers over 18 were run, with sex used as explanatory variables. The adjusted r-square is 0.29. A slightly better fit is obtained with a regression on the logarithm of the weekly wage, but the results are similar.

14 Many of those who did not work full time year round did not leave the labor market, but had a spell of involuntary unemployment.

15 Corcoran & Duncan (1979).

16 The data set also gives information on male workers' children, but I have assumed that men's work behavior and therefore their pay is not affected by the presence of children.

17 Jane Waldfogel has found large and persistent negative effects on women's hourly wages of dropping out of the labor force, which in most cases is for the purposes of child rearing. However, her sample included full-time and part-time workers. The latter were more likely to have dropped out, and part-time work is typically paid less than full-time work. See Waldfogel, J. (1998). Understanding the "family gap" in pay for women with children. *The Journal of Economic Perspectives, 12,* 137–156.

18 One plausible explanation is that the high cost of child care causes some mothers to opt for part-time jobs or to stay home, and that this is particularly true of women who have reason to believe that their earnings will be sub-par given their education.

19 Daniel Hamburg, in a private communication, points out that some women workers whose children are over 18 may in the past have dropped out of the labor force to care for them, or worked part time, and that part of the currently existing gap may be due to that.

20 A small part of the pay gap between women and men is due to this fact, because African Americans constitute a higher proportion of the female work force than of the male work force. However, the opposite is true of Hispanic workers – they are a higher proportion of the male than of the female work force. Altogether race and ethnicity differences in the male and female work force account for only $3 of the gap between women's and men's wages in 2002.

21 Based on data from U.S. Department of Labor, Bureau of Labor Statistics (August, 2001) *Highlights of women's earnings in 2000*, BLS Report 952, Table 3. Retrieved June 22, 2006, from www.bls.gov/cps/cpswom2000.pdf. New average wages for full-time male and female workers were calculated on the assumption that (1) the total number of engineers would have been the same, (2) women would have had engineering jobs in proportion to their share of all professional jobs, and (3) that the additional women engineers would have earned what women engineers actually earned in that year ($949 per week), instead of the average pay of women professional workers ($725). This would have resulted in average female wages rising from $491 to $495, and male wages falling from $645 to $643.

22 See Becker, G. S. (1985). Human capital, effort, and the sexual division of labor. *Journal of Labor Economics*, 3(1, Part 2), S33–S58. The quotation is from page S35.

23 Becker, G. S. (1991). *A treatise on the family*. Cambridge, MA: Harvard University Press.

24 See Bielby, D. D., & Bielby, W. T. (1988). She works hard for the money: Household responsibilities and the allocation of work effort. *American Journal of Sociology*, 93, 1031–1059.

25 See Riach, P. A., & Rich, J. (2002). Field experiments of discrimination in the market place. *Economic Journal, 112*, 480–518.

26 King, R. (1997, April 27). Bias lawsuit has LA roots. *New Orleans Times-Picayune*.

27 King (1997).

28 Bloomberg News (September 20, 1997). Home Depot settles four sex bias lawsuits; retail chain will take $104 million charge. *The Houston Chronicle*.

29 Again, as is typical in cases settled without trial, no fault was admitted.

30 Greenhouse, S. (February 16, 2003). Wal-Mart faces lawsuit over sex discrimination. *The New York Times*, p. 18.

31 Valásquez, M. (n.d.). *The national litigious environment*. Retrieved June 22, 2006, from www.diversitydtg.com.

32 Massachusetts Institute of Technology (1999). *A study on the status of women faculty in science at MIT*. Boston, MA: Massachusetts Institute of Technology. The quotation is from p. 8.

33 Massachusetts Institute of Technology (1999), p. 3.

34 Bergmann, B. R. (1971). The effect on white incomes of discrimination in employment. *Journal of Political Economy*, 79, 294–313; Bergmann, B. R. (1974). Occupational segregation, wages and profits when employers discriminate by race and sex. *Eastern Economic Journal, 1*(2), 103–110; and Bergmann (2005b).

35 Tomaskovic-Devey, D. (1993). *Gender and racial inequality at work: The sources and consequences of job segregation*. Ithaca, NY: ILR Press.

36 This proportion of women changing (PWC) is calculated as

@max(0, f(i)/F − (f(i) + m(i))/(F + M)) summed over i,

where f(i) and m(i) are the number of female and male workers in the ith industry, and F and M are the total number of female and male workers.

The "index of dissimilarity" (DI) from these same data is .52. calculated as

$$\tfrac{1}{2}*@abs(f(i)/F - m(i)/M) \text{ summed over } i$$

The DI is usually described as the proportion of women or men who would have to change occupations, but that is incorrect. See Anker, R. (1998). *Gender and jobs: Sex segregation in occupations in the world.* Geneva: International Labor Office. Beller calculated the index of dissimilarity as .63 for 1981 and as .71 for 1950 (Beller, A. H. (1984). Trends in occupational segregation by sex and race, 1960–1981. In Barbara F. Reskin (Ed.), *Sex segregation in the workplace* (pp. 11–26). Washington, DC: National Academy Press.)

37   Sometimes economists speak of a single labor market divided into segments, based on sex, and also on class and human capital differences. Workers are compartmentalized into particular segments, and cannot move from one segment to another. The idea of a "dual labor market" is similar. See Doeringer, P., & Piore, M. J. (1971). *Internal labor markets and manpower analysis.* Lexingon, MA: D. C. Heath & Co.

38   See Chapter 7 of England, P., & Farkas, G. (1985). *Households, employment, and gender: A social, economic and demographic view.* New York: Aldine.

39   Perhaps this is a better interpretation of Becker's (1957) discrimination coefficient.

40   See Doeringer & Piore (1971).

41   Letter of Jay Allen, Wal-Mart Senior Vice President for Corporate Affairs (2003, September 10). *Washington Post*, p. A18.

42   Some researchers mistakenly use the rate of promotion by sex in judging whether women are discriminated against. See, for example, McCue, K. (1996). Promotions and wage growth. *Journal of Labor Economics, 14*(2), 175–209.

43   One of those quoting Leviticus, and in a journal not usually given to citing God's word, was Fuchs, V. (1986, April). Sex differences in economic well-being. *Science, 25,* 459–464.

44   These data are from the Bureau of Labor Statistics, and refer to full-time wage and salary workers. See http://www.bls.gov

45   The portraits were reprinted in the book *Portraits 9/11/01: The collected "Portraits of Grief" from* The New York Times (2002). New York: Times Books.

46   Trying to Fill a Fallen Husband's Boots: Widow of Firefighter Killed on 9/11 Wants to Join the Department. (April 2, 2003). *New York Times*, p. A19. The *Times* editorial staff clearly know about the extreme segregation in the fire department in the fall of 2001, having published the page of photographs, but only reported on that segregation almost two years later, and only in the context of a human interest story about a particular woman.

15

Legal Perspectives on Employment Discrimination

Deborah L. Rhode and Joan C. Williams

It has been four decades since passage of legislation guaranteeing equal pay and equal employment opportunity between women and men, and the nation is nowhere close to achieving either. Despite significant progress, the workplace remains highly gender-segregated and gender-stratified, with women overrepresented at the bottom and underrepresented at the top in terms of status, power, and income. The annual pay gap between full-time female and male workers is about 20 percent, and significant disparities persist even among those with equivalent education, experience, and job responsibilities.

The present chapter addresses the disjuncture between legal principles and workplace realities. The first section provides a brief review of the law and the inequalities it has failed to address in the paid labor market. The second section of the chapter offers explanations for the disjuncture between the law's aspirations and achievements. The third documents recent developments in the legal campaign for sexual equality, with a particular focus on litigation challenging the "maternal wall." The final section concludes with reform proposals that might help narrow the distance between principles and practices concerning gender equity in the workplace.

Legal Rules and Workplace Realities

Legal prohibitions against sex discrimination

Statutes and case law In 1963, Congress passed the Equal Pay Act (EPA), which requires employers to pay men and women the same salaries for substantially equal work.[1] A year later, Title VII of the Civil Rights Act of 1964 prohibited discrimination on grounds of sex. Early Title VII cases involved explicit exclusions of women from jobs traditionally held by men, in an era when want ads were commonly divided by sex. Examples were lawsuits challenging requirements that flight attendants be female[2] and railroad switchworkers be male.[3] As a consequence, explicit exclusion of women became decreasingly common. However, contemporary case law suggests that some employers still discriminate openly against mothers; women have been told that they belong at home with their children,[4] or that they should choose between having children and having a career.[5] Contemporary Title VII cases generally take two forms: disparate impact cases, which involve facially neutral employment policies that have a disproportionate effect on one sex, or disparate treatment cases, which involve intentionally different treatment on the basis of sex.

Disparate impact cases stem from the Supreme Court's interpretation of Title VII in the landmark case of *Griggs v. Duke Power*. Under this interpretation, the statute prohibits facially neutral practices that disproportionately affect a protected group unless they are job related or justified by business necessity.[6] These disparate impact cases typically turn on a statistical showing that the proportion of qualified women in the relevant labor pool is lower than the proportion of women in the workplace at issue. This remedial structure was sharply constricted by two Supreme Court decisions in the late 1980s but partially restored in the Civil Rights Act of 1991.[7] A typical disparate impact case might involve a female applicant for a blue-collar position who shows that qualifying tests disproportionately excluded women and demanded more physical strength than the position in fact required.

The traditional wisdom is that while disparate impact cases turn on statistics, disparate treatment cases turn on intent. In general, disparate treatment cases require proof that the employer intentionally treated similarly qualified women and men differently, and that the women otherwise would have obtained particular jobs or benefits. For example, a female manager might attempt to demonstrate that she was left out of informal business networks and that she lost a promotion to a male colleague with lower performance evaluations. A key question is what constitutes "intent" for Title VII purposes. While some courts understand "intent" under Title VII to require discrimination that is self-conscious and malicious, this interpretation is far from universal. The decisive issue in a disparate treatment case is whether men and women were treated differently. The traditional method in a case involving a female plaintiff is to identify a similarly situated man who was treated better. This can, but need not, involve proof of conscious intentional bias. As noted below, a new trend has emerged in which parties can prove disparate treatment through evidence of sex-based stereotypes, even in the absence of a comparably qualified worker who received better treatment.

Moreover, a number of important Title VII theories do not fit readily under either disparate impact or disparate treatment frameworks. The best known is sexual harassment law, which prohibits both "quid pro quo harassment" (insisting on sexual favors as a condition of employment) and a hostile work environment based on gender.[8] The Pregnancy Discrimination Act, an amendment to Title VII, also requires employers to treat pregnant employees "the same" as other employees.[9]

A related Title VII theory is constructive discharge. Such a discharge occurs when an employer imposes intolerable working conditions precipitated by unlawful discrimination or harassment that lead a reasonable employee to resign.[10] Prevailing constructive discharge plaintiffs are entitled to all damages available under Title VII for an unlawful termination, including back pay. In some federal circuits, proving constructive discharge requires proof that the employer deliberately created the intolerable working conditions in an effort to compel the plaintiff to resign.[11]

Finally, Title VII does not just disallow discrimination; it also prohibits employers from retaliating against a worker who has engaged in activity protected under Title VII, such as an informal complaint of gender discrimination.[12] For example, in *Snodgrass v. Brown*, a federal district court in Kansas allowed a plaintiff to sue based on a claim that her employer had retaliated for her threat to file a discrimination claim; his retaliation allegedly involved a sudden schedule change that she was unable to keep due to an inability to find last-minute child care. Parties often add retaliation claims to their Title VII cases wherever possible, because it is actually easier in some contexts to prove retaliation than it is to prove the underlying discrimination claim.[13]

The Civil Rights Act of 1991 strengthened Title VII by allowing plaintiffs to recover not only compensatory damages such as lost wages, but also punitive damages and damages for emotional distress. However, such damages are only available in disparate treatment suits, and are subject to caps of between $50,000 and $300,000, depending on the size of the employer.[14]

In addition to the EPA and Title VII, the Family and Medical Leave Act (FMLA) attempts to reduce workplace barriers that disproportionately affect women. FMLA requires employers with more than 50 workers to provide up to 12 weeks unpaid leave to employees who have worked at least 1,250 hours in the prior year; the leave may be used for serious illness of employees or their family members or for parental care following childbirth or adoption. FMLA not only prohibits covered employers from refusing to grant FMLA leaves, it also prohibits them from "interfering" with leaves. For example, *Liu v. Amway Corporation* allowed a woman scientist to sue when she was pressured to reduce her maternity leave and was denied another family leave to care for her dying father, after which she received a poor performance review and was laid off.[15]

U. S. Constitution   Employees who work for a state or local government can sue not only under federal statutes but also under the Fourteenth Amendment to the United States Constitution. The Amendment applies only to government, not private employers; by its terms it prevents states from denying equal protection of the laws. Like federal and state equal employment statutes, the Fourteenth Amendment bars gender discrimination against men as well as women.

A celebrated example is *Knussman v. Maryland*, in which a state trooper sued successfully when he was denied a paid parental leave routinely granted to women holding the same position.[16]

Executive measures: Affirmative action   In 1965, President Lyndon Johnson signed Executive Order (EO) 11246. It requires federal contractors over a certain size to take action affirmatively to end both racial and gender discrimination. More specifically, any organization with more than 50 employees doing more than $50,000 of business with the federal government must monitor their workforce to make sure that they employ qualified women and minorities in proportion to their availability in the relevant labor pool. If the organization's self-monitoring reveals that the organization is utilizing a smaller percentage of women or minorities in any job classification, given the pool of qualified employees, the organization must devise goals and timetables for remedying the situation and must demonstrate that it is making a good faith effort to meet those goals. Many local, state, and federal agencies also require some form of affirmative action, and large numbers of employers have initiated voluntary plans.[17]

Economic realities

In spite of these laws, substantial sex-based inequalities persist in the American workforce.

The wage gap   Although the gap between women's and men's earnings has been slowly eroding over the past quarter century, the disparity remains significant. Adjusting for hours worked (but not for differences in education or experience), women's median weekly earnings in 1979 were 63 percent those of men. In 2004, those earnings were 80 percent.[18] With the exception of Asians, women of color are at the bottom of the economic scale. In 2004, median weekly earnings broken down by race, ethnicity, and sex were: Asian men, $708, Asian women, $613; white men, $657, white women, $584; African American men, $525, African American women, $505; and Hispanic or Latino men, $456 and Hispanic or Latino women, $419.[19] At current rates of change, it would take an estimated half century to achieve gender parity.[20]

Part of the explanation for the gender gap in wages is the concentration of women in lower-paying occupations. More than three-quarters of women work in two of five job categories: technical, sales, and administrative support; and managerial and professional specialties. Within these categories, almost two-thirds work in the lowest-paying area of administrative support.[21] Women make up the vast majority of the labor force in poorly paying fields such as secretarial assistance (98%) and child care (96%).[22] Although women now constitute about half of the workforce in occupations typified by high earnings (executive, administrative, and managerial positions), these female employees earn only 71% of what their male colleagues earn and are underrepresented in the best-paid positions. So too, women in managerial and professional fields are more likely to work in relatively lower-paying areas. For example, women constitute about 14% of architects and engineers, but 86% of paralegals.

Even in the same fields, women earn less. For example, among lawyers, women earn 73% of what men earn; among CEOs, 70%; among bartenders, 81%; and among nurses, 87%.[23] Much of the disparity is hard to explain in terms of qualifications and job responsibilities. Even female dishwashers earn on average $2,000 less per year than male dishwashers.[24] The gap widens further at the highest earning levels. According to IRS data, the ratio of men to women earning over $1 million is 13:1; among those earning $200,000 to $1,000,000 the ratio is slightly less than 10:1.[25]

The actual wage disparity between all female and male employees is considerably greater than the gender gap between full-time female and male employees because women are far more likely to work part time, or for only part of the year. For example, around 25% of women in wage and salary jobs are part-time employees, compared with only 11% of men.[26] These jobs are paid significantly less on a pro-rata basis than full-time jobs and carry fewer benefits. As noted below, women are also more likely to take time out of the labor force, typically for family reasons, which disrupts their earning potential.

Recent research by economists Stephen J. Rose and Heidi Hartmann suggests the extent of the real gap. They examined the 15-year earning patterns of women and men from the Michigan Panel Study of Income Dynamics. Over the period 1983–1998 women on average earned only 38% of what men did. Even women who were in the paid labor force for the entire period earned only 57%. Men without high school diplomas earned more than women with college degrees; women with graduate degrees earned about the same as male high school graduates.[27]

How much of the disparities within occupational fields can be attributed to differences in qualifications, experience, and job responsibilities is a matter of dispute. Lawyers are a case in point. As noted earlier, Department of Labor statistics on weekly earnings for lawyers find that women earn 73% of what men earn.[28] Although some qualitative evidence suggests that law firm interviewers are more concerned about the marital status and reproductive intentions of women than of men, female and male law graduates seem to fare about the same in initial hiring and compensation processes. However, a gap grows over time. A representative study of Colorado lawyers found that salaries for full-time female lawyers during their first three years of practice were 92% of salaries of full-time male lawyers when controlled for years of experience. For lawyers with 10–20 years of practice, the figure was 74%.[29] Similarly, a study of University of Michigan Law School graduates found that salaries of female lawyers were, on average, 71% of salaries of male lawyers with equivalent years in practice. For lawyers with 15 years of experience, the gap was 61%. In both the Colorado and Michigan studies, the gap for more experienced lawyers had not narrowed over the previous 6–10 years.[30] Such patterns are consistent with earlier data on gender disparities in lawyers' earnings.[31]

Some of these disparities are attributable to gender differences in qualifications, position, and hours worked.[32] However, studies controlling for various personal characteristics such as education and experience, or employment context, such as sector, specialty, or firm size, consistently leave some portion of the disparity unexplained.[33] Researchers also generally find significant differences in the returns to women and men for factors influencing income. For example, one study found that in both small and large firms, men received large income premiums from attaining partnership while the impact of partnership on women's incomes was statistically insignificant. Men also obtained higher income premiums from attending a prestigious law school.[34] So too, when controlling for hours worked and other work-related factors, marriage and children are associated with a rise in income for male but not female lawyers.[35] Although part of the gender disparity in earning reflects women's overrepresentation in lower-earning specialties such as family law, public interest law, and government service, most research finds that occupational segregation is not the primary cause of the gender wage gap.[36]

The glass ceiling   Much of the disparity in female and male earnings is attributable to women's underrepresentation in positions of greatest economic rewards. For example, in management, where women constitute about half the new entrants to the field, they represent only 16% of board members and officers, 8% of top leadership positions, and 2% of chief executive officers. In law, women also account for about half of all new entrants to the legal profession, but only 17% of law firm partners, 16% of federal district court judges, and 15% of law school deans and general counsels. The gap widens for women of color, who constitute 3% of the profession, and only 1% of deans, general counsels, and law firm partners.[37] Women comprise over half of the voting public, but only 16% of their congressional representatives and governors and 20% of their state legislators. The United States ranks sixty-sixth in the world in electing female political leaders.

One effort to quantify the extent of the glass ceiling across occupations involved a national survey of equal opportunity data from some 160,000 employers with about 37 million workers. The study identified establishments that were so far below the average utilization of women or minorities for the industry and metropolitan area that there was only one chance in a hundred that the underrepresentation occurred randomly. Such a disparity would be sufficient to trigger a legal presumption of employment discrimination. The study revealed that about 60,000 organizations employing some 925,000 women had gender imbalances sufficient to suggest discrimination.[38]

The maternal wall   Women with substantial caretaking commitments in the home pay an especially substantial price in the world outside it. For women, but not men, the more years children are present in the household, the lower the number of working years and hours, and the lower the income.[39] Married working mothers average about half of what their husbands earn.[40] Most research finds that men who have children also have higher earnings than men who do not. The reverse is true for women.[41] Efforts to quantify this "motherhood penalty" have varied in methodologies and results, but generally find a decline between 4% and 7% for one child.[42] Some, but not all of these studies control for experience and related factors; one that does so finds the penalty drops so that it is only about 5%.[43] According to another study, the penalty has not declined between the mid 1970s and late 1990s.[44] For high-achieving women who drop out, the losses are severe: an 11% decline in earnings after a one-year absence; 37% for three or more years out.[45]

Various explanations have been offered for this penalty. Child rearing may cause women to leave the workforce, to be less productive on the job, to choose family-friendly positions that pay less, and to experience bias from employers and co-workers.[46] Similar accounts have been offered for the glass ceiling and the wage gap generally, and all deserve at least a brief summary here. In order to understand the capacities and limitations of law in addressing employment inequalities, it is necessary to understand their underlying causes.

Explaining the Inequalities

The vast majority of Americans support gender equity and their legislators have enacted a wide range of laws to promote it. But substantial inequalities remain. What explains their persistence? We offer two primary explanations. The first focuses on the limitations of current laws and enforcement structures. The second explores how stereotypes sustain gender differences, encourage gendered choices, and perpetuate gender hierarchies.

Limits of the law

American employment law concerning gender equity is a complex, multilayered system of federal and state legislation, administrative regulation, and judicial rulings. Largely in response to these formal legal mandates, employers have also developed their own internal policies and dispute resolution processes. Although this body of regulation has played a central role in expanding women's workplace opportunities, it is limited in key respects. Certain crucial statutes relating to women's employment, notably the EPA and FMLA, are severely restricted in scope. A second limitation of current regulatory structures involves the gap between formal policies and actual practices. Many guarantees that look effective in principle are ineffectual in fact. A third limitation concerns the expense and evidentiary hurdles in enforcing legal rights. These limitations help explain the persistence of gender inequality despite decades of legal reforms.

Selective scope of formal rights The first and one of the most important legal protections for women in the workplace is the EPA of 1963. By its terms, the act requires equal compensation for jobs that require the same effort, skill, and responsibility and are performed under similar working conditions. However, as noted above, the American workplace remains highly gender segregated, so the vast majority of male and female workers are not in the same occupations or the same job classifications within those occupations. Moreover, courts have interpreted EPA requirements in highly restrictive ways, and largely excluded white-collar occupations from coverage.[47] A representative example is *Georgen-Saad v. Texas Mutual Insurance Co.*[48] There, the plaintiff, a Senior Vice President of Finance, alleged underpayment in comparison with other senior vice presidents in the company. The court dismissed that claim without factual analysis on the ground that "the assertion that any one of these jobs requires 'equal skill, effort, and responsibility'. . . cannot be taken seriously . . . These are Senior Vice Presidents in charge of different aspects of Defendant's operation; these are not assembly-line workers or customer-service representatives." In the trial judge's view, the EPA could deal only with "commodity-like" work, not the functions of high-level executives.

On similar reasoning, courts have consistently rejected efforts to enforce standards of comparable worth, or pay equity. In effect, these standards rely on expert evaluations to assess the skills, responsibilities, and working conditions of jobs that are not identical, and require comparable pay for work of comparable worth. Although this approach has been widely adopted in the public sector and in many other industrialized nations, American courts and legislatures have dismissed it as a radical departure from market principles and an invitation to a "hopeless morass."[49]

Another illustration of partial policies involves the 1993 FMLA. It requires employers with more than 50 workers to provide up to 12 weeks unpaid leave to employees who have worked at least 1,250 hours in the prior year; the leave may be used for serious illness of employees or their family members or for parental care following childbirth or adoption. The restricted scope of the act leaves about half the workforce unprotected; it excludes individuals who work for small employers or in temporary or part-time positions. Moreover, unpaid leave benefits only those who can afford to take it, and one Department of Labor study found that 88 percent of those who were eligible for leave did not exercise the option.[50]

Only one state, California, mandates paid leave, leaving the United States virtually alone among developed nations in failing to provide this benefit. Ironically, because women are overrepresented in part-time jobs, they are less likely than men to be eligible for family leave, even though they are far more likely to want it. They are also short-changed by policies that provide only full-time workers with other benefits like unemployment insurance and health care coverage.

The gap between policies and practices Organizations often circumvent legal requirements. William Bielby, one of the nation's leading experts in employment discrimination, notes that "wired searches," "preselected promotion candidates," "perfunctory performance evaluations," and cosmetic corrective plans are common even in organizations with policies that look effective on paper.[51] Lawyers and consultants routinely coach employers about how to create an appropriate paper trail in order to minimize the risk of legal liability. One strategy is to ensure that performance reviews always include discussions of employee weaknesses. Another is to establish internal dispute resolution processes that seek to defuse grievances and to redefine incidents of perceived discrimination as "misunderstandings."[52] Policies designed to promote equal opportunity too often serve to mask its absence.

Another gap between policies and practices involves parental leave. Although virtually all organizations over a certain size now offer some form of parental leave, fewer than 15 percent of Fortune 100 companies offer the same paid leave to fathers as mothers.[53] Moreover, the vast majority of eligible employees cannot afford to exercise the option of unpaid leave, or fear the stigma and marginalization that may attach to doing so. A wide array of research underscores the hostility from supervisors and co-workers that workers experience when they try to limit their hours in response to family needs.[54] Similarly, although a growing proportion of employers permit a reduced schedule, relatively few women or men in upper-level managerial or professional positions feel able to take one.

The legal profession provides a good example. About 95 percent of surveyed law firms permit part-time work, but only about 4 percent of lawyers take advantage of the opportunity.[55] About three-quarters of surveyed women believe that a reduced schedule would jeopardize their prospects for partnerships.[56] There is ample basis for such concern. Associates commonly report that "no time . . . is the right time" to get pregnant,[57] and reports of stigma associated with part-time work are common.[58] Lawyers at all stages of their careers find that reducing their schedules or taking time off, even for a brief parental leave, can result in the loss of challenging work and career development opportunities.[59] In addition to isolation and marginalization, many part-time lawyers report "schedule creep." "Reduced hours are not respected, 'unexpected emergencies' become expected events, and attorneys can often end up with full-time work for part-time pay."[60]

Barriers to enforcement   Effective legal rules require effective enforcement structures. Aside from affirmative action as established by Executive Order 11246, most antidiscrimination law in the United States requires victims to seek a remedy. Few do so. A national survey of some one thousand workers demonstrated the reluctance of workers to take action. Of those who reported unfair treatment in the workplace, about a third did nothing. Slightly over a quarter reported the incident to a supervisor. Only a fifth filed an internal complaint and only 3 percent brought a legal action.[61]

That reluctance to take action reflects several factors. A wide array of social science research makes clear that most individuals do not like to present themselves as victims; it erodes their sense of control and self-esteem and involves the unpleasantness of identifying a perpetrator.[62] Other individuals are deterred by the high costs of taking action and the low probability of being rewarded or reinforced for doing so. Workers who wish to file a sex discrimination lawsuit generally must first file a complaint with a state or federal equal employment opportunity commission (EEOC). The federal EEOC facilitates remedies for only about a fifth of complainants, and the damages they receive are modest, averaging less than \$14,000.[63] State remedies are similar. If the defendant in a sex discrimination suit can show that, despite discriminatory considerations, the decisions or outcomes would have been the same irrespective of gender, then the recoveries available to a plaintiff are limited to attorney's fees and to injunctive relief. It is common for discrimination lawsuits to drag on for years, cost thousands of dollars, and seriously strain an individual's personal relations and personal resources.

Complainants who file suit face significant evidentiary hurdles. Proving discrimination often requires a pool of similarly qualified male and female applicants that is large enough to permit sex-based comparisons; it may also require expensive statistical studies and expert witnesses. Evidentiary barriers may be insurmountable in contexts involving smaller workforces or upper-level positions, which do not lend themselves to statistical comparisons. Winning such cases frequently demands fairly explicit evidence of bias, which may be hard to come by. Colleagues who could corroborate discrimination may be reluctant to expose it for fear of jeopardizing their own positions. Employers of even "minimal sophistication will neither admit discriminatory . . . [conduct] nor leave a paper trail demonstrating it."[64] Even when plaintiffs can produce direct evidence of bias, some courts deny its significance. "Stray remarks" in the workplace are insufficient to establish liability if the defendant can demonstrate some legitimate reason for the unfavorable treatment.[65]

A sobering example of the difficulties of proof involves the first sex discrimination case to go to trial against a law firm or any professional partnership. The lawsuit involved Nancy Ezold, a litigation associate at a prominent Philadelphia firm. At the time she was rejected for partnership, the firm's litigation department had one female partner; nationally, about 11 percent of partners at large firms were female. The trial court found for Ezold, based on uniformly positive evaluations by the partners for whom she had worked, and a comparison with other male associates who had been promoted despite performance concerns similar to those expressed about Ezold. The court also relied on evidence of gender stereotypes, such as some partners' belief that she was too "assertive" and too preoccupied with "women's issues."

The court of appeals reversed that decision. In its view, the performance concerns of the two-thirds of partners who voted against Ezold were not so "obvious or manifest" a pretext as to justify liability. The appellate judges also criticized the trial court for its "pick and choose" selection of comments to compare, even as they engaged in the same process themselves to overturn the ruling.[66]

Sex discrimination complainants may also arbitrate claims rather than sue in court, but face comparable barriers when they do. A growing number of employment contracts now include provisions requiring arbitration of discrimination claims, although the EEOC, the American Arbitration Association (AAA) and the National Academy of Arbitration all oppose the practice. Currently, several million employees are subject to mandatory arbitration agreements.

Arbitration includes structural defects that disfavor employees. First, employers are "repeat players" who have more information about arbitrators than employees, and more incentives to acquire it. Arbitrators are also likely to be influenced by the fact that employers, not complainants are the source of future business, and by the lack of accountability for decisions. Opinions often are not written and awards are overturned only for egregious procedural problems such as fraud, not for substantive errors.[67] The underrepresentation of women is also a concern; only 6 percent of some 50,000 AAA arbitrators are female. Significant recoveries for discrimination complainants are so infrequent that plaintiff lawyers seldom find it worthwhile to pursue such matters, which reduces incentives for employers to prevent grievances.[68] Arbitration can also be expensive. Unlike judges, whose time is free to the parties, arbitrators generally charge by the hour, often upwards of $350. Complaining parties frequently must prepay an administrative fee to file, and then share the cost of the arbitrator's charges.

The role of stereotypes

Barriers to enforcement of antidiscrimination laws are only part of the explanation for the disjuncture between legal rights and workplace realities. A full explanation of the gap must take into account social norms: the ideologies, preconceptions, prejudices that people bring to employment settings.

Gender bias   Legal scholars have begun to take cognizance of a phenomenon that has long been central to the research of many social sciences: "cognitive" or "unexamined" bias.[69] Such bias builds on group-based stereotypes and operates in ways that are often outside the awareness of the individual. At very early ages, children learn stereotypical attributes that are associated with particular social groups. These stereotypes predispose individuals to perceive and characterize information about group members in ways that conform to pre-existing associations. People can remain vulnerable to these effects even if their conscious beliefs are relatively free of such prejudices.[70]

Gendered assumptions about competence   Social status predicts perceived competence. Men, as measured by body language and patterns of deference, typically are accorded more status than women. In large national surveys, between half and three-quarters of female attorneys believe that they are held to higher standards than their male counterparts or have to work harder for the same results.[71] In some contexts, women may be held to a lower level of competence than men when they first apply for a position, but they usually find it harder to advance through organizations. Psychologist Monica Biernat has explained this "shifting standard of competence" as outgrowths of the same underlying assumption that females are simply less talented and valuable than males.[72]

The dynamics of gendered assumptions about competence are generally not apparent to everyday observation. Most Americans remain unaware of the different interpretations they place on identical behaviour by women and men. However, by focusing on specific instances of behavior at work, people can see if they give the same meaning to male and female conduct. Social bonding behaviors are a case in point. For men, such behaviors may be perceived as mentoring, rainmaking, negotiating. By contrast, women may be seen to be chatting with friends, or gossiping on the phone. Similarly, when a man is absent at 5 pm, he may be assumed to be at a business meeting; when a woman is absent, she may be assumed to be at home with her family.[73]

Also important are the explanations given for male and female success. The same performance by a woman is frequently perceived as less indicative of competence than by a man. Women's achievements are often attributed not to merit but to luck, special effort, or special treatment.[74]

Women in predominantly male environments tend to experience polarized evaluations. A few female superstars will attract special notice and receive higher evaluations than their male counterparts, but women who are just below that level tend to get disproportionately lower evaluations.[75] At the same time, the presence of a few highly regarded women at the top creates the illusion that the glass ceiling has been shattered for everyone else.

Women of color are often doubly disadvantaged because of negative assumptions about competence associated with race as well as gender. Their small numbers frequently place them under a special spotlight. The achievements of women of color are particularly likely to be attributed to affirmative action rather than "merit."[76]

Gender mismatches The stereotypical characteristics traditionally associated with women are at odds with many of the characteristics traditionally associated with effective performance at work, such as assertiveness, competitiveness, and technical expertise. People see warmth as inconsistent with competence in female workers, which gives rise to what psychologists Susan Fiske and Peter Glick term "ambivalent sexism."[77] Women who depart from traditional stereotypes are viewed as abrasive and unpleasant to work with; consequently, they have difficulty enlisting respect, support, and cooperation from co-workers.[78] As a result, female workers often face a double standard and a double bind. They risk appearing too "soft" or too "strident," too "aggressive" or insufficiently "assertive." Ambivalent sexism creates a "catch-22" that can leave women with the choice of being liked but not respected, or respected but not liked – in workplaces that typically require candidates to be both in order to succeed.

Madeline Heilman's research on "lack of fit" points in similar directions.[79] The qualities associated with being an effective manager closely track those associated with a typical man, but diverge sharply from those associated with a typical woman. In her studies, workers described high-achieving women as more "interpersonally hostile" than their male counterparts, and as more likely to be "bitter, quarrelsome and selfish . . . [with] an unbridled ambition for power and achievement."[80]

The literatures on ambivalent sexism and lack of fit offer important insights into workplace environments in which hard-driving women receive labels like "Attila the Hen," "Ice Queen," and "Battle Ax."[81] These literatures also help to explain the attribution bias at work when identical behavior is seen as admirably "assertive" in men but distastefully "aggressive" in women.[82] The perception of ambitious "career women" as "bitchy" and "difficult" has given rise to a profitable consulting industry, which aims to transform "bully broads" into softer, gentler feminine versions of their managerial selves.[83]

Attitudes toward self-promotion reflect a related mismatch between competence and femininity. Being perceived as a "go getter" is a prerequisite for success in many jobs. Yet psychological research finds that self-promoting behaviors viewed as appropriate in men are often viewed as distasteful and inappropriate in women; he is self-confident, she is arrogant and overbearing. The unexamined norm that women should be nurturing not self-serving creates another double bind that perpetuates gender inequality.[84]

Maternal wall   A rapidly growing literature documents that women experience distinctive kinds of stereotyping and bias once they become mothers. Some of these biases involve negative assumptions about the competence of those who are pregnant, mothers, and part-time workers. Social psychological research finds that although "businesswomen" are rated as highly competent and similar in ability to "businessmen," "housewives" are rated extremely low in competence, alongside the elderly, blind, "retarded," and "disabled."[85] "Working mothers" are viewed as more similar in competence to "housewives" than to "businesswomen."[86] It is not without significance that Americans rarely refer to working fathers.

Pregnancy and part-time work also give rise to negative assumptions about competence. When women become mothers, they are held to more rigorous standards of competence – and have to work longer hours to establish competence – than women without children. By contrast, when men become fathers, they have to work shorter hours and are held to lower standards of competence, than childless men.[87] One representative study found that the job evaluations of female managers "plummeted" after they announced their pregnancy, partly because pregnancy triggered the stereotype of women as irrational and overly emotional.[88]

Some evidence suggests that part-time workers may be subject to similar adverse stereotypes, which is a particular problem for women who comprise the majority of those on reduced schedules.[89] Multiple studies find stigma associated with part-time work.[90] In one illuminating psychology experiment, women who worked part time were viewed as less warm and nurturing than homemakers, but as having the same lack of go-getter qualities: they seemed to have the worst of both worlds. In addition, reduced schedules can trigger leniency and attribution biases. Part-time lawyers often report that they are assumed not to be working if they are not at their desk; they also lose any "benefit of the doubt" if they cannot give a co-worker as fast a turnaround as requested.[91]

Madeline Heilman's "lack of fit" analysis and Alice Eagly's "role incongruity" framework both provide insight into a common cultural message: women are often told (formally or informally) that they cannot be both good mothers and effective workers. This incongruity emerges in sharp relief in jobs where the ideal worker is defined as someone available 24/7, because the same expectation is made of the "good mother": she should be "willing to always be there and to do anything for the children."[92] Even employees in traditionally feminine jobs, such as school psychologist, have encountered this form of stereotyping.[93] Such biases are also apparent in workplaces where the accepted truth is that some (typically highly valued, demanding) jobs "just aren't suitable for mothers," while other (typically low-status, low-paid) jobs "just are."

Glick and Fiske's findings about ambivalent sexism have special significance when working mothers are the object of people's attitudes.[94] As Williams has noted, both hostile and benevolent sexism affect working mothers.[95] Hostile stereotyping involves strident criticism of women who do not adhere to traditionalist norms of selfless, stay-at-home motherhood. Benevolent stereotyping involves assumptions about mothers' availability or suitability for particular tasks. For example, employers may fail to consider a mother for a promotion because the higher-level job requires travel, but without asking the woman in question about her preferences. In fact, some mothers who object to a steady diet of long hours do not mind some out of town assignments, which can provide a welcome break in routines as well as an uninterrupted night's sleep.

In-group favoritism   While the sexist attitudes and assumptions of everyone, female and male, impede the advance of gender equality at work, another process, well documented by social scientists, known as "in-group favoritism" will present a problem only so long as men monopolize positions of power. In-group favoritism is apparent in the informal networks of mentoring, contacts, and support that are critical for workplace rewards. Employees generally feel most comfortable with those who are like them in important respects, including gender. Women in traditionally male-dominated fields often remain out of the loop of advice, favorable assignments, and professional development opportunities.[96] Women of color also experience particular difficulties because they are often treated as outsiders by white colleagues, and potential competitors by minority men.[97]

Not only do people prefer to associate with others like themselves, they also accord preferences to members of their own identity groups. Loyalty, cooperation, favorable evaluations, and allocation of rewards and opportunities all increase in likelihood for in-group members.[98] A key example is the presumption of competence that dominant groups accord to their members but not to outsiders. Members of in-groups tend to attribute accomplishments of fellow members to intrinsic characteristics, such as intelligence, drive, and commitment. By contrast, the achievements of out-group members are often ascribed to luck or to special treatment.[99]

One important form of in-group favoritism is leniency bias, which gives members of in-groups a more flexible application of a given standard in areas such as hiring, mentoring, promotion, performance evaluations, and merit reviews. For example, male employers may decline to promote a female worker who lacks a specific qualification, but give the benefit of the doubt to a similarly situated man due to his promising potential.[100] The scope for such bias is especially great in employment sectors where criteria for selection are subjective and network hiring is common; in these contexts, mentoring is crucial.[101]

Fundamental attribution error   Psychologists have long known that in Western nations, including the United States, individuals tend to overestimate the extent to which they are in control of their own actions. One aspect of the phenomenon is known as "the fundamental attribution error," and occurs when observers underestimate the situational constraints on individual behavior.[102] The misperception is pronounced in discussions of working mothers.

For example, within economics, "human capital" theorists argue that women "self-select" into occupations that require lower levels of skill and less educational investment because they anticipate working fewer years than men, with more interruptions.[103] Women are also said to choose occupations that offer lower pay in exchange for more pleasant and less hazardous working conditions, and for more flexible schedules that will accommodate family responsibilities.[104]

The empirical data concerning these theories are mixed. Economist Jane Friesen notes that evidence of compensating differentials for jobs with less favorable working conditions is "weak," except where risk of fatality is involved.[105] Other gender differences in work patterns are, however, well established. A comprehensive study by the General Accounting Office concluded that about half the gap between women and men's earnings is due to differences in work patterns, primarily men's longer hours and more continuous work histories, as well as differences in employee experience, education, occupation, and industry.[106] Other research suggests that women choose, at a higher rate than men, non-wage compensations, particularly forms that are family related. One study of workers between the ages of 24 and 36 across seven industries found that if earnings were adjusted to include not just salaries but also the value of fringe benefits (such as insurance coverage, training/education subsidies, profit sharing, maternity/paternity leave, flexible hours, employer-subsidized child care, and retirement benefits), then the gender gap narrowed from 87 percent to 96 percent.[107] In another study of some 3,000 high achieving women and men, defined as those with graduate or professional degrees or high honors undergraduate degrees, nearly four in ten women reported leaving the work force voluntarily over their careers and the same proportion reported choosing a job with lesser compensation and fewer responsibilities than they were qualified to assume in order to accommodate family responsibilities.[108]

Surveys reveal considerable variation in the number of women who cite family responsibilities as the primary reason for stepping out of the labor force; findings range from 12% to 75%.[109] However, one other consistent finding is that far fewer men report this concern. In the survey of highly qualified employees noted above, 44% of the women, but only 12% of the men cited caretaking responsibilities as the reason for leaving the workforce. For a majority of men, the main reasons were career changes and additional training, factors cited by fewer women.[110] In another study, 12% of the women emphasized family considerations, a reason that men rarely mentioned.[111]

A related economic theory is that profit-maximizing employers often "sort" women into lower-paying occupations through barriers in hiring and promotion. This "wage efficiency" model posits that firms use gender (or other observable characteristics) as an indicator of productivity when it is too costly or difficult to obtain perfect information about employees' willingness to work hard and their commitment to the labor force. Employers screen women out of high-paying employment when the cost of turnover or employee "monitoring" is expensive because they assume that women are more likely to leave the workforce and less willing to work extended hours.[112]

The evidence here is also mixed. It is clear that women have more discontinuous work histories than men. One study found that female employees left the paid labor force at a rate approximately three times that of male employees.[113] Economists Stephen Rose and Heidi Hartmann, using national data from the Michigan Panel Study of Income Dynamics, found that over a 15-year period, 52% of women, but only 16% of men, had at least one full calendar year with no earnings.[114] Almost a fifth of women with graduate or professional degrees are not in the paid labor force; only 5% of similarly credentialed men have opted out. One in three women with MBAs are not working full time, compared with one in twenty for their male peers.[115]

The implications of these data are, however, not conclusive because of the interrelationship between turnover, wages, and employment opportunities. Causality may run in both directions: women may leave the workforce at higher rates because of lower income and fewer opportunities, and also may experience lower incomes and opportunities because of workforce absences. Some evidence finds that the difference in women's and men's turnover is eliminated or reversed when researchers control for factors such as age, training, salary, and job characteristics.[116] Other surveys of highly qualified women find explanations such as inadequate flexibility, and limited opportunities for impact and career development.[117] A recent study on professional women who had opted out found that only about 16 percent were "new traditionalists" with strong unconstrained preferences to become full-time mothers. Over four-fifths of the sample (86%) cited work-related reasons for quitting their jobs, such as the expectation that they would be available 24/7, and the "schedule creep" common in part-time jobs where time constraints were not respected. These patterns privileged men with stay-at-home wives.[118] Other research similarly underscores the obvious: that women do not have the same choices as men in workplaces that enshrine as the ideal worker someone who is perpetually available – typically a man with a wife who has no paid employment.[119]

This research demonstrates a central difficulty with economic models built on women's choice: they incorporate the very bias they attempt to refute. Inequalities in the workplace, home, and culture generally influence the decisions that women make, including how they develop their human capital. For example, Rose and Hartmann note that when women "choose" to take more time out of the paid labor market than their husbands for family reasons, we need to ask "how much of that choice is constrained by lack of affordable, good quality alternative care, women's lower pay or inferior working conditions on the job, their expectations that they won't be promoted anyway, or social norms . . . ?[120]

Similar problems arise in the way that media generally present the "choice" framework formalized in human capital theory. For example, a cover story in the *New York Times Magazine* on the "opt-out revolution" claimed that women are underrepresented in leadership positions less because "the workplace has failed women" than because "women are rejecting the workplace." "Why don't women run the world?," asked author Lisa Belkin. "Maybe it's because they don't want to."[121] More recently, this viewpoint was reiterated by Warren Farrell in discounting discrimination as an explanation for women's disadvantaged economic position, and arguing that it reflects their choice for less demanding jobs, more pleasant working conditions, and a better work–life balance.[122] A front-page story in the *Times* suggested similar explanations based on a scarcely representative profile of Yale college women, who expected for some period to be stay-at-home mothers.[123]

Yet what is too often missed or marginalized in such accounts is the extent to which those choices are socially constructed and constrained. What drops out of the "opt-out" narrative are the complex forces that drive women's decisions. And what are equally notable for their absence are the choices that men make, as parents, policy leaders, and managers, that also limit the choices available to women. Many husbands are committed to equality more in principle than in practice, and are unwilling to structure their own lives to promote it. In one study of highly qualified women, close to four in ten felt that their husbands created more work around the house than they performed.[124] If women are "choosing" not to "run the world," it is partly because men are choosing not to run the washer/dryer.

In short, the disjuncture between legal aspirations and social realities is in part a function of the limited scope of equal opportunity laws and enforcement structures. But it is also partly attributable to cultural assumptions, attitudes, and ideologies. Significant progress in securing gender equity needs to take all of these dynamics into account.

Promising Developments in Employment Law

Despite the limitations sketched out above, employment law continues to play an important role in remedying and deterring discrimination, and encouraging proactive diversity initiatives. One of the most promising developments concerns the series of cases regarding discrimination against employed mothers.[125]

The Center for WorkLife Law has documented a sharp rise in litigation by mothers and other adults with family responsibilities, and has christened this phenomenon "family responsibilities discrimination," or FRD. Over 600 cases of workplace discrimination against caregivers have been identified, as well as a 419 percent increase in the past ten years, as compared with the prior decade.[126] Liability in these cases can be substantial. Over 67 cases have resulted in verdicts or settlements of over $100,000; the largest individual verdict was $11.65 million.[127]

Explaining the line of cases

How can one explain the successes achieved in these cases? Two factors seem quite important. First, the prejudices displayed by defendants have often been of the overt, not covert, variety. Second, cases that involve a challenge to the maternal wall often appeal, although perhaps for different reasons, to both conservative and liberal judges and jurors.

Bias against caregivers has often been extraordinarily open "1970s-style discrimination" that provides direct evidence that men and women (or mothers and fathers) are being treated differently. Many of the cases involve overt hostile stereotypes, both prescriptive and descriptive. For example, in *Bailey v. Scott-Gallaher, Inc.*, the plaintiff was fired when she contacted her employer to find out when she should return to work following the birth of her daughter. Her employer told her she was being discharged because she was "no longer dependable since she had delivered a child [and] that [her] place was at home with her child . . ." As is common, this prescriptive stereotyping was linked with descriptive stereotyping: the supervisor added that the plaintiff was not dependable since "babies get sick . . . and [she] would have to miss work to care for her child."[128] Such overt bias reappears in many other cases, fueled by a widespread (and misguided) sense that such talk is "tough love" rather than gender discrimination.[129]

A second major factor in the success of these maternal wall claims is that they often encounter a sympathetic hearing from both conservative and liberal judges. An apt illustration of the broad political appeal of these cases is a federal appellate case involving a mother whose son had so many ear infections that he ultimately suffered partial hearing loss. As the attorney for the plaintiff *Walsh v. National Computer Systems* put it, "[t]he story we told was that Shireen [Walsh] was made to choose between her job and being a good mother, and that made the jury really mad."[130] Walsh received $625,526 in damages, plus attorneys' fees.

Maternal wall cases appeal to conservative judges because they involve family values; they appeal to liberal judges because they involve gender discrimination. The author of the leading opinion in the landmark U.S. Supreme Court case (*Nevada Department of Human Resources v. Hibbs*) was former Chief Justice William Rehnquist, a noted conservative.[131] The leading federal appellate decision was authored by Guido Calabresi, a noted liberal.[132]

Hibbs stunned constitutional law commentators because Justice Rehnquist reined in a strain of constitutional law that he had carefully crafted for decades. One of the chief legacies of the Rehnquist court is its novel use of the Constitution's 11th Amendment to foster federalism by limiting Congressional authority to trump states' rights.[133] Given Rehnquist's well-documented federalism concerns, the holding in *Hibbs* was surprising; his opinion for the court found that Congress could require states to honor the protections of the FMLA. Even more surprising than the holding of the case was its language, some adopted directly from the brief of Hibbs, the male state employee seeking leave to care for his wife. According to the majority:

> Stereotypes about women's domestic roles are reinforced by parallel stereotypes presuming a lack of domestic responsibilities for men . . . These mutually reinforcing stereotypes created a self-fulfilling cycle of discrimination that forced women to continue to assume the role of primary family caregiver, and fostered employers' stereotypical views about women's commitment to work and their value as employees.[134]

The opinion also included sweeping language condemning the persistent "fault line between work and family – precisely where sex-based overgeneralization has been and remains strongest."[135]

Justice Rehnquist's majority included Justice Sandra Day O'Connor, a frequent member of the Courts' conservative decisions, but a liberal on many gender issues. O'Connor herself worked part time for seven years while her children were young, and has written often about the acute problems that women face in balancing work and family obligations.[136] Justice Rehnquist also had considerable personal experience with family caregiving. His wife died in her sixties and news reports indicated that he sometimes left the Supreme Court early to pick up his granddaughter when his daughter, a single mother, could not do so. *Hibbs* is part of a larger trend in which powerful and often conservative men take a particular interest in family care issues because of challenges faced by their daughters.[137]

Hibbs was quickly followed by the landmark federal appellate opinion in *Back v. Hastings-on-Hudson*, 365 F. 3d 107.[138] *Back* involved a school psychologist who received strong reviews and appeared to be headed for tenure. Her fate changed dramatically as her tenure review approached. "Please do not get pregnant until I retire," the head of personnel advised her when she returned from maternity leave; Back was also asked whether she was "planning on spacing offspring" and was told to "maybe . . . reconsider whether she could be a mother and do this job . . ." The school principal said she "did not know how [Back] could do this job with little ones." Back was also told that it was "not possible for [her] to be a good mother and have this job," and that her "apparent commitment" to her job was "an act" that would end once she got tenure.

The appellate court ruled for Back, reversing the trial court's decision that had prevented her case from proceeding to trial. Calabresi's opinion relied on an earlier Supreme Court decision on gender stereotyping, *Price Waterhouse v. Hopkins*.[139] As the court interpreted that ruling, employers can no more assume "that a woman *will* conform to a gender stereotype (and therefore will not, for example, be dedicated to her job)," than they can assume "that a woman is unqualified for a position because she does *not* conform to a gender stereotype." In social science terminology, this extends *Price Waterhouse*'s ruling on prescriptive stereotyping to descriptive stereotyping.[140] Like *Hibbs*, and for that matter, *Price Waterhouse*, *Back* treated evidence of stereotypes as a matter of common sense rather than a technical field accessible only to specialists. The risk of this approach, of course, is that some judges' intuitions may be at odds with social science research findings on cognitive bias. But if courts, juries, and the lawyers who argue before them are willing to consider such research, it will have the advantage of avoiding the need for expensive testimony from experts and burdensome evidentiary battles over the scope and admissibility of such testimony.[141]

Back's most important holding was that the plaintiff had stated a cause of action for gender discrimination under an intentional discrimination theory despite her failure to present evidence of a similarly situated man who had been treated differently. In effect, *Back* asked "whether stereotyping about the qualities of mothers is a form of gender discrimination, and whether this can be determined in the absence of evidence about how the employer in question treated fathers." The court "answer[ed] both questions in the affirmative":[142]

> It was eminently clear by 2001, when the alleged discrimination took place . . . that adverse actions taken on the basis of gender stereotypes can constitute sex discrimination. It was also eminently clear that it is unconstitutional to treat men and women differently simply because of presumptions about the respective roles they play in family life. [citation omitted] On the facts alleged, a jury could find that [the defendants] stereotyped the plaintiff as a woman and mother of young children, and thus treated her differently than they would have treated a man and father of young children.[143]

The defendants may have "believed their stereotypes . . . to be *true*," but, under the court's analysis, such a belief is not "objectively reasonable"; "it can never be objectively reasonable for a government official to act with the intent that is prohibited by law."[144] In essence, evidence of stereotyping can be conclusive proof of the discriminatory intent required to establish disparate treatment under the Constitution and Title VII – without the need for a similarly situated man. This is a crucial holding because it is often impossible to find a similarly situated man, given the high level of sex segregation in the workplace noted earlier.

Back was quickly followed by another significant federal appellate ruling in a maternal wall case. *Lust v. Sealy*,[145] involved a Sealy mattress sales representative who had lost a promotion to a man. The jury awarded $100,000 in compensatory damages and $1 million in punitive damages and the defendant appealed. Lust's supervisor had a history of making "sexist comments," including "isn't that just like a woman to say something like that," "you're being a blonde again today," and "it's a blonde thing."[146] "More important," noted the appellate court, when Lust expressed interest in the promotion, her supervisor expressed surprise and asked why her husband "wasn't going to take care" of her.[147] "Most important," her supervisor "admitted that he didn't consider recommending Lust for the [promotion, which required a move from Madison, Wisconsin to] Chicago . . . because she had children and he didn't think she'd want to relocate her family, though she hadn't told him that. On the contrary, she had told him again and again how much she wanted to be promoted, even though there was no indication that a Key Account manager's position would open up in Madison any time soon."[148]

In the appellate court's view, "realism" required acknowledging that "the average mother is more sensitive than the average father to the possibly disruptive effect (of a move) on children." However, the supervisor should have asked Lust about her interest because the law insists that employees be evaluated as individuals. Although the supervisor claimed that "she would have told me no," the court tartly pointed out that he "had not been qualified as a mind reader."[149]

Lust, written by the conservative Judge Richard Posner, is an important signpost in several respects. It illustrates courts' increased understanding of the role of stereotyping in sex discrimination contexts, and their willingness to treat assumptions about *mothers* as part and parcel of stereotypes about *women*. If such assumptions can be aggregated with other evidence of bias, such as the quips about blondes, it will be easier for plaintiffs to prove actionable gender discrimination. Of further significance is the court's recognition of the attribution bias inherent in the supervisor's reasoning: when a man expressed an interest in the promotion, the supervisor assumed that he would relocate; but when Lust expressed an interest in the promotion, the supervisor assumed that she would not relocate. Thus, as the court noted, the supervisor "drew two very different inferences from similar conversations." In this respect, *Lust* extends the *Back* court's more traditional use of hostile stereotypes and opens the way to proving discrimination based primarily on statements about what mothers should not, or cannot, do.

A final, significant maternal wall case is *Washington v. Illinois Department of Revenue*.[150] There, the plaintiff, Chrissie Washington, worked a 7 a.m. to 3 p.m. schedule in order to get home to care for her Downs-syndrome child when he returned from school. She alleged that she had been transferred to a nonflexible time schedule in retaliation after she had filed a race discrimination complaint. In response, Washington took two hours of vacation time every day, in order to leave at 3 o'clock, until her vacation time ran out; then she took a leave of absence until she found a supervisor willing to let her work her original schedule. The federal appellate court, in an opinion written by a leading conservative judge, Frank Easterbrook, allowed the plaintiff to go to trial.

The case is noteworthy both because it recognizes the importance of flexible schedules, and it extends that recognition to make new law on the issue of what constitutes retaliation. To prevail on such a claim, plaintiffs must show that they suffered some "adverse employment action." Prior cases had often held that a transfer to the same job with a different schedule (a "lateral transfer") did not constitute such an action. *Washington*, however, rejects such a "bright line" rule in determining whether a personnel action is "adverse," and replaces it with a flexible approach based on the individual circumstances of the plaintiff. In Washington's case, the court noted:

> Working 9-to-5 was a materially adverse change *for her*, even though it would not have been for 99% of the staff. In practical effect the change cut her wages by 25%, because it induced her to use leave for two hours per day (her salary remained the same, but her vacation and sick leave drained away, which is an effective reduction in salary). When her leave ran out, her pay fell to zero for five months, until she found a supervisor willing to let her go at 3.[151]

It would have been easy for the court to find that a 9-to-5 schedule was not a hardship sufficient to demonstrate retaliation. The willingness to consider how such a schedule affected someone with significant caretaking responsibilities signals an important trend in the continuing struggle for gender equality at work. This case, like other maternal wall rulings, offers a promising strategy for those whose responsibilities in the home have unduly limited their opportunities outside it.

Implications

Whatever the reasons for the recent legal successes, they sound a positive note for those who seek truly equal opportunities in employment. Taken as a whole, the series of decisions suggests that judges are increasingly likely to interpret at least some obstacles facing workers with family obligations as problems to be addressed by law, and not as unfortunate dilemmas simply to be left to individual "choice."[152] The concept of shared social responsibility for the balancing of home and work, of reproductive and productive work, has long been identified as central to the erosion of sex discrimination.[153]

Further Reform

The current legal landscape reflects partial progress in American society's gradual transformation of gender roles. In this, as in other contexts, the law mirrors broader cultural aspirations and ambivalences about the rights and responsibilities of women, and the opportunities and obligations of courts. For reasons noted earlier, employment law has limits as a strategy for social change, but neither have we realized its full potential. Inadequacies in legal doctrine, employer policies, and enforcement structures suggest obvious directions for reform.

Not all of the suggested reforms are feasible in the current political climate. But we note them here to suggest a template for guiding our continuing egalitarian agenda. The template also allows us to measure our progress, an activity which in and of itself helps to promote positive change.[154]

Expanding legal protections

One obvious strategy is to expand the scope of law. Current doctrine focuses on ensuring that female and male employees who are similarly situated receive similar opportunities and compensation. That approach is inadequate to address the gender roles, norms, and stereotypes that prevent men and women from being similarly situated. A more realistic framework would promote pay equity and structural changes in the workplace.

To reduce the gender gap in earnings, the law should ensure not just equal compensation for identical work, but equivalent compensation for comparable work. This approach would rely on systems of evaluation that compare jobs in terms of skills, effort, responsibilities, and working conditions. Such systems have been widely available in both the public employment and private sector since World War II. By the beginning of the twenty-first century, about 20 states had relied on job evaluation studies to correct for sex or race bias in public sector. Others had commissioned research to identify such bias. Two states, Minnesota and Iowa, currently require comparable pay for equal work in state employment, and Maine requires it for private sector jobs as well. Other countries, including Sweden, England, Australia, and the province of Ontario, Canada, also have pay equity requirements. A European Council Directive interprets the principle of equal pay under the European Economic Council Treaty to encompass "work to which equal value is attributed."[155] Such initiatives have had moderate success. A study by the Institute for Women's Policy Research found that pay equity strategies in all 20 surveyed states had modest effects in closing the female–male wage gap without substantial negative side effects such as increased unemployment. Wage ratios rose to between 74 and 88 percent, compared to the national average of 71 percent.[156]

Federal legislation that could achieve similar results has been proposed repeatedly over the past decade. One such proposal, the Fair Pay Act, would extend current law by requiring equal pay for "equivalent jobs" in terms of "skills, effort, responsibility, and working conditions." The Act would also expand class action enforcement procedures and permit punitive damages for violations. Other strategies are also possible. One is to require that federal contractors implement a form of pay equity through an Executive Order paralleling the one that now mandates corrective plans in occupations where women are underrepresented.[157] A less coercive approach would be to provide recognition and incentives for employers to conduct their own pay equity audits and implement appropriate responses.[158] Women would also benefit from gender-neutral reforms such as minimum wage increases and expanded benefit coverage for low-paying and part-time jobs, which are disproportionately held by female workers.

Reforms in workplace structures

A traditional way to think about work–family issues involves recognizing women's "need for accommodation of their family responsibilities."[159] We believe that the "accommodation" metaphor miscasts the problem and the solution. Many of the key obstacles that women face stem from the traditional design of good jobs around ideal workers who are employed, full time and full force, for their entire working lives. This ideal reflects men's biology and life patterns; they need take no time off for childbearing and they can generally count on wives and mothers to assume the major share of family responsibilities.[160] Designing jobs – explicitly or implicitly – around the male norm constitutes a form of gender discrimination.

What women need is not accommodation but equality. That will require a redefinition of norms to take into account women's, as well as men's, biology, preferences, and life patterns. Only then will women – as well as men who share traditionally feminine values of caregiving – have truly equal employment opportunity.

This brief overview is not the occasion for a detailed blueprint of work–family reforms. What constitutes the appropriate mix of legal requirements, public subsidies, tax incentives, and voluntary employer initiatives is a complex question with obvious political as well as socioeconomic dimensions. However, in weighing the plausible options, two general principles bear emphasis.

First, opportunities such as paid parental leave should be gender neutral, and men should be encouraged to take advantage of them. This is a departure from current patterns. Encouraging male employees to use family policies is critical in broadening their base of support, minimizing potential backlash, and challenging the perception that caretaking is women's responsibility. Experience here and abroad indicates that "use it or lose it" paid leave, coupled with educational campaigns and managerial support, can help increase men's involvement in the home, which widens women's opportunities in the world outside it.

A second key principle involves oversight and accountability. Work–family policies should be formalized, publicized, and monitored. Employers need to collect information about usage and satisfaction. How many men and women take advantage of options such as parental leaves and part-time schedules? What are their experiences in terms of promotion, turnover, assignments, and so forth? Are reduced hours respected? Is pay proportional to time worked? What problems do employees and their colleagues encounter? Only through such systematic assessment can employers craft policies that are effective in practice. And only by holding supervisors accountable for the results in evaluations and compensation will workplaces make good on their professed commitments to equal opportunity.

Accountability   Accountability is also critical for all gender-equity initiatives. Greater internal and external oversight is essential, and that will, in turn, require more systematic collection and disclosure of information. At the internal level, decision makers need to be held responsible for standards, processes, and practices concerning hiring, evaluation, assignments, promotion, and work–family accommodation. At the external level, employers need to be held responsible for results by regulatory agencies, professional organizations, and public interest groups.

A wide array of social science research indicates that increasing individuals' accountability for the fairness of decision making reduces the scope for bias.[161] Multiple strategies can serve that objective. One is to ensure that the criteria for hiring, evaluation, compensation, and advancement are as objective and specific as possible, and do not inadvertently perpetuate gender inequalities. Narrowing the discretion of decision makers reduces the possibilities for in-group favoritism and unexamined stereotypes. A second essential strategy is to collect data and monitor progress. Employers should compile information on recruitment, hiring, promotion, retention, and quality of life issues broken down by sex, as well as race and ethnicity. They should oversee evaluation, work assignment, and mentoring practices to prevent unintended biases. Where possible, employers should assess their progress in light of the relevant labor pool and the records of similar organizations. Surveys of current and former employees can also provide valuable feedback on equity and quality of life issues. Systematic evaluation of various diversity initiatives is equally critical. Experts have questioned the value of some initiatives, such as bias training programs, and little concrete data is available concerning their effectiveness.[162]

The law can do more to foster such accountability by requiring or encouraging employers to disclose such information and by removing disincentives for its collection. One unintended and unwelcome byproduct of current liability structures is that they can discourage employers from collecting data on problems because that material could be useful to plaintiffs in subsequent discrimination lawsuits. The result is to deter informed problem solving, which might prevent such claims from arising in the first instance.[163] One way to neutralize this deterrent is to require employers over a certain size, or those that are government contractors, to collect and disclose such data. Leading experts have argued that such requirements are essential to assessing the effectiveness of equal opportunity programs.[164]

In the absence of mandatory reporting responsibilities, other strategies will be necessary to encourage data collection. Courts and legislatures could create confidentiality safeguards that would avoid penalizing employers for obtaining information that can improve their own internal processes. Professional organizations, women's rights groups, and the media could request and publish data on gender equity. For example, employers could be asked for information about the representation and advancement of women, and the utilization of alternative schedule policies. Recognition could also be available to organizations that adopt specified "best practices" concerning gender equity. One illustration is the "No Glass Ceiling Initiatives" of various bar associations. These initiatives call on participating law firms to commit to specific goals concerning the representation of women in partnership and leadership positions. Some large corporate clients have assisted these efforts by pledging to consider the diversity of law firms when selecting outside counsel.[165]

Finally, we need to increase the accountability of governmental decision makers for their action, and inaction, on gender equity issues. Current equal opportunity law is insufficient to guarantee equal opportunity in fact. Legislation is needed to fill in the gaps, and to broaden coverage in areas such as pay equity and paid parental leave. More resources also need to be available to government enforcement agencies, such as the EEOC, and more generous assistance needs to be available for programs that recruit, train, and mentor women in nontraditional decently paying occupations.

Child care Affordable quality child care also needs to be public priority. Although women have the most direct interest in this agenda, these are not exclusively "women's issues." They affect the productivity of our workforce and the care of our families.

Conclusion

Ours is not a modest agenda. But to maintain its position in an increasingly competitive global environment, American society can afford no less. For reasons not only of justice, but also economic well-being, the United States must do more to translate equal opportunity principles into workplace practices. At stake is not only equality for women but the quality of life for us all.

Notes

1   Equal Pay Act of 1963, 29 U.S.C. § 206 (d) (1996).
2   Diaz v. Pan American World Airlines, 442 F.2d 385(5th Cir. 1971).
3   Weeks v. Southern Bell Telephone & Telegraph Co., 408 F.2d 228 (5th Cir. 1969).
4   Bailey v. Scott-Gallaher, Inc., 480 S.E. 2d 502 (Va. 1997).
5   Hallberg v. Aristech Chemical Corp. (1999). Discussed in Ann Belser, Mommy Track Wins: $3 Million Awarded to Mom Denied Promotion, *Pittsburgh Post-Gazette*, April 30, 1999, at B1.
6   Griggs v. Duke Power Co., 401 U.S. 424 (1971); Teamsters v. United States, 431 U.S. 324 (1977).

7   Watson v. Fort Worth Bank & Trust, 487 U.S. 977 (1988); Ward's Cove v. Atonio, 490 U.S. 642 (1989); Civil Rights Act of 1991, Pub. L. No. 102-166, 105 Stat. 1071 (1991).
8   Meritor Savings Bank, FSB v. Vinson, 477 U.S. 57 (1986).
9   Pregnancy Discrimination Act of 1978, Pub. L. No. 95-555, 92 Stat. 20706 (Oct. 31, 1978).
10 Suders v. Easton, et al., 325 F.3d 432,445 (3rd Cir. 2003), 124 S.Ct. 2342, 2351 (2004).
11 Calvert, C. T., & Williams, J. C. (2006). *WorkLife law's guide to family responsibilities discrimination.* San Francisco: University of California, Hastings College of the Law, Center for WorkLife Law (available from www.worklifelaw.org).
12 Snodgrass v. Brown, No. 80-1171-K, 1990 WL 198431, U.S. Dist Lexis 16418 (D. Kan. Nov. 26, 1990).
13 Calvert & Williams (2006).
14 Zimmer, M. J., Sullivan, C. A., Richards, R. F., & Calloway, D. (1997). *Cases and materials on employment discrimination.* New York: Aspen.
15 Liu v. Amway Corporation, 347 F.3d 1125 (9th Cir. 2003).
16 Knussman v. Maryland, 65 F. Supp. 2d 353 (D. Md. 1999), aff'd in part, vacated in part, and remanded by 272 F.3d 625 (4th Cir. 2001).
17 Crosby, F. J. (2004). *Affirmative action is dead: Long live affirmative action.* New Haven, CT: Yale University Press; Schuck, P. (2003). Diversity in America: Government at a safe distance. *Ethnic and racial studies, 28*(1), 192–193.
18 U.S. Department of Labor, Bureau of Labor Statistics (2005). *Women in the labor force: A databook,* retrieved at www.bls.gov/cps/wlf-databook2005.htm
19 U.S. Department of Labor (2005), p. 46, Table 16.
20 Institute for Women's Policy Research (IWPR) (2004). *Women's economic status in the states: Wide disparities by race, ethnicity, and region.* Washington, DC: IWPR.
21 U.S. Department of Labor (2001). *Highlights of women's earnings in 2000, Report 952.* Washington, DC: Bureau of Labor Statistics, p. 2.
22 U.S. Census Bureau (2004). *Evidence from census 2000 about earnings by detailed occupation for men and women.* Washington, DC: U.S. Census Bureau, p. 11.
23 U.S. Department of Labor (2004). *Household data, annual averages.* Washington, DC: Bureau of Labor Statistics, Table 39.
24 U.S. Department of Labor (2004), p. 11.
25 Sailer, P., Yau, E., & Rehula, V. (2002). *Income by gender and age from information returns.* Washington, DC: Internal Revenue Service.
26 U.S. Department of Labor (2005), p. 2.
27 Rose, S. J., & Hartmann, H. I. (2004). *Still a man's labor market: The long term earnings gap.* Washington, DC: Institute for Women's Policy Research, pp. iii–iv.

28 U.S. Department of Labor (2004).

29 Reichman, N., & Sterling, J. S. (2004a). *Gender penalties revisited.* Denver, CO: Women's Bar Association. Retrieved July 13, 2006, from http://www.cwba.org, pp. 8–11; Reichman, N. J., & Sterling, J. S. (2004b). Sticky floors, broken steps, and concrete ceilings in legal careers. *Texas Journal of Women and the Law, 14,* 27–76, p. 27.

30 Reichman & Sterling (2004a), pp. 9, 11.

31 Valian, V. (1999). The cognitive basis of gender bias. *Brooklyn Law Review, 65,* 1037–1061, p. 1039.

32 Lentz, B. F., & Laband, D. N. (1995). *Sex discrimination in the legal profession.* Westport, CT: Quorum Books, p. 32.

33 Reichman & Sterling (2004a), pp. 10–11; Rhode, D. L. (2001). *The unfinished agenda: Women and the legal profession.* Chicago, IL: American Bar Association, pp. 14–15.

34 Huang, W. R. (1997). Gender differences in the earnings of lawyers. *Columbia Journal of Law and Social Problems, 30,* 267–325, p. 302.

35 Hersch, J. (2003). The new labor market for lawyers: Will female lawyers still earn less? *Cardozo Women's Law Journal, 10*(1), 1–59, p. 3.

36 Huang (1997), pp. 301, 308, 309; Reichman & Sterling (2004a), pp. 10–11.

37 Patton, P. A. (2005). Women lawyers: Their status, influence, and retention in the legal profession. *William and Mary Journal of Women and the Law, 11*(2), 173–194, pp. 173–174; American Bar Association (ABA) Commission on Women in the Profession (2003). *A current glance at women and the law.* Chicago, IL: American Bar Association, p. 1; Chambliss, E. (2005). *Miles to go: Progress of minorities in the legal profession.* Chicago, IL: American Bar Association; National Association of Law Placement (NALP) (2004). *Women and attorneys of color at law firms,* Washington, DC: NALP; Women's Bar Association of Massachusetts (2000). *More than part time: The effect of reduced-hours arrangements on the retention, recruitment, and success of women attorneys in law firms.* Retrieved from http://www.womenlaw.stanford.edu/mass.rpt.html

38 Blumrosen, A. W., & Blumrosen, R. G. (2002). *The reality of intentional job discrimination in metropolitan America – 1999.* Newark, NJ: Rutgers State University of New Jersey, p. xiii.

39 Rose & Hartmann (2004), p. 26.

40 Crittenden, A. (2002). *The price of motherhood.* New York: Owl Books, p. 111.

41 Avellar, S., & Smock, P. J. (2003). Has the price of motherhood declined over time? A cross-cohort comparison of the motherhood wage penalty. *Journal of Marriage and the Family, 65*(3), 597–607, p. 604; Budig, M. J., & England, P. (2001). The wage penalty for motherhood. *American Sociological Review, 66*(2), 204–225, p. 205; Hewlett, S. A. (2002). *Creating a life: Professional women and the quest for children.* New York: Talk Miramax Books, pp. 140–141.

42   Avellar & Smock (2003), p. 598; Budig & England (2001), p. 206.

43   Budig & England (2001), p. 219.

44   Avellar & Smock (2003).

45   Hewlett, S. A., & Luce, C. B. (2005). Off-ramps and on-ramps: keeping talented women on the road to success. *Harvard Business Review, 83*(3), 43–54.

46   Budig & England (2001).

47   James, J. (2004). The equal pay act in the courts: A de facto white-collar exemption. *New York University Law Review, 79*(5), 1873–1901; Graham, M. E., & Hotchkiss, J. L. (2002). A systematic assessment of employer equal employment opportunity efforts as a means of reducing the gender earnings gap. *Cornell Journal of Law and Public Policy, 12*(1), 169–201.

48   Georgen-Saad v. Texas Mutual Insurance Co., 195 F. Supp. 2d 853 (W. D. Tex. 2002).

49   Lemons v. City of Denver, 17 Fair Employment Practice Cases 906, aff'd, Lemons v. City of Denver, 620 F. 2d 228 (10th Cir. 1978), p. 909.

50   Mory, M., & Pistilli, L. (2001). The failure of the family and medical leave act: Alternative proposals for contemporary American families. *Hofstra Labor and Employment Law Journal, 18*(2), 689–720, p. 689.

51   Bielby, W. T. (2000). Minimizing workplace gender and racial bias, *Contemporary Sociology, 29*(1), 120–129.

52   Edelman, L. B., Erlanger, H. S., & Lande, J. (1993). Internal dispute resolution: The transformation of civil rights in the workplace. *Law and Society Review, 27*(3), 497–534.

53   Rhode (2001), p. 18.

54   Rhode (2001), pp. 17–18; Butler, A. B., & Skattebo, A. L. (2004). What is acceptable for women may not be for men: The effect of family conflicts with work on job performance ratings. *Journal of Organizational Psychology, 77*, 553–564.

55   Patton (2005), p. 189; Berkowitz, E. (2005, October 4). Part-time lawyers find their own glass ceiling. *San Francisco Daily Journal*, p. 6.

56   Catalyst (2001). *Women in law: Making the case.* New York: Catalyst, p. 19.

57   Patton (2005), p. 180.

58   Epstein, C. F., Pfahlert, J., Oglensky, B., Saute, R., & Seron, C. (1999). *The part-time paradox: Time norms, professional lives, family and gender.* New York: Routledge; Eagly, A. H., & Steffen, V. J. (1986). Gender stereotypes, occupational roles, and beliefs about part-time employees. *Psychology Women Quarterly, 10*, 252–262, (p. 259); Williams, J. C. & Calvert, C. T. (2002). Balanced hours: Effective part-time policies for Washington law firms: The project for attorney retention. *William and Mary Journal of Women and the Law, 8*(3), 376–378; Women's Bar Association of Massachusetts (2000).

59   Rhode, D. L. (2002a). *Balanced lives: Changing the culture of legal workplaces.* Chicago, IL: American Bar Association, pp. 15–16; Reichman & Sterling (2004b), pp. 35, 43.

60   Berkowitz (2005); Rhode, D. L. (2002b). Balanced lives for lawyers. *Fordham Law Review*, *70*(6), 2207–2220, p. 2213; Giglio, P. (2004). Rethinking the hours, *Legal Times*, 33, p. 1; Williams, J. C. (2002). Canaries in the mine: Work/family conflict and the law. *Fordham Law Review*, *70*(6), 2221–2239, p. 2224.

61   Dixon, K. A., Storen, D., & Van Horn, C. E. (2002). *A workplace divided: How Americans view discrimination and race on the job.* New Brunswick, NJ: John J. Heldrich Center for Workplace Development, Rutgers University, p. 15.

62   Rhode, D. L. (1997). *Speaking of sex: The denial of gender inequality.* Cambridge, MA: Harvard University Press, p. 9.

63   Major & Kaiser (2006).

64   Riordan v. Kaminers, 831 F. 2d 690 (7th Cir. 1987), p. 697.

65   Heim v. State of Utah, 8 F. 3d 1541 (10th Cir. 1993), p. 1546.

66   Ezold v. Wolf, Block, Schorr & Solis-Cohen, 983 F.2d 509 (3d Cir. 1992), *cert. denied*, 510 U.S. 826 (1993); Rhode, D. L. (2005). What's sex got to do with it: Diversity in the legal profession. In D. L. Rhode & D. Luban (Eds.), *Law Stories* (pp. 233–254). New York: Foundation Press.

67   Montwieler, N. (1997). EEOC policy guidance reaffirms opposition to mandatory arbitration, *U.S. Law Week* (BNA), 66, 2055–2066, pp. 2055–2056; Bartlett, K., & Rhode, D. L. (2006). *Gender and the law: Theory, doctrine, commentary.* Boston: Aspen Press.

68   Bartlett & Rhode (2006).

69   Blasi, G. (2002). Advocacy against the stereotype: Lessons from cognitive social psychology. *University of California, Los Angeles Law Review*, *49*(5), 1241–1281, p. 1243; Krieger, L. H. (1995). The content of our categories: A cognitive bias approach to discrimination and equal employment opportunity. *Stanford Law Review*, *47*, 1161–1248; Williams, J. C. (2003). Litigating the glass ceiling and the maternal wall: Using stereotyping and cognitive bias evidence to prove gender discrimination: The social psychology of stereotyping: Using social science to litigate gender discrimination cases and defang the cluelessness defense. *Employment Rights and Employment Policy*, *7*(2), 401–458, pp. 439–449.

70   Bielby (2000); Bodenhausen, G. V., Macrae, C. N., & Garst, J. (1998). Stereotypes in thought and deed: Social cognitive origins of intergroup discrimination. In C. Sedikides, J. Schopler, & C. A. Insko (Eds.), *Intergroup cognition and intergroup behavior* (pp. 311–335). Mahwah, NJ: Lawrence Erlbaum; Krieger, L. H. (2004). The intuitive psychologist behind the bench: Models of gender bias in social psychology and employment discrimination law. *Journal of Social Issues*, *60*, 835–848; Williams (2003).

71   Samborn, H. V. (2000). Higher hurdles for women. *American Bar Association Journal*, *86*, 30–33, p. 34; American Bar Association (ABA) Commission on Women in the Profession (1997). *Fair measure: Toward effective attorney evaluation.* Chicago, IL: American Bar Association; Foschi, M.

(2000). Double standards for competence: Theory and research. *Annual Review of Sociology, 26*, 21–42, p. 25.

72 Biernat, M. (2003). Toward a broader view of social stereotyping. *American Psychologist, 58*(12), 1019–1027.

73 Heilman, M. E. (2001). Description and prescription: How gender stereotypes prevent women's ascent up the organizational ladder. *Journal of Social Issues, 57*(4), 657–674, p. 662; Hunt, J. S., Borgida, E., Kelly, K. A., & Burgess, D. (2002). Gender stereotyping: Scientific status. In D. L. Faigman, D. H. Kaye, M. J. Saks, & J. Sanders (Eds.), *Modern scientific evidence: The law and science of expert testimony* (pp. 374–426). St. Paul, MN: West Publishing Co., p. 401.

74 Ridgeway, C. L. (2001). Gender, status, and leadership. *Journal of Social Issues, 57*(4), 637–655, p. 646; Ridgeway, C. L., & Correll, S. J. (2000). Limiting inequality through interaction: The end(s) of gender. *Contemporary Sociology, 29*, 110–120, p. 113; Ridgeway, C. L., & Smith-Lovin, L. (1999). The gender system and interaction. *Annual Review of Sociology, 25*, 191–216, p. 2030; Ridgeway & England, this volume.

75 Biernat, M., & Kobrynowicz, D. (1997). Gender and race-based standards of competence: Lower minimum standards but higher ability standards for devalued groups. *Journal of Personality and Social Psychology, 72*, 544–557, p. 555; Heilman (2001), p. 666; Heilman, M. E., Martell, R. F., & Simon, M. C. (1998). The vagaries of sex bias: Conditions regulating the underevaluation, equivaluation, and overvaluation of female job applicants. *Organizational Behavior and Human Decision Processes, 41*, 98–110, p. 98–99.

76 Chambliss (2005); Williams, J. C. (2000). *Unbending gender: Why work and family conflict and what to do about it.* New York: Oxford University Press, pp. 152–153; Kennelly, I. (1999). "That single-mother element": How white employers typify black women. *Gender and Society, 13*(2), 168–192.

77 Glick, P., & Fiske S. T. (2001). Ambivalent sexism. In M. P. Zanna (Ed.), *Advances in experimental social psychology* (Vol. 33, pp. 115–188). Thousand Oaks, CA: Academic Press; Fiske, S. T., Xu, J., Cuddy, A. C., & Glick, P. (1999). (Dis)respecting versus (dis)liking: Status and interdependence predict ambivalent stereotypes of competence and warmth. *Journal of Social Issues, 55*(3), 473–489.

78 Glick & Fiske, this volume.

79 Heilman (2001), p. 661.

80 Heilman, M. E., & Block, C. J. (1989). Has anything changed? Current characterizations of men, women, and managers. *Journal of Applied Psychology, 74*, 935–942, p. 941.

81 Eagly, A. H., & Karau, S. J. (2002). Role congruity theory of prejudice toward female leaders. *Psychology Review, 109*, 573–598, p. 574; Glick & Fiske, this volume.

82 Rhode (2001), p. 15; Ridgeway (2001).

83 Banerjee, V. (2001, August 10). Some "bullies" seek ways to soften up: Toughness has risks for women executives. *New York Times*, p. C1; Taylor, S. E. (1981). A categorization approach to stereotyping. In D. L. Hamilton (Ed.), *Cognitive processes in stereotyping and intergroup behavior* (pp. 83–114). Mahwah: NJ: Lawrence Earlbaum, p. 111.

84 Eagley & Karau (2002), p. 111.

85 Fiske et al. (1999); Eckes, T. (2002). Paternalistic and envious gender stereotypes: Testing predictions from the stereotype content model. *Sex Roles*, *47*(3–4), 99–114, p. 110; Williams, J. C. & Segal, N. (2003). Beyond the maternal wall: Relief for family caregivers who are discriminated against on the job. *Harvard Women's Law Journal, 26*, 77–162; Cuddy, A. J. C., Fiske, S. T., & Glick, P. (2004). When professionals become mothers, warmth doesn't cut the ice. *Journal of Social Issues, 60*(4), 701–718.

86 Cuddy et al. (2004).

87 Fuegen, K., Biernat, M., Haines, E., & Deaux, K. (2004). Mothers and fathers in the workplace: How gender and parental status influence judgments of job-related competence. *Journal of Social Issues, 60*(4), 737–754; Correll, S. J., & Bernard, S. (2005). Getting a job: Is there a motherhood penalty? Paper presented at the American Sociological Association, Philadelphia.

88 Halpert, J. A., Wilson, M. L., & Hickman, J. L. (1993). Pregnancy as a source of bias in performance appraisals. *Journal of Organizational Behavior, 14*(7), 649–663, pp. 650–655.

89 Spain, D., & Bianchi, S. (1996). *Balancing act: Motherhood, marriage, and employment among American women.* New York: Russell Sage Foundation; Becker, P., & Moen, P. (1999). Scaling back: dual earner couples: Work-family strategies. *Journal of Marriage and the Family, 61*, 995–1007.

90 Epstein et al. (1999); Eagley & Steffen (1986), p. 259.

91 Williams & Segal (2003), p. 97.

92 Ganong, L. H., & Coleman, M. (1995). The content of mother stereotypes. *Sex Roles, 32*, 495–512, p. 507; Kobrynowicz, D., & Biernat, M. (1997). Decoding subjective evaluations: How stereotypes provide shifting standards. *Journal of Experimental Psychology, 33*, 579–601, p. 592.

93 Back v. Hastings-on-Hudson Union Free School District, 365 F. 3d. 107 (2d Cir. 2004).

94 Glick & Fiske, this volume.

95 Williams (2003), pp. 427–430.

96 Abbott, I. O. (2000). *The lawyer's guide to mentoring.* Washington, DC: National Association for Law Placement.

97 Catalyst (1999). *Women of color in corporate management: dynamics of career advancement.* New York: Catalyst, p. 15; Wilkins, D., & Gulati, M. G. (1996). Why are there so few black lawyers in corporate law firms: An institutional analysis. *University of California Law Review, 84*, 493–625; Rhode (2001), p. 16.

98   Brewer, M. B., & Brown, R. J. (1998). Intergroup relations. In D. T. Gilbert, S. T. Fiske, & G. Lindzey (Eds.), *The handbook of social psychology* (4th ed., Vol. 2, pp. 554–594). Boston: McGraw Hill; Fiske, S. T. (1998). Stereotyping, prejudice and discrimination. In D. T. Gilbert, S. T. Fiske, & G. Lindzey (Eds.), *The handbook of social psychology* (4th ed., Vol. 2, pp. 357–411). Boston: McGraw-Hill.

99   Crocker, J., Major, B., & Steel, C. (1998). Social stigma. In D. T. Gilbert, S. T. Fiske, & G. Lindzey (Eds.), *The handbook of social psychology* (4th ed., Vol. 2, pp. 504–553). Boston: McGraw Hill; Dovidio, J. F., & Gaertner, S. L. (1993). Stereotypes and evaluative intergroup bias. In D. M. Mackie & D. L. Hamilton (Eds.), *Affect, cognition, and stereotyping* (pp. 167–193). San Diego, CA: Academic Press; Foschi (2000); Krieger (1995); Ridgeway, C. L. (1997). Interaction and the conservation of gender inequality: Considering employment. *American Sociological Review, 62*(2), 218–235.

100 Brewer, M. B. (1996). In-group favoritism: The subtle side of intergroup discrimination. In D. M. Messick & A. E. Tenbrunsel (Eds.), *Codes of conduct: Behavioral research into business ethics* (pp. 160–171). New York: Russell Sage Foundation; Krieger (1995), pp. 1200, 1204.

101 Bielby (2000); Reskin, B. F., & McBrier, D. B. (2000). Why not ascription? Organizations' employment of male and female managers. *American Sociological Review, 65*(2), 210–233; Rhode (2001), p. 16; Wilkins & Gulati (1996), p. 570.

102 Ross, L. (1977). The intuitive psychologist and his shortcomings: Distortions in the attribution process. In L. Berkowitz (Ed.), *Advances in experimental social psychology* (Vol. 10, pp. 174–214). New York: Academic Press.

103 Polachek, S. W. (1981). Occupational self-selection: A human capital approach to sex differences in occupational structure. *Review of Economics and Statistics, 63*(1), 60–69.

104 Farrell, W. (2005). *Why men earn more: The startling truth behind the pay gap and what women can do about it.* New York: American Management Association; Friesen, J. (1993). Alternative economic perspectives on the use of labor market policies to redress the gender gap in compensation. *Georgetown Law Journal, 82,* 31–68.

105 Friesen (1993), p. 38.

106 General Accounting Office (October 2003). *Women's earnings: Work patterns partially explain difference between men's and women's earnings.* GAO-04-35. Washington, DC: U.S. Government Printing Office.

107 Solberg, E., & Laughlin, T. (1995). The gender pay gap, fringe benefits, and occupational crowding. *Industrial and Labor Relations Review, 48*(4), 692–708, pp. 706–707.

108 Hewlett & Luce (2005).

109 Compare Sicherman, N. (1996). Gender differences in departures from a large firm. *Industrial and Labor Relations Review, 49*(3), 484–503, p. 493;

McGrath, M., Driscoll, M., & Gross, M. (2005). *Back in the game: Returning to business after a hiatus; experiences and recommendations for women, employers, and universities.* Philadelphia, PA: Wharton Center for Leadership and Change and the Forte Foundation, p. 7.

110   Hewlett & Luce (2005).

111   Sicherman (1996), p. 493.

112   Friesen (1993), pp. 45–50.

113   O'Neill, J., & Polachek, S. (1993). Why the gender gap in wages narrowed in the 1980s. *Journal of Labor Economics, 11*(1), 205–228, p. 219.

114   Rose & Hartmann (2004), pp. iii, 41.

115   Wallis, C. (March 22, 2004). The case for staying home, *Time,* 51–52, p. 53.

116   Friesen (1993), p. 47; Sicherman (1996), p. 493.

117   Catalyst (1998). *Women entrepreneurs: Why companies lose female talent and what they can do about it.* New York: Catalyst; Korn/Ferry International (2001). *What women want in business: A survey of executives and entrepreneurs.* New York: Korn Ferry International.

118   Stone, P., & Lovejoy, M. (2004). Fast-track women and the "choice" to stay home. *The annals of the American Academy of Political and Social Science, 596*(1), 62–83, p. 68.

119   Williams, J. C. (1989) Deconstructing gender. *Michigan Law Review, 87*(4), 797–845, (p. 833).

120   Rose & Hartmann (2004), p. 2.

121   Belkin, L. (2003, October 26). The opt-out revolution. *New York Times Magazine, 6,* 42, pp. 43–44.

122   Farrell (2005).

123   Story, L. (2005, September 20). Many women at elite colleges set career path to motherhood. *New York Times,* p. A1.

124   Hewlett (2002), p. 107.

125   Williams, J. C., & Cooper, H. C. (2004). The public policy of motherhood. *Journal of Social Issues, 60*(4), 849–865.

126   Still, M. C. (forthcoming). *Demography of the maternal wall.* Center for WorkLife Law Working Paper. San Francisco: University of California, Hastings College of the Law, Center for WorkLife Law (available from www.worklifelaw.org).

127   Calvert & Williams (2006); Schultz v. Advocate Health and Hospitals Corp., No. 01 C 702, 2002 U.S. Dist. LEXIS 9517 (N.D. Ill. Eastern Div., May 24, 2002).

128   Bailey v. Scott-Gallaher (1997), p. 505.

129   Williams, J. C., & Calvert, C. T. (2006). Family responsibilities discrimination: What plaintiffs' attorneys, management attorneys and employees need to know. *Women Lawyers Journal, 91*(2), 24–28.

130   Walsh v. National Computer Systems, Inc., 332 F.3d 1150, 1160 (8th Cir. 2003); Kaster, J. (2003, January 24). Oral comments of Jim Kaster, Plaintiff Shirleen Walsh's Attorney, at Symposium, *The New Glass Ceiling: Litigating Bias Against Parents at Work.* American University, Washington

College of the Law, Washington, DC (unpublished symposium presentations, on file with *American University Journal of Gender, Social Policy and
the Law*).

131 Nevada Department of Human Resources v. Hibbs, 538 U.S. 721 (2003).
132 Back v. Hastings-on-Hudson (2004).
133 Williams & Cooper (2004).
134 Nevada Department of Human Resources v. Hibbs (2003), p. 736.
135 Nevada Department of Human Resources v. Hibbs (2003), p. 738.
136 O'Connor, S. D. (2003). *The majesty of the law: Reflections of a Supreme
Court justice*. New York: Random House.
137 Williams & Cooper (2004).
138 Back v. Hastings-on-Hudson (2004).
139 Price Waterhouse v. Hopkins, 490 U.S. 228 (1989).
140 Heilman (2001); Burgess, D., & Borgida, E. (1999). Who woman are,
who women should be: Descriptive and prescriptive gender stereotypes
in sex discrimination. *Psychology, Public Policy and Law*, 5, 665–692; Eagly,
A. H., Wood, W., & Johannesen-Schmidt, M. C. (2000). Social role theory
of sex differences and similarities: A current appraisal. In A. H. Eagly, T.
Eckes, A. E. Beall, R. J. Sternberg, & H. M. Trautner (Eds.), *The developmental social psychology* (pp. 123–174). Mahwah, NJ: Lawrence
Erlbaum.
141 Hunt et al. (2002).
142 Back v. Hastings-on-Hudson (2004), p. 113.
143 Back v. Hastings-on-Hudson (2004), p. 130.
144 Back v. Hastings-on-Hudson (2004), p. 130.
145 Lust v. Sealy, 383 F.3d 580 (7th Cir. 2004).
146 Lust v. Sealy (2004), p. 583.
147 Lust v. Sealy (2004), p. 583.
148 Lust v. Sealy (2004), p. 583.
149 Lust v. Sealy (2004), p. 583.
150 Washington v. Illinois Department of Revenue, 420 F.3d 658 (7th Cir.,
2005).
151 Washington v. Illinois Department of Revenue (2005), p. 662.
152 Williams (2000), pp. 13–39.
153 Crosby, F. J. (1991). *Juggling: The unexpected advantages of balancing home
and work for women and their families*. New York: MacMillan.
154 Crosby, F. J., Iyer, A., & Sincharoen, S. (2006). Understanding affirmative action. *Annual Review of Psychology*, 57, 585–611.
155 Bartlett & Rhode (2006); MacKinnon, C. A. (2001). *Sex equality*. New
York: Foundation Press, p. 186.
156 Hartmann, H. I., & Aaronson, S. (1994). Pay equity and women's wage
increases: Success in the states, a model for the nation. *Duke Journal of
Gender Law and Policy*, 1, 69–87, p. 80.
157 Nelson, R., & Bridges, W. (1999). *Legalizing gender inequality: Courts,
markets, and unequal pay for women in the United States*. New York:
Cambridge University Press.

158   Bartlett & Rhode (2006).
159   Smith, P. R. (1999). Regulating paid household work: Class, gender, race, and agendas of reform. *American University Law Review, 48,* 851–924; Kessler, L. T. (2001). The attachment gap: Employment discrimination law, women's cultural caregiving, and the limits of economic and liberal legal theory. *University of Michigan Journal of Law Reform, 34*(3), 371–468.
160   Williams & Cooper (2004).
161   Bielby (2000).
162   Bielby (2000); Bisom-Rapp, S. (1999a). Bulletproofing the workplace: Symbol and substance in employment discrimination law practice. *Florida State University Law Review, 26*(4), 969–1047.
163   Sturm, S. (2001). Second generation employment discrimination: A structural approach. *Columbia Law Review, 101,* 458–568.
164   Bielby (2000); Sturm (2001).
165   Pigat, J. D. R., & Jones, S. (2004). *Walking the talk: Creating a law firm culture where women succeed.* Chicago, IL: American Bar Association, pp. 2, 11.

Part IV

Potential Solutions to the Problems of Sex Discrimination in Employment

16

A Critical Look at Organizational Responses to and Remedies for Sex Discrimination

Susan Bisom-Rapp,
Margaret S. Stockdale, and
Faye J. Crosby

Many factors influence how organizations and the people within them respond to sex discrimination. Sex-role stereotyping and other forms of conscious and non-conscious prejudice exert a powerful influence, as has been amply documented by the contributors to Parts II and III of this volume.[1] Reluctance on the part of men, who comprise the majority of corporate decision makers, to give up the privileges they enjoy has also slowed organizational progress toward gender equity.[2] Neither prejudice nor bald self-interest, whether on the part of oneself or one's member group, is an attractive motive to ascribe to a decision maker.

It is our contention that another motive, one generally considered to be quite laudable, has also interfered with the readiness of American work organizations to correct and remedy sex discrimination in employment. Specifically, we contend that the American adherence to justice, linked with certain preconceptions about individual initiative, has – ironically – sometimes hindered efforts to promote gender equity at work.

Our thesis is developed in four sections of our chapter. In the first section, we briefly outline some of the major findings of social psychologists who study social justice issues. We then look at how organizations have enacted policies designed to allow them to conform to the Civil Rights legislation of 1964. The third section of the chapter reviews judicial reactions to sexual harassment lawsuits as an example of how the courts deal with challenges to the persistence of sex discrimination in American organizations. We conclude with a brief examination of the benefits of monitoring the results of procedures as well as the procedures themselves, finding that a concern with distributive justice must be coupled with the concern for procedural justice if organizations are to achieve in fact the gender equity implicitly promised by civil rights legislation four decades ago.

Social Psychology of Social Justice: What We Know About How Americans React to Injustices

Over the last four or five decades, social and organizational psychologists have expended considerable energy theorizing and investigating how people form perceptions of justice and injustice and how those perceptions influence interpersonal behavior. Although there is a clear distinction between studies of justice, on the one hand, and, on the other, legal studies, it seems obvious that research into social justice might yield insights of use to organizations grappling with questions of sex discrimination. By looking at the conceptual and empirical advances within psychological studies of social justice, we can find and understand obstacles to the achievement of gender equity at work.

Belief in a just world

Melvin Lerner[3] helped launch social psychological studies of social justice when he documented the regularity with which people sought to justify their actions. In a classic set of experiments, Lerner extended the observation about justification by placing individuals in the peculiar situation of witnessing the unjustified suffering of another person. When given the opportunity, the participants readily compensated the hapless victim. But, oddly, when (and only when) they were denied the opportunity to compensate the victim, participants in the experiment engaged instead in victim derogation. It seemed that individuals had a need to convince themselves that those who suffer deserve to suffer. Other experiments showed the inverse: when one bears witness to good fortune, one comes to elevate the recipient of the good fortune.

Lerner's general conclusions about people's need to believe in a just world have been substantiated by other researchers.[4] Contemporary researchers have emphasized individual differences, studying the correlates of a strong need to believe that the world is just.[5] Yet, 40 years after the germinal experiments, Lerner's basic insight about "the fundamental illusion" of justice remains unchallenged.

Special case of denial   One particular form of the belief in the just world has received a great deal of attention by researchers: the tendency of people in disadvantaged groups to imagine that they are personally exempt from the discrimination that they know to affect their membership group. When Crosby first stumbled across the phenomenon in the late 1970s, she dubbed it "the denial of personal disadvantage."[6] Twenty years later, the phenomenon has been documented by two dozen studies, conducted by a number of research teams investigating attitudes and feelings among a variety of populations.[7] The phenomenon has formed the basis of Crosby's endorsement of affirmative action as the one antidiscrimination measure that does not require the aggrieved to come forward on their own behalf.[8]

Several factors enable people to convince themselves that they are personally exempt from the forces of discrimination. First, a great deal of employment information remains confidential or private. Often employees do not know the wages or salaries of their fellow workers. Second, even when information is shared, most comparisons are local. Thus, women workers typically compare themselves to other women workers, shielding themselves from the distress that they could feel upon making cross-gender comparisons.[9] Finally, direct comparisons can be ambiguous as long as they are multi-dimensional.[10] For example, a woman manager in Department X who does not obtain a raise and who knows that her male colleague has obtained one may avoid anger by focusing on his greater seniority and ignoring her greater education while her sister in Department Y in the same situation can avoid frustration by concentrating on her male colleague's greater education and downplaying her own greater seniority.

The ability to explain away apparent inequities by emphasizing one trait and downplaying another is not limited to people appraising their own situations. As Crosby and colleagues have documented, individuals have extreme difficulty detecting sex (or other) discrimination when the relevant information is presented in a manner that is analogous to the way individuals in organizations would typically encounter it – on a case-by-case basis.[11]

Distributive justice

Distributive justice refers to the perceived fairness of the distribution of outcomes, such as pay, promotions, and decisions about grievances. Research has shown that perceptions of fairness are affected by the type of allocation norm that is salient in a given situation.[12] Equity norms (e.g., the person who contributes the most, gets the most), are generally preferred when economic productivity is the primary goal; equality norms (everyone gets the same) guide situations where group harmony is important; and need-based norms (the neediest gets the most) are important under conditions of personal development or social welfare.[13]

Research on distributive justice and related theories, such as equity theory, has generally shown that people react to distributions of rewards and of burdens in predictable ways.[14] When people are made to see that the ratio between their own rewards (e.g., pay) and their own qualifications (e.g., education, effort, seniority) is less than the ratio of rewards and qualifications obtained by a specific or generalized other individual, people experience anger or resentment and engage in behaviors designed to alleviate the distress, such as sabotage and revenge. Research has found, for example, that employees have even resorted to theft and sabotage in reaction to perceptions of pay inequity.[15] Similarly, when people are made to feel that their own ratio of rewards to qualifications is greater than that enjoyed by another or others, they experience guilt and then engage in behaviors (e.g., working extra hard) that alleviate guilt.

Procedural justice

Early theorizing and research concentrated on people's reactions to the outcomes of social interactions, but it ran into difficulty when researchers noticed patterns of findings for which there were no readily available accounts. David Messick and colleagues noted that when people are asked to describe examples of unfairness, concerns about pay and promotions and other forms of allocation rank lower than concerns about how one has been treated[16] – a form of justice that came to be known as procedural justice.

Research and theory on procedural justice and related concepts has been abundant, with Thibaut and Walker providing the seminal treatise.[17] These researchers were interested in individuals' reactions to dispute-resolution procedures in legal arenas, and argued that what mattered most to disputants was whether they had a sense of control over final decisions. *Process control* refers to the ability to control the information that is presented on one's behalf – a concept that has been labeled "voice."[18] *Decision control*, or "choice," is the ability to have a say in how the outcome is determined.

Thibaut and Walker's interest in procedural justice has been elaborated on and modified by Tom Tyler. Like Thibaut and Walker, Tyler and his colleagues envision people as being much more concerned with issues of procedural justice than with issues of distributive justice. Where Tyler parts company from Thibaut and Walker is in his understanding of the reasons for the concern with procedural justice. Whereas Thibaut and Walker emphasized the instrumental aspects of a concern with procedural justice, Tyler has insisted on the relational aspects. In a long series of studies, Tyler has developed the theme that procedural justice helps individuals to satisfy their concerns about their status within a group and also their concerns about the group's position within society.[19]

Although Tyler has been unwilling to claim that some aspects of procedures are universally seen as fair, he has noted that individuals assume that they are being treated with fairness when they are treated with respect.[20] Other theorists, some of whom seek to make a distinction between interactional justice (which looks at how procedures are enacted) and procedural justice (which also looks at how procedures are developed), have echoed the importance of interpersonal respect.[21]

A great deal of empirical research has now confirmed the importance of procedural justice issues. Individuals like to have allocations that go in their favor. Yet, they tend to accept allocation decisions that are not in their favor if they believe that the rules that guided those decisions were procedurally fair.[22]

One group of researchers examined a sample of 996 recently fired or laid off workers to determine what factors accounted for their making a wrongful termination charge.[23] Being treated poorly by one's supervisor at the time of termination and being given an insufficient explanation for the termination – both essential elements of interpersonal justice – were the strongest predictors of making a charge. Similarly, Goldman, Paddock, and Cropanzano in a qualitative interview study of 34 individuals who had filed Equal Employment Opportunity Commission (EEOC) complaints found that while concerns for distributive injustice played a role in the decision to file a claim, procedural injustice concerns were paramount to their decision to continue pursuing the claim.[24]

Of special interest to researchers of procedural justice is the issue of voice. Individuals deeply value having an opportunity to give voice to their perspectives, even when decisions have already been made so that the information is of no instrumental value.[25] Being listened to, even just ceremonially, has been found to be a strong predictor of job satisfaction and of pro-organizational behaviors and attitudes. Conversely, being denied an opportunity to voice opinions about how they were treated on the job or being treated with disrespect when voicing their complaint to authorities within their organizations has been found to be an impetus for filing complaints with the EEOC.[26]

Retributive justice

Recently some psychological justice researchers have articulated another dimension to justice motives not adequately explained by distributive and procedural concepts. Asking the provocative question, "Why do people seek to punish others?" Darley and Pittman have concluded that punishment occurs as a means for repairing rents in the social fabric.[27] Punishment is meant to enforce symbolic messages of culturally relevant justice values.

Darley's conceptualizations bear some similarity to the jurisprudence of tort law, the foundational basis of employment discrimination doctrine. Darley notes that when a wrong is committed, individuals assess the intentions and degree of fault of the person who caused the harm to decide the magnitude of punishment warranted or compensation owed. If the harm-doer did not intend to cause harm and acted within reasonable bounds that would normally not cause harm, the act is viewed as accidental. Accidental harms, Darley posits, direct attention less at issues of punishment of the harm-doer and more toward the compensatory goal of making the victim whole. If the harm-doer knew or should have known her or his acts would cause harm or did not follow normal standards of care, then the harm-doer is viewed as negligent and thus deserving of some punishment. Finally, when the harm-doer desires or knows that his or her acts may lead to harm and nonetheless proceeds to engage in the activity to cause that harm, the acts are viewed as intentional and deserving of severe punishment.

The emphasis on intentions and fault, evident in Darley's analysis of retributive justice, sheds light on why it is so difficult to diminish discriminatory practices in organizations. Leaders in contemporary American business organizations almost never set out to harm a specified group of employees or potential employees. Rather, they usually intend to behave in ways that they might describe as upholding standards. To uphold standards is surely not an act worthy of correction, let alone punishment.

The problem is that standards have a way of maintaining the status quo and of excluding the disenfranchised, even as they do so without individuals' awareness or conscious intention. Norton, Vandello, and Darley[28] describe a process they call "casuistry," which is the unconscious shift in emphasizing seemingly objective criteria to justify a social-category-based selection decision. In one of their six studies documenting and testing the parameters of casuistry, Norton et al. found that male undergraduates, acting as managers in a personnel selection task where they chose between a highly qualified male and female applicant for a construction-related job, not only overwhelmingly chose the male candidate, but justified their decision on the criterion on which the male candidate scored higher. In one condition the male candidate had more experience than the female candidate (she had better educational credentials), and in another condition, these criteria were reversed, with the male candidate having the greater educational credentials. In justifying their selection decision, participants almost always mentioned the "justified" criterion (education or experience), and rarely mentioned gender as a factor in their decision making. These studies suggest that we can fool ourselves into believing we are following procedurally just principles, such as using objective criteria for decision making, when in fact we are still operating in a biased fashion.

In sum

Volumes of research studies conducted in the US and Canada show that people care a great deal about justice, and especially about procedural justice. It is also clear that even well-intentioned policies and procedures can perpetuate discriminatory practices because fair-looking procedures can be inaccurately conflated with nondiscriminatory working conditions. As long as people are treated with respect, they may never even notice, let alone lodge complaints about, the ways in which they are ill treated. And as long as decision makers can imagine themselves to be pure of motive, they may never even look to see what results are wrought by their policies and procedures.

Organizational Responses to Civil Rights Legislation

Before the civil rights revolution, employers, unless they were unionized, operated with considerable discretion. Antidiscrimination legislation, particularly Title VII of the Civil Rights Act of 1964 (Title VII), represented an unprecedented limitation on managerial authority. The product of a vibrant political movement, civil rights legislation also gave rise to expectations of bias-free workplaces and fair treatment. The desire to avoid legal battles and the quest for public legitimacy – an effort to bring organizations in line with society's emergent values – served as catalysts for organizations to create equal employment opportunity (EEO) compliance mechanisms to signal their adherence to the new laws.[29] Given the importance of procedures in creating the impression that justice obtains, and given the importance of the appearance of justice for people's trust in and loyalty to organizations, it is hardly surprising that employers' responses to antidiscrimination legislation consisted of implementing procedures intended to show that previously disadvantaged people are now fairly treated.

Some procedures have been codified in organizational policies and supported by organizational structures. Sociologists offer persuasive evidence that Title VII was the impetus for the development and broad implementation of a range of personnel practices that today are viewed as commonplace. These practices include non-union grievance procedures and disciplinary hearings;[30] the establishment of EEO offices;[31] the use of formal performance evaluations and salary classification;[32] the writing of employment at-will clauses in employment contracts designed to forestall wrongful discharge suits;[33] the use of sexual harassment grievance procedures,[34] maternity leave policies,[35] and the creation of diversity training.[36]

The legacy of the 1960s manifests itself in another way as well. Executive Order 11246, signed by President Johnson in 1965, requires non-construction (service and supply) contractors with 50 or more employees and federal government contracts of $50,000 or more to develop written affirmative action programs. Affirmative action employers must monitor their workforces to make sure that they employ qualified female workers and qualified ethnic minority workers in proportion to their availability for various job classifications. When self-monitoring reveals discrepancies between the availability of female talent and the utilization of female talent, corrective steps must be taken.[37]

Although affirmative action law has always provided employers with considerably more guidance than has EEO law, both forms of civil rights measures initially allowed and still do allow employers some latitude in terms of implementation. Title VII, in particular, presented employers with a broad, undefined prohibition, leaving uncertain the scope of the practices that would ultimately be deemed illegal.[38] It is only over time, and often through the compliance efforts of employers themselves, that the vague contours of Title VII's proscriptions have taken firmer shape.[39] Indeed, no less an authority than the U.S. Supreme Court has proclaimed that one of the purposes of antidiscrimination law is to encourage employers to adopt effective organizational structures for the purpose of lessening discrimination.[40]

Into the uncertain legal atmosphere stepped human resource professionals and management lawyers. These allied professional groups responded opportunistically to the civil rights changes in the legal landscape. Soon after Title VII's passage, such professionals began calling for and developing solutions to what they described as looming legal threats to employers.[41]

The success of antidiscrimination efforts was uneven. Although many business leaders felt discomfort about being seen as out of step with American society's changing norms, there was often palpable managerial resistance to changing the status quo and organizational procedures perceived as tried and true. In some instances, managers were truly disturbed by what they saw as changing the rules of conduct in the middle of a set of interactions.[42] One way that some companies resolved the tension between the forces for stasis and the forces for change was to announce symbolic adherence to EEO law while minimally disturbing the firm's existing operations.[43] General remedial measures can be, and in many instances demonstrably have been, easily decoupled from a firm's day-to-day activities.[44] This is not to say that organizations enacting cosmetic compliance measures necessarily regard their efforts in this light. As noted above, adherence to justice principles can mask the presence of bias and make discrimination very difficult to detect.

Studies of success

Although there is an impressive literature documenting the rise and spread of EEO policies and procedures, much less is known about their effectiveness. Several scholars have sought to identify the elements of civil rights compliance that are associated with increasing representation of women in employment and particularly within the managerial ranks. Konrad and Linnehan surveyed human resource executives at over 100 firms in the Philadelphia area, asking them to report the extent to which their organizations had adopted various affirmative action or EEO practices. These practices were categorized as either identity blind or identity conscious. Identity-blind practices included processes designed to treat people the same regardless of gender or race. Identity-conscious practices, in contrast, formally recognize gender or race in an attempt to remedy current discrimination, redress past injustices, and/or achieve fair and visible representation of women and minorities in leadership positions.[45]

As one would expect, government contractors, who were all affirmative action employers, were significantly more likely than other employers to use identity-conscious practices. Interestingly, being subject to an EEO lawsuit in the last five years and being subject to a compliance review were also positively associated with the adoption of identity-conscious programs and structures. Konrad and Linnehan found, in turn, the adoption of identity-conscious practices was positively related to the percentage of women in management and the level of the highest-ranking woman in the organization. Adoption of identity-blind structures was not associated with these or related criteria.

Similar findings were obtained in a study of the workforce participation of women and minorities in 207 different organizations.[46] Organizations that had general structures like EEO offices and affirmative action plans were more likely than others to embrace specialized practices like affirmative action recruitment programs. Yet, in the absence of such specialized programs, general antidiscrimination efforts lost their potency. Indeed, when an organization's affirmative action plans were largely symbolic, rather than substantive, women tended to be underrepresented in the organization, a finding consistent with an earlier study.[47] General corporate EEO offices and training programs designed to convey needed skills to underrepresented groups did not seem to better the position of women either.

A more recent study makes the important point that the most effective antidiscrimination measures are those that require someone in an organization to take responsibility both for identifying local causes of bias and for monitoring changes in the conditions that create inequality.[48] Using changes in the representation of women and minorities in management as the measure of success, a study by Kalev, Dobbin, and Kelley of 810 work establishments concluded that structures designed to combat individual bias – diversity training, mentoring and networking programs, and diversity performance evaluations – lack the positive impact of those that require analyzing and monitoring organizational-level diversity outcomes.

Some of the details of Kalev et al.'s study are especially revealing. They discovered that firms adopting diversity-training programs actually see a decline in the odds of women achieving management status. Companies that evaluate managers on the basis of their performance in promoting diversity are likely to see slight increases in the percentages of white women entering managerial ranks but also some decreases in the chances for black men. Firms with networking programs experience increases in the representation of white women but no significant effects for other groups. Mentoring programs appear to increase the representation of African American women, leaving other underrepresented groups untouched. In contrast, firms with affirmative action plans, diversity committees, and diversity staff tend to experience across the board increases in underrepresented groups. These latter programs, argue the study authors, establish organizational responsibility for the changes necessary to realize a diverse workforce.

Efforts to reduce subjectivity in recruitment and hiring processes also appear to affect female representation in the managerial ranks. A study of over 500 randomly selected organizations in the US found the adoption of formal policies, such as open recruitment, is associated with a higher percentage of women managers.[49] Conversely, reliance on informal recruitment and market competition for managerial jobs is related to less female representation in managerial ranks. Formalized practices appear to decrease discrimination by removing subjectivity in the appraisal process.

Two independent examinations of promotion decisions in the Senior Executive Service (SES) of the federal government suggest that utilizing the principles of procedural justice combined with a progressive, EEO-supportive culture shows promise for creating and sustaining true gender equity. The SES is a corps of senior executives and agency managers who serve just below the top presidential appointees. SES members act as a conduit between the President's appointees and the federal workforce of agencies with representation in the President's cabinet. Examining selection decisions from 1987 to 1992,[50] and then expanding their analysis to include promotion decisions from 1995 to 1999,[51] a team of researchers found female candidates proportionately more likely to be promoted than male candidates, despite the fact that between 84 and 88 percent of the candidates were men. Women's higher qualifications tended to account for their promotion success.

The more recent Powell and Butterfield study (2002) sought to determine whether women's advancement into the SES represented truly substantive gains. That study surveyed a sample of 1,000 male and female SES members across all federal agencies. It found that women and men were almost equally likely to be located in agencies that had considerable discretionary power. Women, moreover, tended to rate their job responsibilities higher than did men.[52] The positive political environment for women in government generally, along with that particular public employer's strong commitment to equal opportunity, may well account for this success.[53] Likewise, these encouraging results may be attributable to formal processes, such as fair and open recruitment procedures, uniform selection procedures, and open record keeping of the decision-making process.[54]

More research is needed before a given antidiscrimination structure can comfortably be deemed to produce positive effects for disadvantaged groups. Nonetheless, the preliminary studies described above assess the effectiveness of various antidiscrimination measures across organizations and begin to enumerate the characteristics of policies that are positively associated with progress for working women. Read together, they indicate that the most effective remedies are formal and identity-conscious policies that promote concrete organizational responsibility for change and are most difficult to segregate from daily organizational life.

Assessing the climate generally

EEO policies do not exist in the abstract. They are embedded in real organizations, and their effectiveness is influenced by organizational climate. A policy or practice deemed generally effective by researchers may have limited utility when adopted by a particular employer.

One way of gauging organizational climate is to assess employees' beliefs about the legitimacy of their employers' compliance efforts; those beliefs are a key component of assessing the everyday impact of civil rights law. Employees' interpretations of their employer's compliance efforts may affect their willingness to make use of existing structures to pursue their rights.[55] If an organizational climate sends the message that antidiscrimination efforts are not taken seriously or that complainants face potential retaliation, no amount of policy promulgation will bring about substantive change. Additionally, gender differences may be operative in the way employees react to specific organizational practices. Such differences, for example, have appeared in studies of grievance resolution procedures.[56] Employers who are serious about creating conditions of gender equality must, in designing institutional responses to civil rights law, take into account which groups may be reluctant to avail themselves of such structures and take steps to reduce employee hesitancy.

It might seem logical to look at the number of lawsuits as a gauge of progress toward equity in employment. One might naively assume that as efforts to eliminate sex discrimination are increasingly successful, the number of lawsuits would decrease. Such a point of view does not, however, take into account the inconvenient fact that individuals are loath to seek redress for wrongs when they know that their efforts are unlikely to reap benefit and likely to cause distress to themselves.

A recent study of Nielson and Nelson[57] is especially instructive about the likelihood that aggrieved parties might seek to improve their situation through legal action. Included in the study is an analysis of data available on employment discrimination litigation in the federal courts from 1990 to 2001. Nielsen and Nelson conceptualize employment discrimination litigation as a "disputing pyramid." The base is comprised of a large number of people with perceived injuries, a subset of that group go on to become informal claims, fewer still become full-blown disputes between the parties, even fewer result in a formal filing, and the smallest number are those cases that actually go to trial.[58] Reviewing the empirical research relevant to each of the categories that make up the pyramid, Nielsen and Nelson come to stark conclusions about the practical effect of antidiscrimination law. Few workers who perceive they are discriminated against take informal or formal action to redress their grievances, most of those who do sue their employers never reach trial, those who reach the trial phase lose over 60 percent of the time, and those victorious at trial receive only modest awards.[59] The picture revealed by Nielson and Nelson varies considerably from popular and media accounts of employment discrimination litigation, which frighten employers and have even helped create a market for employment practice liability insurance.[60]

Court Responses to Complaints Against Employers: What Happens in Sexual Harassment Suits

Up to this point, our analysis has relied on social scientific explanations of why discrimination is easily masked and difficult to detect, rendering many policies adopted to eliminate bias as more symbolic than substantive. As we examine the role of the courts in this section, it is worth noting that current employment discrimination law imposes barriers on the ability of plaintiffs to successfully litigate bias claims. A disparate treatment claim, the most common form of employment discrimination claim, requires proof of discriminatory intent. Unconscious bias, often a factor in organizational decision making that disadvantages out-groups, can be difficult to address under this legal theory.[61] Other complex forms of disadvantage, such as organizational culture,[62] patterns of workplace interaction that over time exclude women,[63] and sex segregation of occupational categories[64] fit uneasily within prevailing legal conceptions of discrimination.

Apart from these significant limitations, a question arises: Within the confines of existing legal theories, do the courts distinguish adequately between organizational compliance that is merely symbolic and organizational compliance that is, in fact, substantive? If the courts can tell the difference between real programs and procedures and those that are only cosmetic, legal remedies may serve as a sharp instrument for social change. If the courts are generally unable to differentiate between organizations that are going through the motions of change and organizations that are making a sincere effort to bring about change, then lawsuits will, at best, serve as blunt instruments against discrimination.

A number of studies have looked at how the courts treat at least one antidiscrimination measure: sexual harassment policies. However, the process by which courts came to equate corporate grievance procedures and antiharassment policies as compelling evidence of nondiscrimination is detailed convincingly by sociologist Lauren Edelman and her colleagues.[65] The story is not one of judicial innovations, but instead involves the interventions of human resource professionals and management attorneys. In the early 1980s, when there was little legal support for their assertions, these professionals began recommending grievance procedures as mechanisms for avoiding liability claiming, among other things, that courts were favorably disposed toward employers who implement internal procedures.[66]

Courts, with the U.S. Supreme Court taking the lead, over time responded by acting in conformity with the stated expectations of the personnel and legal professions. More specifically, courts ultimately embraced a grievance procedure defense to sexual harassment claims where the victim's employment environment has been adversely affected but he or she has suffered no tangible employment action such as termination, demotion, or a cut in pay.[67] In order to avoid legal liability in such cases, the defense requires the employer to prove: (1) that it exercised reasonable care to prevent and correct promptly any harassing behavior; and (2) that the employee unreasonably failed to avail herself of preventative or corrective opportunities provided or to avoid harm otherwise.[68] The sexual harassment grievance procedure, first recommended by human resources and legal professionals as a litigation prevention device, has thus become the primary evidence used by employers to demonstrate they acted reasonably to prevent harassment. Similarly, the employee's failure to make use of such procedures is a major way of establishing the affirmative defense's second prong. Through a process Edelman dubs "legal endogeneity," the meaning of sexual harassment law compliance has been determined not by the courts charged with enforcing Title VII but by the very organizations that the law was designed to regulate.[69]

Edelman and her colleagues see this judicial deference to organizational practice as problematic. The existence of a sexual harassment grievance procedure has come to be equated by judges with legal compliance. Judicial deference to organizational policies typically exists apart from any searching inquiry into whether these common structures function effectively overall or in a given workplace.

The possibility that legal compliance might be merely symbolic rather than substantive is especially troubling to those who envision civil rights law as a potentially transformative force because courts are unlikely to be aware of the organizational dynamics that may undermine employees' rights.[70] For example, procedures may lack due process protections or the full panoply of remedies available in litigation. Additionally, employees concerned about retaliation or bias may decide not to use such procedures, even though the failure to lodge a grievance when a procedure is available can be fatal to an employee's harassment suit.[71] Perhaps the most significant danger, however, is that the absence or presence of a harassment grievance procedure may be used as the yardstick for legal compliance rather than a court undertaking an inquiry into the effectiveness of the device in eliminating workplace harassment.

Recent analyses by legal scholars confirm Edelman's fears. Reviewing courts' approach to the defense, one legal analyst has identified a judicial preoccupation with procedural matters.[72] Rather than assessing whether harassment policies are generally effective, the courts concentrate on procedural details such as whether employer complaint mechanisms include a bypass procedure clearly identifying personnel to whom complainants can go when they might otherwise need to lodge the complaint with their harassers.[73] Beiner has found courts tremendously unsympathetic to plaintiffs who fail to use existing grievance procedures, notwithstanding their very rational concerns about the repercussions of lodging a formal complaint.[74] Similarly, West reports that despite language in the Supreme Court decisions establishing the necessity of adopting effective preventive policies to create nondiscriminatory environments, the focus in harassment litigation is on what transpires after harassment occurs. The employer's duty to prevent harassment is easily satisfied by creating and disseminating an antiharassment policy with a grievance procedure.[75]

The courts' form over substance approach to employers' compliance efforts is also evident in the unthinking acceptance by employment lawyers and judges of harassment and diversity training as a vaccination against and antidote for discriminatory work environments.[76] Judges have embraced the pedagogical approach by incorporating it into civil rights doctrine – educational efforts like training are relevant to the availability of punitive damages – by citing training as favorable employer evidence in litigation, and by making it a regular component of consent decrees, without ever inquiring about whether training accomplishes what it purports to accomplish. Yet social scientists confess that we know very little about how and when these educational programs actually work and in some cases their use can give the impression that discrimination is being meaningfully addressed when in fact it is not.[77]

We do not discount the role of litigation in providing incentives for some employers to undertake meaningful steps to eliminate workplace bias. Yet the tendency of many organizations to create structures that are purely ceremonial, coupled with evidence that courts defer to some of these devices as evidence of nondiscrimination, underscores the need to move beyond litigation to identify strategies that create and sustain gender equity. As many have noted, monitoring the outcomes of one's policies and procedures is a vital component of positive change.[78] Careful monitoring of results is at the heart of affirmative action as established by Executive Order 11246.

Monitoring

Affirmative action

If the process of bringing a lawsuit is reactive, occurring in reaction to a perceived problem, the policy of affirmative action is proactive, intended to ward off probable problems. Affirmative action is not a policy that differs from the majority of American law, but it is a controversial and often poorly understood policy.

Several factors contribute to the confusion that the American public seems to feel about affirmative action. First, the label applies to a number of different practices in education and employment. Second, the media has tended to seek heat rather than light, emphasizing the extent of controversy and failing to provide definitions or explanations of how affirmative action operates.[79]

Although poorly understood, affirmative action in employment, as established by Executive Order 11246, applies to 20 to 25 percent of the American workforce. All 3 million federal government employees are covered by affirmative action as are the employees of the roughly 200,000 establishments that do business with the federal government. About half of the federal contractors are in the construction industry and half are not.

The central principles of affirmative action are surprisingly simple. In essence, every affirmative action employer commits to being both gender conscious and race conscious and commits to monitoring how well it is doing in terms of employing people from targeted classes. Along the dimension of race, the targeted classes include African Americans, Hispanic Americans, Asian Americans, and Native Americans. Along the dimension of gender, women constitute the targeted class. For each targeted class, and for every relevant job classification, an affirmative action employer must calculate two statistics: availability and incumbency (or utilization). Availability refers to the proportion of the qualified workforce for each job classification to come from each targeted class. An organization might, for example, determine that women comprise 30 percent of the people with the qualifications to be lawyers but only 2 percent of the people qualified to be welders. The calculation of availability statistics allows for some small measure of discretion, but the process is by now rather well defined and routine. Even more constrained is the calculation of incumbency.

When incumbency figures fall short of availability, the organization must consider remediation. Sensible plans and timetables are devised. As long as the organization makes a good faith effort to correct its deficiencies, no punitive measures are taken. Organizations that flagrantly flout the responsibility to bring incumbency into line with availability can be disbarred from receiving federal contracts. Disbarment occurs very rarely.

Republican administrations are not known to apply affirmative action law with the same vigor as Democratic administrations. Nonetheless, affirmative action has been credited with a portion of women's economic advances over the past four decades. Contrasts between federal contractors and other companies in the same sectors of the economy show the former to provide more jobs and better jobs to women than do the latter.[80] Given the importance of monitoring for the advancement of women, and given the centrality of monitoring to affirmative action, the salutary effect of affirmative action is not surprising. One of the ways in which affirmative action policy proves especially effective is in its insistence on examining outcomes or results of procedures as well as the procedures themselves.

Court-ordered monitoring

Another example of the promise of monitored remediation is that of court-ordered monitoring, which is also an expression of litigation's potential for bringing about meaningful change. Here, the case of Mitsubishi Motor Manufacturing of America is instructive. In 1998 Mitsubishi set out to transform its auto plant in Normal, Illinois from an environment of rampant sexual abuse and harassment to one where women could work under conditions of equality, dignity, and respect. After years of allowing horrendous conditions to flourish, the automaker changed course in the face of vigilant government prosecution, high-profile publicity, and an aggressive consumer campaign spearheaded by the National Organization for Women. As part of a $34 million lawsuit settlement with the EEOC, Mitsubishi extensively revised its existing sexual harassment policy to ensure convenient mechanisms for reporting harassment, prompt investigation and resolution of complaints, progressive discipline for those retaliating against complainants, and written communication of investigatory findings. An appeal mechanism for complainants dissatisfied with the company's findings or proposed remedial actions was established.

Managers and supervisors were informed of their duty to actively monitor compliance with the new policy. Handling EEO issues became a criterion for supervisory performance evaluation and was linked to the bonus/salary structure. A significant percentage of the Normal plant workforce – from new assembly-line workers to supervisory employees and even senior managers – was given mandatory sexual harassment training. A nursing room for nursing mothers was created.[81]

Although there is some question about the depth of the change in organizational climate at the Normal plant,[82] and indeed some of the steps taken by the company have been found generally by researchers as unhelpful in bringing about gender equity, there is no doubt that Mitsubishi has taken very seriously the need for organizational change. Not only has it agreed to undertake changes, it has also acknowledged the need to expose the plant to outside scrutiny. The company agreed for three years to allow three court-appointed monitors to observe, investigate, and report on its efforts to eradicate sexual harassment. In May 2001, Mitsubishi received a clean bill of organizational health from them.[83]

The Mitsubishi case, however, was unusual. Most successful discrimination suits or negotiated settlements, in contrast, culminate with more common legal remedies like back pay, reinstatement, and the provision of job training to those denied it. These devices are designed to correct discrete legal violations rather than to bring about large-scale transformation of a particular workplace, and provisions for employer accountability are noticeably absent.

Parting Thoughts

Whether transformation comes dramatically as in the case of Mitsubishi Motors or slowly and steadily as in the case of most federal contractors and other organizations practicing affirmative action, change can be sustained only when those in and around the organization feel that both the goals and the means to reach the goals are fair. Given the prevalence of procedural justice issues, as distinct from issues of distributive justice, those who would make American employers as just in substance as they are in slogan need to engage in a special balancing act. On the one hand, they must never lose sight of the need to collect and assess the hard data of achieved results. On the other hand, they must be constantly ready to educate people about the fairness of the procedures by which results are assessed.

Notes

This chapter benefited from participation in a research working group entitled, "Social Scientific Perspectives on Employment Discrimination in Organizations," which is part of the Discrimination Research Group, a joint effort funded by the American Bar Foundation, the Center for Advanced Study in the Behavioral Sciences, and the Ford Foundation (grant #1045–0189).

1   Kimmel, this volume; Glick & Fiske, this volume.
2   Hopkins, this volume; Ridgeway & England, this volume.
3   Lerner, M. J. (1980). *The belief in a just world: A fundamental delusion*. New York: Plenum.
4   Lerner, M., & Miller, D. T. (1978). Just world research and the attribution process: Looking back and ahead. *Psychological Bulletin, 85*(5), 1030–1051.
5   Dalbert, C. (2001). *The justice motive as a personal resource: Dealing with challenges and critical life events*. New York: Kluwer Academic/Plenum Publishers.

6   Crosby, F. J. (1982). *Relative deprivation and working women*. New York: Oxford University Press; and Crosby, F. J. (1984). The denial of personal discrimination. *American Behavioral Scientist, 27*, 371–386.

7   Crosby, F. J., Iyer, A., Clayton, S., & Downing, R. A. (2003). Affirmative action: Psychological data and the policy debates. *American Psychologist, 58*, 93–115.

8   Clayton, S. D., & Crosby, F. (1992). *Justice, gender and affirmative action*. Ann Arbor, MI: University of Michigan Press; Crosby, F. J. (2004). *Affirmative action is dead: Long live affirmative action*. New Haven, CT: Yale University Press; and Crosby, F. J., Iyer, A., & Sincharoen, S. (2006). Understanding affirmative action. *Annual Review of Psychology, 57*, 586–611.

9   Zanna, M. P., Crosby F., & Loewenstein, G. (1987). Male reference groups and discontent among female professionals. In B. A. Gutek, & L. Larwood (Eds.), *Pathways to women's career development* (pp. 28–41). Beverly Hills: Sage Publications.

10 Crosby (1984).

11 Crosby, F., Clayton, S., Hemker, K., & Alksnis, O. (1986). Cognitive biases in the perception of discrimination: The importance of format. *Sex Roles, 14*, 637–646.

12 Deutsch, M. (1975). Equity, equality, and need: What determines which value will be used as a basis of distributive justice. *Journal of Social Issues, 31*, 137–149.

13 Deutsch (1975).

14 Adams, J. S. (1965). Inequity in social exchange. In L. Berkowitz (Ed.), *Advances in experimental social psychology* (Vol. 2. pp. 267–299). New York: Academic Press; Greenberg, J. (1990). Organizational justice: Yesterday, today, and tomorrow. *Journal of Management, 16*, 606–613; Mowday, R. T. (1987). Equity theory and predictions in behavior in organizations. In R. Steers, & L. Porter (Eds.), *Motivation and work behavior* (pp. 89–110). New York: McGraw-Hill; and Walster, E., Walster, G. W., & Berscheid, E. (1978). *Equity theory and research*. Boston: Allyn & Bacon.

15 Greenberg (1990).

16 E.g., Finkel, N. J. (2000). But it's not fair! Commonsense notions of unfairness. *Psychology, Public Policy and Law, 6*, 898–952; Messick, D. M., Bloom, S., Boldizar, J. P., & Samuelson, C. D. (1985). Why we are fairer than others. *Journal of Experimental Social Psychology, 21*, 389–399.

17 Thibaut, J., & Walker, L. (1975). *Procedural justice: A psychological analysis*. Hillsdale, NJ: Lawrence Erlbaum.

18 Folger, R., & Cropanzano, R. (1998). *Organizational justice and human resource management*. Thousand Oaks, CA: Sage.

19 Lind, E. A., & Tyler, T. R. (1988). *The social psychology of procedural justice*. New York: Plenum; Tyler, T. R., & Blader, S. L. (2003). The group engagement model: Procedural justice, social identity, and cooperative behavior. *Personality and Social Psychology Review, 7*, 349–361; and Tyler, T. R., &

Lind, E. A. (1992). A relational model of authority in groups. In M. P. Zanna (Ed.), *Advances in experimental social psychology* (Vol. 25, pp. 115–191). San Diego, CA: Academic Press.

20 Crosby, F. J., & Franco, J. (2003). The ivory tower and the multicultural world. *Personality and Social Psychology Review, 7*, 362–373; and Tyler & Blader (2003).

21 Bies, R. J., & Moag, J. S. (1986). Interactional justice: Communication criteria of fairness. In R. J. Lewicki, B. H. Sheppard, & B. H. Bazerman (Eds.), *Research on negotiation in organizations* (Vol. 1, pp. 43–55). Greenwich, CT: JAI Press; Greenberg (1990); and Greenberg, J., & McCarty, C. (1990). The interpersonal aspects of procedural justice: A new perspective on pay fairness. *Labor Law Journal, 41*, 580–586.

22 Brockner, J., & Wiesenfeld, B. M. (1996). An interactive framework for explaining reactions to decisions: The interactive effects of outcomes and procedures. *Psychological Bulletin, 120*, 189–208.

23 Lind, E. A., Greenberg, J., Scott, K. S., & Welchans, T. D. (2000). The winding road from employee to complainant: Situational and psychological determinants of wrongful-termination claims. Administrative Science Quarterly, *45*, 557–590.

24 Goldman, B. M., Paddock, E. L., & Cropanzano, R. (2004). A transformational model of legal-claiming. *Journal of Managerial Issues, 16*, 417–441.

25 Thibaut & Walker (1975); and Tyler, T. R., Rasinksi, K., & Spodick, N. (1985). The influence of voice on satisfaction with leaders: Exploring the meaning of process control. *Journal of Personality and Social Psychology, 48*, 72–81.

26 Goldman et al. (2004).

27 Darley, J. M., & Pittman, T. S. (2003). The psychology of compensatory and retributive justice. *Personality and Social Psychology Review, 7*, 324–336.

28 Norton, M. I., Vandello, J. A., and Darley, J. M. (2004). Casuistry and social category bias. *Journal of Personality and Social Psychology, 87*, 817–831.

29 Bisom-Rapp, S. (1999b). Discerning form from substance: Understanding employer litigation prevention strategies. *Employee Rights and Employment Policy Journal, 3*, 1–64; and Edelman, L. B. (1992). Legal ambiguity and symbolic structures: Organizational mediation of civil rights law. *American Journal of Sociology, 97*, 1531–1576.

30 Sutton, J. R., Dobbin, F., Meyer, J. W., & Scott, W. R. (1994). The legalization of the workplace. *American Journal of Sociology, 99*, 944–971.

31 Edelman (1992).

32 Dobbin, F., Sutton, J. R., Meyer, J. W., & Scott, W. R. (1993). Equal opportunity law and the construction of internal labor markets. *American Journal of Sociology, 99*, 396–427.

33 Sutton et al. (1994).

34 Edelman, L. B., Uggen, C., & Erlanger, H. S. (1999). The endogeneity of legal regulation: Grievance procedures as rational myth. *American Journal of Sociology, 105*, 406–454.

35 Kelly, E., & Dobbin, F. (1999). Civil rights law at work: Sex discrimination and the rise of maternity leave policies. *American Journal of Sociology, 105*, 455–492.

36 Edelman, L. B., & Petterson, S. M. (1999). Symbols and substance in organizational response to civil rights law. *Research in Social Stratification and Mobility, 17*, 107–135; and Kalev, A., Dobbin, F., & Kelly, E. (2005b). *Two to tango: Affirmative action, diversity programs and women and African-Americans in management.* Unpublished paper on file with author.

37 Crosby (2004); and Edelman & Petterson (1999).

38 Edelman (1992); and Sutton, J. R., & Dobbin, F. (1996). The two faces of governance: Responses to legal uncertainty in U.S. firms, 1955 to 1985. *American Sociological Review, 61*, 794–811.

39 Suchman, M. C., & Edelman, L. B. (1997). Legal rational myths: The new institutionalism and the law and society tradition. *Law and Social Inquiry, 21*, 903–941.

40 Pennsylvania State Police v. Suders, 542 U.S. 129 (2004).

41 Sutton & Dobbin (1996); Suchman & Edelman (1997).

42 Skitka, L. J., & Crosby, F. J. (2003). Trends in the social psychological study of justice. *Personality and Social Psychology Review, 7*, 282–285.

43 Edelman (1992).

44 Edelman & Petterson (1999).

45 Konrad, A. M., & Linnehan, F. (1995a). Race and sex differences in line managers' reactions to equal employment opportunity and affirmative action interventions. *Group and Organizational Management, 20*, 409–39; Konrad, A. M., & Linnehan, F. (1995b). Formalized HRM structures: Coordinating equal employment opportunity or concealing organizational practices? *Academy of Management Journal, 38*, 787–820.

46 Edelman & Petterson (1999).

47 Baron, J. N., Mittman, B. S., & Newman, A. E. (1991). Targets of opportunity: Organizational and environmental determinants of gender integration within the California civil service, 1979–1985. *American Journal of Sociology, 96*, 1362–1401.

48 Kalev et al. (2005).

49 Reskin, B. F., & McBrier, D. B. (2000). Why not ascription? Organizations' employment of male and female managers. *American Sociological Review, 65*(2), 210–233.

50 Powell, G. N., & Butterfield, D. A. (1994). Investigating the "glass ceiling" phenomenon: An empirical study of actual promotions to top management. *Academy of Management Journal, 37*, 68–86.

51 Powell, G. N., Butterfield, D. A. (2002). Exploring the influence of decision makers' race and gender on actual promotions to top management. *Personnel Psychology, 55*, 397–428.

52 Dolan, J. (2004). Gender equity: Illusion or reality for women in the Federal Executive Service. *Public Administration Review, 64,* 299–308.

53 Dolan (2004); Powell & Butterfield (1994).

54 Powell & Butterfield (1994, 2002).

55 Albiston, C. R. (2005). Bargaining in the shadow of social institutions: Competing discourses and social change in workplace mobilization of civil rights. *Law and Society Review, 39,* 11–49; and Fuller, S. R., Edelman, L. B., & Marusik, S. F. (2000). Legal readings: Employee interpretation and mobilization of law. *Academy of Management Review, 25,* 200–216.

56 See, for example Hoffman, E. A. (2005). Dispute resolution in a worker cooperative: Formal procedures and procedural justice. *Law and Society Review, 39,* 51–82; and Marshall, A.-M. (2005). Idle rights: Employees' rights consciousness and the construction of sexual harassment policies. *Law and Society Review, 39,* 83–123.

57 Nielsen, L. B., & Nelson, R. L. (2005). Rights realized? An empirical analysis of employment discrimination litigation as a claiming system. *Wisconsin Law Review,* 663–711.

58 Nielsen & Nelson (2005).

59 Nielsen & Nelson (2005).

60 Bielby, W. T., & Bourgeois, M. (2002, August). *Insuring discrimination: Making a market for employment practice liability insurance.* Paper presented at the Annual Meeting of the American Sociological Association. Chicago, IL.

61 Krieger, L. H. (1995). The content of our categories: A cognitive bias approach to discrimination and equal employment opportunity. *Stanford Law Review, 47,* 1161–1248; and McGinley, A. C. (2000). ¡Viva la evolucion!: Recognizing unconscious motive in Title VII. *Cornell Journal of Law and Public Policy, 9,* 415–492.

62 Green, T. K. (2005). Work culture and discrimination. *California Law Review, 93,* 623–684.

63 Sturm, S. (2001). Second generation employment discrimination: A structural approach. *Columbia Law Review, 101,* 458–568.

64 Schultz, V. (1990). Telling stories about women and work: Judicial interpretations of sex segregation in the workplace in Title VII cases raising the lack of interest defense. *Harvard Law Review, 103,* 1749–1843; and Schultz, V. (2000). Life's work. *Columbia Law Review, 100,* 1881–1964.

65 Edelman et al. (1999).

66 Edelman et al. (1999).

67 Burlington Industries, Inc. v. Ellerth, 524 U.S. 742 (1998); Faragher v. City of Boca Raton, 524 U.S. 775 (1998); Pennsylvania State Police v. Suders (2004).

68 Burlington Industries, Inc. v. Ellerth (1998); Faragher v. City of Boca Raton (1998).

69 Edelman et al. (1999).

70 Edelman et al. (1999).

71   Beiner, T. M. (2005). *Gender myths v. working realities: Using science to refor-mulate sexual harassment law*. New York: New York University Press.

72   Grossman, J. L. (2003). The culture of compliance: The final triumph of form over substance in sexual harassment law. *Harvard Women's Law Journal, 26*, 3–75.

73   Grossman (2003).

74   Beiner (2005).

75   West, M. S. (2002). Preventing sexual harassment: The federal courts' wake-up call for women. *Brooklyn Law Review, 68*, 457–523.

76   Bisom-Rapp, S. (2001). An ounce of prevention is a poor substitute for a pound of cure: Confronting the developing jurisprudence of education and prevention in employment discrimination law. *Berkeley Journal of Employ-ment and Labor Law, 22*, 1–47.

77   Bisom-Rapp (2001).

78   Krieger, this volume.

79   Crosby, F. J., & Cordova, D. (1996). Words worth of wisdom. *Journal of Social Issues, 52*(4), 33–49.

80   Crosby (2004); and Reskin, B. F. (1998). *The realities of affirmative action in employment*. Washington, DC: American Sociological Association.

81   Joint Motion for Entry of Consent Decree, EEOC v. Mitsubishi Motor Mfg. of America (C.D. Ill. June 10, 1998) (No. 96–1192). Retrieved July 5, 2006, from www.eeoc.gov/policy/docs/mmma.html

82   Selmi, M. (2005). Sex discrimination in the nineties, seventies style: Case studies in the preservation of male workplace norms. *Employee Rights and Employment Policy Journal, 9*, 1–50.

83   Final Report to the Parties and the Court, EEOC v. Mitsubishi Motor Mfg. of America, May 17, 2001 (on file with authors).

17

The Watched Variable Improves: On Eliminating Sex Discrimination in Employment

Linda Hamilton Krieger

Since Congress passed the Civil Rights Act of 1964,[1] it has been unlawful for all but the smallest U.S. employers,[2] labor unions,[3] and employment agencies[4] to discriminate against women in hiring, promotion, compensation, union membership, job referral, or other terms and conditions of employment or union membership. And since 1967, when President Johnson amended Executive Order 11246[5] to address sex as well as race discrimination, federal contractors having contracts exceeding $50,000 and 50 or more employees have been required to take affirmative action to ensure that women are accorded equal opportunity in hiring, training, promotion, and other terms and conditions of employment.

These laws, and others like them at the state level, have been enormously successful. It would be hard to argue with the proposition that since the early 1970s, when for example, major newspapers still divided help wanted advertisements into "Women Wanted" and "Men Wanted" sections,[6] women have made great strides in the American labor market. And yet, as earlier chapters in this collection describe,[7] significant problems remain. For example, in the year 2000, women with a four-year college degree who worked full time and year round still, on average, made only 71.5 cents for every dollar made by men.[8] As revealed by a 1992 study by Stroh, Brett, and Reilly, average differences in male and female manager salaries remain significant, even after controlling for education, experience, time-in-job, industry, time off, and other human capital variables.[9] Moreover, women remain significantly underrepresented in careers related to mathematics, science, and engineering,[10] and, as the Department of Labor's Glass Ceiling Commission reported in 1995, at the dawn of the twenty-first century, only 3–5 percent of senior management positions in and 6.9 percent of seats on the boards of Fortune 500 companies were held by women.[11] Women in the U.S. workforce have come a long way, but we have a long way yet to go.

So here is the question: If, as a society, we were truly committed to eliminating sex discrimination in employment, what would we do? What laws would we enact, and what agencies and processes would we design to enforce them? What would we expect – of our government, of employers, of employment agencies and labor unions – as contributions to our collective effort to make equal employment opportunity for women a concrete reality as opposed to a wispy aspiration?

At first, it may seem a daunting question. And yet, the simple fact is we have been down this road before, and we have learned a great deal about how to identify, prevent, and redress sex discrimination in employment. The enormous strides made by women in the 1970s and 1980s – in the skilled trades, in law, medicine, accounting, and the sciences, in business and public management positions – did not just spontaneously happen. Class action lawsuits, equal employment opportunity compliance and affirmative action programs, along with social and political agitation, wrested these advances from a gender-stratified and gender-segregated labor market. We know how to reduce sex discrimination in employment, and it is the goal of this chapter to marshal what we know from past experience and to suggest new ways of applying it in the years ahead.

The Difficulty Inherent in Identifying Employment Discrimination

The *Merriam-Webster Unabridged Collegiate Dictionary* defines discrimination as "the process by which two stimuli differing in some aspect are responded to differently."[12] Title VII of the Civil Rights Act of 1964, in pertinent part, makes it unlawful "to fail or refuse to hire or to discharge any individual, or otherwise to discriminate against any individual with respect to his [sic] compensation, terms, conditions, or privileges of employment, because of such individual's . . . sex."[13] Thus, one "discriminates" in employment "because of sex" if one responds differently to females, as compared to males, in ways that negatively affect their relative employment opportunities.

Once discrimination is understood in this way, it becomes clear why it can be difficult to identify. Many different mental processes can cause an employment decision maker to "respond differently" to males and females in the workplace. At the most blatant end of the spectrum, an employer might refuse to hire or promote a woman to a particular position because he believes that women should not hold jobs of the type in question. We might refer to this type of bias as a "normative stereotype," because it reflects a "norm," a belief about how women "should" behave. Or, the employer might refuse to hire a woman as opposed to a man for a particular job because she believes that, on average, men are more productive than women, and so uses sex as a rough and ready predictor of future productivity. We might refer to this type of bias as a "descriptive stereotype," because it reflects a descriptive belief about how men and women actually behave.

Open, deliberate application of these sorts of explicit normative and descriptive stereotypes is easily recognizable as sex discrimination, but it has also become relatively rare and hard to prove. Few employers, even if they explicitly hold and apply such normative or descriptive beliefs about women, are willing to express them openly, let alone admit that they have applied them in making particular employment decisions.

As earlier chapters in this collection have described,[14] discrimination is not always the product of consciously endorsed sexist beliefs. It can also result from the application of *implicit* stereotypes, networks of mental associations that predispose the stereotype-holder to perceive, characterize, and behave toward men and women in different ways. Discrimination that results from these sorts of stereotypes can be even harder to identify than discrimination resulting from explicit, if hidden, beliefs.

It is particularly difficult to recognize discrimination from case-by-case data. In one well-known experimental illustration, Faye Crosby and her colleagues presented male subjects with a set of materials describing a hypothetical "Company Z," comprising ten different departments.[15] The materials were constructed so that women in the company earned, on average, significantly less than men, even after controlling for input variables like seniority, educational attainment, and performance ratings. In one condition, subjects first received information about employees in aggregated form; data reflecting salary and performance on the input variables for male and female employees in the company as a whole were arranged systematically on a single large page.

After seeing this information in aggregate form, research participants were asked whether there was sex discrimination in the company as a whole. They were then shown the same data on a department-by-department basis, and were asked to make serial judgments about each department. In a second condition, researchers reversed the order of these two steps. Research participants were first shown data on a department-by-department basis, and asked to make judgments about the existence of discrimination in each department. Only then were they shown the aggregate data and asked to make judgments about the company as a whole.

Crosby and her colleagues found that format had a significant effect on subjects' abilities to identify the sex-based disparities embedded in the stimulus materials. When information was presented first on a department-by-department basis, subjects perceived significantly less discrimination than when the same information was presented first in aggregated form.

Crosby's findings were subsequently replicated by other researchers, using slightly modified experimental designs. In one study, Diane Cordova found that both male and female subjects more readily identified sex discrimination embedded in a set of stimulus materials when information about salaries and input variables was presented in an aggregated format. When information was presented on a department-by-department basis, subjects identified sex discrimination far less frequently, in both an immediate-response and a delayed-response condition.[16] In another study, Twiss, Tabb, and Crosby found that even when patterns of input-controlled disparities in men's versus women's salaries were not labeled as "sex discrimination," subjects were still far less likely to identify those patterns in "plant-by-plant" as opposed to company-wide data.[17]

Sex discrimination is hard to detect in case-by-case data because it is almost always possible to attribute less favorable treatment of a particular woman, or small group of women, to factors other than sex. As Twiss et al. describe the problem:

> In the workplace, a number of attributes are considered to be relevant "input variables" for any given outcome. Because any two individuals are likely to differ on a number of input characteristics, a comparison between the outcomes of, say, one female and one male seldom provides sure proof of disparate treatment. As long as the male in the comparison surpasses the female on one input attribute, we may have a plausible explanation of any outcome decision that favors the male. As long as the female can be considered inferior on just one relevant input characteristic, we can theoretically justify an outcome decision that adversely affects the female.[18]

Sex discrimination caused by the application of subtle gender preferences or implicit sex stereotypes may be hard even for the people applying those preferences or stereotypes to detect from case-by-case data. This occurs because the preference or stereotype biases the decision indirectly, by altering the decision maker's perception of the target person's qualifications or performance.

In a dramatic demonstration of this phenomenon in the socio-economic class-bias context, John Darley and Paget Gross showed that subjects who refused to apply stereotypes in predicting the relationship between children's socio-economic status and educational performance were nonetheless influenced by those stereotypes when asked to assess whether a mixed and somewhat ambiguous test performance by a particular working-class or upper middle-class child reflected abilities "below grade level," "at grade level," or "above grade level."[19] In this study, Darley and Gross found that the same test performance was rated as above grade level for the high socio-economic status child and below grade level for the low socio-economic status child. In a more recent illustration of a similar phenomenon, Norton, Vandello, and Darley found that when a selection decision can be based on any of a number of different input variables (such as education and experience), subjects altered their assessments of the relative importance of these different variables to justify decisions actually based on social category membership.[20] In short, discrimination is hard to identify in case-by-case data in part because it is difficult to disentangle the reasons – discriminatory or nondiscriminatory – why a particular decision was made.

This difficulty is exacerbated when patterns of disparate treatment are inconsistent or inconspicuous. In a dramatic illustration of this phenomenon, Susan Clayton showed that subjects had difficulty identifying patterns of sex discrimination in compensation when the pay disparities were small or inconsistent, or when some women were paid more than some men. Subjects were particularly poor at identifying discrimination when women's salaries were slightly lower than or equivalent to men's, but the women were better qualified.[21]

Extending Clayton's results, Christel Rutte and her colleagues demonstrated that sex discrimination is especially difficult to detect when principles of "ordinal equity" are not violated.[22] Ordinal equity is violated when a person who ranks higher on relevant input variables (e.g., qualifications) ranks lower than another person on the relevant outcome variable (e.g., salary, rank, or grade). *Magnitudes* of difference in the input or output variables do not implicate ordinal equity. In Rutte's study, when experimenters gave men systematic but unobtrusive advantages that did not violate principles of ordinal equity, subjects generally failed to recognize that women were being unfavorably treated. And perhaps more importantly, when subjects *did* recognize these less obtrusive forms of sex-based disparity, they were unlikely to label them as unfair.

As we have seen, people have difficulty recognizing sex discrimination when it is not conspicuous and consistent. People also have difficulty identifying discrimination when it manifests as small, seemingly insignificant forms of preference or leniency toward members of one particular group. When we think of discrimination, we think of discrimination *against* members of a group in which group members are treated unfavorably according to some standard metric of fairness. But as social psychologist Marilyn Brewer points out, discrimination can also occur when members of the subordinated group are treated neutrally according to some standard metric of fairness, while members of the privileged group are treated with greater leniency or favor than neutral rules would direct.[23] When these subtle forms of advantage accrete over time, they can be very difficult to detect. For one thing, people are more likely to notice things that *do* happen to them than things that do not.[24] For example, a woman who is not hired into a particular job, not mentored, or not given a raise, is less likely to perceive that she has been treated unfairly than a woman who is fired. Moreover, in order to perceive that she was being treated unfairly, a woman would need, at a minimum, cross-gender comparative information, and this is often unavailable to her. In addition, if a woman does compare herself to other employees, she is more likely to select another woman than a man as a referent.[25]

For all these reasons, it is difficult to identify sex discrimination from case-by-case data, or even from small aggregate groups. But that does not mean that discrimination is impossible to identify. It is simply that, like any complex empirical inquiry, to identify discrimination one needs the right information, organized and analyzed in the right way.

Techniques for Identifying Sex Discrimination

As the prior section described, it is far easier to identify discrimination from aggregated data than from case-by-case data. But in a sense, this observation states rather than solves the central problem: to determine whether sex discrimination is occurring in an employment-related selection system, exactly what data should be aggregated, and how should it be analyzed?

Forty years of equal employment opportunity (EEO) litigation and voluntary EEO compliance programs have produced a set of now widely accepted methods for detecting patterns of sex discrimination in hiring, job assignment, and promotion. The centerpiece of any such inquiry is known as a "utilization analysis."[26] In performing a gender utilization analysis, one first identifies the percentage of women and men hired, assigned, or promoted into a particular job classification. Next, one determines the percentage of men and women in the relevant pool of qualified persons from which employees are selected for the positions in question. The final step in a utilization analysis entails comparing the percentage of women in the relevant selection pool with the percentage of women actually selected for the positions being studied. If women are underrepresented in the positions relative to their representation in the relevant selection pool, and if this underrepresentation is statistically significant,[27] a *prima facie* inference can be raised that some sort of discrimination is operating in the selection procedure.[28] As the Supreme Court explained in 1977, statistical evidence of this kind is indicative of discrimination because "absent explanation, it is ordinarily to be expected that nondiscriminatory (employment) practices will in time result in a work force that is more or less representative of the . . . composition of the population . . . from which employees are drawn."[29]

In *Dukes v. Wal-Mart*, a pending nationwide class action lawsuit alleging systemic discrimination against women in Wal-Mart management, a utilization analysis formed the centerpiece of the plaintiff's case. That analysis reveals that, as of 2001 when the case was filed, women constituted 67% of all hourly workers, 88% of Customer Service Managers, and 78% of Department Managers in Wal-Mart stores in the United States. However, women constituted only 35.7% of Assistant Managers, 23% of Co-Managers, and 14.3% of Store Managers in those same stores.[30] Given the large number of positions being analyzed, and the extent of the disparity between availability of women and their selection into the positions in question, the results of this analysis are statistically significant at a very high level.

Of course, in any situation in which selection decisions are premised on specific input variables (i.e., qualifications), it is always possible that observed gender disparities could be caused not by sex discrimination, but rather by an unequal distribution of those input variables among males and females in the relevant selection pool. Consequently, once a statistically significant utilization disparity has been observed, one needs to assess whether that disparity will remain significant after controlling for other input variables, such as experience, education, or past performance.

Here again, 40 years of equal employment opportunity litigation and compliance programs provide widely accepted methods for extending the utilization analysis to account for nondiscriminatory factors that could be causing systematic gender-based disparities in employment outcomes. Specifically, we can use a statistical technique known as multiple regression analysis to determine whether, even after controlling for nondiscriminatory factors the employer claims to use in making selections, a candidate's sex still predicts selection outcomes at a statistically significant level.[31]

Once a statistically significant utilization disparity has been observed, and regression analysis has shown that it cannot readily be attributed to legitimate nondiscriminatory factors, the next step in a utilization analysis is to determine what aspects of the selection process might be leaving room for the operation of gender bias. Drawing again on the *Dukes v. Wal-Mart* litigation, for example, in their class certification motion, the Wal-Mart plaintiffs pointed to the following aspects of Wal-Mart's promotion practices that might be operating as "built-in headwinds"[32] to women's advancement:

- Wal-Mart's policy of allowing managers to select employees for the company's management training program based on subjective criteria, with little guidance and no objective selection guidelines;
- Wal-Mart's failure to post openings in its management training program, or systematically describe management training opportunities to employees;
- the absence of any application procedure for the management training program and reliance, instead, on an informal, "tap-on-the-shoulder" selection system;
- Wal-Mart's policy requiring management employees to certify that they would be willing to relocate, despite the absence of any demonstrated business justification for the policy;
- Wal-Mart's failure to monitor promotion and salary decisions to assure that systematic gender-linked disparities were not developing; and
- Wal-Mart's failure to institute policies and practices that would in any way hold managers accountable for such gender disparities when and if they did develop.[33]

Various additional types of information are useful in identifying sex discrimination in employment decision-making systems. These include patterns of discrimination complaints, the making of comments evincing stereotyped or other gender-biased attitudes on the part of decision makers, and information about what, if any, steps the organization has taken to identify and remedy under-utilization of women in various parts of the organization.[34] But by far the most important tool for identifying sex discrimination in employment is to examine aggregated statistical data for results. At the end of the day, as we will see, in EEO policy as in so many other places, it is the watched variable that improves.

Combating Sex Discrimination in Employment: The Available Tools

Since Title VII was enacted in 1964, a variety of enforcement tools have been developed and used to prevent, identify, and remedy sex discrimination in employment. Before we can assess what society might do in the future to eliminate sex discrimination in employment, it is useful to have at least a rudimentary understanding of how these various tools work, and what existing research tells us about their relative efficiency and effectiveness.

Enforcement activities by administrative agencies: The Equal Employment Opportunity Commission and its state counterparts

In addition to prohibiting sex, race, national origin, and religious discrimination in employment, Title VII of the Civil Rights Act of 1964 established a federal enforcement agency, the Equal Employment Opportunity Commission, or EEOC.[35] Originally, Title VII empowered the EEOC to enforce the Act only through statutory interpretation, education, complaint investigation, and persuasion. In 1972, Congress also gave the EEOC authority to bring lawsuits in federal court to enforce and remedy violations of the statute on behalf of discrimination victims.[36]

Most of the EEOC's resources are spent receiving and investigating individual complaints of discrimination filed by persons claiming to be aggrieved under Title VII or the other statutes the Commission enforces. So, for example, in 2005, the EEOC received 75,428 charges of discrimination, of which 23,094 (30.6%) involved complaints of sex discrimination.[37] Once the EEOC receives a charge of discrimination, it is required to investigate the charge, determine whether there is reasonable cause to believe that discrimination actually occurred, and if so, to attempt conciliation between the parties. If conciliation efforts are not successful, the Commission is permitted, but not required, to initiate litigation on behalf of the charging party against the respondent.

In 2005, of the 23,094 sex discrimination charges filed, 4,019 were quickly settled or withdrawn by the charging party. Another 4,188 were abandoned or closed for other non-merits based reasons. Of the remaining charges, the Commission made a reasonable cause finding in 1,693 cases (7.1% of all charges filed), successfully conciliated 454 cases (1.9%), and provided monetary benefits to charging parties during the administrative (as opposed to litigation) process in the amount of 91.3 million dollars.[38]

Most discrimination charges filed with the EEOC are filed by individuals alleging discrimination against themselves alone. Likewise, most of the lawsuits filed by the EEOC seek redress for individual discrimination grievants.[39] However, the EEOC has the authority to expand individual investigations to determine whether the employer is engaging in a pattern and practice of discrimination of the type alleged in an individual charge. If the Commission finds reasonable cause to believe that this is so, it can sue on behalf of an entire class and seek both monetary and structural remedies.

On the whole, class-based litigation, also known as pattern and practice litigation, provides far more remedy for the enforcement agency dollar than individual victim-oriented enforcement efforts. For example, in 2004, the EEOC obtained a number of multimillion dollar recoveries in lawsuits alleging patterns and practices of sex discrimination.[40] The largest of these was a $54 million consent decree obtained in a pattern and practice sex discrimination suit against Morgan Stanley. In addition to providing $52 million in monetary relief to women who were members of the class, the consent decree also provided extensive injunctive relief in the form of promotion, pay equity, and other EEO-related goals, and required the appointment, at Morgan Stanley's expense, of an ombudsperson to monitor compliance with the decree's terms and investigate any further complaints of sex discrimination.[41] This one 2004 settlement of $54 million equaled over half of the $100.8 million obtained in administrative conciliations by the EEOC during the same fiscal year. The relative efficiency of class-based litigation is only accentuated when one considers that the EEOC's entire litigation support budget for the 2004 fiscal year totaled a mere $3.36 million.[42]

Enforcement activities by administrative agencies: Executive Orders 10925, 11246, 11375 and the Federal Contract Compliance Program

Ever since World War II, when President Roosevelt issued an executive order prohibiting race discrimination in defense contractors' employment practices,[43] some form of nondiscrimination obligation has been imposed on federal contractors. Executive Order 10925, issued by President Kennedy in 1961, and Executive Order 11246, issued by President Johnson in 1965, for the first time required federal contractors not only to refrain from discrimination based on race, but also to take "affirmative action" to ensure that race discrimination did not occur. Both Orders provided specific sanctions for violations, up to termination of existing contracts and debarment from future federal contracting opportunities. In 1967, through Executive Order 11375, President Johnson amended Executive Order 11246 to prohibit sex as well as race discrimination and to require sex-based affirmative action as well. However, little was done until the 1970s to enforce these provisions, particularly the Orders' affirmative action mandates.

Surprisingly, it was Richard M. Nixon that made affirmative action a key element of the country's civil rights enforcement strategy. In 1969, Nixon's Labor Department promulgated detailed regulations spelling out exactly what the Executive Orders' affirmative action obligations entailed.[44] Among other things, these regulations, as amended in 1972 to cover women as well as racial minorities, required all federal contractors having 50 or more employees and contracts worth $50,000 or more to undertake systematic utilization analyses to determine whether they were employing women and members of minority groups in numbers proportional to their representation in the qualified, relevant labor market.[45] To the extent that contractors identified areas of under-utilization, Nixon's affirmative action regulations required that contractors undertake specific remedial measures designed to correct the observed disparities. These measures included the setting of goals and timetables for reaching parity between utilization and availability, and the identification and removal of unnecessary obstacles to full utilization of minorities and women.[46] Although the Regulations made clear that the goals were not to be treated as quotas, contractors with availability–utilization disparities were expected to report annually on the measures they were taking, and the progress they were making, to correct any observed utilization deficiencies.[47]

In addition, all contractors meeting the 50/50 threshold were required to develop, annually update, and provide to the relevant federal enforcement agency an affirmative action plan. Regulations required that the plan establish clear organizational lines of authority for implementing the contractor's affirmative action obligations. Specifically, the Regulations required that a specific management-level employee be assigned responsibility for plan oversight, and that "[h]e or she must have the authority, resources, support of and access to top management to ensure the effective implementation of the affirmative action program."[48] Employers subject to the Executive Order were required, as part of their affirmative action planning, to design internal organizational audit and reporting systems to measure the effectiveness of the plan, and to identify strategies for recruiting minorities and women not currently in the workforce who might, through special training or other community-based programs, be successfully employed.[49]

Over the 1970s, federal enforcement of the Executive Orders became increasingly aggressive. The various federal contract compliance agencies were reorganized into the Office of Federal Contract Compliance Programs (OFCCP), which enforced the Orders through desk audit and on-site compliance reviews, complaint investigation, and information sharing with the EEOC. These compliance reviews involved a comprehensive analysis of contractors' nondiscrimination and affirmative action efforts, including reviews of utilization analyses, recruitment and training programs, and internal affirmative action program implementation efforts.

Contractors were targeted for review through a variety of screens. First, a compliance review could be triggered by the OFCCP's automated equal employment data system (EEDS), which alerted the agency when representation of women or minorities fell below benchmarks set by other contractors in the same industry, or labor market representation statistics on the representation of qualified women and minorities in the contractor's recruitment area.[50] Compliance review would also be triggered whenever a contract or first-tier subcontract of one million dollars or more was first awarded by a federal agency, or whenever a discrimination complaint or series of discrimination complaints caused the OFCCP to believe that either the Executive Order or its implementing regulations were being violated.[51]

If an OFCCP review resulted in a finding of noncompliance, the agency had a number of remedial options at its disposal. By far the most common remedy was the signing of a commitment or conciliation agreement between the contractor and the OFCCP specifying the particular steps the contractor would take to remedy the problems identified. These sometimes involved the provision of monetary relief to applicants or employees, but more often they required changes to the contractor's hiring, promotion, or compensation practices and more aggressive utilization monitoring. At the extreme, the Secretary of Labor, upon the recommendation of the OFCCP and following a hearing, was empowered to withhold government payments to the contractor, cancel or terminate the contract in whole or in part, or even debar the contractor from future contracting opportunities.[52]

Substantial research shows that the affirmative action provisions of the federal contract compliance program had substantial salutary effects. They played a significant role in integrating the American labor force during the 1970s, and their positive influence on the employment of minorities and women – especially women of color – continue to this day.

Much of this research has been conducted by UC Berkeley labor economist Jonathan Leonard. Using a massive government data set covering 68,690 employment establishments during the period 1974–1980, Leonard demonstrated that the annual growth rate of black male and black female employment at federal contractors covered by the Executive Orders significantly exceeded corresponding growth rates for black males and females in the labor market as a whole.[53] For black males, relative to white males, employment growth rates at contractor firms were 3.8% faster, for other minority males, 7.9% faster, for minority females, 12.3% faster, and for white females, 2.8% faster.[54]

At contracting firms that underwent compliance reviews during the 1970s, the results were even more dramatic for minority men and women, though not for white women. At these firms, Leonard showed, the growth rate for black male employment was 7.9% faster than at other firms. Corresponding figures were 15.2% for other minority males, and 6.2% for minority women. Compliance reviews had a net negative effect on the employment growth rates of both white women and white men.[55]

More recently, legal sociologists Alexandra Kalev, Frank Dobbin, and Erin Kelly have shown that OFCCP affirmative action enforcement efforts undertaken during the 1970s (when executive order enforcement was at its most vigorous) are associated with strong, lasting gains in minority and women's employment. In their analysis of a massive data set consisting of utilization ("EEO-1") reports filed with the EEOC, and organizational survey data, Kalev et al. showed that OFCCP compliance reviews designed to change organizational routines had far stronger and more lasting effects on minority *and* female employment than any other EEO intervention, including individual lawsuits, the establishment of antidiscrimination policies and diversity training regimes, or networking programs.[56] Systemic approaches to identifying and eliminating discrimination can be, and have been, effective in reducing levels of discrimination in the American labor market.

Unfortunately, the advent of the Reagan years saw the almost immediate demise of the kinds of systemic government enforcement programs researchers like Leonard and Kalev et al. have shown to be most effective in bringing minorities and women into those parts of the labor force where they had previously been underrepresented. In 1979, William Bradford Reynolds, Reagan's choice to head the Civil Rights Division of the Department of Justice, reported to Congress that the Department would no longer seek goals and timetables as remedies in pattern and practice employment discrimination cases brought by the federal government.[57] Less than three years later, Reynold's Civil Rights Division filed an amicus brief in *Williams v. City of New Orleans*, a private suit against the New Orleans police department, arguing that racial goals and timetables, which it consistently referred to as "quotas," were *per se* unlawful.[58] This marked a dramatic shift in Justice Department policy. Soon, the Department was arguing in cases across the country that goals and timetables relief was *per se* illegal under both Title VII and the U.S. Constitution as a form of "reverse discrimination."[59]

At the EEOC, Reagan-appointed Chairman Clarence Thomas brought similar policy changes to the Commission's enforcement programs. Thomas eliminated the EEOC's policy of seeking goals and timetables relief in EEOC litigation,[60] dramatically scaled back the EEOC's systemic investigation program, and went so far as to question the use of statistical methods in the litigation of pattern and practice discrimination cases.[61] By 1984, the EEOC was litigating less than half the number of Title VII suits than it had pending during the mid-1970s, and those cases it did bring almost all alleged discrimination against individuals.[62]

At the OFCCP, enforcement of Executive Order 11246 came to a virtual standstill during the Reagan years. Agency staffing levels and budgets were drastically reduced, back pay awards and other sanctions were phased out, and compliance reviews became virtual rubber-stamps of contractor submissions.[63] With the Justice Department arguing in courts around the country that goals and timetables were illegal, it was perhaps understandable that contractors began dismantling their internal affirmative action programs.[64] Not surprisingly, with the demise of the contract compliance programs, progress toward full workplace inclusion for underrepresented groups slowed, and in some cases reversed, during the 1980s.[65]

Private enforcement activities: Individual and class action litigation

Individual and organizational plaintiffs do not have to depend on the government to enforce women's rights under Title VII or other antidiscrimination laws; they can file private lawsuits in the state and federal courts. Organizations like the National Organization for Women (NOW) can,[66] and have, filed charges of discrimination on behalf of groups of women being denied equal employment opportunity by employers or unions. When administrative procedures fail to resolve such a charge, Title VII permits private parties, including organizations acting on behalf of their members,[67] to file suit in federal district court. Such suits can allege individual discrimination, or a pattern and practice of discrimination against an entire class.[68]

In a private employment discrimination class action, a named plaintiff sues on behalf of herself and on behalf of other "similarly situated" women. So, for example, in *Dukes v. Wal-Mart*, Betty Dukes and five other women have sued Wal-Mart on behalf of a nationwide class of 1.6 million female Wal-Mart employees allegedly discriminated against because of their sex in promotion and pay.[69] To proceed as a class action, a case must satisfy the requirements of Rule 23 of the Federal Rules of Civil Procedure. Roughly speaking, these include: (1) that the members of the class are sufficiently numerous; (2) that common questions of law and fact predominate over those unique to the individual class members; (3) that the claims of the named plaintiffs are typical of those of the class they seek to represent; and (4) that the named plaintiffs will adequately represent the interests of the class.[70]

A pattern and practice discrimination suit filed and successfully certified as a class action proceeds much like systemic suits brought by the EEOC, and proof of discrimination is proven (or disproven) in the same ways in both contexts. So, as with EEOC pattern and practice litigation, the centerpiece of a private class action is a statistical utilization analysis demonstrating that women's representation in the positions at issue is lower than their relative representation in the relevant selection pool, controlling for factors like education, experience, or other qualifications.[71] Where pay is at issue, the centerpiece of a plaintiff's case is a regression analysis showing that, even controlling for the factors defendant claims determine compensation, the independent variable of sex has a significant predictive effect on the dependent variable of salary.[72]

Other types of evidence used by plaintiffs to prove private pattern and practice discrimination suits, whether alleging sex or other grounds of discrimination, include:

- evidence that the defendant employer uses employment practices, like unstructured subjective decision-making systems, conducive to bias;
- evidence of comments evincing bias made or tolerated by decision makers;
- evidence of how individual women were treated in comparison to similarly situated men; or
- the existence of a pattern of unresolved or meritorious sex discrimination complaints filed by female applicants or employees.[73]

Where plaintiffs succeed in proving pattern and practice discrimination, Title VII provides not only instatement into jobs and back pay to individual discrimination victims, but also structural remedies similar to those required of contractors under the Executive Order 11246 Regulations. Thus, remedies in sex (and race) discrimination class actions – often provided in voluntary settlements known as "consent decrees"[74] – include goals and timetables for correcting under-utilization or under-compensation of women in at-issue positions, provisions for periodic reporting by the defendant on progress toward those goals, restructuring of selection procedures or criteria to remove unnecessary barriers to women's advancement, and the appointment of a special master to monitor employer progress in complying with the decree.[75] Successful plaintiffs in Title VII suits are also entitled to an award of attorney's fees, which in suits of the complexity common to pattern and practice class actions can easily run into millions of dollars.[76]

Numerous researchers have provided evidence for the proposition that private pattern and practice sex discrimination class actions – or the threat that they might be filed – played a significant role in advancing women's position in the labor force during the 1970s.[77] Unfortunately, however, in 1982, just as Reagan administration appointees at the Justice Department, the EEOC, and the OFCCP were shutting down the government's systemic and pattern and practice oriented enforcement programs, the United States Supreme Court tightened considerably the requirements for certification of private employment discrimination class actions under Rule 23. Specifically, in *General Telephone Company of the Southwest v. Falcon*, the Court rejected the idea, previously cited by courts in certifying discrimination class actions, that sex, race, or national origin discrimination was so inherently class-based that certification should be easier in discrimination cases than in many other types of litigation.[78] *Falcon* established a high bar for the certification of private class action pattern and practice cases, making it particularly difficult for a named plaintiff to represent individuals outside of her particular job category or geographical unit.[79]

The effect of *Falcon* on private class actions was dramatic. In 1975, federal district courts received 1,106 motions for class certification. By 1989, the number had dropped to 51,[80] and by 1990 to only 20.[81] In short, the 1980s saw the demise of the EEOC's systemic enforcement programs, the OFCCP's affirmative action-oriented enforcement of Executive Order 11246, a precipitous drop in the number of class action pattern and practice cases brought by either private or government plaintiffs, and an aggressive rhetorical attack on the utilization analysis/goals and timetables approach to EEO enforcement that had animated all of these policy initiatives.

By 1991, when economists John Donohue and Peter Siegelman reported the results of their research examining changes in the nature of federal employment discrimination litigation,[82] the pattern and practice class action had been almost completely replaced by individual disparate treatment and sexual harassment suits, in which one plaintiff claimed, and attempted to prove, discrimination against herself alone. And most of the time, particularly in the disparate treatment suits, she lost. Even in cases that made it through the EEOC's administrative process, attracted a lawyer willing to assume the expenses and risks of litigation, defeated the defendant's summary judgment motion and got all the way to trial, plaintiff success rates ranged from 36 to 44 percent in jury trial cases. The success rate was significantly lower for cases tried to a judge – a mere 14 to 33 percent.[83]

For many reasons, relying on individual victims of discrimination to bring, and successfully litigate, individual disparate treatment lawsuits as the primary way of enforcing federal EEO policy is benighted at best, disastrous at worst. As discussed earlier in this chapter, it is very difficult to identify discrimination in case-by-case data. In any individual sex discrimination case there may be a number of plausible reasons other than the plaintiff's sex to which an employer can attribute a challenged employment decision. Determining whether the plaintiff's sex played a role in any particular employment decision will in most cases be very expensive, if not impossible, given that employers seldom admit when they are taking sex into account or leave a "paper trail" evincing bias.[84] Thus, even if they were accurate, individualized adjudications would be an extremely inefficient way of eliminating sex discrimination from the labor market.[85]

There is little evidence that individual discrimination lawsuits actually result in increased compliance with antidiscrimination laws over time. As Alexandra Kalev and Frank Dobbin have shown, employers who during the 1970s were subjected to OFCCP compliance reviews designed to change organizational routines and effect measurable improvements in utilization remained more diverse than comparable organizations that were not. However, having been a defendant in EEO lawsuits, Kalev and Dobbin reported, had no measurable lasting effects.[86]

There is no research evidence indicating that the people who bring individual disparate treatment lawsuits are even the people who are actually being discriminated against. On the other hand, there is a great deal of research evidence indicating that many people who are subjected to discrimination take no action to obtain a remedy. As the following section will demonstrate, society cannot rely on victims of discrimination to recognize that they have been discriminated against or to take the individual action needed to remedy the wrong done to them.

Perceiving and Claiming Discrimination

Here is an apparent paradox: Between 1992 and 2002, the number of charges filed with the EEOC rose by over 16 percent, and the number of employment discrimination lawsuits over 161 percent.[87] In reaction to statistics like these, some social commentators argue that there is too much discrimination claiming going on in American society, that women and members of minority groups too readily allege that they have been discriminated against.[88] But on the other hand, as this section will describe, a great deal of social science research indicates that people are unlikely to perceive that they have been discriminated against, even when they have been. Moreover, even after they do view themselves as having been subjected to discrimination, people are unlikely to seek redress. How can we explain this apparent paradox, and what does it suggest about what, as a society, we should do about eliminating sex discrimination in employment?

First, the research evidence. Social psychologists have known for over two decades now that women are much more likely to think that women in general are subject to sex discrimination than they are to think that they *themselves* have ever been discriminated against. This phenomenon, known as the "denial of personal discrimination" was first identified by Faye Crosby, whose research findings have been replicated in a number of different contexts.[89]

There are a number of possible explanations for the denial of personal discrimination effect. First, as Crosby suggested 20 years ago, the phenomenon might result from the same factors that make it difficult to detect discrimination in case-by-case data. In any individual situation involving a non-selection of a woman for a particular employment opportunity, a variety of factors other than sex are available to explain the action or decision. Only through aggregate data can one detect the discrimination "signal" within the "noise" of situation-specific differences between the male and female candidates.

This presents a problem for women who find themselves on the losing end of employment decisions. Aggregated information is rarely available to individual women who are attempting to figure out why they didn't get a particular assignment, job, or promotion. The problem is even worse in the day-to-day decisions that build people's skill sets and professional reputations. People often don't know the extent to which other employees are being mentored. They don't know what their superiors are saying to others in the work environment or broader professional community about their or their male colleagues' talents, potential, accomplishments, or shortcomings. And when it comes to compensation levels, the situation is all but hopeless. Few women even *know* how much money their colleagues are making, and so can not possibly tell whether they are being discriminated against in compensation.

There are other reasons why people might fail to identify their own negative employment outcomes as discrimination, even when discrimination has, in fact, occurred. As Kristin Bumiller found from a series of in-depth interviews with female and minority workers in the 1980s, people are reluctant to label their experiences as discrimination because they do not want to think of themselves as victims.[90] Numerous other researchers have found much the same thing: the psychological costs of viewing oneself as a victim of discrimination are steep.

The notion that individuals control their own destiny is a core ideological tenet of American culture.[91] Beliefs in individual mobility and meritocracy, that reward will flow from hard work and perseverance, provide Americans with a sense of self-efficacy, of control over their social world.[92] This sense of control and self-efficacy, in turn, conduces to feelings of well-being, and to increased motivation, hope, and mastery orientation.[93]

These ideological and psychological pressures are so powerful that they influence the social justice-related perceptions of even subordinated members of society. Research on this phenomenon, variously referred to as "just-world hypothesis,"[94] "system justification theory"[95] or the "status-legitimacy hypothesis,"[96] helps explain why low-status members of society are unlikely to view themselves as victims of discrimination. It also helps explain the somewhat surprising finding that among whites, the more subjects endorsed beliefs in individual mobility, the more likely they were to believe that they and other whites had been subjected to race or national origin discrimination.[97]

In general, most people are confident that if they experienced discrimination, they would report it or take other remedial action.[98] But this is not how people actually behave. Even when people perceive themselves to have been victims of discrimination, they are unlikely to share those perceptions with other people, and they are even more unlikely to file a formal complaint or grievance.[99] Why? Because claiming discrimination is socially costly, even among members of one's own group.[100] Generally speaking, people think poorly of others, especially members of their own group, who blame their negative outcomes on discrimination.[101] Because claiming discrimination causes reputational damage, people tend not to do it.

So back to the apparent paradox. If people are hesitant publicly to claim that they have been discriminated against, why are there more discrimination charges and lawsuits, than there were 15 years ago?

First, it may be that the increase in discrimination charges and claims between 1992 and 2002 is attributable to developments that have little to do with the prevalence of discrimination or with an increased tendency on the part of people who have actually been discriminated against to pursue legal redress. Charge and litigation rates have gone up, at least in substantial part, because in the early 1990s, Congress expanded legal protection against employment discrimination to new groups,[102] namely people with disabilities, through the Americans with Disabilities Act of 1990,[103] and long-term employees denied family and medical care leaves, through the Family and Medical Leave Act of 1993.[104]

Second, in 1991, Congress amended Title VII[105] to provide for awards of compensatory and punitive damages, and an accompanying right to jury trial in some types of discrimination cases, a change that made those cases (primarily those alleging egregious harassment or discriminatory termination of employment) more attractive to lawyers working on a contingent fee basis.[106] As various commentators have observed, the availability of compensatory and punitive damages has altered the *types* of cases in which claims of discrimination are made, skewing the distribution toward disparate treatment termination and harassment cases, which tend to yield relatively higher compensatory damage awards, at the expense of those involving failures to hire or promote.[107]

Third, the Clarence Thomas Supreme Court confirmation hearings in 1992 raised awareness of sexual harassment, leading to a dramatic rise in the filing of harassment claims.[108] There are more sexual harassment claims, more disability discrimination claims, and more discriminatory termination claims than there were in 1990. But there are far fewer systemic discrimination claims seeking structural remedies that can bring meaningful change to women's opportunities in the labor market.

Specifically, the incidence of hiring, promotion, and compensation discrimination claims has dropped dramatically since Title VII's early days. So has the incidence of disparate impact claims, in which practices like minimum height and weight requirements or word of mouth recruitment systems were challenged as neutral in form but discriminatory in practice and therefore illegal under Title VII. In the 1960s and 1970s, charges of hiring and promotion discrimination, many of them brought on behalf of a class of similarly situated individuals, dominated the federal civil rights caseload, but they have now been largely replaced by individual cases involving alleged harassment and discriminatory termination.[109]

The prospect of high damages, the difficulties and expenses attending class certification, the influx into the employment discrimination bar of personal injury lawyers with little expertise or interest in statistical proof of discrimination or in the design and implementation of structural remedies, have all combined to transform the employment discrimination lawsuit from a civil rights action to an individual personal injury claim. Law professor and long-time civil rights advocate Michael Selmi puts the matter succinctly:

> Not so long ago, class action employment discrimination suits were defined as a quintessential form of public law litigation where monetary relief was generally viewed as one component of necessary remedial relief, and a far less important component than the institutional reform the suit ultimately produced. Yet today the lawsuits have largely become just another variation of a tort claim where monetary relief is the principal, and often the only, goal of the litigation. Along with this shift in emphasis has come a dramatic change in our perspective on the persistence of discrimination. There is no longer any concerted effort to eliminate discrimination; instead, efforts are directed at providing monetary compensation for past discrimination without particular concern for preventing future discrimination, or even remedying past discrimination, through injunctive relief. For firms, discrimination claims are now like accidents – a cost of doing business, which necessarily implies that a certain level of discrimination will persist.[110]

On Solutions: Toward the Elimination of Sex Discrimination in Employment

Returning to the question with which the chapter began: If as a society, we were truly committed to eliminating sex discrimination in employment, what would we do? Most importantly, we would abandon our present misplaced reliance on individual, *ex post facto* claims of discrimination as our primary EEO policy enforcement tool. Instead, we would return to the proactive approach to labor market integration based on the systematic aggregation of information, on utilization analysis and the setting of goals and timetables for achieving gender parity, the close, results-oriented monitoring of progress toward those goals, and the identification and removal of process barriers to inclusion of women in jobs where they are underrepresented.

Not only should we return to this approach, we should expand on it. Taking a page from the regulation of financial markets, we should require not only that Title VII-covered employers and labor unions provide meaningful EEO compliance information to the federal government, we should require the government to provide it to the public.

More specifically, if we were really committed to eliminating sex discrimination in employment, we would reform EEO enforcement policy in two broad ways. First, we would insist upon more vigorous enforcement of existing laws by federal regulatory agencies. Congress would provide the OFCCP with the resources required to ramp up dramatically the quantity and the quality of on-site audits and compliance reviews. Where a compliance review reveals under-utilization of women in any job category, contractors should be required, as a condition of continued contract eligibility, to set full inclusion goals and to make steady, meaningful progress toward achieving them.

Additionally, a comprehensive system of information sharing between the EEOC and the OFCCP should be implemented to enable the EEOC to target for systemic investigation and discrimination litigation companies whose contract compliance reports reveal under-utilization of women. The EEOC would, in turn, provide the OFCCP with company-specific charge data, so that the OFCCP could target for contract compliance review companies with high rates of EEOC complaints. Similar programs would be established and vigorously enforced at the state and local government levels.

Unfortunately, in the present political environment, it may be unrealistic to assume that vigorous, 1970s style enforcement of EEO/affirmative action mandates will be returning to the executive branch's agenda in the foreseeable future. So the question becomes: What policy innovations might serve at least some of the same ends furthered by vigorous Executive Order enforcement, yet be more practically achievable in the current political environment? How, in other words, might we liberate gender equity policy from the vicissitudes of executive branch ideology?

Here the second element of the proposed reform strategy comes into play. If the federal government is unwilling to use the information it has the power to obtain from companies, unions, and employment agencies to squeeze sex discrimination out of the American labor market, that information should be made available to the public, so that individual women, and women's organizations, can more effectively take EEO enforcement into our own hands. Along these lines, Title VII and Executive Order 11246 should be amended so as to put into place rigorous EEO compliance information disclosure requirements, analogous to the financial and management practice disclosure requirements that now characterize federal regulation of financial markets. Our financial markets work, in large measure, because publicly held companies are required to provide a tremendous amount of information about their operations to both securities regulators and the investing public. This information allows investors to make better decisions about where to invest their money, reducing risks of financial harm. It also allows investors who think they were defrauded or otherwise harmed by a particular company to more easily pursue a legal remedy.

Under the new legislative and administrative initiatives this section proposes, Title VII, the Executive Order Regulations, and the Federal Rules of Civil Procedure would be amended to make publicly available the data from which female prospective and incumbent employees could better assess the female friendliness of the various firms competing for their services. Under a meaningful EEO information disclosure regime, women who have some measure of labor market power, or advocacy organizations representing the interests of women who lack labor market power, would be able to review promotion rates, pay equity data, and sex discrimination complaint and dispute resolution information for different employers in the labor market. This is not currently possible, because the information needed to make an accurate assessment of an employer's real gender equity climate is not publicly available.

As the following discussion will describe, virtually every aspect of EEO enforcement currently occurs behind a veil of legally sanctioned secrecy. Hard data on corporate EEO compliance is simply not available to women who are entering, or considering moving between employers in, the labor market, or to women's organizations that are trying to target their advocacy efforts.

Lacking meaningful EEO compliance information, women entering the workforce, or seeking to move within it, have no way of knowing which employers will limit their employment opportunities and which will not. Thus, even women who by virtue of educational and professional attainment might have at least some labor market power can not effectively use that power to drive down levels of sex discrimination in the market for their services. Under certain circumstances, market forces can play some role in squeezing discrimination out of a labor market. But in order for that to happen, information asymmetries between the sellers of employment opportunities (in this case, employers) and the buyers of employment opportunities (in this case, prospective employees) must be eliminated, or at least greatly reduced.

Of course, not all women in the labor market have the kind of market power that would enable them to make effective use of information about different employers' commitment to gender equality. But a mandatory utilization information disclosure regime would benefit these women, too. Without meaningful utilization and other EEO-related information, women's advocacy organizations like Equal Rights Advocates in San Francisco, or the NOW Legal Education and Defense Fund in Washington, DC, which are in a position to represent disempowered women's interests, are also unable to determine which employers, employment agencies, and labor unions are discriminating against women. This lack of information prevents women's organizations from effectively and efficiently targeting their advocacy efforts, including the filing of systemic sex discrimination charges with the EEOC, class action lawsuits, or public education campaigns.

The case for a new information disclosure oriented approach to EEO policy set out in the remainder of this chapter proceeds in the following steps. The first subsection describes the various laws and institutionalized practices that encourage, permit, and in some cases even require EEO enforcement activities to operate behind a veil of secrecy and obfuscation. Under such conditions, employers know (or have the ability to learn) whether women are being hired, mentored, promoted, and paid in proportion to their representation in the available labor pool and in comparison with similarly situated men, but women themselves do not have access to this information. This creates what economists refer to as an *information asymmetry* between women workers and their current or potential employers. The following subsection examines the predictable negative consequences of this information asymmetry, and outlines the basic contours of a mandatory EEO data disclosure regime that could remedy them.

On the present unavailability of EEO compliance information

In 2005, the EEOC received over 23,000 charges of sex discrimination in employment.[111] Of these, approximately 5,700 were resolved through voluntary settlement involving some sort of remedy to the charging party.[112] Just under 1,700 led to a formal administrative finding of discrimination by the EEOC.[113]

Under Title VII's Section 706(b), however, the EEOC is prohibited from making public any information that would identify the employers, labor unions, or employment agencies against whom those charges of discrimination were filed or those formal findings of discrimination made. So, if women employees of Company X filed sex discrimination charges against it at a rate ten times higher than any company of comparable size, a woman considering going to work for Company X would never know. In fact, were an EEOC employee to make such information public, he or she could be charged with a federal crime carrying a maximum sentence of imprisonment for up to one year.[114]

The same confidentiality mandate cloaks other important EEO compliance information. For example, all private Title VII employers with 100 or more employees and all federal contractors who have 50 or more employees are required to file annual EEO-1 reports that specify the proportion of women and minorities employed in each of nine job categories. Multi-facility employers must file separate reports for each facility at which 50 or more employees are employed.[115]

These reports yield aggregated data from which patterns of under-utilization by particular employers can be identified. However, the public has no access to these data. Under Title VII's Section 709(e), no information from EEO-1 reports may be publicly disclosed in any way that would identify patterns of gender, race, or national origin-related under-utilization by individual companies.[116]

Similar disclosure restrictions govern the OFCCP's compliance programs. The OFCCP refuses to disclose to the public the affirmative action plans, compliance review-related submissions, or annual Equal Opportunity Surveys it obtains from contractor employers, and it takes the position that these materials are exempt from disclosure under the federal Freedom of Information Act (FOIA).[117]

Increasingly, employers are also finding ways to keep out of the public sphere the kinds of EEO-compliance-related information that would ordinarily surface in sex discrimination lawsuits. As numerous legal commentators have observed, secrecy in American civil litigation is no longer the exception but the rule.[118] As we will see, secrecy is accomplished through a number of specific devices, including mandatory, pre-dispute arbitration agreements imposed by employers as a condition of employment, confidentiality provisions in settlement agreements, and civil discovery related protective orders.

Many employers now require applicants, as a condition of employment, to agree that they will resolve any employment disputes, including claims of sex discrimination, through private arbitration rather than through access to the court system. In addition to depriving employees of a right to jury trial, these mandatory arbitration arrangements allow employers to keep the existence and resolution of sex discrimination claims out of the public eye. Toward this end, many mandatory pre-dispute arbitration agreements require employees to promise that they will maintain confidentiality during an arbitration, and after it has concluded.

Second, it is now almost universally the case that when individual discrimination lawsuits settle, either before a case is actually filed or after it is filed but before a verdict is rendered, the settlement is conditioned on the employee/plaintiff's promise not to disclose the terms of the settlement. Given that over 95 percent of civil cases settle before trial,[119] the impact of routine confidentiality agreements in settlements can hardly be overstated. Other than the occasional high-profile, high-value jury award or government consent decree, the public has virtually no access to information about the nature or amounts of settlements in sex discrimination lawsuits.

Finally, protective orders issued by judges during the course of a civil lawsuit are also used by employers to keep important evidence reflecting noncompliance with EEO laws out of the public view. As was described earlier in this chapter, the centerpiece of any pattern and practice sex discrimination lawsuit is a utilization analysis that compares the representation of women in the at-issue jobs with their availability in the relevant labor market. To prove discrimination, plaintiffs often supplement this utilization analysis with evidence of other discrimination charges or findings against the employer, or employer records or statements reflecting gender bias on the part of the decision makers.

The information from which a sex discrimination plaintiff can prove her case is generally obtained from the employer during a part of the lawsuit called "discovery." Through the discovery process, employers are legally required to provide statistical and other information from which the plaintiff's lawyers – and ultimately the court – can assess whether the employer is systematically treating women less favorably than men and, if so, whether that difference in treatment can reasonably be attributed to gender bias. Absent a court order specifically prohibiting disclosure, once an employer provides this information to a sex discrimination plaintiff, the information can be shared with the public, with advocacy organizations, or with other aggrieved individuals and their counsel.

Increasingly, however, defendants in sex discrimination and other civil cases are obtaining broad protective orders, through which the court prohibits plaintiffs from disclosing EEO compliance-related information obtained during the discovery process. In their strongest form, these protective orders can require not only promises not to disclose information obtained in discovery (violations of which can be punished as contempt of court), but also the sealing of testimony, pleadings, exhibits, court transcripts, and other lawsuit-related documents, and the return of those materials to the employer after the litigation is concluded – often by confidential settlement agreement.

These three devices – mandatory arbitration agreements with confidentiality provisions imposed as a condition of hiring, confidentiality clauses in settlement agreements, and the issuance of protective orders prohibiting disclosure of EEO compliance-related information obtained in discovery – combine with EEOC and OFCCP confidentiality provisions to keep from the public virtually all employer-specific, systematically aggregated EEO compliance data. Neither individual women in the labor market, nor the advocacy organizations that advance their interests, have any way of knowing which employers are systematically treating women less favorably than men, and which are not.

The wages of secrecy and the benefits of disclosure

In 1914, in a book urging passage of laws mandating public disclosure of financial information by firms selling stocks and other securities to the public, Louis Brandeis wrote, "Sunshine is said to be the best of disinfectants, electric light the most efficient policeman."[120] Two decades later, after the great stock market crash of 1929 and in the grip of the Great Depression, Congress finally took Brandeis' advice, and passed the Securities Act of 1933 and the Securities Exchange Act of 1934.[121]

These two laws, which have provided a framework for the regulation of financial markets in the United States for the past 70 years, are based on a straightforward concept: that investors cannot make rational decisions about buying securities, and financial markets can therefore not operate efficiently, unless potential buyers have access to a common pool of meaningful information that they can use to decide whether a particular company's securities, priced at a particular level, represent a good investment. Absent mandatory public disclosure of relevant financial and management practices information, companies selling securities for sale will possess bargain-relevant information that potential buyers lack. Information asymmetries between contracting parties systematically disadvantage the parties lacking information and prevent market forces from optimally pricing securities offered for sale.[122]

The financial disclosure mandates of the Securities Act and the Securities Exchange Act function primarily to equalize (not perfectly, of course, but serviceably) informational asymmetries between the sellers of securities and the buying public, and, perhaps more importantly, to make investment-relevant information available to those professionals (securities analysts, brokers, mutual fund managers) who are in a position to scrutinize, evaluate, and present the disclosed information in a form that makes it more useful to the lay investing public. Legally mandated disclosure, as opposed to voluntary disclosure, is necessary because corporate managers have inadequate incentives to disclose unfavorable information about their performance and because the disclosure of financial information in general can alert competitors to a firm's particular strengths or vulnerabilities, possibly resulting in proprietary injury.[123]

Labor markets, like financial markets, cannot be expected to operate efficiently or fairly if "sellers" of employment opportunities (employers, labor unions, employment agencies) and "buyers" of employment opportunities (potential or actual employees) are operating under conditions of informational asymmetry. But that is precisely the present case with respect to equal employment opportunity in the American labor market. Under present conditions, it is very difficult, perhaps impossible, for women choosing among various potential employment opportunities to know which employers, unions, or employment agencies will discriminate against them and which will not.

This state of affairs harms women both individually and collectively in a number of serious, tangible ways. Unable to distinguish discriminating employers from nondiscriminating employers, women may unknowingly take jobs where their prospects for equitable treatment are in fact quite bleak. Lacking comparative information about how men are treated, they will be disadvantaged in bargaining over wages or promotional opportunities. Women are collectively disadvantaged as well. With EEO compliance information hidden behind a veil of secrecy, companies have no real need to compete with each other to optimize employment opportunity for women. Absent meaningful disclosure, reputational pressures will not be brought to bear on employers either; the information that might shame them into improving their gender equity performance is confidential. And without access to EEO-related information, women and women's advocacy organizations will not know whether they have reasonable grounds for filing charges or lawsuits alleging sex discrimination. This state of affairs conduces to under-enforcement of Title VII, particularly in relation to discrimination in hiring and compensation, where women have the least access to comparative information indicative of discriminatory treatment.

For these reasons, if we were really serious about eliminating sex discrimination in the labor market, we would, in addition to the steps described earlier, implement mandatory EEO information disclosure requirements analogous to those regulating U.S. financial markets. Moreover, we would amend state and federal rules of civil procedure and professional ethics to make confidentiality provisions in discrimination settlement and arbitration agreements unlawful. Protective orders would be granted in discrimination litigation only in limited circumstances implicating trade secrets or the constitutional privacy rights of individual employees.

As described earlier in this chapter, four decades of employment discrimination litigation have yielded a set of widely accepted methods for identifying patterns of gender in (equality) in hiring, job assignment, compensation, and promotion. In the hiring and promotion context, the cornerstone of any such inquiry is a utilization analysis that compares the representation of women in particular job categories with their availability in the relevant selection pool. To the extent that disparities are found, the next step involves identifying and remedying the disparities' causal antecedents.

Pay equity studies follow a similar pattern. First, the average salaries of men and women in the same job categories are calculated. Then, using multiple regression analysis, the inquiry seeks to determine whether, controlling for variables like education, tenure, and so on, sex remains a significant predictor of salary. To the extent that it does, attempts are then made to identify and eliminate those features of the compensation system – including discrimination – that systematically disadvantage women.

As we have seen, other types of evidence are also relevant in a gender equity review, in either the litigation or the regulatory compliance context. These include evidence regarding the existence and disposition of prior sex discrimination complaints, the nature of the procedures used to make hiring, promotion, training, and compensation decisions, whether any of the relevant selection criteria themselves have a demonstrable disparate impact on women, and whether the employer has a history of tolerating harassment or other negative treatment of female employees. As earlier described, this is precisely the type of information that federal contractors already provide to the OFCCP.

The same categories of information should also be provided to the public for any employer, employment agency, or labor union large enough to make the information meaningful (the Executive Order sets this threshold at 50 employees). On an annual basis, covered employers, employment agencies, labor unions, and joint labor-management apprenticeship programs should be required to file disclosure statements including the following components:

- utilization analyses comparing the percentage of women in each job group with their availability in the relevant selection pool;
- an explanation of how, for each job group, relevant selection pool statistics were compiled, presented in sufficient detail that a reasonably sophisticated reader could evaluate whether the availability pool had been properly constructed;
- statistics showing, for each job group and at each level up the job ladder, the comparative selection rates and odds ratios of women versus men being promoted or otherwise advanced from one level or step to the next;
- for each compensation classification, statistics showing the average wage or salary gap, if any, between male and female employees in a particular job group at each step up the job ladder;

- for each job group in which women are under-utilized relative to their representation in the available selection pool, goals and timetables for eliminating the disparity;
- for each job group in which women are under-utilized relative to their representation in the available selection pool, an analysis of the current obstacles to women's inclusion or advancement and a specific plan for removing them;
- statistics disclosing, on a facility-by-facility basis, the number of sex discrimination charges filed with either the EEOC, the OFCCP, or any other EEO enforcement agency (state or federal), with a description of the issue alleged in each complaint (i.e., promotion, compensation, harassment, termination), and an indication of whether and if so, how, the complaint was resolved.

For each covered entity, the EEOC and the OFCCP should make these reports, along with the affirmative action plans filed by federal contractors, publicly available on the internet. Providing this information would allow civil rights groups like NOW to target their organizing, public pressure, and class action litigation efforts, making enforcement less vulnerable to the vagaries of executive branch ideology.

Perhaps as importantly, making hard EEO data information available on the internet could unleash the considerable power that intelligent markets can exercise in squeezing sex discrimination out of the labor market. As mentioned earlier, our financial markets work (perhaps not perfectly, but certainly better than they otherwise would) at least in part because publicly held companies must provide a tremendous amount of investment-relevant information about their operations to both securities regulators and the investing public. The same could be done with labor markets.

Under a meaningful EEO-information disclosure regime, women would be able to review promotion rates, pay equity data, and sex discrimination complaint information for the various companies competing for their services, something they cannot now do because all the relevant information is publicly unavailable. They could review their own company's gender equity performance, and compare it to what would be expected in a nondiscriminatory world. They could compare their own employer's gender equity performance with that of the company's competitors, and from those comparisons make decisions about whether to negotiate for better terms with their present employer or seek employment in more female-friendly quarters.

In sum, if as a society we are really serious about eliminating sex discrimination in employment, we should return to and expand upon the systemic, proactive approach to labor market integration characterizing EEO enforcement policy in the 1970s. Forget the diversity training programs. Forget the 1–800 stop sexual harassment hotlines. Forget even the occasional "so-big-it's-like-somebody-just-won-the-lottery" jury verdict. If you want to eliminate sex discrimination in employment, don't rely on individual *ex post facto* claims of discrimination. Instead, demand, scrutinize, and act on systematically aggregated utilization data. The watched variable improves.

Notes

1   Title VII of the Civil Rights Act of 1964, 42 U.S.C. §2000e *et. seq.* (2003).
2   To be covered by Title VII, an employer must have 15 or more employees for each working day in each of 20 or more calendar weeks in the current or preceding calendar year. 42 U.S.C. §2000e-2(a) (2003).
3   Section 703(c) of Title VII, 42 U.S.C. §2000e-2(c) prohibits sex discrimination by labor unions.
4   Section 703(b) of Title VII, 42 U.S.C. §2000e-2(b) prohibits sex discrimination by employment agencies.
5   Executive Order 11246 was codified in the Federal Register at 30 Fed. Reg. 12,319.
6   For an example of this practice, see, e.g., Hailes v. United Air Lines, 464 F.2d 1006 (5th Circuit 1972) (describing "Help Wanted – Male" and "Help Wanted – Female" sections in New Orleans newspaper employment advertisements); Brush v. San Francisco Newspaper Printing Company, 469 F.2d 89 (9th Cir. 1972) (describing sex segregated help wanted ads in the *San Francisco Chronicle* and *San Francisco Examiner* newspapers).
7   Bergmann; Glick & Fiske; Rhode & Williams this volume.
8   American Association of University Women Educational Foundation (2003). *Women at Work*, table: State-by-state data on women's and men's educational attainment and earnings by educational attainment, downloaded November 19, 2005, from http://www.aauw.org/research/statedata/table_data.pdf
9   Stroh, L. K., Brett, J. M., & Reilly, A. H. (1992). All the right stuff: A comparison of female and male managers' career progression. *Journal of Applied Psychology, 77*, 251–260.
10 General Accounting Office (2004). *Report to Congressional requesters – Gender issues: Women's participation in the sciences has increased, but agencies need to do more to ensure compliance with Title IX.* Washington, DC: General Accounting Office.
11 U.S. Department of Labor, Glass Ceiling Commission (1995). *Good for business: Making full use of the nation's human capital.* District of Columbia: United States Government Printing Office.
12 *The Online Merriam-Webster Unabridged Collegiate Dictionary* (2005). http://unabridged.merriam-webster.com/cgi-bin/collegiate?va=discrimination
13 Title VII, Section 703(a)(1), 42 U.S.C.A. §2000e-2(a) (1) (2003).
14 Glick & Fiske, this volume.

15   Crosby, F. J., Clayton, S., Hemker, K., & Alksnis, O. (1986). Cognitive biases in the perception of discrimination: The importance of format. *Sex Roles, 14*, 637–646.

16   Cordova, D. I. (1992). Cognitive limitations and affirmative action: The effects of aggregate versus sequential data in the perception of discrimination. *Social Justice Research, 5*, 319–333.

17   Twiss, C., Tabb, S., & Crosby, F. J. (1989). Affirmative action and aggregate data: The importance of patterns in the perception of discrimination. In F. A. Blanchard, & F. J. Crosby (Eds.), *Affirmative Action in Perspective* (pp. 159–176). New York: Springer-Verlag.

18   Twiss et al. (1989), p. 160.

19   Darley, J. M., & Gross, P. H. (1983). A hypothesis-confirming bias in labeling effects. *Journal of Personality and Social Psychology, 44*, 20–33.

20   Norton, M. I., Vandello, J. A., & Darley, J. M. (2004). Casuistry and social category bias. *Journal of Personality and Social Psychology, 87*, 817–831.

21   Clayton, S. D. (1989). *The recognition of discrimination in a minimal-information format.* Unpublished paper presented at the 97th meeting of the American Psychological Association, described in S. D. Clayton, & F. J. Crosby, (Eds.), *Justice, gender, and affirmative action*, Ann Arbor, MI: University of Michigan Press, pp. 79–81.

22   Rutte, C. G., Diekmann, K. A., Polzer, J. T., Crosby, F. J., & Messick, D. M. (1994). Organization of information and the detection of gender discrimination. *Psychological Science, 5*, 226–231.

23   Brewer, M. B. (1996). In-group favoritism: The subtle side of intergroup discrimination. In D. M. Messick, & A. E. Tenbrunsel (Eds.), *Codes of conduct: Behavioral research and business ethics* (pp. 160–179). New York: Russell Sage Foundation.

24   Taylor, S. E., & Fiske, S. T. (1978). Salience, attention, and attribution: Top of the head phenomena. In L. Berkowitz (Ed.), *Advances in experimental social psychology* (Vol. 11, pp. 249–288). New York: Academic Press.

25   Clayton, S. D., & Crosby, F. J. (1992). *Justice, gender, and affirmative action.* Ann Arbor, MI: University of Michigan Press.

26   Utilization analysis, also sometimes referred to as "under-utilization analysis" or "availability/incumbency" analysis, is described at 41 C.F.R. §60-2.15, a portion of the federal regulations implementing Executive Order 11246, which is discussed in greater detail below.

27   A disparity is considered statistically significant if the likelihood that it occurred as a result of random variation is less than 1 in 20 (5%). The particular test used to assess the statistical significance of a hiring, job assignment, or promotion disparity is the test for significance of differences in population proportions, also known as the "Z test." The Supreme Court endorsed this statistical approach in Castaneda v. Partida, 430 U. S. 482, 496–497, n. 17 (1977) and again in Hazelwood School District v. United States, 433 U.S. 299 (1977).

28 The leading case establishing this approach is still Teamsters v. United States, 431 U.S. 324 (1977). For an accessible explanation of the role of statistics in determining whether an employment selection system is being influenced by discriminatory motivation, see Zimmer, M. J., Sullivan, C. A, & White, R. H. (2003). *Cases and materials on employment discrimination law*. New York: Aspen Publishers.

29 Teamsters v. United States, 431 U.S. 324, 339, n. 20 (1977).

30 Impact Fund, The (2005). *Dukes v. Wal-Mart* statistical charts: Percent women in store management and hourly Supervisors, 2001. Retrieved November 26, 2005, from http://www.WalMartclass.com/staticdata/charts/table7.html; http://www.WalMartclass.com/staticdata/WalMartclass/brief2.html

31 The leading case on the use of multiple regression analysis in determining whether disparities in employment outcome are reasonably attributable to protected group status (e.g. race, sex, national origin) is the Supreme Court's 1986 decision in Bazemore v. Friday, 478 U.S. 385. Additional information about the use of regression analysis in employment discrimination litigation and EEO compliance programs can be found in Zimmer et al. (2003).

32 The term "built in headwinds" originates in the Supreme Court's 1971 decision in Griggs v. Duke Power Co., 401 U.S. 424, 431 (1971), which held that, under certain circumstances, even facially neutral practices can constitute unlawful discrimination if they function as "built in headwinds" against the advancement of Title VII protected groups.

33 Dukes v. Wal-Mart, Memorandum of Points and Authorities in Support of Plaintiffs' Motion for Class Certification, (n.d.). Retrieved May 17, 2006, from http://www.walmartclass.com/staticdata/walmartclass/brief2.html

34 Lindemann, B., & Grossman, P. (1996). *Employment discrimination law* (3rd ed.). Washington, DC: BNA Books.

35 Title VII of the Civil Rights Act of 1964, §706, 42 U.S.C.A. §2000e-5.

36 Title VII of the Civil Rights Act of 1964, §706(f), 42 U.S.C.A. §2000e-5(f).

37 United States Equal Employment Opportunity Commission (n.d.). *Charge statistics FY 1992–2005*, retrieved May 17, 2006, from http://www.eeoc.gov/stats/charges.html

38 Equal Employment Opportunity Commission. (2005, January 27). *Sex-based charges FY 1992–2005*. Retrieved July 15 from http://www.eeoc.gov/stats/sex.html

39 In 2004, for example, the EEOC filed a total of 375 discrimination suits in federal district court. Of these, 146 were brought on behalf of a class, while 233 were brought on behalf of an individual charging party. United States Equal Employment Opportunity Commission, Office of General Counsel (n.d.) *Fiscal year 2004 annual report*. Retrieved October

18, 2005, from http://www.eeoc.gov/litigation/04annrpt/index.html#IB4 (Last modified October 18, 2005).

40   For a thorough description of these cases and the amounts recovered for the charging party class, see http://www.eeoc.gov/litigation/04annrpt/index.html#IB4 (accessed October 18, 2005).

41   EEOC Office of General Counsel (n.d.).

42   EEOC Office of General Counsel (n.d.).

43   Executive Order No. 8802, 3 C.F.R. §957 (1938–43 Comp.).

44   The regulations implementing Executive Order 11246, as amended by Executive Order 11375 were codified in the Code of Federal Regulations at 41 C.F.R. §§60. They remain located in the same section, but have been amended.

45   For a description of the changes made to the executive order enforcement program in the late 1960s and early 1970s, see Shaeffer, R. G. (1973). *Nondiscrimination in employment: Changing perspectives, 1963–1972.* New York: The Conference Board.

46   The utilization analysis provisions of the Executive Order Regulations are located at Affirmative Action Programs. Subpart B – Purpose and Contents of Affirmative Action Programs 41 C.F.R. §60-2.11.

47   41 C.F.R. §60-2.30.

48   41C.F.R. §60-2.17.

49   41 C.F.R. §60-2.13.

50   Lindemann & Grossman (1996).

51   Lindemann & Grossman (1996).

52   Executive Order #11246, §209(a)(6), reprinted as amended in BNA (n.d.) *Affirmative Action Compliance Manual*, http://www.bna.com/products/labor/aacm.htm, 101, 103; 41 C.F.R. §60-1.4(a), 1–26 to 1–27, 250.28, & 741.28. For a discussion of the Labor Secretary's debarment power, see Uniroyal, Inc. v. Marshall, 482 F. Supp. 364, 375 (D.D.C. 1979).

53   Leonard, J. S. (1984). The impact of affirmative action on employment. *Journal of Labor Economics, 2*, 439–463; Leonard, J. S. (1985). What promises are worth: the impact of affirmative action goals. *Journal of Human Resources, 20*, 3–20; Leonard, J. S. (1990). The impact of affirmative action regulation and equal employment law on black employment. *Journal of Economic Perspectives, 4*, 47–63.

54   Leonard, J. S. (1986). What was affirmative action? *American Economic Review, 76*, 359–363.

55   Leonard (1986).

56   Kalev, A., & Dobbin, F. (2006). Enforcement of civil rights in private workplaces: Compliance reviews and lawsuits before and after Reagan. *Law and Social Inquiry, 31*(4) (December); Kalev, A., Dobbin, F., & Kelly, E. (2005a). *Best practices or best guesses? What works in diversity management.* Unpublished paper on file with author; Kalev, A., Dobbin, F., & Kelly, E. (2005b). *Two to tango: Affirmative action, diversity programs and*

women and African-Americans in management. Unpublished paper on file with author.

57   Oversight Hearings, note 153, at 136–139 (testimony of William Bradford Reynolds, assistant Attorney General for Civil Rights).

58   See Williams v. City of New Orleans, 729 F.2d 1554 (5th Cir. 1984).

59   Rose, D. L. (1989). Twenty-five years later: Where do we stand on equal employment opportunity law? *Vanderbilt Law Review, 42,* 1121–1181.

60   Thomas pledged in 1984 to make "concerted efforts to set forth the Reagan Administration's position on affirmative action – favoring victim-specific remedies and moving away from quotas and proportional representation . . ." Policy Changes, Aggressive Enforcement, Will Mark Next Term at EEOC, Thomas Says. (1984, November 15). *221 Daily Lab. Rep. (BNA),* p. A-6.

61   Policy changes (1984).

62   Leonard, J. S. (1989a). The changing face of employees and employment regulation. *California Management Review, 31,* 29–34.

63   Leonard (1990).

64   Leonard (1989a).

65   Leonard (1990).

66   Title VII Section 706(b) provides that a charge of discrimination may be filed with the EEOC "by or on behalf of a person claiming to be aggrieved." 42 U.S.C. §2000e-5(b).

67   NOW v. Sperry Rand Corp., 457 F. Supp. 1338 (D. Conn. 1978) (holding that NOW had standing to sue on behalf of its members to redress hiring, recruitment, discharge, and retaliation against its members).

68   Examples of Title VII suits litigated by NOW on behalf of women allegedly discriminated against in employment, include NOW v. Bank of California, 680 F.2d 1291 (9th Cir. 1982); NOW v. Sperry Rand Corp., 457 F. Supp. 1338 (D. Conn.); and NOW v. Minnesota Mining & Mfg. Co., 11 Fair Empl. Prac. Cases 720 (D. Minn. 1975).

69   As of the writing of this chapter, the Wal-Mart complaints are available online at www.Wal-Martclass.com

70   Federal Rule of Civil Procedure, Rule 23(a); General Telephone Company v. Falcon, 457 U.S. 147, 161 (1982).

71   Statsny v. Southern Bell Tel. & Tel. Co., 458 F. Supp. *314,* 323–339 (W.D.N.C. 1978) (regression analysis used to prove allegations of pattern and practice discrimination in promotion and compensation). See generally, Lindemann & Grossman (1996).

72   Lindemann & Grossman (1996).

73   Teamsters v. United States, 431 U.S. 324 (1977) remains the leading case on proof of pattern and practice discrimination.

74   A consent decree is a settlement entered into voluntarily by the parties to a suit, which is then approved by the judge and thereafter treated as a judicial order, enforceable through further proceedings in court. It has the same effect as a remedial judgment entered after trial and a verdict

for the plaintiff. See, e.g., Firefighters Local 93 v. City of Cleveland, 487 U.S. 501 (1986) (upholding legality of goals and timetables remedy in consent decrees entered in private discrimination suits).

75   Section 706(g)(1) of Title VII, 42 U.S.C. §2000e-5(g)(1), provides, in relevant part: "If the court finds that the respondent has intentionally engaged in or is intentionally engaging in an unlawful employment practice charged in the complaint, the court may enjoin the respondent from engaging in such unlawful employment practice, and order such affirmative action as may be appropriate, which may include, but is not limited to, reinstatement or hiring of employees . . . or other equitable relief as the court deems appropriate." For a thorough discussion of structural, as well as individual and monetary, form of relief in Title VII actions, see Lindemann & Grossman (1996), pp. 1741–1914.

76   Title VII, Section 706(k), 42 U.S.C. §2000e-5(k).

77   See, e.g., Belton, R. (1978). A comparative review of public and private enforcement of Title VII of the Civil Rights Act of 1964, *Vanderbilt Law Review, 31,* 905–961 (describing the critical importance of the class action in the enforcement of Title VII's prohibitions against race, sex, and national origin discrimination); Leonard, J. S. (1989b). Women and affirmative action, *Journal of Economic Perspectives, 3,* 61–75 (suggesting that the threat of patterns and practice lawsuits played a relatively greater role in promoting employment opportunities for women than did affirmative action programs enforced by the OFCCP).

78   See, e.g., Bowe v. Colgate-Palmolive Company, 416 F.2d 711, 719 (7th Cir. 1969) (stating that "a suit for violation of Title VII is necessarily a class action as the evil sought to be ended is discrimination on the basis of a class characteristic, *i.e.,* race, sex, religion or national origin."

79   Lindemann & Grossman (1996), pp. 1582–1591.

80   Donohue, J. J., & Siegelman, P. (1991). The changing nature of employment discrimination litigation. *Stanford Law Review, 43,* 983–1030.

81   Nielsen, L. B., & Nelson, R. L. (2005). Rights realized? An empirical analysis of employment discrimination litigation as a claiming system. *Wisconsin Law Review,* 663–711, p. 392.

82   Donohue & Siegelman (1991).

83   Nielsen & Nelson (2005), p. 698.

84   For a more thorough canvassing of the weaknesses of individual disparate treatment adjudications as an EEO policy enforcement tool, see Krieger, L. H. (1998). Civil rights perestroika: Intergroup relations after affirmative action. *California Law Review, 86,* 1251–1333, pp.1302–1329.

85   Strauss, D. A. (1991). The law and economics of racial discrimination in employment: the case for numerical standards. *Georgetown Law Review, 79,* 1619–1657.

86   Kalev & Dobbin (2006).

87   Nielsen & Nelson (2005).

88 See, e.g., Olson, W. (1997). *The excuse factory: How employment law is paralyzing the American workplace.* New York: Free Press.

89 Crosby, F. J. (1984). The denial of personal discrimination. *American Behavioral Scientist, 27,* 371–386; Taylor, D. M., Wright, S. C., & Porter, L. E. (1994). Dimensions of perceived discrimination: The personal/group discrimination discrepancy. In M. P. Zanna, & J. M. Olson, (Eds.), *The psychology of prejudice: The Ontario symposium* (Vol. 7, pp. 233–255). Hillsdale, NJ: Lawrence Erlbaum.

90 Bumiller, K. (1988). *The civil rights society: The social construction of victims.* Baltimore: Johns Hopkins University Press.

91 Fiske, A. P., Kitayama, S., Markus, J. R., & Nisbett, R. E. (1998). The cultural matrix of social psychology. In D. Gilbert, S. T. Fiske, & G. Lindzey (Eds.), *Handbook of social psychology* (4th ed., Vol. 2, pp. 915–981). Boston: McGraw Hill.

92 Major, B., Gramzow, R. H., McCoy, S. K., Levin, S., Schmader, T., & Sidanius, J. (2002). Perceiving personal discrimination: The role of group status and legitimizing ideology. *Journal of Personality and Social Psychology, 82,* 269–282.

93 See, e.g., Tomaka, J., & Blascovich, J. (1994). Effects of justice beliefs on cognitive appraisal of and subjective, physiological, and behavioral responses to stress. *Journal of Personality and Social Psychology, 67,* 732–740.

94 Lerner, M. J. (1980). *The belief in a just world: A fundamental delusion.* New York: Plenum Press.

95 Jost, J. T., & Hunyady, O. (2002). The psychology of system justification and the palliative function of ideology. *European Review of Social Psychology, 13,* 126–128.

96 Major et al. (2002).

97 Major et al. (2002). See also, Shorey, H. S., Cowan, G., & Sullivan, M. P. (2002). Predicting perceptions of discrimination among Hispanics and Anglos. *Hispanic Journal of Behavioral Sciences, 24,* 3–22.

98 Shelton, J. N., & Stewart, R. E. (2004). Confronting perpetrators of prejudice: The inhibitory effects of social costs. *Psychology of Women Quarterly, 28,* 215–223; Swim, J. K., & Myers, L. L. (1999). Excuse me – What did you just say?!: Women's public and private responses to sexist remarks. *Journal of Experimental Social Psychology, 35,* 68–88.

99 Stangor, C., Swim, J. K., Van Allen, K. L., & Secrist, G. B. (2002). Reporting discrimination in public and private contexts. *Journal of Personality and Social Psychology, 82,* 69–74; Stangor, C., Swim, J. K., Sechrist, G. B., Decoster, J., VanAllen, K. L., & Ottenbreit, A. (2003). Ask, answer, and announce: Three stages in perceiving and responding to prejudice. *European Review of Social Psychology, 14,* 277–311. For a recent review of the literature on discrimination claiming behavior, see Nielsen & Nelson (2005).

100 Garcia, D. M., Reser, A. H., Amo, R. B., Redersdorff, S., & Branscombe, N. R. (2005). Perceivers' responses to in-group and out-group members who blame a negative outcome on discrimination. *Personality and Social Psychology Journal, 31*, 769–780; Kaiser, C. R., & Miller, C. T. (2001b). Stop complaining! The social costs of making attributions to discrimination. *Personality and Social Psychology Bulletin, 27*, 254–263.

101 For both a thorough review of the relevant literature, and a vivid experimental demonstration of this effect, see Garcia et. al. (2005).

102 See Nielsen & Nelson (2005) for a discussion of the impact of new statutory rights on the increasing numbers of EEO lawsuits filed over the course of the 1990s.

103 Americans with Disabilities Act of 1990, 42 U.S.C §12101–12213.

104 Family and Medical Leave Act of 1993, 29 U.S.C. §2601–2654.

105 Civil Rights Act of 1991, 42 U.S.C §1981a.

106 Under a contingent fee agreement, a lawyer represents a plaintiff without charging an hourly fee or waiting to receive fees from the court after a judgment for plaintiff on the merits. Instead, the lawyer receives a percentage of the settlement or recovery after judgment as compensation for his or her services.

107 Jones, G. T. (2002). Testing for structural change in legal doctrine: An empirical look at the plaintiff's decision to litigate employment disputes a decade after the Civil Rights Act of 1991. *Georgia State University Law Review, 18*, 997–1029.

108 By 2002, sexual harassment charges represented 55% of the sex discrimination charges filed with the EEOC. Nielsen & Nelson (2005).

109 Donohue & Siegelman (1991); Nielsen & Nelson (2005).

110 Selmi, M. (2003). The price of discrimination: The nature of class action employment discrimination litigation and its effects. *Texas Law Review, 81*, 1249–1335, pp. 1251–1252. Reprinted by permission of Michael Selmi and the *Texas Law Review* Association.

111 For fiscal year 2005, the precise number was 23,094. United States Equal Employment Opportunity Commission, *Sex-based charges FY 1992–2005*. Retrieved May 17, 2006 from http://www.eeoc.gove/stats/charges.html

112 EEOC, *Sex-based charges* (2005). The precise number was 5,702.

113 EEOC, *Sex-based charges* (2005). The precise number was 1,683.

114 Title VII of the Civil Rights Act of 1964, 42 U.S.C. §2000e-5(b).

115 Title VII of the Civil Rights Act of 1964, §709(c), 42 U.S.C. 2000e-8(c); 29 C.F.R. §1602.7.

116 29 C.F.R. Section 1601.22 of the Code of Federal Regulations provides that, unless the Commission actually files a federal lawsuit against a particular employer, union, or employment agency, "Neither a charge, nor information obtained during the investigation of a charge of employment discrimination . . . nor information obtained from records required to be kept or reports required to be filed . . . shall be made matters of public information by the Commission."

117   41 C.F.R. 60–1.20, 60–2.18(d) (2000).

118   Brenowitz, S. (2004). Deadly secrecy: The erosion of public information under private justice. *Ohio State Journal on Dispute Resolution, 19,* 679–708; Doré, L. K. (2004). Settlement, secrecy, and judicial discretion: South Carolina's new rules governing the sealing of settlements. *South Carolina Law Review, 55,* 791–827.

119   In a 1996 study, Samuel Gross and Kent Syverud reported a combined state-federal civil pre-trial settlement rate of 98%. Gross, S. R., & Syverud, K. D. (1996). Don't try: Civil jury verdicts in a system geared to settlement. *UCLA Law Review, 4,* 1–64.

120   L. Brandeis (1914). *Other people's money and how the bankers use it,* New York: F.A. Stokes, p. 92.

121   The Securities Act of 1933, 15 U.S.C. §§77a–77aa (2000 & Supp. II 2002); The Securities Exchange Act of 1934, 15 U.S.C. §78a–78nn (2000 & Supp. II 2002).

122   On these points, readers are referred to Coffee, J. C., Jr. & Seligman, J. (2003). *Securities regulation: Cases and materials* (9th ed.). New York: Foundation Press, pp. 2–8. The germinal work on the effects of information asymmetries on market efficiency is well-represented by Akerlof, G. A. (1970). The market for lemons. *The Quarterly Journal of Economics, 84,* 448–500.

123   Coffee & Seligman (2003), pp. 4–5.

References

Abbott, I. O. (2000). *The lawyer's guide to mentoring.* Washington, DC: National Association for Law Placement.

Acker, J. (1990). Hierarchies, jobs, and bodies: A theory of gendered organizations. *Gender and Society, 4*, 139–158.

Adams, J. S. (1965). Inequity in social exchange. In L. Berkowitz (Ed.), *Advances in experimental social psychology* (Vol. 2. pp. 267–299). New York: Academic Press.

Affirmative Action Programs. Subpart B – Purpose and Contents of Affirmative Action Programs 41 CFR §§60-2.11, 60-2.13, 60-2.17, 60-2.30.

Akerlof, G. A. (1970). The market for lemons. *The Quarterly Journal of Economics, 84*, 448–500.

Albiston, C. R. (2005). Bargaining in the shadow of social institutions: Competing discourses and social change in workplace mobilization of civil rights. *Law and Society Review, 39*, 11–49.

Allport, G. W. (1954). *The nature of prejudice.* Reading, MA: Addison-Wesley.

American Arbitration Association. (1995, May 9). *A due process protocol for mediation and arbitration of statutory disputes arising out of the employment relationship.* Retrieved July 26, 2005, from http://www.adr.org/sp.asp?id=22078

American Arbitration Association. (2004, January 1). *National rules for the resolution of employment disputes.* Retrieved July 26, 2005, from http://www.adr.org/sp.asp?id=22075

American Arbitration Association. (2006, July 1). *Employment arbitration rules and mediation procedures.* Retrieved July 15, 2006, from www.adr.org/sp.asp?id=28481

American Association of University Women Educational Foundation. (2003). *Women at Work*, table: State-by-state data on women's and men's educational attainment and earnings by educational attainment, downloaded November 19, 2005, from http://www.aauw.org/research/statedata/table_data.pdf

American Bar Association (ABA) Commission on Women in the Profession. (1997). *Fair measure: Toward effective attorney evaluation.* Chicago, IL: American Bar Association.

American Bar Association (ABA) Commission on Women in the Profession. (2003). *A current glance at women and the law.* Chicago, IL: American Bar Association.

American Psychological Association. (2002). Ethical principles of psychologists and code of conduct. In D. N. Bersoff (Ed.), *Ethical conflicts in psychology* (pp. 28–45). Washington, DC: American Psychological Association.

Americans with Disabilities Act of 1990, 42 U.S.C. §12101–12213.

Anker, R. (1998). *Gender and jobs: Sex segregation in occupations in the world.* Geneva: International Labor Office.

Asch, S. E. (1955). Opinions and social pressure. *Scientific American,* 31–35.

Avellar, S., & Smock, P. J. (2003). Has the price of motherhood declined over time? A cross-cohort comparison of the motherhood wage penalty. *Journal of Marriage and the Family,* 65(3), 597–607.

Back v. Hastings-on-Hudson Union Free School District, 365 F. 3d. 107 (2d Cir. 2004).

Bailey v. Scott-Gallaher, Inc., 480 S.E.2d 502 (Va. 1997).

Bales, R. A. (2004). The laissez-faire arbitration market and the need for a uniform federal standard governing employment and consumer arbitration. *Kansas Law Review,* 52, 583–630.

Banaji, M. R., & Greenwald, A. G. (1995). Implicit gender stereotyping in judgments of fame. *Journal of Personality and Social Psychology,* 68, 181–198.

Banaji, M. R., & Hardin, C. D. (1996). Automatic stereotyping. *Psychological Science,* 7, 136–141.

Banerjee, V. (2001, August 10). Some "bullies" seek ways to soften up: Toughness has risks for women executives. *New York Times,* p. C1.

Bargh, J. A., & Raymond, P. (1995). The naïve misuse of power: Nonconscious sources of sexual harassment. *Journal of Social Issues,* 51, 85–96.

Bargh, J. A., Chen, M., & Burrows, L. (1996). Automaticity of social behavior: Direct effects of trait construct and stereotype activation on action. *Journal of Personality and Social Psychology,* 71, 230–244.

Baron, J. N., Hannan, M. T., Hsu, G., & Kocak, O. (2002). Gender and the organization-building process in young, high-tech firms. In M. Guillen, R. Collins, P. England, & M. Meyer (Eds.), *The new economic sociology: Developments in an emerging field* (pp. 245–273). New York: Russell Sage Foundation.

Baron, J. N., Mittman, B. S., & Newman, A. E. (1991). Targets of opportunity: Organizational and environmental determinants of gender integration within the California civil service, 1979–1985. *American Journal of Sociology,* 96, 1362–1401.

Baron, J. N., & Newman, A. E. (1989). Pay the man: Effects of demographic composition on prescribed wage rates in the California civil service. In R. T.

Michael, H. I. Hartmann, & B. O'Farrell (Eds.), *Pay equity: Empirical inquiries* (pp. 107–130). Washington, DC: National Academy Press.

Baron, J. N., & Pfeffer, J. (1994). The social psychology of organizations and inequality. *Social Psychology Quarterly, 57*(3), 190–209.

Bartlett, K., & Rhode, D. L. (2006). *Gender and the law: Theory, doctrine, commentary.* Boston: Aspen Press.

Bazemore v. Friday, 478 U.S. 385 (1986).

Beck et al. v. The Boeing Company, 203 F.R.D. 459 (W.D.WA. 2001).

Beck et al. v. The Boeing Company, Boeing's motion *in limine* to exclude expert report, opinions, and testimony of plaintiffs' expert Eugene Borgida, Ph.D. April 12, 2004.

Beck et al. v. The Boeing Company, Boeing's reply on motion to strike expert report, opinion, and testimony of plaintiffs' expert Eugene Borgida, Ph.D. April 29, 2004.

Beck et al. v. The Boeing Company, Deposition of Dr. Eugene Borgida, Ph.D. December 11, 2003.

Beck et al. v. The Boeing Company, Order denying defendant's motion to exclude expert report, opinions, and testimony of plaintiffs' expert Eugene Borigda, Ph.D. May 14, 2004.

Beck et al. v. The Boeing Company, Plaintiffs' opposition to Boeing's motion in limine to exclude expert report, opinions, and testimony of plaintiffs' expert Eugene Borgida, Ph.D. April 26, 2004.

Beck, J. (2006). Entity liability for teacher-on-student sexual harassment: Could state law offer greater protection than federal statutes? *Journal of Law and Education, 35*, 141–151.

Becker, G. S. (1957). *The economics of discrimination.* Chicago: University of Chicago Press.

Becker, G. S. (1985). Human capital, effort, and the sexual division of labor. *Journal of Labor Economics, 3*(1, Part 2), S33–S58.

Becker, G. S. (1991). *A treatise on the family.* Cambridge, MA: Harvard University Press.

Becker, P., & Moen, P. (1999). Scaling back: dual earner couples: Work-family strategies. *Journal of Marriage and the Family, 61*, 995–1007.

Beiner, T. M. (2001). Sex, science and social knowledge: The implications of social science research on imputing liability to employers for sexual harassment. *William and Mary Journal of Women and the Law, 7*, 273–339.

Beiner, T. M. (2005). *Gender myths v. working realities: Using social science to reformulate sexual harassment law.* New York: New York University Press.

Belkin, L. (2003, October 26). The opt-out revolution. *New York Times Magazine, 6*, 42.

Beller, A. H. (1984). Trends in occupational segregation by sex and race, 1960–1981. In Barbara F. Reskin (Ed.), *Sex segregation in the workplace* (pp. 11–26). Washington, DC: National Academy Press.

Belton, R. (1978). A comparative review of public and private enforcement of Title VII of the Civil Rights Act of 1964, *Vanderbilt Law Review, 31*, 905–961.

Berger, J., Rosenholtz, S. J., & Zelditch, M., Jr. (1980). Status organizing processes. *Annual Review of Sociology*, 6, 479–508.

Bergman, M. E., Langhout, R. D., Palmieri, P. A., Cortina, L. M., & Fitzgerald, L. F. (2002). The (un)reasonableness of reporting: Antecedents and consequences of reporting sexual harassment. *Journal of Applied Psychology*, 87, 230–242.

Bergmann, B. R. (1971). The effect on white incomes of discrimination in employment. *Journal of Political Economy*, 79, 294–313.

Bergmann, B. R. (1974). Occupational segregation, wages and profits when employers discriminate by race and sex. *Eastern Economic Journal*, 1(2), 103–110.

Bergmann, B. R. (1995). Becker's theory of the family: Preposterous conclusions. *Feminist Economics*, 1(1), 141–150.

Bergmann, B. R. (2005a). The state of economics: Needs lots of work. *Annals of the American Academy of Political and Social Science*, 600, 52–67.

Bergmann, B. R. (2005b). *The economic emergence of women.* New York: Palgrave.

Berkman v. New York, 812 F.2d 52 (2d Cir. 1987).

Berkman v. New York, 536 F.Supp 177 (E.D.N.Y, 1982).

Berkowitz, E. (2005, October 4). Part-time lawyers find their own glass ceiling. *San Francisco Daily Journal*, p. 6.

Bernard, T. H. & Rapp, A. L. (2005). Are we there yet? Forty years after the passage of the civil rights act: Revolution in the workforce and the unfulfilled promises that remain. *Hofstra Labor and Employment Law Journal*, 22, 627–670.

Bersoff, D. N. (2003). *Ethical conflicts in psychology* (3rd ed.). Washington, DC: American Psychological Association.

Bielby, D. D., & Bielby, W. T. (1988). She works hard for the money: Household responsibilities and the allocation of work effort. *American Journal of Sociology*, 93, 1031–1059.

Bielby, W. T. (2000). Minimizing workplace gender and racial bias. *Contemporary Sociology*, 29(1), 120–129.

Bielby, W. T. (2003). Can I get a witness? Challenges of using expert testimony on cognitive bias in employment discrimination. *Employee Rights and Employment Policy Journal*, 7, 377–397.

Bielby, W. T., & Baron, J. N. (1986). Men and women at work: Sex segregation and statistical discrimination. *American Journal of Sociology*, 91, 759–799.

Bielby, W. T., & Bielby, D. (2002). Telling stories about gender and effort: Social science narratives about who works hard for the money. In M. Guillen, R. Collins, P. England, & M. Meyer (Eds.), *The new economic sociology: Developments in an emerging field* (pp. 193–217). New York: Russell Sage Foundation.

Bielby, W. T., & Bourgeois, M. (2002, August). *Insuring discrimination: Making a market for employment practice liability insurance.* Paper presented at the Annual Meeting of the American Sociological Association. Chicago, IL.

Biernat, M. (2003). Toward a broader view of social stereotyping. *American Psychologist*, 58(12), 1019–1027.

Biernat, M., & Kobrynowicz, D. (1997). Gender- and race-based standards of competence: Lower minimum standards but higher ability standards for devalued groups. *Journal of Personality and Social Psychology*, 72, 544–557.

Biernat, M., & Manis, M. (1994). Shifting standards and stereotype-based judgments. *Journal of Personality and Social Psychology*, 66, 5–20.

Biernat, M., & Vescio, T. K. (2002). She swings, she hits, she's great, she's benched: Implications of gender-based shifting standards for judgment and behavior. *Personality and Social Psychology Bulletin*, 28, 66–77.

Bies, R. J., & Moag, J. S. (1986). Interactional justice: Communication criteria of fairness. In R. J. Lewicki, B. H. Sheppard, & B. H. Bazerman (Eds.), *Research on negotiation in organizations* (Vol. 1, pp. 43–55). Greenwich, CT: JAI Press.

Bingham, L. B. (1998). On repeat players, adhesive contracts, and the use of statistics in judicial review of employment arbitration awards. *McGeorge Law Review*, 29, 223–259.

Bisom-Rapp, S. (1999a). Bulletproofing the workplace: Symbol and substance in employment discrimination law practice. *Florida State University Law Review*, 26(4), 969–1047.

Bisom-Rapp, S. (1999b). Discerning form from substance: Understanding employer litigation prevention strategies. *Employee Rights and Employment Policy Journal*, 3, 1–64.

Bisom-Rapp, S. (2001). An ounce of prevention is a poor substitute for a pound of cure: Confronting the developing jurisprudence of education and prevention in employment discrimination law. *Berkeley Journal of Employment and Labor Law*, 22, 1–47.

Black v. City & County of Honolulu, 2000 WL 1275818 (D. Hawaii 2000).

Blair, I. V., & Banaji, M. R. (1996). Automatic and controlled processes in stereotype priming. *Journal of Personality and Social Psychology*, 70, 1142–1163.

Blasi, G. (2002). Advocacy against the stereotype: Lessons from cognitive social psychology. *University of California, Los Angeles Law Review*, 49(5), 1241–1281.

Blau, F. D., Ferber, M. A., & Winkler, A. E. (2006). *The economics of women, men, and work* (5th ed.). Upper Saddle River, NJ: Pearson/Prentice-Hall.

Bloomberg News (September 20, 1997). Home Depot settles four sex bias lawsuits; retail chain will take $104 million charge. *The Houston Chronicle*.

Blumrosen, A. W., & Blumrosen, R. G. (2002). *The reality of intentional job discrimination in metropolitan America – 1999*. Newark, NJ: Rutgers State University of New Jersey.

BNA (n.d.) *Affirmative Action Compliance Manual*, http://www.bna.com/products/labor/aacm.htm

Bodenhausen, G. V., Macrae, C. N., & Garst, J. (1998). Stereotypes in thought and deed: Social cognitive origins of intergroup discrimination. In C. Sedikides, J. Schopler, & C.A. Insko (Eds.), *Intergroup cognition and intergroup behavior* (pp. 311–335). Mahwah, NJ: Lawrence Erlbaum.

Boeing pays a biggie. (2006, May 29). *Business Week*, p. 30.

Bond, C. A. (1997). Shattering the myth: Mediating sexual harassment disputes in the workplace. *Fordham Law Review*, 65, 2489–2533.

Borgida, E., Hunt, C., & Kim, A. (2005). On the use of gender stereotyping research in sex discrimination litigation. *Journal of Law and Policy*, 13(2), 613–628.

Borgida, E., Rudman, L. A., & Manteufel, L. L. (1995). On the courtroom use and misuse of gender stereotyping research. *Journal of Social Issues*, 51, 181–192.

Bowe v. Colgate-Palmolive Company, 416 F.2d 711, 719 (7th Cir. 1969).

Brake, D. L. (2005). Retaliation. *Minnesota Law Review*, 90, 18–105.

Brandeis, L. (1914). *Other people's money and how the bankers use it*. New York: F. A. Stokes.

Brenowitz, S. (2004). Deadly secrecy: The erosion of public information under private justice. *Ohio State Journal on Dispute Resolution*, 19, 679–708.

Brewer, M. B. (1996). In-group favoritism: The subtle side of intergroup discrimination. In D. M. Messick & A. E. Tenbrunsel (Eds.), *Codes of conduct: Behavioral research and business ethics* (pp. 160–179). New York: Russell Sage Foundation.

Brewer, M. B., & Brown, R. J. (1998). Intergroup relations. In D. T. Gilbert, S. T. Fiske, & G. Lindzey (Eds.), *Handbook of social psychology* (4th ed., Vol. 2, pp. 554–594). New York: McGraw-Hill.

Brewer, M. B., & Lui, L. (1989). The primacy of age and sex in the structure of person categories. *Social Cognition*, 7, 262–274.

Brockner, J., & Wiesenfeld, B. M. (1996). An interactive framework for explaining reactions to decisions: The interactive effects of outcomes and procedures. *Psychological Bulletin*, 120, 189–208.

Brodsky, S. L. (1999). *The expert witness: More maxims and guidelines for testifying in court*. Washington, DC: American Psychological Association.

Broomfield v. Lundell, 159 Ariz. 349 (Ct. App. Div. 1 1988).

Brown v. Scott Paper Worldwide Co., 98 Wash. App. 349 (Div. 1 1999).

Brunet, E. (1992). Arbitration and constitutional rights. *North Carolina Law Review*, 71, 81–120.

Brush v. San Francisco Newspaper Printing Company, 469 F.2d 89 (9th Cir. 1972).

Budig, M. J. (2002). Male advantage and the gender composition of jobs: Who rides the glass escalator? *Social Problems*, 49, 258–277.

Budig, M. J., & England, P. (2001). The wage penalty for motherhood. *American Sociological Review*, 66(2), 204–225.

Bumiller, K. (1988). *The civil rights society: The social construction of victims*. Baltimore: Johns Hopkins University Press.

Burgess, D., & Borgida, E. (1999). Who women are, who women should be: Descriptive and prescriptive gender stereotyping in sex discrimination. *Psychology, Public Policy, and Law*, 5, 665–692.

Burlington Industries, Inc. v. Ellerth, 524 U.S. 742 (1998).

Butler v. Home Depot, 984 F. Supp. 1257 (N.D. Cal. 1997).

Butler, A. B., & Skattebo, A. L. (2004). What is acceptable for women may not be for men: The effect of family conflicts with work on job performance ratings. *Journal of Organizational Psychology*, 77, 553–564.

Calvert, C. T., & Williams, J. C. (2006). *WorkLife Law's guide to family responsibilities discrimination.* San Francisco: University of California, Hastings College of the Law, Center for WorkLife Law (available from www.worklifelaw.org).

Canadian Human Rights Commission. (1983). *Unwanted sexual attention and sexual harassment.* Montreal: Minister of Supply and Services of Canada.

Carli, L. L. (2001). Gender and social influence. *Journal of Social Issues*, 57, 725–741.

Carpenter, D. (2006, July 5). Boeing's chief ethics champ. *The Denver Post*, p. 2C.

Cascio, W. F., & Aguinis, H. (2005). *Applied psychology in human resource management* (6th ed.). Upper Saddle River, NJ: Prentice-Hall.

Castaneda v. Partida, 430 U. S. 482 (1977).

Casellas, G. F., & Hill, I. L. (1998). *Sexual harassment: Prevention and avoiding liability.* Society for Human Resource Management Legal Report.

Catalyst (1998). *Women entrepreneurs: Why companies lose female talent and what they can do about it.* New York: Catalyst.

Catalyst (1999). *Women of color in corporate management: Dynamics of career advancement.* New York: Catalyst.

Catalyst (2001). *Women in law: Making the case.* New York: Catalyst.

Catania, A. (1983). State employment discrimination remedies and pendent jurisdiction under Title VII: Access to federal courts. *American University Law Review*, 32, 777–838.

Cavico, F. J. (2003). The tort of intentional infliction of emotional distress in the private employment sector. *Hofstra Labor and Employment Law Journal*, 21, 109–182.

Cejka, M. A., & Eagly, A. H. (1999). Gender-stereotypic images of occupations correspond to the sex segregation of employment. *Personality and Social Psychology Bulletin*, 25, 413–423.

Chamallas, M. (2004). Title VII's midlife crisis: The case of constructive discharge. *Southern California Law Review*, 77, 307–396.

Chamberlin v. 101 Realty, Inc., 915 F.2d 777 (1st Cir. 1990).

Chambers v. TrettcoW, Inc., 614 N.W.2d 910 (Mich. 2000).

Chambliss, E. (2005). *Miles to go: Progress of minorities in the legal profession.* ABA Commission on Racial and Ethnic Diversity in the Legal Profession. Chicago, IL: American Bar Association.

Charles, M., & Grusky, D. B. (2004). *Occupational ghettos: The worldwide segregation of women and men.* Stanford, CA: Stanford University Press.

Cialdini, R. B., & Trost, M. R. (1998). Social influence: Social norms, conformity, and compliance. In D. T. Gilbert, S. T. Fiske, & G. Lindzey. *The handbook of social psychology* (4th ed., Vol. 2, pp. 151–192). New York: McGraw Hill.

Circuit City Stores, Inc. v. Adams, 279 F.3d 889 (9th Cir. 2002).

Circuit City Stores, Inc. v. Adams, 532 U.S. 105 (2001).

Civil Rights Act of 1991, 42 U.S.C.A. §§1981, 2000 et seq. (West 2003).

Clayton, S. D. (1989). *The recognition of discrimination in a minimal-information format.* Unpublished paper presented at the 97th meeting of the American Psychological Association.

Clayton, S. D., & Crosby, F. J. (1992). *Justice, gender, and affirmative action.* Ann Arbor, MI: University of Michigan Press.

Clermont, K. M., & Eisenberg, T. (1992). Trial by jury or judge: Transcending empiricism. *Cornell Law Review, 77,* 1124–1177.

Coffee, J. C., Jr., & Seligman, J. (2003). *Securities regulation: Cases and materials* (9th ed.). New York: Foundation Press.

Cohen, B. P., & Zhou, X. (1991). Status processes in enduring work groups. *American Sociological Review, 56*(2), 179–188.

Cole v. Burns Int'l Security Services, 105 F.3d 1465 (D.C. Cir. 1997).

Conley, F. (1998). *Walking out on the boys.* New York: Farrar, Straus & Giroux.

Connecticut General Statutes Annotated §46a-104 (West 2004).

Conway, M., Pizzamiglio, M. T., & Mount, L. (1996). Status, communality, and agency: Implications for stereotypes of gender and other groups. *Journal of Personality and Social Psychology, 71,* 25–38.

Cooper, L. J., Nolan, D. R., & Bales, R. A. (2005). *ADR in the workplace* (2nd ed.). St. Paul, MN: Thomson West.

Copus, D. (2005). A lawyer's view: Avoiding junk science. In F. J. Landy (Ed.), *Employment discrimination litigation: Behavioral, quantitative, and legal perspectives* (pp. 450–462). San Francisco: Jossey-Bass.

Corcoran, K. O., & Melamed, J. C. (1990, Summer). From coercion to empowerment: Spousal abuse and mediation. *Mediation Quarterly, 7,* 303–316.

Corcoran, M., & Duncan G. J. (1979). Work history, labor force attachment, and earnings differences between the sexes. *Journal of Human Resources, 14*(1, Winter), 3–20.

Cordova, D. I. (1992). Cognitive limitations and affirmative action: The effects of aggregate versus sequential data in the perception of discrimination. *Social Justice Research, 5,* 319–333.

Correll, S. J. (2001). Gender and the career choice process: The role of biased self-assessments. *American Journal of Sociology, 106,* 1691–1730.

Correll, S. J. (2004). Constraints into preferences: Gender, status and emerging career aspirations. *American Sociological Review, 69*(1), 93–113.

Correll, S. J., & Bernard, S. (2005). *Getting a job: Is there a motherhood penalty?* Paper presented at the American Sociological Association, Philadelphia.

Cortina, L. M., & Wasti, S. A. (2005). Profiles in coping: Responses to sexual harassment across persons, organizations, and cultures. *Journal of Applied Psychology, 90,* 182–192.

Cota, A. A., & Dion, K. L. (1986). Salience of gender and sex composition in ad hoc groups: An experimental test of distinctiveness theory. *Journal of Personality and Social Psychology, 50,* 770–776.

Cotter, D., Hermsen, J. M., & Vanneman, R. (2004). *Gender inequality at work.* New York: Russell Sage Foundation.

Crandall, C. S., & Eshleman, A. (2003). A justification-suppression model of the expression and experience of prejudice. *Psychological Bulletin, 129,* 414–446.

Craver, C. B. (2001). The use of non-judicial procedures to resolve employment discrimination claims. *Kansas Journal of Law and Public Policy, 11,* 141–176.

Crittenden, A. (2002). *The price of motherhood.* New York: Owl Books.

Crocker, J., Major, B., & Steel, C. (1998). Social stigma. In D. T. Gilbert, S. T. Fiske, & G. Lindzey (Eds.), *The handbook of social psychology* (4th ed., Vol. 2, pp. 504–553). Boston: McGraw Hill.

Crosby, F. J. (1982). *Relative deprivation and working women.* New York: Oxford University Press.

Crosby, F. J. (1984). The denial of personal discrimination. *American Behavioral Scientist, 27,* 371–386.

Crosby, F. J. (1991). *Juggling: The unexpected advantages of balancing home and work for women and their families.* New York: MacMillan.

Crosby, F. J. (2004). *Affirmative action is dead: Long live affirmative action.* New Haven, CT: Yale University Press.

Crosby, F. J., Clayton, S., Hemker, K., & Alksnis, O. (1986). Cognitive biases in the perception of discrimination: The importance of format. *Sex Roles, 14,* 637–646.

Crosby, F. J., & Cordova, D. (1996). Words worth of wisdom. *Journal of Social Issues, 52*(4), 33–49.

Crosby, F. J., & Franco, J. (2003). The ivory tower and the multicultural world. *Personality and Social Psychology Review, 7,* 362–373.

Crosby, F. J., Iyer, A., Clayton, S., & Downing, R. A. (2003). Affirmative action: Psychological data and the policy debates. *American Psychologist, 58,* 93–115.

Crosby, F. J., Iyer, A., & Sincharoen, S. (2006). Understanding affirmative action. *Annual Review of Psychology, 57,* 585–611.

Crosby, F. J., Williams, J., & Biernat, M. (2004). The maternal wall. *Journal of Social Issues, 60,* 675–682.

Cuddy, A. J. C., Fiske, S. T., & Glick, P. (2004). When professionals become mothers, warmth doesn't cut the ice. *Journal of Social Issues, 60*(4), 701–718.

Cuddy, A. J. C., Fiske, S. T., & Glick, P. (In press). The BIAS map: Behaviors from intergroup affect and stereotypes. *Journal of Personality and Social Psychology.*

Culbertson, A. L., Rosenfeld, P., Booth-Kewley, S., & Magnusson, P. (1992). *Assessment of sexual harassment in the Navy: Results of the 1989 Navy-wide survey* (Report No. TR-92-11). San Diego, CA: Navy Personnel Research and Development Center.

Czopp, A. M., & Monteith, M. J. (2003). Confronting prejudice (literally): Reactions to confrontations of racial and gender bias. *Personality and Social Psychology Bulletin, 29,* 532–544.

Dalbert, C. (2001). *The justice motive as a personal resource: Dealing with challenges and critical life events.* New York: Kluwer Academic/Plenum Publishers.

Dansky, B. S., & Kilpatrick, D. G. (1997). Effects of sexual harassment. In W. O'Donohue (Ed.), *Sexual harassment: Theory, research, and treatment* (pp. 152–174). Needham Heights, MA: Allyn & Bacon.

Darley, J. M., & Gross, P. H. (1983). A hypothesis-confirming bias in labeling effects. *Journal of Personality and Social Psychology, 44*, 20–33.

Darley, J. M., & Pittman, T. S. (2003). The psychology of compensatory and retributive justice. *Personality and Social Psychology Review, 7*, 324–336.

Daubert v. Merrell Dow Pharmaceuticals, Inc., 113 S. Ct. 2786 (1993).

Davison, H. K., & Burke, M. J. (2000). Sex discrimination in simulated employment contexts: A meta-analytic investigation. *Journal of Vocational Behavior, 56*, 225–248.

Day, N. E., & Schoenrade, N. (2000). The relationship among reported disclosure of sexual orientation, anti-discrimination policies, to management support and work attitudes of gay and lesbian employees. *Personnel Review, 29*, 346–363.

Deaux, K., & LaFrance, M. (1998). Gender. In D. T. Gilbert, S. T. Fiske, & G. Lindzey (Eds), *The handbook of social psychology* (4th ed., Vol. 2, pp. 788–827). New York: McGraw-Hill.

DeLoach v. American Red Cross, 967 F. Supp. 265 (N.D. Ohio 1997).

Deutsch, M. (1975). Equity, equality, and need: What determines which value will be used as a basis of distributive justice. *Journal of Social Issues, 31*, 137–149.

Devine, P. G. (1989). Stereotypes and prejudice: Their automatic and controlled components. *Journal of Personality and Social Psychology, 56*, 5–18.

Devine, P. G., Plant, E. A., Amodio, D. M., Harmon-Jones, E., & Vance, S. L. (2002). The regulation of explicit and implicit race bias: The role of motivations to respond without prejudice. *Journal of Personality and Social Psychology, 82*, 835–848.

Diaz v. Pan American World Airlines, 442 F.2d 385(5th Cir. 1971).

Dixon, K. A., Storen, D., & Van Horn, C. E. (2002). *A workplace divided: How Americans view discrimination and race on the job.* New Brunswick, NJ: John J. Heldrich Center for Workplace Development, Rutgers University.

Dobbin, F., & Kelly, E. (2005). *Two to tango: affirmative action, diversity programs and women and African-Americans in management.* Unpublished paper on file with author.

Dobbin, F., Sutton, J. R., Meyer, J. W., & Scott, W. R. (1993). Equal opportunity law and the construction of internal labor markets. *American Journal of Sociology, 99*, 396–427.

Dobbs, D. B. (2000). *The Law of Torts.* St. Paul, MN: West Group.

Doeringer, P., & Piore, M. J. (1971). *Internal labor markets and manpower analysis.* Lexingon, MA: D. C. Heath & Co.

Dolan, J. (2004). Gender equity: Illusion or reality for women in the Federal Executive Service. *Public Administration Review, 64*, 299–308.

Donohue, J. J., & Siegelman, P. (1991). The changing nature of employment discrimination litigation. *Stanford Law Review, 43,* 983–1030.

Doré, L. K. (2004). Settlement, secrecy, and judicial discretion: South Carolina's new rules governing the sealing of settlements. *South Carolina Law Review, 55,* 791–827.

Dovidio, J. F. (2001). On the nature of contemporary prejudice: The third wave. *Journal of Social Issues, 57,* 829–849.

Dovidio, J. F., & Gaertner, S. L. (1993). Stereotypes and evaluative intergroup bias. In D. M. Mackie, & D. L. Hamilton (Eds.), *Affect, cognition, and stereotyping* (pp. 167–193). San Diego, CA: Academic Press.

Dovidio, J. F., Kawakami, K., & Gaertner, S. L. (2002). Implicit and explicit prejudice and interracial interaction. *Journal of Personality and Social Psychology, 82,* 62–68.

Dukes et. al. v. Wal-Mart Stores, Inc., Memorandum of Points and Authorities in Support of Plaintiffs' Motion for Class Certification, United States District Court for the Northern District of California, Case No. C-01–2252 MJJ, filed July 25, 2003 retrieved May 23, 2006 from http://www.walmartclass.com/staticdata/walmartclass/brief2.html

Dunlop, J. T., & Zack, A. M. (1997). *Mediation and arbitration of employment disputes.* San Francisco, CA: Jossey-Bass.

Eagly, A. H. (1987). *Sex differences in social behavior: A social role interpretation.* Hillsdale, NJ: Erlbaum.

Eagly, A. H., Ashmore, R. D., Makhijani, M. G., & Longo, L. C. (1991). What is beautiful is good, but . . . A meta-analytic review of research on the physical attractiveness stereotype. *Psychological Bulletin, 110,* 109–128.

Eagly, A. H., & Karau, S. J. (2002). Role congruity theory of prejudice toward female leaders. *Psychological Review, 109,* 573–598.

Eagly, A. H., Makhijani, M. G., & Klonsky, B. G. (1992). Gender and evaluation of leaders: A meta-analysis. *Psychological Bulletin, 111,* 3–22.

Eagly, A. H., & Mladinic, A. (1993). Are people prejudiced against women? Some answers from research on attitudes, gender stereotypes, and judgments of competence. In W. Strobe & M. Hewstone (Eds.), *European review of social psychology* (Vol. 5, pp. 1–35). New York: Wiley.

Eagly, A. H., & Steffen, V. J. (1984). Gender stereotypes stem from the distribution of women and men into social roles. *Journal of Personality and Social Psychology, 46,* 735–754.

Eagly, A. H., & Steffen, V. J. (1986). Gender stereotypes, occupational roles, and beliefs about part-time employees. *Psychology Women Quarterly, 10,* 252–262.

Eagly, A. H., Wood, W., & Diekman, A. B. (2000). Social role theory of sex differences and similarities: A current appraisal. In T. Eckes & H. M. Trautner (Eds.), *The developmental social psychology of gender* (pp. 123–174). Mahwah, NJ: Lawrence Erlbaum.

Eagly, A. H., Wood, W., & Johannesen-Schmidt, M. C. (2000). Social role theory of sex differences and similarities: A current appraisal. In A. H. Eagly, T.

Eckes, A. E. Beall, R. J. Sternberg, & H. M. Trautner (Eds.), *The developmental social psychology* (pp. 123–174). Mahwah, NJ: Erlbaum.

Eccles, J. S. (1989). Bringing young women to math and science. In M. Crawford & M. Gentry (Eds.), *Gender and thought: Psychological perspectives* (pp. 36–58). New York: Springer-Verlag.

Eckes, T. (2002). Paternalistic and envious gender stereotypes: Testing predictions from the stereotype content model. *Sex Roles, 47*(3–4), 99–114.

Edelman, L. B. (1992). Legal ambiguity and symbolic structures: Organizational mediation of civil rights law. *American Journal of Sociology, 97,* 1531–1576.

Edelman, L. B., Erlanger, H. S., & Lande, J. (1993). Internal dispute resolution: The transformation of civil rights in the workplace. *Law and Society Review, 27*(3), 497–534.

Edelman, L. B., & Petterson, S. M. (1999). Symbols and substance in organizational response to civil rights law. *Research in Social Stratification and Mobility, 17,* 107–135.

Edelman, L. B., Uggen, C., & Erlanger, H. S. (1999). The endogeneity of legal regulation: Grievance procedures as rational myth. *American Journal of Sociology, 105,* 406–454.

EEOC v. Waffle House, 534 U.S. 279 (2002).

Eighth Circuit Gender Fairness Task Force. (1997). Final report and recommendations of the Eighth Circuit Gender Fairness Task Force. *Creighton Law Review, 31,* 9–181.

Eller, M. E. (1990). Sexual harassment: Prevention, not protection. *Cornell Hotel and Restaurant Administration Quarterly, 30,* 84–89.

Ellison v. Brady, 924 F.2d 872 (9th Cir. 1991).

England, P. (1982). The failure of human capital theory to explain occupational sex segregation. *Journal of Human Resources* (Spring), 358–70.

England, P. (1992). *Comparable worth: Theories and evidence.* New York: Aldine.

England, P., Budig, M. J., & Folbre, N. (2002). The wages of virtue: The relative pay of care work. *Social Problems, 49,* 455–473.

England, P., & Farkas, G. (1985). *Households, employment, and gender: A social, economic and demographic view.* New York: Aldine.

England, P., Hermsen, J. M., & Cotter, D. A. (2000). The devaluation of women's work: A comment on Tam. *American Journal of Sociology, 105,* 1741–1751.

Epstein, C. F., Pfahlert, J., Oglensky, B., Saute, R., & Seron, C. (1999). *The part-time paradox: Time norms, professional lives, family and gender.* New York: Routledge.

Equal Employment Opportunity Commission. (1999). *Enforcement guidance on vicarious employer liability for unlawful harassment by supervisors,* EEOC Notice No. 915–002, 14.

Equal Employment Opportunity Commission. (2001, February 13). *State and local agencies.* Retrieved July 15, 2005, from http://www.eeoc.gov/employers/stateandlocal.html

Equal Employment Opportunity Commission. (2003, November 19). *History of the EEOC mediation program.* Retrieved July 15, 2005, from http://www. eeoc.gov/mediate/history.html

Equal Employment Opportunity Commission. (2004, November 1). *Facts about mediation.* Retrieved May 27, 2005, from http://www.eeoc.gov/mediate. facts.html

Equal Employment Opportunity Commission. (2004). *Glass ceilings: The status of women as officials and managers in the private sector.* Washington, DC: EEO.

Equal Employment Opportunity Commission. (2005, January 27). *All statutes FY 1992–2004.* Retrieved June 13, 2006, from http://www.eeoc.gov/ stats/all.html

Equal Employment Opportunity Commission. (2005, January 27). *Sex-based charges FY 1992–2005.* Retrieved July 15, 2005, from http://www.eeoc.gov/ stats/sex.html

Equal Employment Opportunity Commission. (2005, March 21). *Questions and answers about mediation.* Retrieved June 13, 2006, from http://www.eeoc.gov/ mediate/mediation-qa.html

Equal Employment Opportunity Commission. (2005, April 22). *Litigation statistics, FY 1992–2004.* Retrieved July 15, 2005, from http://www.eeoc.gov/stats/ litigation.html

Equal Employment Opportunity Commission. (n.d.). *Charge statistics FY 1992–2005,* retrieved May 17, 2006, from http://www.eeoc.gov/stats/ charges.html

Equal Employment Opportunity Commission v. Dial Corporation (2002, September 17) WL 31061088, N. D. Ill.

Equal Employment Opportunity Commission (EEOC) v. Dial Corporation (2002, November 17). Northern District, Ill., No. 99 C 3356.

Equal Employment Opportunity Commission, Office of General Counsel (n.d.) *Fiscal year 2004 annual report.* Retrieved October 18, 2005, from http://www. eeoc.gov/litigation/04annrpt/index.html#IB4

Equal Pay Act of 1963, 29 U.S.C. §206 (d) (1996).

Estriecher, S. (2001). Saturns for rickshaws: The stakes in the debate over predispute arbitration agreements. *Ohio State Journal on Dispute Resolution, 16,* 559–570.

Evans, M. R. (2001). Women and mediation: Toward a formulation of an interdisciplinary empirical model to determine equity in dispute resolution. *Ohio State Journal on Dispute Resolution, 17,* 145–183.

Executive Order No. 8802, 3 C.F.R. §957 (1938–43 Comp.).

Ezold v. Wolf, Block, Schorr & Solis-Cohen, 983 F.2d 509 (3d Cir. 1992), *cert. denied,* 510 U.S. 826 (1993).

Faigman, D. L., Kaye, D. H., Saks, M. J., & Sanders, J. (2002). *Modern scientific evidence: The law and science of expert testimony.* St. Paul, MN: West Publishing Co.

Faigman, D. L., & Monahan, J. (2005). Psychological evidence at the dawn of the law's scientific age. *Annual Review of Psychology, 56,* 631–660.

Family and Medical Leave Act of 1993, 29 U.S.C. §2601–2654.

Faragher v. City of Boca Raton, 524 U.S. 775 (1998).

Farrell, W. (2005). *Why men earn more: The startling truth behind the pay gap and what women can do about it.* New York: American Management Association.

Federal Arbitration Act, 9 U.S.C.A. §2 et seq. (West 2003).

Fernandez, R. M., & Sosa, M. L. (2005). Gendering the job: Networks and recruitment at a call center. *American Journal of Sociology, 115,* 859–904.

Finkel, N. J. (2000). But it's not fair! Commonsense notions of unfairness. *Psychology, Public Policy and Law, 6,* 898–952.

Firefighters Local 93 v. City of Cleveland, 487 U.S. 501 (1986).

Fiske, A. P., Kitayama, S., Markus, J. R., & Nisbett, R. E. (1998). The cultural matrix of social psychology. In D. Gilbert, S. T. Fiske, & G. Lindzey (Eds.), *The handbook of social psychology* (4th ed., Vol. 2, pp. 915–981). Boston: McGraw Hill.

Fiske, S. (1993). Controlling other people: The impact of power on stereotyping. *American Psychologist, 48,* 621–628.

Fiske, S. (1998). Stereotyping, prejudice, and discrimination. In D. T. Gilbert, S. T. Fiske, & G. Lindzey (Eds.), *The handbook of social psychology* (4th ed., Vol. 2, pp. 357–411). Boston: McGraw-Hill.

Fiske, S. (2000). Interdependence and the reduction of prejudice. In S. Oskamp (Ed.), *Reducing prejudice and discrimination* (pp. 115–135). Mahwah, NJ: Erlbaum.

Fiske, S., Bersoff, D. N., Borgida, E., Deaux, K., & Heilman, M. E. (1991). Social science research on trial: Use of sex stereotyping research in Price-Waterhouse v. Hopkins. *American Psychologist, 46,* 1049–1060.

Fiske, S., & Borgida, E. (1999). Social framework analysis as expert testimony in sexual harassment suits. In S. Estreicher (Ed.), *Sexual harassment in the workplace* (pp. 575–583). Boston: Kluwer Law International.

Fiske, S., Cuddy, A. J. C., Glick, P., & Xu, J. (2002). A model of (often mixed) stereotype content: Competence and warmth respectively follow from perceived status and competition. *Journal of Personality and Social Psychology, 82,* 878–902.

Fiske, S., & Glick, P. (1995). Ambivalence and stereotypes cause sexual harassment: A theory with implications for organizational change. *Journal of Social Issues, 51,* 97–115.

Fiske, S., & Neuberg, S. L. (1990). A continuum of impression formation, from category-based to individuating processes: Influences of information and motivation on attention and interpretation. In M. P. Zanna (Ed.), *Advances in experimental social psychology* (Vol. 23, pp. 1–74). New York: Academic Press.

Fiske, S., & Ruscher, J. B. (1993). Negative interdependence and prejudice: Whence the affect? In D. M. Mackie & D. L. Hamilton (Eds.), *Affect, cognition, and stereotyping: Interactive processes in group perception* (pp. 239–268). San Diego, CA: Academic Press.

Fiske, S., & Stevens, L. E. (1993). What's so special about sex? Gender stereotyping and discrimination. In S. Oskamp & M. Costanzo (Eds.), *Gender issues in contemporary society: Applied social psychology annual* (pp. 173–196). Newbury Park, CA: Sage.

Fiske, S., Xu, J., Cuddy, A. C., & Glick, P. (1999). (Dis)respecting versus (dis)liking: Status and interdependence predict ambivalent stereotypes of competence and warmth. *Journal of Social Issues, 55*(3), 473–489.

Fitzgerald, L. F. (1993). Sexual harassment: Violence against women in the workplace. *American Psychologist, 48,* 1070–1076.

Fitzgerald, L. F., & Shullman, S. L. (1993). Sexual harassment: A research analysis and agenda for the 90's. *Journal of Vocational Behavior, 42,* 5–29.

Fitzgerald, L. F., Swan, S., & Fischer, K. (1995). Why didn't she just report him? The psychological and legal implications of women's responses to sexual harassment. *Journal of Social Issues, 51,* 117–138.

Folger, R., & Cropanzano, R. (1998). *Organizational justice and human resource management.* Thousand Oaks, CA: Sage.

Foschi, M. (2000). Double standards for competence: Theory and research. *Annual Review of Sociology, 26,* 21–42.

Franke, K. M. (1997). What's wrong with sexual harassment? *Stanford Law Review, 49,* 691–772.

Friesen, J. (1993). Alternative economic perspectives on the use of labor market policies to redress the gender gap in compensation. *Georgetown Law Journal, 82,* 31–68.

Frieze, I. H., Olson, J. E., & Russell, J. (1991). Attractiveness and income for men and women in management. *Journal of Applied Social Psychology, 21,* 1039–1057.

Fuchs, V. (1986, April). Sex differences in economic well-being. *Science, 25,* 459–464.

Fuegen, K., Biernat, M., Haines, E., & Deaux, K. (2004). Mothers and fathers in the workplace: How parental status influences judgments of job-related competence. *Journal of Social Issues, 60*(4), 737–754.

Fuller, S. R., Edelman, L. B., & Marusik, S. F. (2000). Legal readings: Employee interpretation and mobilization of law. *Academy of Management Review, 25,* 200–216.

Gaertner, S. L. & Dovidio, J. F. (1986). The aversive form of racism. In J. F. Dovidio, & S. L. Gaertner (Eds.), *Prejudice, discrimination, and racism* (pp. 61–89). San Diego: Academic Press.

Galinsky, A. D., Gruenfeld, D. H., & Magee, J. C. (2003). From power to action. *Journal of Personality and Social Psychology, 85,* 453–466.

Ganong, L. H., & Coleman, M. (1995). The content of mother stereotypes. *Sex Roles, 32,* 495–512.

Garcia, D. M., Reser, A. H., Amo, R. B., Redersdorff, S., & Branscombe, N. R. (2005). Perceivers' responses to in-group and out-group members who blame a negative outcome on discrimination. *Personality and Social Psychology Journal, 31,* 769–780.

Gazeley, B. J. (1997). Venus, Mars, and the law: On mediation of sexual harassment cases. *Willamette Law Review, 33,* 605–647.

General Accounting Office. (October 2003). *Women's earnings: Work patterns partially explain difference between men's and women's earnings.* GAO-04-35. Washington, DC: U.S. Government Printing Office.

General Accounting Office. (2004). *Report to Congressional requesters – Gender issues: Women's participation in the sciences has increased, but agencies need to do more to ensure compliance with Title IX.* Washington, DC: General Accounting Office.

General Telephone Company of the Southwest v. Falcon, 457 U.S. 147, 161 (1982).

Georgen-Saad v. Texas Mutual Insurance Co., 195 F. Supp. 2d 853 (W. D. Tex. 2002).

Giglio, P. (2004). Rethinking the hours. *Legal Times*, 33.

Gill, M. J. (2004). When information does not deter stereotyping: Prescriptive stereotypes foster bias under conditions that deter descriptive stereotyping. *Journal of Experimental Social Psychology, 40*, 619–632.

Gilmer v. Interstate/Johnson Lane Corp., 500 U.S. 20 (1991).

Glick, P. (1991). Trait-based and sex-based discrimination in occupational prestige, occupational salary, and hiring. *Sex Roles, 25*, 351–378.

Glick, P., Diebold, J., Bailey-Werner, B., & Zhu, L. (1997). The two faces of Adam: Ambivalent sexism and polarized attitudes toward women. *Personality and Social Psychology Bulletin, 23*, 1323–1334.

Glick, P., & Fiske, S. T. (1996). The Ambivalent Sexism Inventory: Differentiating hostile and benevolent sexism. *Journal of Personality and Social Psychology, 70*, 491–512.

Glick, P., & Fiske S. T. (2001). Ambivalent sexism. In M. P. Zanna (Ed.), *Advances in experimental social psychology* (Vol. 33, pp. 115–188). Thousand Oaks, CA: Academic Press.

Glick, P., Fiske, S. T., et al. (2000). Beyond prejudice as simple antipathy: Hostile and benevolent sexism across cultures. *Journal of Personality and Social Psychology, 79*, 763–775.

Glick, P., Larsen, S., Johnson, C., & Branstiter, H. (2005). Evaluations of sexy women in low and high status jobs. *Psychology of Women Quarterly, 29*, 389–395.

Glick, P., Wilk, K., & Perreault, M. (1995). Images of occupations: Components of gender and status in occupational stereotypes. *Sex Roles, 32*, 564–582.

Glick, P., Zion, C., & Nelson, C. (1988). What mediates sex discrimination in hiring decisions? *Journal of Personality and Social Psychology, 55*, 178–186.

Godfrey v. Perkin-Elmer Corp., 794 F.Supp. 1179 (D.N.H. 1992).

Goldin, C. (1995). *Career and family: College women look to the past.* Working Paper 5188. Cambridge, MA: National Bureau of Economic Research.

Goldman, B. M., Paddock, E. L., & Cropanzano, R. (2004). A transformational model of legal-claiming. *Journal of Managerial Issues, 16*, 417–441.

Goodwin, S. A., Fiske, S. T., Rosen, L. D., & Rosenthal, A. M. (2002). The eye of the beholder: Romantic goals and impression biases. *Journal of Experimental Social Psychology, 38*, 232–241.

Gorman, E. H. (2005). Gender stereotypes, same-gender preferences, and organizational variation in the hiring of women: Evidence from law firms. *American Sociological Review*, *70*(4), 702–728.

Graham, M. E., & Hotchkiss, J. L. (2002). A systematic assessment of employer equal employment opportunity efforts as a means of reducing the gender earnings gap. *Cornell Journal of Law and Public Policy*, *12*(1), 169–201.

Green, M. Z. (2000). Debunking the myth of employer advantage from using mandatory arbitration for discrimination claims. *Rutgers Law Journal*, *31*, 399–471.

Green, T. K. (2005). Work culture and discrimination. *California Law Review*, *93*, 623–684.

Greenberg, J. (1990). Organizational justice: Yesterday, today, and tomorrow. *Journal of Management*, *16*, 606–613.

Greenberg, J., & McCarty, C. (1990). The interpersonal aspects of procedural justice: A new perspective on pay fairness. *Labor Law Journal*, *41*, 580–586.

Greenhouse, S. (February 16, 2003). Wal-Mart faces lawsuit over sex discrimination. *The New York Times*, p. 18.

Griggs v. Duke Power Co., 401 U.S. 424 (1971).

Gross S. R., & Syverud, K. D. (1996). Don't try: Civil jury verdicts in a system geared to settlement. *UCLA Law Review*, *4*, 1–64.

Grossman, J. L. (2003). The culture of compliance: The final triumph of form over substance in sexual harassment law. *Harvard Women's Law Journal*, *26*, 3–75.

Gruber, J. E. (1989). How women handle sexual harassment: A literature review. *Sociology and Social Research*, *74*, 3–9.

Gruber, J. E. (1995). Women's response to sexual harassment: A multivariate analysis. *Basic and Applied Social Psychology*, *17*, 543–562.

Gruber, J. E., & Bjorn, L. (1986). Women's response to sexual harassment: An analysis of sociocultural, organizational, and personal resource models. *Social Science Quarterly*, *67*, 814–825.

Gruber, J. E., & Smith, M. D. (1995). Women's response to sexual harassment: A multivariate analysis. *Basic and Applied Social Psychology*, *17*, 543–562.

Gutek, B. A. (1985). *Sex and the workplace: The impact of sexual behavior and harassment on women, men, and organization.* San Francisco: Jossey-Bass.

Gutek, B. A. (1997). Sexual harassment policy initiatives. In W. O'Donohue (Ed.), *Sexual harassment: Theory, research, treatment* (pp. 185–198). New York: Allyn & Bacon.

Gutek, B. A., & Done, R. (2001). Sexual harassment. In R. K. Unger (Ed.), *Handbook of the psychology of women and gender* (pp. 367–387). New York: Wiley.

Gutek, B. A., & Done, R. (2005). What influences evaluations of sexual harassment policy effectiveness? University of Arizona, unpublished manuscript.

Gutek, B. A., Murphy, R. O., & Douma, B. (2004). A review and critique of the Sexual Experiences Questionnaire (SEQ). *Law and Human Behavior*, *28*, 457–482.

Gutek, B. A., O'Connor, M., Melançon, R., Stockdale, M., Geer, T. M., & Done, R. S. (1999). The utility of the reasonable woman standard in hostile environment sexual harassment cases: A multimethod, multistudy examination. *Psychology, Public Policy and the Law, 5*(3), 596–629.

Gutek, B. A., & Stockdale, M. S. (2005). Sex discrimination in employment. In F. J. Landy (Ed.), *Employment discrimination litigation: Behavioral, quantitative, and legal perspectives* (pp. 229–255). San Francisco: Jossey-Bass.

Guthrie, C., & Levin, J. (1998). "Party satisfaction" perspective on comprehensive mediation statute. *Ohio State Journal of Dispute Resolution, 13,* 885–907.

Hailes v. United Air Lines, 464 F.2d 1006 (5th Cir. 1972).

Hall v. Consolidated Freightways Corp. of Delaware, 337 F.3d 669 (6th Cir. 2003).

Hall v. State Farm. Ins. Co., 18 F. Supp. 2d 751 (E.D. Mich. 1998).

Hallberg v. Aristech Chemical Corp. (1999). Discussed in Ann Belser, Mommy Track Wins: $3 Million Awarded to Mom Denied Promotion, *Pittsburgh Post-Gazette,* April 30, 1999, at B1.

Halligan v. Piper Jaffray, Inc., 148 F.3d 197 (2d Cir. 1998).

Halpert, J. A., & Burg, J. H. (1997). Mixed messages: Co-worker responses to the pregnant employee. *Journal of Business and Psychology, 12,* 241–253.

Halpert, J. A., Wilson, M. L., & Hickman, J. L. (1993). Pregnancy as a source of bias in performance appraisals. *Journal of Organizational Behavior, 14*(7), 649–663.

Harkavay, J. (1999). Privatizing workplace justice: The advent of mediation in resolving sexual harassment disputes. *Wake Forest Law Review, 34,* 135–169.

Harris v. Forklift Systems, Inc., 510 U.S. 17 (1993).

Hartmann, H. I., & Aaronson, S. (1994). Pay equity and women's wage increases: Success in the states, a model for the nation. *Duke Journal of Gender Law and Policy, 1,* 69–87.

Hawai'i Civil Rights Commission. Fair employment practices agencies in other states. Retrieved May 27, 2005, from http://www.state.hi.us/here/OtherStates.htm

Hazelwood School District v. United States, 433 U.S. 299 (1977).

Hebl, M. R., King, E., Glick, P., Singletary, S. L., & Kazama, S. M. (Accepted pending revisions). Hostile and benevolent discrimination toward pregnant women: Complementary interpersonal punishments and rewards that maintain traditional roles. *Journal of Applied Psychology.*

Heilman, M. E. (1983). Sex bias in work settings: The lack of fit model. *Research in Organizational Behavior, 5,* 269–298.

Heilman, M. E. (1984). Information as a deterrent against sex discrimination: The effects of sex and information type on preliminary employment decisions. *Organizational Behavior and Human Performance, 33,* 174–186.

Heilman, M. E. (2001). Description and prescription: How gender stereotypes prevent women's ascent up the organizational ladder. *Journal of Social Issues, 57*(4), 657–674.

Heilman, M. E., & Block, C. J. (1989). Has anything changed? Current characterizations of men, women, and managers. *Journal of Applied Psychology, 74*, 935–942.

Heilman, M. E., Martell, R. F., & Simon, M. C. (1998). The vagaries of sex bias: Conditions regulating the underevaluation, equivaluation, and overvaluation of female job applicants. *Organizational Behavior and Human Decision Processes, 41*, 98–110.

Heilman, M. E., & Stopek, M. H. (1985). Being attractive, advantage or disadvantage? Performance-based evaluations and recommended personnel actions as a function of appearance, sex, and job type. *Organizational Behavior and Human Decision Processes, 35*, 202–215.

Heim v. State of Utah, 8 F. 3d 1541 (10th Cir. 1993).

Hersch, J. (2003). The new labor market for lawyers: Will female lawyers still earn less? *Cardozo Women's Law Journal, 10*(1), 1–59.

Hewlett, S. A. (2002). *Creating a life: Professional women and the quest for children.* New York: Talk Miramax Books.

Hewlett, S. A., & Luce, C. B. (2005). Off-ramps and on-ramps: Keeping talented women on the road to success. *Harvard Business Review, 83*(3), 43–54.

Hill, E. (2003). Due process at low cost: An empirical study of employment arbitration under the auspices of the American Arbitration Association. *Ohio State Journal on Dispute Resolution, 18*, 777–827.

Hishon v. King & Spalding, 467 U.S. 69 (1984).

Hoffman, C., & Hurst, N. (1990). Gender stereotypes: Perception or rationalization? *Journal of Personality and Social Psychology, 58*, 197–208.

Hoffman, E. A. (2005). Dispute resolution in a worker cooperative: Formal procedures and procedural justice. *Law and Society Review, 39*, 51–82.

Hoffman-LaRoche, Inc. v. Zeltwanger, 144 S.W.3d 438 (Tex. 2004).

Holmes, S. (2004, April 26). A new black eye for Boeing? *Business Week*, pp. 90–92.

Holmes, S., & France, M. (2004, June 28). Coverup at Boeing? *Business Week.* Retrieved June 10, 2006, from www.businessweek.com/print/magazine/content/04_26/b3889088.htm

Hooters of America, Inc. v. Phillips, 173 F.3d 933 (4th Cir. 1999).

Hopkins v. Price Waterhouse, 618 F. Supp. 1109 (D.C.D.C., 1985).

Hopkins v. Price Waterhouse, 920 F.2d 967 (C.A.D.C., 1990).

Hopkins, A. B. (1996). *So ordered: Making partner the hard way.* Amherst, MA: University of Massachusetts Press.

Howard, W. M. (1995, Oct.–Dec.). Arbitrating claims of employment discrimination: What really does happen? What really should happen? *Dispute Resolution Journal, 50*, 40–50.

Huang, W. R. (1997). Gender differences in the earnings of lawyers. *Columbia Journal of Law and Social Problems, 30*, 267–325.

Huffman, M. L., & Torres, L. (2002). It's not only "who you know" that matters: Gender, personal contacts and job lead quality. *Gender and Society, 16*, 793–813.

Hulin, C. L., Fitzgerald, L. F., & Drasgow, F. (1996). Organizational influences on sexual harassment. In M. S. Stockdale (Ed.), *Sexual harassment in the workplace: Perspectives, frontiers, and response strategies* (pp. 127–150). Thousand Oaks, CA: Sage.

Hunt, J. S., Borgida, E., Kelly, K. A., & Burgess, D. (2002). Gender stereotyping: Scientific status. In D. L. Faigman, D. H. Kaye, M. J. Saks, & J. Sanders (Eds.), *Modern scientific evidence: The law and science of expert testimony* (pp. 374–426). St. Paul, MN: West Publishing Co.

Hyde, J. S. (2005). The gender similarities hypothesis. *American Psychologist, 60*(6), 581–592.

Impact Fund, The (2005). *Dukes v. Wal-Mart* statistical charts: Percent women in store management and hourly Supervisors, 2001. Retrieved November 26, 2005, from http://www.WalMartclass.com/staticdata/charts/table7.html; http://www.WalMartclass.com/staticdata/WalMartclass/brief2.html

Institute for Women's Policy Research (IWPR). (2004). *Women's economic status in the states: Wide disparities by race, ethnicity, and region.* Washington, DC: Institute for Women's Policy Research.

Institute for Women's Policy Research. (2005). *The gender wage ratio: Women's and men's earnings.* IWPR Fact Sheet #C350. Washington, DC: Institute for Women's Policy Research.

Irvine, M. (1993). Mediation: Is it inappropriate for sexual harassment grievances? *Ohio State Journal on Dispute Resolution, 9,* 27–53.

Jackson, L. M., Esses, V. M., & Burris, C. T. (2001). Contemporary sexism and discrimination: The importance of respect for men and women. *Personality and Social Psychology Bulletin, 27*(1), 48–61.

Jacobs, J. E., Davis-Kean, P., Bleeker, M., Eccles, J. S., & Malanchuck, O. (2005). "I can, but I don't want to": The impact of parents, interests, and activities on gender differences in math. In A. M. Gallagher & J. C. Kaufman (Eds.), *Gender differences in mathematics* (pp. 246–263). Cambridge: Cambridge University Press.

James, J. (2004). The equal pay act in the courts: A de facto white-collar exemption. *New York University Law Review, 79*(5), 1873–1901.

Joint Motion for Entry of Consent Decree, EEOC v. Mitsubishi Motor Mfg. of America (C.D. Ill. June 10, 1998) (No. 96–1192). Retrieved July 5, 2006, from www.eeoc.gov/policy/docs/mmma.html

Jones, G. T. (2002). Testing for structural change in legal doctrine: An empirical look at the plaintiff's decision to litigate employment disputes a decade after the Civil Rights Act of 1991. *Georgia State University Law Review, 18,* 997–1029.

Jost, J. T., & Hunyady, O. (2002). The psychology of system justification and the palliative function of ideology. *European Review of Social Psychology, 13,* 126–128.

Kaiser, C. R., & Miller, C. T. (2001a). Reacting to impending discrimination: Compensation for prejudice and attributions to discrimination. *Personality and Social Psychology Bulletin, 27,* 1357–1367.

Kaiser, C. R., & Miller, C. T. (2001b). Stop complaining! The social costs of making attributions of discrimination. *Personality and Social Psychology Bulletin, 27,* 254–263.

Kaiser, C. R., & Miller, C. T. (2003). Derogating the victim: The interpersonal consequences of blaming events on discrimination. *Group Processes and Intergroup Relations, 6,* 227–237.

Kalev, A. & Dobbin, F. (2006). Enforcement of civil rights in private workplaces: Compliance reviews and lawsuits before and after Reagan. *Law and Social Inquiry, 31*(4) (December).

Kalev, A., Dobbin, F., & Kelly, E. (2005a). *Best practices or best guesses? What works in diversity management.* Unpublished paper on file with author, Department of Sociology, Harvard University.

Kalev, A., Dobbin, F., & Kelly, E. (2005b). *Two to tango: Affirmative action, diversity programs and women and African-Americans in management.* Unpublished paper, Department of Sociology, Harvard University.

Kanter, R. M. (1977). *Men and women of the corporation.* New York: Basic Books.

Kaster, J. (2003, January 24). Oral comments of Jim Kaster, Plaintiff Shirleen Walsh's Attorney, at Symposium, *The New Glass Ceiling: Litigating Bias Against Parents at Work.* American University, Washington College of the Law, Washington, DC (unpublished symposium presentations, on file with *American University Journal of Gender, Social Policy and the Law*).

Kelly, E., & Dobbin, F. (1999). Civil rights law at work: Sex discrimination and the rise of maternity leave policies. *American Journal of Sociology, 105,* 455–492.

Kennelly, I. (1999). "That single-mother element": How white employers typify black women. *Gender and Society, 13*(2), 168–192.

Kessler, L. T. (2001). The attachment gap: Employment discrimination law, women's cultural caregiving, and the limits of economic and liberal legal theory. *University of Michigan Journal of Law Reform, 34*(3), 371–468.

Kidder, L. H., Lafleur, R. A., & Wells, C. V. (1995). Recalling harassment, reconstructing experience. *Journal of Social Issues, 51,* 53–67.

Kief, S. C. (2000). Individual liability of supervisors, managers, officers or co-employees for discriminatory actions under state civil rights act. *American Law Reports 5th, 83,* 1–102.

Kilbourne, B. S., England, P., Farkas, G., Beron, K., & Weir, D. (1994). Returns to skill, compensating differentials, and gender bias: Effects of occupational characteristics on the wages of white women and men. *American Journal of Sociology, 100,* 689–719.

Kimmel, E., Harlow, D. N., & Topping, M. (1979). Training women for administrative roles: A positive response to Title IX. *Educational Leadership, 37,* 229–231.

King, R. (1997, April 27). Bias lawsuit has LA roots. *New Orleans Times-Picayune.*

Knapp, D. E., Faley, R. H., Ekeberg, S. E., & Dubois, C. L. Z. (1997). Determinants of target responses to sexual harassment: A conceptual framework. *Academy of Management Review, 22,* 687–729.

Knussman v. Maryland, 65 F. Supp. 2d 353 (D. Md. 1999), aff'd in part, vacated in part, and remanded by 272 F.3d 625 (4th Cir. 2001).

Kobrynowicz, D., & Biernat, M. (1997). Decoding subjective evaluations: How stereotypes provide shifting standards. *Journal of Experimental Psychology, 33,* 579–601.

Kolstad v. American Dental Association, 527 U.S. 526 (1999).

Konrad, A. M., & Linnehan, F. (1995a). Race and sex differences in line managers' reactions to equal employment opportunity and affirmative action interventions. *Group and Organizational Management, 20,* 409–39.

Konrad, A. M., & Linnehan, F. (1995b). Formalized HRM structures: Coordinating equal employment opportunity or concealing organizational practices? *Academy of Management Journal, 38,* 787–820.

Korn/Ferry International (2001). *What women want in business: A survey of executives and entrepreneurs.* New York: Korn Ferry International.

Kotter, J., & Heskett, J. (1992). *Corporate culture and performance.* New York: The Free Press.

Kowalski, R. M. (1996). Complaints and complaining: Functions, antecedents, and consequences. *Psychological Bulletin, 119,* 179–196.

Krieger, L. H. (1995). The content of our categories: A cognitive bias approach to discrimination and equal employment opportunity. *Stanford Law Review, 47,* 1161–1248.

Krieger, L. H. (1998). Civil rights perestroika: Intergroup relations after affirmative action. *California Law Review, 86,* 1251–1333.

Krieger, L. H. (2004). The intuitive psychologist behind the bench: Models of gender bias in social psychology and employment discrimination law. *Journal of Social Issues, 60,* 835–848.

Kryeski v. Schott Glass Technologies, Inc., 426 Pa.Super. 105, A.2d 595 (1993).

Lacy, D. A. (2002). Alternative dispute resolution or appropriate dispute resolution: Will ADR help or hinder the EEOC complaint process? *University of Detroit Mercy Law Review, 80,* 31–59.

Landrum, M. A., & Trongard, D. A. (1998). Judicial marphallaxis: Mandatory arbitration of statutory rights. *William Mitchell Law Review, 24,* 345–406.

Langlois, J. H., Kalakanis, L., Rubenstein, A. J., Larson, A., Hallam, M., & Smoot, M. (2000). Maxims or myths of beauty: A meta-analysis and theoretical review. *Psychological Bulletin, 26,* 390–423.

Latanè, B. (1981). The psychology of social impact. *American Psychologist, 36,* 343–356.

Lemons v. City of Denver, 17 Fair Employment Practice Cases 906, aff'd, Lemons v. City of Denver, 620 F. 2d 228 (10th Cir. 1978).

Lenhart, S. A., & Shrier, D. K. (1996). Potential costs and benefits of sexual harassment litigation. *Psychiatric Annals, 26,* 132–138.

Lentz, B. F., & Laband, D. N. (1995). *Sex discrimination in the legal profession.* Westport, CT: Quorum Books.

Leonard, J. S. (1984). The impact of affirmative action on employment. *Journal of Labor Economics, 2,* 439–463.

Leonard, J. S. (1985). What promises are worth: The impact of affirmative action goals. *Journal of Human Resources, 20,* 3–20.

Leonard, J. S. (1986). What was affirmative action? *American Economic Review, 76,* 359–363.

Leonard, J. S. (1989a). The changing face of employees and employment regulation. *California Management Review, 31,* 29–38.

Leonard, J. S. (1989b). Women and affirmative action. *Journal of Economic Perspectives, 3,* 61–75.

Leonard, J. S. (1990). The impact of affirmative action regulation and equal employment law on black employment. *Journal of Economic Perspectives, 4,* 47–63.

Lerner, M. J. (1980). *The belief in a just world: A fundamental delusion.* New York: Plenum.

Lerner, M., & Miller, D. T. (1978). Just world research and the attribution process: Looking back and ahead. *Psychological Bulletin, 85*(5), 1030–1051.

Letter of Jay Allen, Wal-Mart Senior Vice President for Corporate Affairs (2003, September 10). *Washington Post,* p. A18.

Lind, E. A., Greenberg, J., Scott, K. S., & Welchans, T. D. (2000). The winding road from employee to complainant: Situational and psychological determinants of wrongful-termination claims. *Administrative Science Quarterly, 45,* 557–590.

Lind, E. A., & Tyler, T. R. (1988). *The social psychology of procedural justice.* New York: Plenum.

Lindemann, B., & Grossman, P. (1996). *Employment discrimination law* (3rd ed.). Washington, DC: BNA Books.

Linebaugh v. Sheraton Michigan Corp., 198 Mich.App. 335 (1993).

Lipsett v. University of Puerto Rico (1988). 864 F.2d 881, 889, n.19, 1st Cir.

Liu v. Amway Corporation, 347 F.3d 1125 (9th Cir. 2003).

Livingston, J. A. (1982). Responses to sexual harassment on the job: Legal, organizational, and individual actions. *Journal of Social Issues, 38,* 5–22.

Locksley, A., Borgida, E., Brekke, N., & Hepburn, C. (1980). Sex stereotypes and social judgment. *Journal of Personality and Social Psychology, 39,* 821–831.

Long, A. B. (2006). "If the train should jump the track . . .": Divergent interpretations of state and federal employment discrimination statutes. *Georgia Law Review, 40,* 469–557.

Lord, C. G., Saenz, D. S., & Godfrey, D. K. (1987). Effects of perceived scrutiny on participant memory for social interactions. *Journal of Experimental Social Psychology, 23,* 498–517.

Los Angeles Dept. of Water & Power v. Manhart, 435 U.S. 702 (1978).

Lunsford, J. L. (2004, July 19). Boeing to change pay plan to settle sex-bias lawsuit. *The Wall Street Journal,* p. B2.

Lust v. Sealy, 383 F.3d 580 (7th Cir. 2004).

Maass, A., Cadinu, M., Guarnieri, G., & Grasselli, A. (2003). Sexual harassment under social identity threat: The computer harassment paradigm. *Journal of Personality and Social Psychology, 85,* 853–870.

MacKinnon, C. A. (2001). *Sex equality*. New York: Foundation Press.

Magnuson v. Peak Technical Services, Inc., 808 F.Supp. 500 (E.D. Va. 1992).

Major, B., Gramzow, R. H., McCoy, S. K., Levin, S., Schmader, T., & Sidanius, J. (2002). Perceiving personal discrimination: The role of group status and legitimizing ideology. *Journal of Personality and Social Psychology*, *82*, 269–282.

Major, B., & Vick, S. B. (2005). The psychological impact of prejudice. In J. F. Dovidio, P. Glick, & L. A. Rudman (Eds.), *On the nature of prejudice: Fifty years after Allport* (pp. 244–261). Malden, MA: Blackwell.

Maltby, L. L. (2003). Employment arbitration and workplace justice. *University of San Francisco Law Review*, *38*, 105–118.

Marshall, A.-M. (2005). Idle rights: Employees' rights consciousness and the construction of sexual harassment policies. *Law and Society Review*, *39*, 83–123.

Martini v. Federal Nat'l Mortgage Ass'n, 178 F.3d 1336 (D.C. Cir. 1999).

Massachusetts Institute of Technology. (1999). *A study on the status of women faculty in science at MIT*. Boston, MA: Massachusetts Institute of Technology.

Maume, D. J., Jr. (1999). Glass ceilings and glass escalators: Occupational segregation and race and sex differences in managerial promotions. *Work and Occupations*, *26*, 483–509.

McCann, M. W. (1994). *Rights at work*. Chicago, IL: University of Chicago Press.

McCue, K. (1996). Promotions and wage growth. *Journal of Labor Economics*, *14*(2), 175–209.

McDermott, E. P., et al. (2001, August 1). *The EEOC mediation program: Mediators' perspective on the parties, processes, and outcomes*. Retrieved February 10, 2005, from http://www.eeoc.gov/mediate/mcdfinal.html

McDermott, E. P., & Obar, R. (2004). "What's going on" in mediation: An empirical analysis of the influence of a mediator's decision style on party satisfaction and monetary benefit. *Harvard Negotiation Law Review*, *9*, 75–113.

McGinley, A. C. (2000). ¡Viva la evolucion!: Recognizing unconscious motive in Title VII. *Cornell Journal of Law and Public Policy*, *9*, 415–492.

McGrath, M., Driscoll, M., & Gross, M. (2005). *Back in the game: Returning to business after a hiatus; experiences and recommendations for women, employers, and universities*. Philadelphia, PA: Wharton Center for Leadership and Change and the Forte Foundation.

McIlwee, J. S., & Robinson, J. G. (1992). *Women in engineering: Gender, power, and workplace culture*. Albany, NY: SUNY Press.

McKenzie-Mohr, D., & Zanna, M. P. (1990) Treating women as sexual objects: Look to the (gender schematic) male who has viewed pornography. *Personality and Social Psychology Bulletin*, *16*, 296–308.

McKinney, K. (1990). Sexual harassment by university faculty by colleagues and students. *Sex Roles*, *23*, 421–438.

McPherson, J. M., Smith-Lovin, L., & Cook, J. M. (2001). Birds of a feather: Homophily in social networks. *Annual Review of Sociology*, *27*, 415–444.

Meritor Savings Bank, FSB v. Vinson, 477 U.S. 57 (1986).

Merle, R. (2005, March 8). Boeing CEO resigns over affair with subordinate. *The Washington Post*, p. A1.

Messick, D. M., Bloom, S., Boldizar, J. P., & Samuelson, C. D. (1985). Why we are fairer than others. *Journal of Experimental Social Psychology, 21*, 389–399.

Milgram, S. (1974). *Obedience to authority*. New York: Harper Perennial.

Mill, J. S. (2004). *Principles of Political Economy* (1848). Amherst, NY: Prometheus Books. (Original work published 1848.)

Millbrook v. IBP, Inc., 280 F.3d 1169, 1180–1181 (7th Cir. 2002).

Miller, R. C. (2001). Liability, under state law claims, of public and private schools and institutions of higher learning for teacher's, other employee's, or student's sexual relationship with, or sexual harassment or abuse of, student. *American Law Reports 5th, 86*, 1–57.

Mincer, J., & Polachek, S. (1974). Family investments in human capital: Earnings of women. *Journal of Political Economy, 82*(2, Part 2), S76–S108.

Montwieler, N. (1997). EEOC policy guidance reaffirms opposition to mandatory arbitration, *U.S. Law Week* (BNA), 66, 2055–2066.

Moore, C. W. (2003). *The mediation process: Practical strategies for resolving conflict*. San Francisco, CA: Jossey-Bass.

Morehouse v. Berkshire Gas Co., 989 F. Supp. 54 (D. Mass. 1997).

Morgan v. Hertz Corp., 542 F.Supp. 123 (1981).

Morrison v. Circuit City Stores, 317 F.3d 646, (6th Cir. 2003) (en banc).

Mory, M., & Pistilli, L. (2001). The failure of the family and medical leave act: Alternative proposals for contemporary American families. *Hofstra Labor and Employment Law Journal, 18*(2), 689–720.

Mowday, R. T. (1987). Equity theory and predictions in behavior in organizations. In R. Steers & L. Porter (Eds.), *Motivation and work behavior* (pp. 89–110). New York: McGraw-Hill.

Mullen, B. (1983). Operationalizing the effect of the group on the individual: A self-attention perspective. *Journal of Experimental Social Psychology, 19*, 295–322.

Munson, L. J., Miner, A. G., & Hulin, C. (2001). Labeling sexual harassment in the military: An extension and replication. *Journal of Applied Psychology, 86*, 293–303.

National Association of Law Placement (NALP). (2004). *Women and attorneys of color at law firms*. Washington, DC: NALP.

Nelson, R., & Bridges, W. (1999). *Legalizing gender inequality: Courts, markets, and unequal pay for women in America*. New York: Cambridge University Press.

Nevada Department of Human Resources v. Hibbs, 538 U.S. 721 (2003).

Nielsen, L. B., & Nelson, R. L. (2005). Rights realized? An empirical analysis of employment discrimination litigation as a claiming system. *Wisconsin Law Review*, 663–711.

Nieva, V. F., & Gutek, B. A. (1981). *Women and work: A psychological perspective*. New York: Praeger.

Nisbett, R. E., & Wilson, T. D. (1977). Telling more than we can know: Verbal reports on mental processes. *Psychological Review, 84,* 231–259.

Norton, M. I., Vandello, J. A., & Darley, J. M. (2004). Casuistry and social category bias. *Journal of Personality and Social Psychology, 87,* 817–831.

NOW v. Bank of California, 680 F.2d 1291 (9th Cir. 1982).

NOW v. Minnesota Mining & Mfg. Co., 11 Fair Empl. Prac. Cases 720 (D. Minn. 1975).

NOW v. Sperry Rand Corp., 457 F. Supp. 1338 (D. Conn. 1978).

O'Connor, M., Gutek, B. A., Stockdale, M., Geer, T. M., & Melançon, R. (2004). Explaining sexual harassment judgments: Looking beyond gender of the rater. *Law and Human Behavior, 28*(1), 9–27.

O'Connor, M., & Vallabhajosula, B. (2004). Sexual harassment in the workplace: A legal and psychological framework. In B. J. Cling (Ed.), *Sex, Violence and Women: A Psychology and Law Perspective* (pp. 115–147). New York: Guilford Press.

O'Connor, S. D. (2003). *The majesty of the law: Reflections of a Supreme Court justice.* New York: Random House.

Offerman, L. R., & Malamut, A. B. (2002). When leaders harass: The impact of target perceptions of organizational leadership and climate on harassment reporting and outcomes. *Journal of Applied Psychology, 87,* 885–893.

Olson, W. (1997). *The excuse factory: How employment law is paralyzing the American workplace.* New York: Free Press.

Online Merriam-Webster Unabridged Collegiate Dictionary (2005). Retrieved May 16, 2006, from http://unabridged.merriam-webster.com/noauth/mwlogin. php?return=/cgi-bin/collegiate?va=discrimination

O'Neill, J., & Polachek, S. (1993). Why the gender gap in wages narrowed in the 1980s. *Journal of Labor Economics, 11*(1), 205–228.

Outtz, J. L., & Landy, F. J. (2005). Concluding thoughts. In F. J. Landy (Ed.), *Employment discrimination litigation: Behavioral, quantitative, and legal perspectives* (pp. 575–590). San Francisco: Jossey-Bass.

Padavic, I., & Reskin, B. F. (2002). *Women and men at work.* Thousand Oaks, CA: Pine Forge Press.

Patton, P. A. (2005). Women lawyers: Their status, influence, and retention in the legal profession. *William and Mary Journal of Women and the Law, 11*(2), 173–194.

Peeters, G. (2002). From good and bad to can and must: Subjective necessity of acts associated with positively and negatively valued stimuli. *European Journal of Social Psychology, 32,* 125–136.

Pennsylvania State Police v. Suders, 542 U.S. 129 (2004).

Petersen, T., & Morgan, L. (1995). Separate and unequal: Occupation, establishment, sex segregation, and the gender wage gap. *American Journal of Sociology, 101,* 329–365.

Petersen, T., & Saporta, I. (2004). The opportunity structure for discrimination. *American Journal of Sociology, 109*(4), 852–901.

Pigat, J. D. R., & Jones, S. (2004). *Walking the talk: Creating a law firm culture where women succeed*. Chicago, IL: American Bar Association.

Poehlman, T. A., Uhlmann, E., Greenwald, A. G., & Banaji, M. R. (submitted for publication). Understanding and using the Implicit Association Test: III. Meta-analysis of predictive validity.

Polachek, S. W. (1981). Occupational self-selection: A human capital approach to sex differences in occupational structure. *Review of Economics and Statistics, 63*(1), 60–69.

Policy Changes, Aggressive Enforcement, Will Mark Next Term at EEOC, Thomas Says. (1984, November 15). *Daily Lab. Rep. (BNA), 221,* p. A-6.

Portraits 9/11/01: The collected "Portraits of Grief" from The New York Times (2002). New York: Times Books.

Powell, G. N., & Butterfield, D. A. (1994). Investigating the "glass ceiling" phenomenon: An empirical study of actual promotions to top management. *Academy of Management Journal, 37,* 68–86.

Powell, G. N., & Butterfield, D. A. (2002). Exploring the influence of decision makers' race and gender on actual promotions to top management. *Personnel Psychology, 55,* 397–428.

Powers, Kinder, & Keeney. (1999). Prevent sexual harassment the right way. *Rhode Island Employment Law Letter, 4*(4), 6–8.

Pratto, F., Stallworth. L. M., Sidanius, J., & Siers, B. (1997). The gender gap in occupational role attainment: A social dominance approach. *Journal of Personality and Social Psychology, 72,* 37–53.

Pregnancy Discrimination Act of 1978, Pub. L. No. 95–555, 92 Stat. 20706 (Oct. 31, 1978).

Price Waterhouse v. Hopkins, 109 S.Ct. 1775 (1989).

Price Waterhouse v. Hopkins, 490 U.S. 228 (1989).

Pryor v. U. S. Gypsum Co., 585 F.Supp. 311 (W.D. Mo., 1984).

Pryor, J. B., Giedd, J. L., & Williams, K. B. (1995). A social psychological model for predicting sexual harassment. *Journal of Social Issues, 51,* 69–84.

Pryor, J. B., LaVite, C. M., & Stoller, L. M. (1993). A social psychological analysis of sexual harassment: The person/situation interaction. *Journal of Vocational Behavior, 42,* 68–83.

Ray v. Miller Meester Advertising, Inc. 664 N.W.2d 355 (Minn. 2003).

Reichman, N., & Sterling, J. S. (2004a). *Gender penalties revisited*. Denver, CO: Women's Bar Association. Retrieved July 13, 2006, from http://www.cwba.org

Reichman, N. J., & Sterling, J. S. (2004b). Sticky floors, broken steps, and concrete ceilings in legal careers. *Texas Journal of Women and the Law, 14,* 27–76.

Reskin, B. F. (1998). *The realities of affirmative action in employment*. Washington, DC: American Sociological Association.

Reskin, B. F. (2000). The proximate causes of employment discrimination. *Contemporary Sociology, 29*(2), 319–328.

Reskin, B. F., & McBrier, D. B. (2000). Why not ascription? Organizations' employment of male and female managers. *American Sociological Review, 65*(2), 210–233.

Reskin, B. F., McBrier, D. B., & Kmec, J. A. (1999). The determinants and consequences of workplace sex and race composition. *Annual Review of Sociology*, *25*, 335–361.

Reskin, I., & Padavic, B. (2002). *Women and men at work* (2nd ed.). Thousand Oaks, CA: Pine Forge Press.

Reskin, B. F., & Roos, P. (1990). *Job queues, gender queues*. Philadelphia: Temple University Press.

Reskin, B. F., & Ross, C. E. (1995). Jobs, authority, and earnings among managers: The continuing significance of sex. In J. A. Jacobs (Ed.), *Gender inequality at work* (pp. 127–151). Thousand Oaks, CA: Sage.

Reuben, R. C. (1996, August). The lawyer turns peacemaker. *ABA Journal*, *82*, 54–62.

Rhode, D. L. (1997). *Speaking of sex: The denial of gender inequality*. Cambridge, MA: Harvard University Press.

Rhode, D. L. (2001). *The unfinished agenda: Women and the legal profession*. American Bar Association Commission on Women in the Profession. Chicago, IL: American Bar Association.

Rhode, D. L. (2002a). *Balanced lives: Changing the culture of legal workplaces*. American Bar Association Commission on Women in the Profession. Chicago, IL: American Bar Association.

Rhode, D. L. (2002b). Balanced lives for lawyers. *Fordham Law Review*, *70*(6), 2207–2220.

Rhode, D. L. (2005). What's sex got to do with it: Diversity in the legal profession. In D. L. Rhode & D. Luban (Eds.), *Law Stories* (pp. 233–254). New York: Foundation Press.

Riach, P. A., & Rich, J. (2002). Field experiments of discrimination in the market place. *Economic Journal*, *112*, 480–518.

Ridgeway, C. L. (1997). Interaction and the conservation of gender inequality: Considering employment. *American Sociological Review*, *62*(2), 218–235.

Ridgeway, C. L. (2001). Gender, status, and leadership. *Journal of Social Issues*, *57*(4), 637–655.

Ridgeway, C. L., & Correll, S. J. (2000). Limiting inequality through interaction: The end(s) of gender. *Contemporary Sociology*, *29*, 110–120.

Ridgeway, C. L., & Correll, S. J. (2004). Unpacking the gender system: A theoretical perspective on gender beliefs and social relations. *Gender and Society*, *18*(4), 510–531.

Ridgeway, C. L., & Smith-Lovin, L. (1999). The gender system and interaction. *Annual Review of Sociology*, *25*, 191–216.

Riger, S. (1991). Gender dilemmas in sexual harassment policies and procedures. *American Psychologist*, *46*, 497–505.

Riordan v. Kaminers, 831 F. 2d 690 (7th Cir. 1987).

Robbennolt, J. K. (2004, Spring). Apology – Help or hindrance? An empirical analysis of apologies' influence on settlement making. *Dispute Resolution Magazine*, *10*, 33–34.

Robinson v. Jacksonville Shipyards, Inc., 760 F. Supp. 148 (1991).

Rogers, N. H., & McEwen, C. A. (1989). *Mediation: Law, policy, practice.* Eagan, MN: West Group.

Rose, D. L. (1989). Twenty-five years later: Where do we stand on equal employment opportunity law? *Vanderbilt Law Review, 42,* 1121–1181.

Rose, S. J., & Hartmann, H. I. (2004). *Still a man's labor market: The long term earnings gap.* Washington, DC: Institute for Women's Policy Research.

Rosenberg, S., & Lipman, J. (2005). Survey: Developing a consistent standard for evaluating a retaliation case under federal and state civil rights statutes and state common law claims: An Iowa model for the nation. *Drake Law Review, 53,* 359–420.

Ross, L. (1977). The intuitive psychologist and his shortcomings: Distortions in the attribution process. In L. Berkowitz (Ed.), *Advances in experimental social psychology* (Vol. 10, pp. 174–221). New York: Academic Press.

Ross, L., & Nisbett, R. E. (1991). *The person and the situation: Perspectives of social psychology.* New York: McGraw-Hill.

Roy, B. (Producer). (2006, March 28). *Taking the heat: The first women firefighters of New York City.* New York: Public Broadcasting Service.

Rudman, L. A. (1998). Self-promotion as a risk factor for women: The costs and benefits of counterstereotypical impression management. *Journal of Personality and Social Psychology, 74,* 629–645.

Rudman, L. A. (2005). Rejection of women? Beyond prejudice as antipathy. In J. F. Dovidio, P. Glick, & L. A. Rudman (Eds.), *On the nature of prejudice: Fifty years after Allport* (pp. 107–120). Malden, MA: Blackwell.

Rudman, L. A., & Borgida, E. (1995). The afterglow of construct accessibility: The behavioral consequences of priming men to view women as sexual objects. *Journal of Experimental Social Psychology, 6,* 493–517.

Rudman, L. A., & Fairchild, K. (2004). Reactions to counterstereotypic behavior: The role of backlash in cultural stereotype maintenance. *Journal of Personality and Social Psychology, 87,* 157–176.

Rudman, L. A., & Glick, P. (1999). Feminized management and backlash toward agentic women: The hidden costs to women of a kinder, gentler image of middle-managers. *Journal of Personality and Social Psychology, 77,* 1004–1010.

Rudman, L. A., & Glick, P. (2001). Prescriptive gender stereotypes and backlash toward agentic women. *Journal of Social Issues, 57,* 743–762.

Rudman, L. A., & Kilianski, S. E. (2000). Implicit and explicit attitudes toward female authority. *Personality and Social Psychology Bulletin, 26,* 1315–1328.

Ruggiero, K. M., & Taylor, D. M. (1995). Coping with discrimination: How disadvantaged group members perceive the discrimination that confronts them. *Journal of Personality and Social Psychology, 68,* 826–838.

Ruggiero, K. M., & Taylor, D. M. (1997). Why minority group members perceive or do not perceive the discrimination that confronts them: The role of self-esteem and perceived control. *Journal of Personality and Social Psychology, 72,* 373–389.

Rutte, C. G., Diekmann, K. A., Polzer, J. T., Crosby, F. J., & Messick, D. M. (1994). Organization of information and the detection of gender discrimination. *Psychological Science, 5,* 226–231.

Sailer, P., Yau, E., & Rehula, V. (2002). *Income by gender and age from information returns.* Washington, DC: Internal Revenue Service.

Samborn, H. V. (2000). Higher hurdles for women. *American Bar Association Journal, 86,* 30–33.

Schein, E. H. (1983). The role of the founder in creating organization culture. *Organization Dynamics, 11,* 13–28.

Schein, E. H. (1985). *Organizational culture and leadership.* San Francisco: Jossey-Bass.

Schmader, T., & Johns, M. (2003). Converging evidence that stereotype threat reduces working memory capacity. *Journal of Personality and Social Psychology, 85,* 440–452.

Schneider, B. (Ed.). (1990). *Organizational climate and culture.* San Francisco: Jossey-Bass.

Schuck, P. (2003). Diversity in America: Government at a safe distance. *Ethnic and racial studies, 28*(1), 192–193.

Schultz v. Advocate Health and Hospitals Corp., No. 01 C 702, 2002 U.S. Dist. LEXIS 9517 (N.D. Ill. Eastern Div., May 24, 2002).

Schultz, T. W. (March, 1960). Investment in human capital. *American Economic Review, 51*(1), 1–17.

Schultz, V. (1990). Telling stories about women and work: Judicial interpretations of sex segregation in the workplace in Title VII cases raising the lack of interest defense. *Harvard Law Review, 103,* 1749–1843.

Schultz, V. (2000). Life's work. *Columbia Law Review, 100,* 1881–1964.

Schwartz, D. S. (1997). Enforcing small print to protect big business: Employee and consumer rights claims in an age of compelled arbitration. *Wisconsin Law Review,* 33–132.

Sechrist, G. B., Swim, J. K., & Stangor, C. (2004). When do the stigmatized make attributions to discrimination occurring to the self and others: The roles of self-presentation and need for control. *Journal of Personality and Social Psychology, 87,* 111–122.

Securities Act of 1933, 15 U.S.C. §§77a-77aa (2000 & Supp. II 2002).

Securities Exchange Act of 1934, 15 U.S.C. §78a-78nn (2000 & Supp. II 2002).

Selmi, M. (2003). The price of discrimination: The nature of class action employment discrimination litigation and its effects. *Texas Law Review, 81,* 1249–1335.

Selmi, M. (2005). Sex discrimination in the nineties, seventies style: Case studies in the preservation of male workplace norms. *Employee Rights and Employment Policy Journal, 9,* 1–50.

Shaeffer, R. G. (1973). *Nondiscrimination in employment: Changing perspectives, 1963–1972.* New York: The Conference Board.

Shelton, J. N., & Stewart, R. E. (2004). Confronting perpetrators of prejudice: The inhibitory effects of social costs. *Psychology of Women Quarterly, 28,* 215–223.

Sherwyn, D. (2003). Because it takes two: Why post-dispute voluntary arbitration programs will fail to fix the problems associated with employment discrimination law adjudication. *Berkeley Journal of Employment and Labor Law, 24,* 1–69.

Shih, M., Pittinsky, T. L., & Ambady, N. (1999). Stereotype susceptibility: Identity salience and shifts in quantitative performance. *Psychological Science, 10,* 80–83.

Shorey, H. S., Cowan, G., & Sullivan, M. P. (2002). Predicting perceptions of discrimination among Hispanics and Anglos. *Hispanic Journal of Behavioral Sciences, 24,* 3–22.

Sicherman, N. (1996). Gender differences in departures from a large firm. *Industrial and Labor Relations Review, 49*(3), 484–503.

Simmons, A. M. (2005). Sixth annual review of gender and sexuality law: IV. Employment law chapter: State sexual harassment. *The Georgetown Journal of Gender and the Law, 6,* 597–613.

Simons, D. F. (2005). Employment law that fits our state. *Hawaii Bar Journal, March,* 4–12.

Sinclair, L., & Kunda, Z. (2000). Motivated stereotyping of women: She's fine if she praised me but incompetent if she criticized me. *Personality and Social Psychology Bulletin, 26,* 1329–1342.

Six, B., & Eckes, T. (1991). A closer look at the complex structure of gender stereotypes. *Sex Roles, 24,* 57–71.

Skitka, L. J., & Crosby, F. J. (2003). Trends in the social psychological study of justice. *Personality and Social Psychology Review, 7,* 282–285.

Skogan, W. (1976). Citizen reporting of crime: Some national panel data. *Criminology, 13,* 535–549.

Smith, P. R. (1999). Regulating paid household work: Class, gender, race, and agendas of reform. *American University Law Review, 48,* 851–924.

Smith, R. (2002). Race, gender, and authority in the workplace: Theory and research. *Annual Review of Sociology,* 509–542.

Smith, T. W. (1999). *The emerging 21st century American family.* GSS Social Change Report no. 42. Chicago, IL: National Opinion Research Center.

Snodgrass v. Brown, No. 80–1171-K, 1990 WL 198431, U.S. Dist Lexis 16418 (D. Kan. Nov. 26, 1990).

Society for Human Resource Management. (1999). *Sexual harassment survey.* SHRM Management Program.

Solberg, E., & Laughlin, T. (1995). The gender pay gap, fringe benefits, and occupational crowding. *Industrial and Labor Relations Review, 48*(4), 692–708.

Spain, D., & Bianchi, S. (1996). *Balancing act: Motherhood, marriage, and employment among American women.* New York: Russell Sage Foundation.

Spence, J. T., & Buckner, C. E. (2000). Instrumental and expressive traits, trait stereotypes, and sexist attitudes: What do they signify? *Psychology of Women Quarterly, 24,* 44–62.

Spence, J. T., & Helmreich, R. (1972). The Attitudes Toward Women Scale. *JSAS Catalog of Selected Documents in Psychology, 2,* ms. #153.

Spencer, S. J., Steele, C. M., & Quinn, D. M. (1999). Under suspicion of inability: Stereotype threat and women's math performance. *Journal of Experimental Social Psychology, 35,* 4–28.

St. Antoine, T. J. (1995). Mandatory arbitration of employee discrimination claims: Unmitigated evil or blessing in disguise? *Thomas M. Cooley Law Review, 15,* 1–19.

St. Mary's Honor Center v. Hicks, 509 U.S. 502 (1993).

Stambaugh, P. M. (1997). The power of law and the sexual harassment complaints of women. *NWSA Journal, 9,* 23–42.

Stangor, C., Lynch, L., Duan, C., & Glass, B. (1992). Categorization of individuals on the basis of multiple social features. *Journal of Personality and Social Psychology, 62,* 207–218.

Stangor, C., Swim, J. K., Sechrist, G. B., Decoster, J., VanAllen, K. L., & Ottenbreit, A. (2003). Ask, answer, and announce: Three stages in perceiving and responding to prejudice. *European Review of Social Psychology, 14,* 277–311.

Stangor, C., Swim, J. K., Van Allen, K. L., & Secrist, G. B. (2002). Reporting discrimination in public and private contexts. *Journal of Personality and Social Psychology, 82,* 69–74.

Statsny v. Southern Bell Tel. & Tel. Co., 458 F. Supp. 314 (W.D.N.C. 1978).

Steele, C. M., Spencer, S. J., & Aronson, J. (2002). Contending with group image: The psychology of stereotype and social identity threat. In M. P. Zanna (Ed.), *Advances in experimental social psychology* (Vol. 34, pp. 379–440). San Diego, CA: Academic Press.

Steinberg, R. J. (1995). Gendered instructions: Cultural lag and gender bias in the hay system of job evaluation. In J. A. Jacobs (Ed.), *Gender inequality at work* (pp. 57–92). Thousand Oaks, CA: Sage.

Steinberg, R., Haignere, L., Possin, C., Chertos, C. H., and Treiman, D. (1986). The New York State pay equity study: A research report. Albany, NY: Center for Women in Government/SUNY Press.

Stender v. Lucky Stores, 803 F.Supp. 259 (N.D. Cal. 1992).

Sternlight, J. R. (2003). The rise and spread of mandatory arbitration as a substitute for the jury trial. *University of San Francisco Law Review, 38,* 17–38.

Sternlight, J. R. (2004). In search of the best procedure for enforcing employment discrimination laws: A comparative analysis. *Tulane Law Review, 78,* 1401–1499.

Still, M. C. (forthcoming). *Demography of the maternal wall.* Center for Work-Life Law working paper. San Francisco: University of California, Hastings College of the Law, Center for WorkLife Law (available from www.worklifelaw.org).

Stockdale, M. S., Bisom-Rapp, S., O'Connor, M., & Gutek, B. A. (2004). Coming to terms with zero tolerance sexual harassment policies. *Journal of Forensic Psychology Practice*, *4*, 65–78.

Stockdale, M. S., & Crosby, F. J. (Eds.). (2004). *The psychology and management of workplace diversity*. Oxford: Blackwell.

Stockdale, M. S., Visio, M., & Batra, L. (1999). The sexual harassment of men: Evidence for a broader theory of sexual harassment and sex discrimination. *Psychology, Public Policy, and Law*, *5*, 630–664.

Stockett v. Tolin, 791 F.Supp. 1536 (S.D. Fl. 1992).

Stone, K. V. (1996). Mandatory arbitration of individual employment rights: The yellow-dog contract of the 1990s. *Denver University Law Review*, *73*, 1017–1050.

Stone, P., & Lovejoy, M. (2004). Fast-track women and the "choice" to stay home. *The annals of the American Academy of Political and Social Science*, *596*(1), 62–83.

Story, L. (2005, September 20). Many women at elite colleges set career path to motherhood. *New York Times*, p. A1.

Strauss, D. A. (1991). The law and economics of racial discrimination in employment: the case for numerical standards. *Georgetown Law Review*, *79*, 1619–1657.

Strickler, G. M. (2004, July 29–31). Arbitration of employment discrimination claims. *ALI-ABA CLE, Current Developments in Employment Law, Course Number SK013*, 801–813.

Stroh, L. K., Brett, J. M., & Reilly, A. H. (1992). All the right stuff: A comparison of female and male managers' career progression. *Journal of Applied Psychology*, *77*, 251–260.

Sturm, S. (2001). Second generation employment discrimination: A structural approach. *Columbia Law Review*, *101*, 458–568.

Suchman, M. C., & Edelman, L. B. (1997). Legal rational myths: The new institutionalism and the law and society tradition. *Law and Social Inquiry*, *21*, 903–941.

Suders et al. v. Easton, 325 F.3d 432, (3rd Cir. 2003).

Summers, C. W. (2004). Mandatory arbitration: Privatizing public rights, compelling the unwilling to arbitrate. *University of Pennsylvania Journal of Labor and Employment Law*, *6*, 685–734.

Sutton, J. R., & Dobbin, F. (1996). The two faces of governance: Responses to legal uncertainty in U.S. firms, 1955 to 1985. *American Sociological Review*, *61*, 794–811.

Sutton, J. R., Dobbin, F., Meyer, J. W., & Scott, W. R. (1994). The legalization of the workplace. *American Journal of Sociology*, *99*, 944–971.

Swim, J. K. & Hyers, L. L. (1999). Excuse me – What did you just say?!: Women's public and private responses to sexist remarks. *Journal of Experimental Social Psychology*, *35*, 68–88.

Swim, J. K., Hyers, L. L., Cohen, L. L., & Ferguson, M. J. (2001). Everyday sexism: Evidence for its incidence, nature and everyday impact from three daily diary studies. *Journal of Social Issues*, *57*, 31–53.

Tajfel, H. (1981). *Social identity and intergroup relations*. Cambridge: Cambridge University Press.

Taylor, D. M., Wright, S. C., & Porter, L. E. (1994). Dimensions of perceived discrimination: The personal/group discrimination discrepancy. In M. P. Zanna & J. M. Olson (Eds.), *The psychology of prejudice: The Ontario symposium* (Vol. 7, pp. 233–255). Hillsdale, NJ: Lawrence Erlbaum.

Taylor, S. E. (1981). A categorization approach to stereotyping. In D. L. Hamilton (Ed.), *Cognitive processes in stereotyping and intergroup behavior* (pp. 83–114). Mahwah, NJ: Lawrence Erlbaum.

Taylor, S. E. & Fiske, S. T. (1978). Salience, attention, and attribution: Top of the head phenomena. In L. Berkowitz (Ed.), *Advances in experimental social psychology* (Vol. 11, pp. 249–288). New York: Academic Press.

Teamsters v. United States, 431 U.S. 324 (1977).

Tetenbaum, T. (1999, Autumn). Beating the odds of merger & acquisition failure. *Organizational Dynamics*, 22–36.

Tetlock, P. E., & Lerner, J. (1999). The social contingency model: Identifying empirical and normative boundary conditions on the error-and-bias portrait of human nature. In S. Chaiken & Y. Trope (Eds.), *Dual process models in social psychology* (pp. 571–585). New York: Guilford Press.

Thibaut, J., & Walker, L. (1975). *Procedural justice: A psychological analysis*. Hillsdale, NJ: Lawrence Erlbaum.

Title VII of the Civil Rights Act of 1964, 42 U.S.C. §2000e *et. seq.* (2003).

Tomaka, J., & Blascovich, J. (1994). Effects of justice beliefs on cognitive appraisal of and subjective, physiological, and behavioral responses to stress. *Journal of Personality and Social Psychology*, *67*, 732–740.

Tomaskovic-Devey, D. (1993). *Gender and racial inequality at work: The sources and consequences of job segregation*. Ithaca, NY: ILR Press.

Torres, L., & Huffman, M. L. (2004). Who benefits? Gender differences in returns to social network diversity. *Research in the Sociology of Work*, *14*, 17–33.

Trying to Fill a Fallen Husband's Boots: Widow of Firefighter Killed on 9/11 Wants to Join the Department. (April 2, 2003). *New York Times*, p. A19.

Tversky, A., & Kahneman, D. (1974). Judgment under uncertainty: Heuristics and biases. *Science*, *185*, 1124–1131.

Twiss, C., Tabb, S., & Crosby, F. J. (1989). Affirmative action and aggregate data: The importance of patterns in the perception of discrimination. In F. A. Blanchard & F. J. Crosby (Eds.), *Affirmative action in perspective* (pp. 159–176). New York: Springer-Verlag.

Tyler, T. R., & Blader, S. L. (2003). The group engagement model: Procedural justice, social identity, and cooperative behavior. *Personality and Social Psychology Review*, *7*, 349–361.

Tyler, T. R., & Lind, E. A. (1992). A relational model of authority in groups. In M. P. Zanna (Ed.), *Advances in experimental social psychology* (Vol. 25, pp. 115–191). San Diego, CA: Academic Press.

Tyler, T. R., Rasinksi, K., & Spodick, N. (1985). The influence of voice on satisfaction with leaders: Exploring the meaning of process control. *Journal of Personality and Social Psychology*, *48*, 72–81.

U.S. Census Bureau. (2004). *Evidence from Census 2000 about earnings by detailed occupation for men and women.* Washington, DC: U.S. Census Bureau.

U.S. Department of Labor. (2001). *Highlights of women's earnings in 2000, Report 952.* Washington, DC: Bureau of Labor Statistics.

U.S. Department of Labor. (2004). *Household data, annual averages.* Washington, DC: Bureau of Labor Statistics.

U.S. Department of Labor, Bureau of Labor Statistics. (2001, August). *Highlights of women's earnings in 2000*, BLS Report 952, Table 3. Retrieved June 22, 2006, from www.bls.gov/cps/cpswom2000.pdf

U.S. Department of Labor, Bureau of Labor Statistics. (2005). *Women in the labor force: A databook*, retrieved at www.bls.gov/cps/wlf-databook2005.htm

U.S. Department of Labor, Bureau of Labor Statistics. (August, 2001). *Highlights of women's earnings in 2000*, BLS Report 952, Table 3. Retrieved June 22, 2006, from www.bls.gov/cps/cpswom2000.pdf

U.S. Department of Labor, Glass Ceiling Commission. (1995). *Good for business: Making full use of the nation's human capital.* District of Columbia: United States Government Printing Office.

U.S. Merit Systems Protection Board. (1981). *Sexual harassment in the federal workplace: Is it a problem?* Washington, DC: U.S. Government Printing Office.

U.S. Merit Systems Protection Board. (1988). *Sexual harassment in the federal workplace: An update.* Washington, DC: U.S. Government Printing Office.

U.S. Merit Systems Protection Board (1995). *Sexual harassment in the federal workforce: Trends, progress, continuing challenges.* Washington, DC: U.S. Merit Systems Protection Board.

Uhlmann, E. L., & Cohen, G. L. (2005). Constructed criteria: Redefining merit to justify discrimination. *Psychological Science*, *16*, 474–480.

Uniform guidelines on employee selection procedures (1978). *Federal Register*, *43*, 38290–38315.

Uniroyal, Inc. v. Marshall, 482 F. Supp. 364 (D.D.C. 1979).

United States v. City of Buffalo, 457 F. Supp. 612 (W.D.N.Y. 1978).

United States Courts. (2004). U.S. district courts: District court profile. Retrieved June 13, 2006, from http://www.uscourts.gov/cgi-bin/cmsd2005.pl

University of South Florida. (1998). *1997–1998 University of South Florida Fact Book.* Tampa, Florida.

Valásquez, M. (n.d.) *The national litigious environment.* Retrieved June 22, 2006, from www.diversitydtg.com

Valian, V. (1999). The cognitive basis of gender bias. *Brooklyn Law Review*, *65*, 1037–1061.

Vescio, T. K., Gervais, S. J., Snyder, M., & Hoover, A. (2005). Power and the creation of patronizing environments: The stereotype-based behaviors of the powerful and their effects on female performance in masculine domains. *Journal of Personality and Social Psychology, 88,* 658–672.

Wagenseller v. Scottsdale Mem'l Hosp., 710 P.2d 1025 (Ariz. 1985).

Wagner, D. G., & Berger, J. (1997). Gender and interpersonal task behaviors: Status expectation accounts. *Sociological Perspectives, 40,* 1–32.

Waldfogel, J. (1998). Understanding the "family gap" in pay for women with children. *The Journal of Economic Perspectives, 12,* 137–156.

Wallace v. Skadden, Arps, Slate, Meagher & Flom, 715 A.2d 873 (D.C. 1998).

Wallis, C. (2004, March 22). The case for staying home. *Time,* 51–52.

Walsh v. National Computer Systems, Inc., 332 F.3d 1150, 1160 (8th Cir. 2003).

Walster, E., Walster, G. W., & Berscheid, E. (1978). *Equity theory and research.* Boston: Allyn & Bacon.

Walton, M. D., Sachs, D., Ellington, R., Hazlewood, A., Griffin, S., & Bass, D. (1988). Physical stigma and the pregnancy role: Receiving help from strangers. *Sex Roles, 18,* 323–331.

Ward's Cove v. Atonio, 490 U.S. 642 (1989).

Washington Revised Code Annotated §49.12.175 (West 2002).

Washington v. Illinois Department of Revenue, 420 F.3d 658 (7th Cir. 2005).

Watson v. Fort Worth Bank & Trust, 487 U.S. 977 (1988).

Weeks v. Southern Bell Telephone & Telegraph Co., 408 F.2d 228 (5th Cir. 1969).

Wegner, D. M., & Bargh, J. A. (1998). Control and automaticity in social life. In D. T. Gilbert, S. T. Fiske, & G. Lindzey, *The handbook of social psychology* (4th ed., Vol. 2, pp. 446–496). New York: McGraw Hill.

West, C., & Zimmerman, D. (1987). Doing gender. *Gender and Society, 1,* 125–151.

West, M. S. (2002). Preventing sexual harassment: The federal courts' wake-up call for women. *Brooklyn Law Review, 68,* 457–523.

Wilkins, D., & Gulati, M. G. (1996). Why are there so few black lawyers in corporate law firms: An institutional analysis. *University of California Law Review, 84,* 493–625.

Williams, C. (1992). The glass escalator: Hidden advantages for men in the "female" professions. *Social Problems, 39*(3), 253–267.

Williams, J. C. (1989) Deconstructing gender. *Michigan Law Review, 87*(4), 797–845.

Williams, J. C. (2000). *Unbending gender: Why work and family conflict and what to do about it.* New York: Oxford University Press.

Williams, J. C. (2002). Canaries in the mine: Work/Family conflict and the law. *Fordham Law Review, 70*(6), 2221–2239.

Williams, J. C. (2003). Litigating the glass ceiling and the maternal wall: Using stereotyping and cognitive bias evidence to prove gender discrimination: The social psychology of stereotyping: Using social science to litigate gender discrimination cases and defang the cluelessness defense. *Employment Rights and Employment Policy, 7*(2), 401–458.

Williams, J. C., & Calvert, C. T. (2002). Balanced hours: Effective part-time policies for Washington law firms: The project for attorney retention. *William and Mary Journal of Women and the Law*, 8(3), 376–378.

Williams J. C., & Calvert, C. T. (2006). Family responsibilities discrimination: What plaintiffs' attorneys, management attorneys and employees need to know. *Women Lawyers Journal*, 91(2), 24–28.

Williams, J. C., & Cooper, H. C. (2004). The public policy of motherhood. *Journal of Social Issues*, 60(4), 849–865.

Williams, J. C., & Segal, N. (2003). Beyond the maternal wall: Relief for family caregivers who are discriminated against on the job. *Harvard Women's Law Journal*, 26, 77–162.

Williams v. City of New Orleans, 729 F.2d 1554 (5th Cir. 1984).

Wojciszke, B. (1994). Multiple meanings of behavior: Construing actions in terms of competence or morality. *Journal of Personality and Social Psychology*, 67, 222–232.

Wolkind, S., & Zajicek, E. (Eds.). (1981). *Pregnancy: A psychological and social study*. New York: Grune & Stratton.

Wolman, B. A. (1988). Verbal sexual harassment on the job as intentional infliction of emotional distress, *Capital University Law Review*, 17, 245–272.

Women's Bar Association of Massachusetts. (2000). *More than part time: The effect of reduced-hours arrangements on the retention, recruitment, and success of women attorney in law firms*. Retrieved from http://www.womenlaw.stanford.edu/mass.rpt.html

Woodford v. Community Action Agency of Greene County, 239 F.3rd 517 (C.A. 2, N.Y., 2001).

Woodzicka, J., & LaFrance, M. (2001). Real versus imagined gender harassment. *Journal of Social Issues*, 57, 15–30.

Wright v. Universal Maritime Service Corp., 525 U.S. 70 (1998).

Yoder, J. D. (1991). Rethinking tokenism: Looking beyond numbers. *Gender and Society*, 5(2), 178–192.

Zanna, M. P., Crosby, F., & Loewenstein, G. (1987). Male reference groups and discontent among female professionals. In B. A. Gutek & L. Larwood (Eds.), *Pathways to women's career development* (pp. 28–41). Beverly Hills: Sage.

Zimmer, M. J., Sullivan, C. A., Richards, R. F., & Calloway, D. (1997). *Cases and materials on employment discrimination*. New York: Aspen.

Zimmer, M. J., Sullivan, C. A., & White, R. H. (2003). *Cases and materials on employment discrimination law*. New York: Aspen Publishers.

Index